Interaction in Cooperative Groups: The Theoretical Anatomy of Group Learning brings together current, related research from education, developmental psychology, and social psychology in an approach that is both integrative and analytical. Its intent is to provide an understanding of the dynamics of processes that are fundamental to group interaction and its outcomes. The editors have pulled together an impressive array of researchers from diverse areas within psychology and education. Many of the most exciting and currently visible research programs are represented.

The book is divided into four parts: (1) developmental foundations and the social construction of knowledge, (2) social skills and classroom factors influencing peer interactions, (3) the effects of task and reward structure on academic achievement, and (4) factors influencing the promotion of positive intergroup relations. A concluding chapter provides recommendations for implementation of the research in applied settings.

Interaction in Cooperative Groups is a valuable resource for the professional community and will serve to initiate a long-overdue unification of distinct, yet conceptually similar, areas of research.

D0216991

Interaction in Cooperative Groups

Interaction in Cooperative Groups

The Theoretical Anatomy of Group Learning

Edited by

RACHEL HERTZ-LAZAROWITZ
School of Education
University of Haifa

NORMAN MILLER
Department of Psychology
University of Southern California

CAMBRIDGE
UNIVERSITY PRESS

Published by the Press Syndicate of the University of Cambridge
The Pitt Building, Trumpington Street, Cambridge CB2 IRP
40 West 20th Street, New York, NY 10011-4211, USA
10 Stamford Road, Oakleigh, Melbourne 3166, Australia

© Cambridge University Press 1992

First published 1992
First paperback edition 1995

Printed in the United States of America

Library of Congress Cataloging-in-Publication Data is available.

A catalog record for this book is available from the British Library.

ISBN 0-521-40303-0 hardback
ISBN 0-521-48376-X paperback

Contents

Contributors

Barbara L. Bershon
Department of Psychology
The American University

Donald F. Dansereau
Department of Psychology
Texas Christian University

Hugh Jordan Harrington
Hughes Aircraft Company
Los Angeles, California

Rachel Hertz-Lazarowitz
School of Education
University of Haifa

David W. Johnson
Cooperative Learning Center
University of Minnesota

Roger T. Johnson
Cooperative Learning Center
University of Minnesota

Valerie Benveniste Kirkus
Graduate School of Education
University of Southern California

Sharon Knechel
Department of Education
McPherson College

Sarah J. McCarthey
College of Education
The University of Texas at Austin

Susan McMahon
College of Education
University of Wisconsin – Madison

Geoffrey M. Maruyama
Department of Educational Psychology
University of Minnesota

Norman Miller
Department of Psychology
University of Southern California

Sharon Nelson-Le Gall
Learning Research and Development
 Center
University of Pittsburgh

Angela M. O'Donnell
Department of Educational Psychology
Rutgers, The State University of New
 Jersey

Renee Petersen
Stillwater Public Schools
Stillwater, Minnesota

Robert E. Slavin
Center for Research on Effective
    Schooling for Disadvantaged
    Students
Johns Hopkins University

Noreen M. Webb
Graduate School of Education
University of California, Los Angeles

An Overview of the Theoretical Anatomy of Cooperation in the Classroom

Rachel Hertz-Lazarowitz, Valerie Benveniste Kirkus, and Norman Miller

Cooperative interdependence in classroom settings is the basis of many interventions designed to improve both academic achievement and social relations in schools and as such has been a primary focus in educational and social psychological literature for more than two decades. Each discipline, however, has given rise to a distinct line of research. The purpose of this volume is to bring together recent work from diverse areas to provide both educators and social psychologists with theoretical foundations for integrating the principles and processes that underlie the cognitive and affective outcomes of cooperative interaction. Its uniqueness lies in its attempt to connect concepts that stem from different approaches. We hope that such a theoretical "anatomy" will facilitate a general understanding of the fundamental conditions for promoting achievement and positive social relations in schools by means of cooperation.

The researchers who have contributed to this volume recognize that it is the natural tendency of children to grow and learn through social interaction, and share the belief that understanding cooperative interactions within school contexts will not only help children achieve educational goals but also create more long-term benefits for humankind. Each chapter examines in detail the dynamics of a specific area of cooperative interaction and its cognitive and/or affective correlates. Though there is some overlap in content, the chapters are organized into four general areas: (1) developmental foundations and the social construction of knowledge, (2) social skills and classroom factors influencing peer interactions, (3) the effects of task and reward structure on academic achievement, (4) factors influencing the promotion of positive intergroup relations.

This introduction provides a brief preview of key ideas discussed in each chapter. In our final chapter we attempt to integrate this research, including other pertinent literature from social, educational, and developmental psychology.

1

Part I   Developmental Foundations and the Social Construction of Knowledge

The first three chapters lay the developmental foundation for the examination of cooperative interactions. Central to each chapter is a social constructivist view of learning based largely on the theories of Piaget (1926) and Vygotsky (1980, 1986). To both theorists the social milieu is pivotal to cognitive growth and knowledge construction. Piaget described the interaction between the factors that are internal and external to the child as necessary for the formation and attainment of increasingly complex stages of cognitive ability. The internal factors are the child's maturational level and intrinsic need for equilibration. These work in concert with the external factors – the social transmission of knowledge and environmental experiences – to influence development. Central to the Vygotskian view is the role of a more knowledgeable other in guiding social interaction and providing the conceptual scaffolding for the gradual internalization of knowledge.

In their respective chapters McCarthey and McMahon, Bershon, and Nelson-Le Gall base their discussion of knowledge development and cognitive growth on the important role of social interactions, suggesting that schools and teachers ought not to fight against, but to work with, the innate tendency of children to interact verbally in social groups.

McCarthey and McMahon (Chapter 1) provide a general discussion of the contribution of social interaction to learning in which, within the context of developing children's writing skills in the classroom, they make clear Damon and Phelps's (1989) distinctions between tutorial, cooperative, and collaborative learning. They elaborate on the appropriateness of each form of group learning as viewed from the perspective of the individual, the purposes of instruction, and the nature of the task. These three components (personal, instructional, and task) influence interaction in distinct ways during each of three identified processes of writing: planning, drafting, and revising.

Operating in tandem with the three types of peer interaction are three process dimensions, each of which has several levels. These interdependent process dimensions are (1) role, (2) interactive structure, and (3) task. Levels of ability have an important influence on student roles, creating patterns of interaction that co-vary as a function of actual and perceived ability differences. For example, students of similar ability may collaborate or cooperate, whereas when one student is clearly more knowledgeable than another, a tutorial exchange will occur. The dimension of interactive structure is defined in terms of mutuality of interaction, which describes the directional flow of discourse. On this continuum, tutorial interaction, which is largely unidirectional knowledge transmission, represents the anchor point of "low mutuality" whereas collaboration represents the "high mutuality" anchor.

Although all three process dimensions are important for understanding and setting the boundary conditions that will influence the type of peer interaction that is enacted, McCarthey and McMahon propose that the task dimension is criterial to the others – that is, the nature of the task defines students' roles and interactive patterns. They explain that in the process of writing, "the demands of the task frame the amount and type of discourse and influence who will have control over the text." They interpret the three variables (role, interactive structure, task) from a social constructivist framework that delineates for practitioners ways to progress through the learning continuum, from static transmission of knowledge to dynamic transformation of knowledge.

Bershon (Chapter 2) discusses social learning from its earliest inception, focusing on the role of inner language in problem solving. She succinctly explains Vygotsky's view of how the transmission of social in*ter*psychic knowledge becomes in*tra*psychic knowledge, which forms new cognitive structures that become a part of the child's problem-solving repertoire. Her discussion centers on the adaptive use of inner language as a natural cognitive tool in problem solving. Vygotskian theoretical distinctions between the development of speech from social to egocentric to inner serve as a springboard for her discussion. Social speech begins through parent-child discourse. From this interaction children learn volitional behavior. Interpersonal egocentric language evolves, again, in the service of directing behavior and solving problems. Inner language then emerges as the internalization of this problem-solving speech. The social in*ter*personal communicative tool becomes an in*tra*personal communicative tool – cognitive thought.

In Bershon's detailed examination of inner speech she specifies four types that may occur during problem solving: task related, self related, other related, and task irrelevant. Further, she identifies a list of the cognitions concomitant with inner speech that, when identified and incorporated into classroom problem-solving tasks, will be useful in improving task performance and in fostering the development of the megacognitive skill of self-regulation. In this manner (and with reference to Marshall, 1988) Bershon envisions a shift of emphasis in the classroom from places of *work* to places of *learning*.

Nelson-Le Gall (Chapter 3) takes us further into the natural social learning strategies of children by examining their help-seeking behaviors. Her analysis of theory and research regarding adaptive and maladaptive perceptions of help-seeking in children (and adults) provides an insightful foundation for understanding the cognitive, motivational, and affective bases that influence situation-specific help-seeking behaviors. Previewing themes that emerge in later chapters, she also discusses impediments to learning inherent in the established organizational structure of schools.

Nelson-Le Gall refers to early literature (e.g., Beller, 1955) showing that negative affect often arises after (or while) seeking help, because help-seeking was interpreted as an indicator of dependency and thus deemed inappropriate beyond earliest childhood. This negative affect, in turn, acts as an obstacle to learning by disinclining further attempts to seek help. She discusses more recent literature, as well, that outlines situational determinants that serve as a barrier to the development of adaptive and appropriate (i.e., instrumental) help-seeking by students in school. Nelson-Le Gall also explains that under certain conditions help-seeking may lead to self-perceptions of low ability, embarrassment, or feelings of indebtedness and dependency.

Other relevant literature in social psychology supports the notion that those receiving help often show decreased liking toward their helpers. Circumstances associated with this and other similar outcomes include those in which the recipient of help does not foresee the opportunity to reciprocate (Castro, 1974; Gergen, Ellsworth, Maslach, & Seipel, 1975; Gross & Latané, 1974; Shumaker & Jackson, 1979), tasks in which performance is believed to reflect an individual's intelligence (Morse, 1972), ego-involving tasks such as those associated with one's personal self-concept (DePaulo & Fisher, 1980; Gergen, Morse, & Kristeller, 1973; Wallston, 1976), tasks in which the relevant experience of donor and recipient is perceived as similar (Fisher, Harrison, & Nadler, 1978; Fisher & Nadler, 1974; Nadler, Fisher, & Streufert 1974), and tasks in which the group or team experiences failure (Ashmore, 1970; Blanchard, Adelman, & Cook, 1975; Blanchard & Cook, 1976).

It is important to note, however, that Cook and Pelfrey (1985) found that a person who received help when working as a member of a cooperating group expressed more liking for a teammate who provided help. In discussing this reversal of the typical negative consequences of dependence, Cook and Pelfrey point to two features that distinguish cooperative group settings from the dyadic relations in which receiving help produces dislike of the helper. One difference is that group settings evoke norms of responsibility toward teammates and the collective, which act to minimize the negative effects that ordinarily occur when one is unable to reciprocate help that is received. A second feature is that help received in the context of group membership increases the recipient's view of his or her own value to the group, which, in turn, has positive consequences for liking of the group as well as the particular member who provided the help.

As indicated, Nelson-Le Gall integrates theories regarding the development of self-perceptions of ability and self-presentational concerns that can act together to deter students from seeking needed help. These are issues that we, also, explore in Chapter 11. Importantly, these factors can act as a barrier to a student's inclination not only to seek help from other students but also to seek help *from teachers*. Nelson-Le Gall's response to this observed dilemma is to reconceptualize help-seeking as a *positive* behavioral option that is instrumental to achievement, learning, and goal attainment. Rather than focus upon the negative costs of seeking help, the model presented here focuses upon the negative costs of *not* doing so. Further, she differentiates help-seeking in terms of dependency-oriented versus mastery-oriented interpersonal negotiation, in which person and task variables are important determinants of behavior. The theoretical orientation of this chapter offers the interventionist a foundation for creating a classroom social climate (by means of classroom norms, adult-sanctioned peer interaction, and teacher behaviors that support mastery orientation) that will help foster natural social learning through instrumental help-seeking.

Part II   Social Skills and Classroom Factors Influencing Peer Interactions

Hertz-Lazarowitz (Chapter 4) provides a comprehensive foundation for understanding social interactions in the classroom. She presents a multidimensional model in which unique patterns of social interaction are dependent on six interrelated classroom "mirrors." These mirrors include the physical organization of the classroom, the learning task, teacher instructional behavior, teacher communicative behavior, student social behavior, and student academic behavior. Each mirror contains a continuum of type of learning, which varies from solitary to interactional to collaborative. Together they provide a model for analyzing activity within a given classroom in terms of the reflections created by its unique combination of mirrors.

Hertz-Lazarowitz describes the conditions that facilitate each type of learning, providing teachers with a practical pathway for the progression from a traditional classroom to one that is interactive and, further, to one that is cooperative. She states that movement along this continuum does not require the discarding of one strategy and substitution of another but, rather, a restructuring of teacher behaviors.

The introduction of four key concepts provides researchers with an organizational tool for observing, describing, and analyzing classrooms within different contexts. The first pivotal notion is that of classroom multidimensionality and the different stages within each dimension. Second is the developing nature of multidimensional complexity, which progresses within each mirror from noninteractive to interactive to cooperative. Third is the sense of harmony or optimal effectiveness that may be established by creating a convergence across mirrors in the stages or levels at which a class operates. And last is the interdependence of these mirrors in producing the combined social and cognitive outcomes that emerge.

Equally pertinent is her discussion of negative outcomes. Low-level, irrelevant interactions suffer from procedural, repetitive, almost "ritualistic" processes, thus lacking the content elaboration associated with effective learning. Also, her research shows that even within the context of cooperatively structured learning, noninteractive behaviors frequently occur and helping behaviors are not always automatic. Hertz-Lazarowitz suggests that looking at *combinations of behaviors* is the key to broadening understanding of the processes that underlie cooperative interaction.

Following this general model for understanding classroom interactions, Webb (Chapter 5) focuses more specifically on interactions among students. Her model of peer interaction describes the types of help-giving and help-receiving interactions that lead to positive or negative learning outcomes and the kinds of responses group members provide when one member experiences difficulty. Based on a taxonomy of type of help exhibited in students' verbal exchanges, which ranges from the offering of information to the presentation of complex elaborations, she analyzes spontaneous student exchanges (in groups of four mixed-ability students) during their learning of mathematics.

Not surprisingly, her data suggest that giving help in the form of supplying information without explanation is weakly correlated with achievement gains. When peer interaction includes elaboration and/or explanations, however, achievement improves correspondingly. Within mixed-ability groups, distinct patterns of interaction and achievement emerge for those at each ability level (low, medium, high). High-ability students always verbalized their thinking, even when incorrect or experiencing difficulty. Medium- and low-ability students sometimes remained silent during problem solving. Silent medium-ability students, however, in general performed well on the delayed posttest, whereas silent low-ability students did not. Webb offers plausible speculations to account for these findings and also refers to the model offered by Nelson-Le Gall to understand possible process variables that may be influential in these patterns of verbal interaction.

Webb's findings regarding the effect of ability status on the social interaction of students should be kept in mind when reading Chapters 9 and 10. Status factors and concomitant perceptions of self-identity (that are partially based on such factors) are powerful determinants of patterns of participation (Berger, Cohen, & Zelditch, 1972; Cohen, 1982, Cohen, Lotan, & Catanzarite, 1990) and of interpersonal and intergroup acceptance (Miller and Harrington, 1990; Tajfel, Flament, Billig, & Bundy, 1971).

Webb's use of both immediate and delayed posttest measures allows for achievement-related inferences about long-term retention as well as short-term recall. She ends her chapter with general principles for shaping student interaction into patterns that optimize achievement in the classroom and provides a list of conditions that will facilitate the exchange of high-level elaboration in groups, which, in turn, promote metacognitive skills that are task general rather than task specific – a central theme in Chapter 6.

O'Donnell and Dansereau (Chapter 6) depart from Webb's model of *sponta-*

neous peer interaction to examine the effects of experimentally manipulated *scripted* interaction between student dyads. Whereas the preceding chapters examined cooperative learning in classroom settings with preschool or elementary school children, O'Donnell and Dansereau (as do Miller and Harrington, and Maruyama, Knechel, and Petersen in Chapters 9 and 10) work with college students in a laboratory setting. In so constraining their research they strive for a level of experimental control that provides for a more exact understanding of process variables that underlie the outcomes of cooperative interactions. Working from a perspective similar to the developmental approach presented in the first part of this book, learning is again construed in terms of metacognitive skills that facilitate learning across a wide variety of content areas. Their model is comprehensive in that it includes both cognitive and affective correlates of cooperative interaction. The full model comprises cognitive, affective, metacognitive, and social variables (CAMS). They delineate the optimal task and process conditions for effective implementation of dyadic cooperative learning, as defined by enhanced student achievement and motivation. Also, their work offers the unique contribution of analysis of *processing* activities engaged in by students, rather than simply the achievement *outcomes* that result from them.

Their *Scripted Cooperation* procedure includes five generic components, many of which have been identified by cognitive psychologists as critical factors for facilitating learning (e.g., Anderson, 1985): (1) dividing a text into discrete and meaningful subsections, (2) having both members of the dyad read the text a section at a time, (3) requiring one partner to recall the pertinent details and information, (4) requiring the other partner to monitor this oral recall to detect errors and omissions (these two roles are evenly interchanged throughout the text), and (5) having both members of the dyad elaborate on this information with methods that may include developing analogies and generating images. Scripted Cooperation encourages the development of metacognitive learning strategies – that is, learning stategies that are content independent or readily transferable from one domain of learning to another, such as skills useful in the content areas of history, science, literature, and so on. O'Donnell and Dansereau contend that content-independent affective outcomes simultaneously develop as a result of observational learning during scripted interaction. For example, one member of the dyad may model a positive affective strategy such as overcoming frustration when confronting a difficult task. The other may model effective ways of coping with anxiety that may occur when confronted by potential evaluation or public performance. In this way, each member of the dyad brings to the cooperative interaction a repertoire of cognitive and affective skills that may be acquired through social modeling and strengthened by rehearsal.

This chapter also notes conditions of cooperative interaction that are associated with possible negative outcomes. Further, it parallels many aspects of the applied field settings described in earlier chapters. For example, CAMS interactions that result in *automatic* information processing promote little new learning; thus, O'Donnell and Dansereau structure their laboratory learning tasks to be moderately challenging to enhance both content-dependent and content-independent learning. This is compatible with the notion of the zone of proximal development advocated by developmentalists (see Chapters 1 and 2). Another negative affective outcome may be a decline in motivation when the learner perceives highly discrepant ability differences between group members. This idea is complementary to, and may help explain, Webb's findings with regard to silent, low-ability students. O'Donnell and Dansereau discuss other differences between individuals that may have negative consequences and inhibit learning (e.g., high anxiety during social interaction that interferes with attention to task).

Overall, however, 10 years of research on Scripted Cooperation shows that it effectively promotes academic success. Although it emphasizes cognitive consequences, it also reports important and interesting results with respect to interpersonal attitudes. Those who participated in experimenter-generated cooperative scripts expressed more positive attitudes toward working with future partners in cooperative situations than those who did not. The combined cognitive and affective measures of CAMS scripted cooperative learning offer a practical basis for understanding process variables underlying these correlates of cooperative interactions in classrooms.

Part III   The Effects of Task and Reward Structures on Academic Achievement

Although the chapters by Slavin and D. W. Johnson and R. T. Johnson discuss some of the process variables (e.g., student interaction and motivation) that were examined in detail in Parts I and II, Part III primarily focuses on the influences of task and reward structures on student achievement.

Slavin (Chapter 7) reviews the literature and theory about the relationship between cooperation and achievement and analyzes the effects of different task and outcome measures in laboratory and field research. Differences in the definition or measurement of achievement may lead to opposing recommendations regarding optimal ways to maximize it, partly because the benefits of cooperative learning result from more than a single theoretical construct. He points out that achievement as measured by individual scores on an exam differs greatly from achievement as measured by the creation of a group product. He argues that measuring the advantage of cooperative over individual achievement on the basis of group performance or problem solving may be misleading, as these reflect *pooled* knowledge or problem-solving ability, which, when measured by the creation of a single product, gives groups an advantage over a single individual.

As do the authors of previous chapters, Slavin briefly discusses circumstances in which achievement may be negatively affected by cooperative interaction. He classifies these conditions under the construct of diffusion of responsibility, a specific source of dysfunction that social psychologists include in the process loss that often accompanies group problem solving (e.g., Steiner, 1972). Slavin emphasizes the role of a cooperative reward structure in conjunction with a cooperative task structure to protect against this negative outcome. The processes by which cooperation acts to enhance achievement are examined from six perspectives: (1) motivation (reward and/or goal structure), (2) social cohesion, (3) developmental level, (4) cognitive elaboration, (5) rehearsal or practice, and (6) classroom organizational efficiency. Slavin's interpretation of the motivational components is largely *extrinsic.* That is, he sees increases in motivation to achieve as driven by strivings for symbolic or tangible external rewards such as certificates, grades, or increases in free-time activities. Similarly, he views motivational gains from social cohesion, such as increased helping behaviors, to be a consequence of creating social norms that make helping appropriately instrumental to the group in their quest to attain extrinsic rewards. His analysis argues for the need for both group rewards and individual accountability to maximize achievement.

Slavin's summary of achievement in cooperative settings reviews some of the constructs described in earlier chapters, such as elaboration (Chapter 6) and practice via verbalization (Chapter 2). To this, he adds the idea of increased organizational efficiency in teachers' use of time. This occurs during cooperatively structured activities because students can assume responsibility for checking each other's work and thereby free the teacher – whether for more direct one-on-one instruction or for other activities. He concludes with an integrative model of these six perspectives. Because each is "demonstrably 'correct' in some circumstances, but none are probably both necessary and sufficient in *all* circumstances," his model describes complementary relations among them that enhance academic achievement.

Reward structure is discussed again by D. W. Johnson and R. T. Johnson (Chapter 8). Whereas a major concern for Slavin was the differences among operational definitions of *achievement,* this chapter focuses on the differences among operational definitions of *cooperation.* Like Slavin, D. W. Johnson and R. T. Johnson acknowledge that cooperation in learning is not always the optimal method for attaining maximal achievement and briefly discuss the conditions under which social loafing is likely to undermine the positive achievement effects of cooperation.

D. W. Johnson and R. T. Johnson describe the effects of task and reward structures on academic achievement by means of a typology of "positive social interdependence." Positive interdependence includes two major types of interdependence: *means* interdependence and *outcome* interdependence. With positive means interdependence a task is structured such that two or more individuals are required to coordinate their efforts to successfully complete it. Outcome interdependence can include either or both *goal* interdependence and *reward* interdependence. In goal interdependence, as previously described by Deutsch (1949), one can attain one's goals if, and only if, other members also attain their goals. Reward interdependence exists when each group member receives an equivalent reward for successful completion of the joint task (e.g., the same grade). Importantly, they noted that it is difficult to assess the relative benefits of reward versus goal interdependence. Although goal interdependence can be structured without reward interdependence, the converse is not true; reward interdependence cannot be structured and/or measured independently of goal interdependence.

Their typology delineates the essential components and boundary conditions of cooperative intervention that will lead to increases in academic achievement. This chapter, as well as Slavin's chapter, provides a framework for understanding causal antecedents to both increases and decreases in learning. A section of Chapter 8 is also devoted to the social benefits of interdependence in cooperative learning.

Part IV   Factors Influencing the Promotion of Positive Intergroup Relations

This section considers cooperative learning from a social psychological perspective. Whereas educational psychologists emphasize the cognitive correlates of cooperation, social psychologists focus on its affective consequences as viewed from intrapersonal, interpersonal, and intergroup perspectives. In our view, academic achievement and interpersonal processes and outcomes are of equal importance: allocating fewer chapters here that are concerned solely with social psychological issues should not be construed as an indication of lesser perceived relevance or significance. Rather, as mentioned previously, we see this lack of balance as a reflection of normative perceptions of the purposes of schooling. The traditional purpose of schools in Western culture has been transmission of academic knowledge, skills, and information. Socialization of children has, by and large, been considered to be the responsibility of the family. As argued in many of the earlier chapters, however, it is self-evident that socialization processes and academic learning are inextricably intertwined and that the formation and nature of interpersonal and intergroup attitudes, as well as the acquisition of social skills, are major components of each child's school experience. Indeed, this is a basic assumption underlying the purpose of this collection.

Miller and Harrington (Chapter 9) lay the foundation for understanding the social psychological processes at work in classroom interactions. Their approach emphasizes the role of identity in interpersonal and intergroup relations and is based on the notion that positive self-identity is a primary motivating factor underlying student behavior. They discuss four principles for the structure and assignment of cooperative work teams in the classroom (or workplace) that are designed to reduce social category salience and, thereby, to promote positive interpersonal and intergroup relations, particularly in culturally or ethnically heterogeneous settings.

Miller and Harrington give the reader an understanding of the principles and processes of ingroup-outgroup socialization that operate in both traditionally and cooperatively structured classrooms. They recognize the central role of the teacher in the formation and successful operationalization of various forms of cooperative learning teams. Central to their approach is the notion that social skills are instrumentally relevant to learning goals. Their four guiding principles are designed for teachers who are forming cooperative groups or making a transition to a cooperative classroom structure. Their first recommendation is to minimize the salience of the social category distinctions among the students in a classroom by assigning them to groups (and to roles within groups) explicitly on the basis of their unique personal attributes or by random assignment, rather than on the basis of their social category membership. Second, they recommend creating a classroom climate that minimizes threats to identity and self-esteem. Third, they suggest that teachers provide opportunities for students to know and be known by others on the basis of their individual attributes by employing tasks and procedures that facilitate mutual self-disclosure. And last, they note the need to provide a structure that will facilitate the development of the social skills necessary for interpersonal cooperation.

Miller and Harrington address the fundamental question of the goals, purposes, and functions served by public education. They argue that the development of positive interpersonal relations that foster appreciation and acceptance of diversity needs to be among the primary goals of schooling in our increasingly pluralistic society. They translate research outcomes into simple rules for practitioners and teachers that do not require intensive investment of human or material resources and can thus be easily implemented in the classroom. With an understanding of the principles underlying these intervention strategies, they hope to maximize the positive effects of cooperative learning within the classroom and lay a foundation for their generalizations not only to other school-related activities but to other social and interpersonal arenas as well.

Maruyama, Knechel, and Petersen (Chapter 10) also focus on intergroup acceptance and cultural diversity in the classroom. They draw on and summarize recent research on (1) cooperative goal structures, (2) controversy and concurrence-seeking in the context of cooperative learning, (3) role reversal and the related literature of ''consider the opposite'' (e.g., Lord, Lepper, & Preston, 1984), and

(4) majority and minority social influence, in order to develop a model of minority empowerment in numerically unbalanced cooperative groups. Their discussion seeks to extend earlier research by D. W. Johnson and R. T. Johnson on structured controversy in cooperative classroom learning (D. W. Johnson, R. T. Johnson, Pierson, & Lyons, 1985; Smith, D. W. Johnson, & R. T. Johnson, 1984).

Maruyama, Knechel, and Petersen (like O'Donnell and Dansereau and Miller and Harrington) test their model in controlled laboratory conditions using college students. Their experimental paradigm focuses on strategies to enable those who argue the minority position on an issue to overcome barriers inherent in minority status. Strategies that lessen pressure toward group conformity and encourage active participation include (1) consistency of opinion, (2) continued focus upon the issues at hand, (3) expression of personal confidence, (4) avoidance of behaviors that indicate the need for, or seeking of, personal acceptance and approval, and (5) appealing to the broader values and beliefs of the group.

Though the authors acknowledge that the testing of their model is still in the beginning stages, they have taken an organized, incremental approach that they believe shows much promise for structuring a classroom culture that fosters adaptive intellectual and social skills as well as intergroup acceptance. By examining issues for which there is no one correct answer, the model provides for the modeling of complex reasoning strategies. By focusing on role reversal in group decision making, they believe that they can provide students with a procedure for understanding how and why members of a group might disagree, and thus remove the stigma of disagreement.

Another way in which role reversal acts to counter possible negative outcomes inherent in conflict is by reducing self-defensiveness. This is complementary to one of the basic tenets of the model outlined by Miller and Harrington, that of reducing threat to self-esteem. Knowing that one's ideas will be carefully repeated back creates a climate in which those ideas will be listened to with attention and without ridicule. This is particularly significant in ethnically heterogeneous settings in which it is important to develop knowledge about and create acceptance of persons as individuals rather than as members of a particular social category. The finding by Maruyama and his colleagues that students working within the minority empowerment paradigm generally expressed satisfaction with the process and interest in working with each other again supports this view.

Part V   Conclusion

In our final chapter additional process events underlying cooperative interaction are discussed. First, we discuss the literature on social facilitation and inhibition of group performance and achievement and review the literature on the development of children's social understanding. Second, we discuss our vision of the merging of this knowledge into established educational practice. In conjunction with all the contributors here, we hope to provide educators and social scientists with a more complete understanding of the social processes operating in the classroom, allowing for the creation and implementation of flexible classroom structures and strategies to meet specific learning and social goals.

References

Anderson, J. R. (1985) *Cognitive psychology and its implications*. New York: W. H. Freeman.

Ashmore, R. D. (1970). Solving the problems of prejudice. In B. E. Collins (ed.), *Social psychology* (pp. 298–340). Reading, MA: Addison-Wesley.

Beller, E. (1955). Dependency and independence in young children. *Journal of Genetic Psychology, 87,* 23–35.

Berger, J., Cohen, B. P., & Zelditch, M., Jr. (1972). Status characteristics and social interaction. *American Sociological Review, 37,* 241–255.

Blanchard, F. A., Adelman, L., & Cook, S. W. (1975). Effect of group success and failure upon interpersonal attraction in cooperating interracial groups. *Journal of Personality and Social Psychology, 31,* 1020–1030.

Blanchard, F. A., & Cook, S. W. (1976). Effects of helping a less competent member of a cooperating interracial group on the development of interpersonal attraction. *Journal of Personality and Social Psychology, 34,* 1245–1255.

Castro, M. A. (1974). Reactions to receiving aid as a function of cost to the donor and opportunity to aid. *Journal of Applied Social Psychology, 4,* 194–209.

Cohen, E. G. (1982). Expectation states and interracial interaction in school settings. *Annual Review of Sociology, 8,* 209–235.

Cohen, E. G., Lotan, R., & Catanzarite, L. (1990). Treating status problems in the cooperative classroom. In S. Sharan (Ed.), *Cooperative learning: Theory and research* (pp. 203–228). New York: Praeger.

Cook, S. W., & Pelfrey, M. (1985). Reactions to being helped in cooperating interracial groups: A context effect. *Journal of Personality and Social Psychology, 49*(5), 1221–1245.

Damon, W., & Phelps, E. (1989). Critical distinctions among three methods of peer education. *International Journal of Educational Research, 58*(2), 9–19.

DePaulo, B. M., & Fisher, J. D. (1980). The costs of asking for help. *Basic and Applied Social Psychology, 1,* 23–35.

Deutsch, M. (1949). A theory of competition and cooperation. *Human Relations, 2,* 129–151.

Fisher, J. D., Harrison, C., & Nadler, A. (1978). Exploring the generalizability of donor-recipient similarity effects. *Personality and Social Psychology Bulletin, 4,* 627–630.

Fisher, J. D., & Nadler, A. (1974). The effect of similarity between donor and recipient on reactions to aid. *Journal of Applied Social Psychology, 4,* 230–243.

Gergen, K. J., Ellsworth, P., Maslach, C., & Seipel, M. (1975). Obligation, donor resources and reactions to aid in three nations. *Journal of Personality and Social Psychology, 3,* 390–400.

Gergen, K. J., Morse, S. J., & Kristeller, J. L. (1973). The manner of giving: Cross-national continuities in reactions to aid. *Psychologia, 16,* 121–131.

Gross, A. E., & Latané, B. (1974). Receiving help, giving help, and interpersonal attraction. *Journal of Applied Social Psychology, 4,* 210–223.

Johnson D. W., Johnson, R. T., Pierson, W. T., & Lyons, V. (1985). Controversy versus concurrence seeking in multi-grade and single grade learning groups. *Journal of Research in Science Teaching, 22*(9), 835–848.

Lord, C. G., Lepper, M. R., & Preston, E. (1984). Considering the opposite: A corrective strategy for social judgment. *Journal of Personality and Social Psychology, 47,* 1231–1243.

Marshall, H. H. (1988). Work or learning: Implications of classroom metaphors. *Educational Researcher, 17,* 9–16.

Miller, N., & Harrington, H. J. (1990). A situational identity perspective on cultural diversity and teamwork in the classroom. In S. Sharan (Ed.), *Cooperative learning: Theory and application* (pp. 39–75). New York: Praeger.

Morse, S. J. (1972). Help, likability and social influence. *Journal of Applied Social Psychology, 2,* 34–46.

Nadler, A., Fisher, J. D., & Streufert, S. (1974). The donor's dilemma: Recipient's reaction to aid from friend or foe. *Journal of Applied Social Psychology, 4,* 275–285.

Piaget, J. (1926) *Language and thought of the child.* New York: Harcourt Brace.

Shumaker, S. A., & Jackson, J. S. (1979). The adverse effects of nonreciprocated benefits. *Social Psychology Quarterly, 42,* 148–158.

Smith, K. A., Johnson, D. W., & Johnson, R. T. (1984). Effects of controversy on learning in cooperative groups. *Journal of Social Psychology, 122,* 119–209.

Steiner, I. (1972). *Group process and productivity.* New York: Academic Press.

Tajfel, H., Flament, C., Billig, M. G., & Bundy, R. F. (1971). Social categorization and intergroup behaviour. *European Journal of Social Psychology, 1,* 149–177.

Vygotsky, L. S. (1978). *Mind in society: The development of higher psychological processes.* Cambridge: Harvard University Press.

    (1986). *Thought and language.* Cambridge: MIT Press.

Wallston, B. S. (1976). The effects of sex-role ideology, self-esteem, and expected future interactions with an audience on male help-seeking. *Sex Roles, 2,* 353–356.

Part I

**Developmental Foundations
and the Social Construction
of Knowledge**

1 From Convention to Invention: Three Approaches to Peer Interactions During Writing

Sarah J. McCarthey and Susan McMahon

In the 1970s a shift in the dominant theory and practice of school writing instruction began. The shift was away from a focus on the written product and form of writing toward an emphasis on the writing process in all of its complexity. During the 1980s greater attention to the social contexts in which people learn to write while interacting with teachers and peers has been added (Freedman, Dyson, Flower, & Chafe, 1987). This paradigm shift in writing is related to the emerging social constructivist views of human learning and development.

This chapter briefly discusses social constructivism and provides a review of the current literature on peer interactions during writing. It then analyzes three types of peer group settings during writing activities using a social constructivist perspective. For this analysis we present scenarios illustrating three types of peer group interactions that might occur in actual classrooms. Several frameworks provide ways to relate peer interactions in writing to social constructivism.

Roots of Social Constructivism

A social constructivist view of learning has its philosophical roots in the work of Wittgenstein (1953) and Mead (1934) and has been further articulated in the work of Harré (1984). These philosophers share with Kuhn (1962) the conceptualization of knowledge as a social artifact that is maintained through a community of peers. Knowledge, then, is not based on an objective reality that can be measured and quantified but rather is consensually formed through social interaction (Bruffee, 1984, 1986).

The psychological roots of social constructivism are based on the theories of Vygotsky (1978, 1986) and others who have modified and developed his views

We wish to thank Annemarie Palincsar and James Gavelek for their contributions to our understanding of social constructivist theory, for their continual support, and for their helpful comments on earlier versions of this chapter. In the spirit of collaboration, the two authors contributed equally to the writing of this chapter.

17

(e.g., Bruner, 1985; Cole, 1985; Rogoff, 1986). Social constructivist views are based on the idea that knowledge is constructed by interactions of individuals within the society and that all thought is social in nature (Vygotsky, 1986; Williams, 1989). Learning is the result of internalization of social interaction; there is a movement from the interpsychological plane (between individuals) to the intrapsychological plane (within an individual). Learning occurs within the "zone of proximal development," defined as "the distance between a child's actual developmental level as determined by independent problem solving and the level of potential development as determined through problem solving under adult guidance or in collaboration with more capable peers" (Vygotsky, 1978, p. 86).

These features of social constructivist perspectives have increased attention to the role of dialogue in learning (Cazden, 1988; Edwards & Mercer, 1987) while focusing on the role of peers in instructional practices (Damon & Phelps, 1989). The rationale for engaging peers in the instruction of others is based on the notion that because learning is social in nature, students ought to be provided with opportunities to interact with one another. The purpose of peer interaction is to make the implicit nature of social learning explicit by encouraging active learning within social settings.

The connections between social constructivism and writing can be clearly linked. Social constructivism incorporates discourse with learning; this learning is internalized. If an individual's thoughts are internalized conversations, writing can be perceived as the reemergence of this internalized interaction (Bruffee, 1984). Further, to enhance one's writing ability, one would need to increase and vary the amounts and types of discourse. The role of peer interaction in writing increasingly becomes an area of inquiry. The following review of peer interactions during writing provides a foundation for an analysis of interactions from a social constructivist viewpoint.

Review of Research of Peer Interactions During Writing

Writing models that include three phases of the writing process – planning, drafting, and revising – have been used in both teaching and research (Hayes & Flower, 1980). Current research in peer interaction in writing can be analyzed not only in terms of these phases of the writing process but also in terms of Saunders's (1989) dimensions of "co-writing," in which peers collaborate on every task; "co-publishing," in which individuals produce a collaborative text based on individual texts; "co-responding," where individuals interact only during the revising process; and "helping," in which writers voluntarily help one another during the writing process. Saunders's categories distinguish roles that students play when working together on writing tasks.

Although some research has been done on the co-writing and helping roles, much of the classroom practice and most of the research on peer interaction during writing has focused on co-responding. Often students are arranged in small groups to respond to the individual texts that each student has produced; these groups are called peer response groups (DiPardo & Freedman, 1988). Research focusing specifically on revision when peers respond to and edit writing has revealed that students can help one another improve their writing through response. For instance, Nystrand's (1986) process-product studies compared several college-level classrooms and measured success through students' achievement based on writing samples. He found that students who responded to one another's writing tended to reconceptualize revision, not as editing, but as a more substantive rethinking of text, whereas students who did not work in groups viewed the task as editing only. An analysis of the talk within groups suggested that the groups were able to address rhetorical problems in writing in a concrete and cooperative way. Nystrand and Brandt (1989) investigated the talk of group members and found that trained raters were able to predict the type of revision a student would make based on the talk about that text, with the extent of the discussion predicting the level of revision.

Gere and Stevens (1985) found that response groups could stay on task and that students' comments attended to the writer's meaning in a way that was more specific and varied than the teacher's comments. Their analysis was based on comparing writing groups in fifth-, eighth-, tenth-, eleventh-, and twelfth-grade classrooms using transcripts of audiotapes of group interactions. In a related study Gere and Abbott (1985) found that grade level affected the topics discussed in groups; older students attended more to form whereas younger students focused on the content of the writing. Students tended to have more content-oriented discussions when they wrote narratives rather than expository texts.

In classrooms studied by Freedman (1987) students had opportunities to work in groups to respond to one another's texts. However, students worked at completing teacher-given tasks rather than responding to one another's writing in one of the classrooms. Freedman hypothesizes that the teacher never relinquished control but gave the students specific assignments to complete and directions on how to assess one another's work. In another classroom, Freedman found that students initiated talk about content and encouraged and questioned one another. The differences between these classrooms suggests that classroom structure affects peer interactions, the degree of control that students will have over their interactions, and, thus, what students can learn from one another.

In a study using microanalysis of peer conferences and interview data, Dahl (1988) found that fourth-grade students exchanged considerable information within writing conferences and were able to help one another. Writers did take into consideration respondents' comments on their drafts. Students expected to receive help in revising from their peers, and their expectations were met.

Group writing conferences influenced revision knowledge and revision activity in a study of 16 first graders (Fitzgerald & Stamm, 1990). The authors found that the extent of the influence of the peer conferences on knowledge was mediated by the student's entry-level knowledge of revision such that there were great gains for students with the least knowledge and little measurable change for students with high amounts of knowledge initially.

The commonality within these studies is the focus on revision of texts written by individual authors. Because the tasks focused on revision and the outcomes of the interactions, it is difficult to assess the interactive nature of the work students did. These studies highlight the complex relationship among the tasks on which students were working and the interactions among peers. The topics about which students wrote, the genre, the ways in which the teachers had framed the task, as well as the interactions among peers seemed to influence one another and affect the outcomes of the revision process.

Differences in tasks affect the interactions of peers, as evidenced in two studies in which students acted as writer-helpers (Carr & Allen, 1987; Heap, 1986). In these studies, students interacted during the writing phase. In Heap's (1986) study of first-grade writer-helpers, writers had the role of composing the texts, and helpers suggested or confirmed each writer's idea. Carr and Allen's study (1987) suggests that kindergartners can elicit help from one another during the writing process and peers will provide direct teaching when a peer asks for help. Children respond positively to direct teaching when they request help, but this teaching-learning relationship takes time to develop. Again, the task of writing individual texts determines to some degree the kind of interaction that students will undertake.

More prolonged interactions occurred under conditions in which students constructed texts together (Daiute, 1989; O'Donnell et al., 1985). O'Donnell and her colleagues examined college students who worked cooperatively to create a set of explicit instructions. Not only did students who wrote cooperatively write more explicit communicative instructions than those who wrote alone, but the students who worked together initially also wrote better instructions alone than those who initially wrote alone. In Daiute's (1989) study of third-, fourth-, and fifth-grade classrooms, students wrote collaborative stories with a partner. When student discourse was analyzed, the researchers found that the children engaged in playful talk that contained elements of critical thinking. After examining the texts the students wrote individually after collaborating, Daiute reported that students' individual writing improved as measured by increased elaboration of characters, plot segments, and images. Improvement occurred when there was a balance between playful talk (e.g., role playing, trying out concepts, and using imagery) and controlled talk (e.g., planning, evaluating, labeling, or controlling the writing process) within the collaboration.

Table 1.1. *Dimensions of peer groups*

	Peer tutoring	Cooperative learning	Peer collaboration
Role	Low on equality	High on equality	High on equality
Interactive structure	Low on mutuality	Medium-to-high on mutuality	High on mutuality
Task	Independent	Multiple contributions to one task	Joint task

As suggested by these studies, the task of composing a single piece together facilitates the interactions among peers. Saunders (1989) argues that co-writers engage in spontaneous, fast-paced, and wide-ranging discussions during the planning phase and that interaction during composing involves discussion, conflict, and debate focused on reaching consensus.

Viewed as a body, these studies suggest a relationship between the tasks and the interaction of peers. Additional research is needed about peer interaction during all of the phases of writing – planning, composing, and revising. To propose potential areas of research, in the following section we present three scenarios that highlight the distinctions among three types of peer interactions. The interactions take place during planning, drafting, and revising. These scenarios will also serve as a springboard for analysis in terms of social constructivist theory. In actual classroom settings, the three types of peer interactions would not remain so distinct. Because the tasks impinge to a high degree on the kinds of peer interaction that take place, we have considered this relationship in the presentation of our scenarios and tried to select tasks appropriate to each type of interaction.

Peer Interaction Scenarios

The three scenarios of peer interactions during writing are used to characterize each of the following: peer tutoring, cooperative learning, and peer collaboration; these three activities have been identified by Damon and Phelps (1989) as three major categories of peer instruction. Three dimensions – role, interactive structure, and task – frame the distinctions among the three approaches to instruction and will be used to connect peer-based instruction to a social constructivist view of learning and development (see Table 1.1). Role refers to the relationship between or among the participants based on who has knowledge and power. In relationship to writing, these roles can be viewed with regard to the degree of ownership over the text and in terms of the dynamics of the relationship between or among the peers. For example, Saunders (1989) discusses the idea of ownership, and Damon and Phelps (1989) use the term *equality* to refer to the degree of control over the text and within the interaction. The individual or individuals with ownership of a text have more control over it. A peer acting merely as an editor of another's writing has less ownership and, therefore, less power to initiate changes. However, if a peer is in the role of peer tutor because of greater knowledge, the individual has more authority because of greater knowledge and may influence subsequent changes.

The second dimension we use to frame our analysis is that of interactive structure (Saunders, 1989). Damon and Phelps (1989) introduced the term *mutuality* to refer to the amount and source of the interaction. As tasks and the roles of members within the group change, the pattern of interaction changes. A group described as "high on mutuality" would have all members contributing to the interaction most of the time, whereas in a group that was "low on mutuality," one member would tend to dominate the interaction.

The third dimension, task, is key because the nature of the task influences the interaction and the types of role relationships among the members of the group (Saunders, 1989). The task of simply editing or responding to another's paper is substantially different from constructing a text together – the demands of the task frame the amount and type of discourse and influence who will have control over the text. Clearly, the three dimensions of role, interactive structure, and task are interdependent.

In addition to using these three dimensions, our analysis includes other frameworks that are specific to each scenario, and it highlights how each type of peer interaction follows from social constructivist philosophy. We continue our analysis comparing and contrasting peer tutoring, cooperative learning, and peer collaboration through an examination of the conceptions of knowledge, the zone of proximal development, and discourse.

In the fourth- and fifth-grade classroom of Ms. Brooks, students are seated in pairs or small groups in different parts of the classroom. Some students are seated in chairs at tables in the middle of the room, and other pairs and groups of students are sitting on pillows or on the rug in the corners of the room. The teacher circulates among the groups of students and asks questions, provides suggestions, and keeps students on tasks. The task on which these students are working is writing about the field trip they had taken the previous day to the Museum of Natural History; the writing assignment is connected to the students' study of animal habitats and adaptations to the environment. Students may select from a variety of genres to produce their pieces, including a narrative form of their personal experiences in the museum, a description of a particular animal and its habitat, or a plan that highlights the most important features of the museum for a visiting tourist.

The teacher has organized three different types of group activities: peer tutoring, cooperative learning, and peer collaboration. Because the teacher has provided many opportunities for students to interact in various ways through the year, the students are quite experienced in writing with one another.

Peer Tutoring

Two girls, Angelique and Tonya, are sitting on the floor by the window. Tonya, a fifth grader, is the more experienced writer. She writes outside class, producing more developed text than many of the other students, and keeps a daily journal on her own that she shares with members of the class. The two girls are discussing the topics they want to write about. Tonya has decided she wants to write a story about the woolly mammoths. Angelique wants to write about the walk to the museum because she had so much fun talking with her friends. Tonya explains that this is not a good topic because it does not really relate to the field trip to the Natural History Museum. She suggests that Angelique select a topic more closely related to the museum. She indicates that it would be easier for her to help Angelique if both girls wrote on the same topic using the same genre. Angelique agrees to write about the woolly mammoths, too. Tonya reminds Angelique about many of the details the guide told them about the ancient creature; however, Tonya soon realizes they do not have enough information to write their papers. She suggests that they go to the library to find a book. When they return, Tonya reads the book she has selected to Angelique while Angelique takes notes. Tonya frequently stops and tells Angelique what to include in the notes.

After she has completed reading the book, Tonya suggests what information they will include. Angelique wants to include everything in the notes, but Tonya suggests ways they should limit the information. When they have completed this, the two girls begin to write their separate papers.

As they write, Angelique frequently asks Tonya for help. Her questions are sometimes about the text but more often about spelling or word choice. When the girls have completed their drafts, Tonya reads Angelique's paper. Tonya questions Angelique about the areas of her paper that are vague. When Angelique seems unclear about the questions, Tonya not only provides explanations about what Angelique should include but also elaborates on why she should include it. Angelique accepts Tonya's suggestions and agrees to incorporate them into her paper. The two girls then separate to work on their revisions. When they pair up again, it is Tonya's turn to provide Angelique with editorial comments. As with the previous meeting, Tonya provides the leadership and takes on the role of the knowledgeable one. Each girl then completes a final draft to be turned in to the teacher.

This scenario demonstrates many of the assumptions that underlie the use of peer tutors. Here, the task is for each girl to write her own paper. This task influences the roles and interactive structures. Because each one is responsible for creating a paper, it might appear that each has ownership over her own text. However, because Tonya has been recognized by both the teacher and Angelique as the more knowledgeable one, she has direct influence over what Angelique writes. As Damon and Phelps (1989) point out, the roles in peer tutoring are "low on equality." Because one child, Tonya, is perceived as the "knowledgeable other," there is limited equality in the partnership. Tonya has more knowledge and more control of the situation and Angelique is the novice with less knowledge and control.

In the scenario, the interactive structure is "low in mutuality" because Tonya is often dominant in the discourse. Angelique seems to contribute very little. However, each child gains from the interaction. Although the novice, who is perceived as the one with the greater need, gets more help, the expert gains from the experience of articulating and reconstructing her own knowledge (Webb, 1989).

Another way to examine the roles and interactive structures within peer tutoring is through what Rogoff (1986) described as "guided participation." Damon and Phelps (1989) connected Rogoff's five steps to the interaction or pattern of peer tutoring that fit the scenario we described. The first of these steps is the creation of a bridge from what is already learned to what needs to be learned. Tonya provides the bridge by questioning and guiding Angelique, as well as by modeling her own thinking through her responses to Angelique's questions. The second step in guided participation is the provision of a structure for problem solving. In the preceding scenario, Tonya realized they did not have enough information to begin writing, and it is she who provides the solution by suggesting to Angelique that they could go to the library to find a book.

The next facet of Rogoff's five-step plan states the need for transference of responsibility from the expert to the novice. This can be seen somewhat when Tonya reads aloud to Angelique. Angelique's role is to take notes. By allowing Angelique to take notes, Tonya transfers some of the responsibility to Angelique. The fourth aspect of the plan calls for both partners to participate in problem solving. This is evidenced in all aspects of the writing process with these two children through the course of their planning, writing, and revising their texts. Rogoff's final step, which states that the interaction may be both tacit and explicit, is displayed in Tonya's explicit suggestions about what to include in the text and the appropriateness of the topic selected.

This scenario demonstrates the interrelationships among role, task, and the resulting interactive structure. The writing task in this scenario influences the girls' roles, and the knowledge that each brings to the task affects these roles as well.

Cooperative Learning

At a round table in the center of the room sit four students – Mei-Lin, Juanita, Roberto, and Jonathan. These children are of mixed abilities and have been grouped by the teacher. Although the children will take on different roles within the group, each is seen by the teacher as an equal partner with something to contribute. This group has more students than some groups in the room because they have decided to complete a larger project. For their report on the day's field trip to the Natural History Museum they will complete a booklet with illustrations.

First they decide that there will be some specific roles that each child will take turns fulfilling. One of these will be to collect the necessary materials the group will need each day; another is to record information that arises in group discussions. Despite the role assignments, each child is required to gather information and complete a section of the final booklet.

In the planning stage, students discuss their ideas about what they want to include in the booklet. Mei-Lin is particularly interested in the exhibit on early humans and wants to write a poem. Juanita loves to draw and has already begun drawing the extinct animals she saw. Roberto and Jonathan each want to write informational texts about dinosaurs. Each child's ideas are given equal voice and consideration. Finally, Juanita discovers that each child's interests could be included under the title of "extinct creatures." They decide this will be their topic; then they discuss what each will contribute to the book. During this discussion they decide ways in which to gather the necessary information. They decide to go to the library.

After the group returns from the library, they begin reading individually. As they begin to discuss what they are learning, Roberto and Jonathan discover that their books give conflicting information about how dinosaurs became extinct. Confused, they ask the girls which information they think should be included in the report. As they discuss this, Mei-Lin suggests they go get another book to see what it says. The third book not only gives some information that is in the other two books but also provides some additional explanation. The group decides to manage this dilemma by stating in their booklet that there seem to be conflicting ideas about why the dinosaurs became extinct. Roberto decides he will handle this information in his paper.

As the children continue to gather information, they sometimes write alone and sometimes share ideas with other members of the group. They might ask each other for help in many different areas. Some share ideas about content; others ask for help spelling words. For example, while trying to draw a dinosaur, Juanita becomes confused. She has forgotten what the dinosaurs at the museum looked like. She remembers they had a lot of bones, but she wants to draw them as they looked when they were alive. She asks Roberto and Jonathan for help. Each boy contributes what he remembers from the visit and shows her pictures from their books. Soon, Juanita has a fairly representative picture.

As they move into the revision stage, each child reads her or his text to the group. Other members make suggestions or ask questions, but each child maintains ownership over her or his own text. As they continue to revise, they exchange papers frequently to help one another with copyediting. Each child sees and comments on every other child's text. The final product is a single booklet with four contributing authors.

Cooperative groups are formed in multiple ways, usually along five dimensions: teacher-imposed task and structure, task interdependence, individual accountability, use or nonuse of competition, and reward interdependence (Slavin, 1980). We described a group in which the first three were included. Because cooperative groups usually work on tasks assigned by the teacher (Damon &

Phelps, 1989), we kept this dimension. Task interdependence and individual accountability were included because they contributed to our presentation of a variety of situations in which peer interaction could be used in classrooms. The interdependence helps foster discussion, and the individual accountability contributes to maintaining some ownership over text.

We also described a noncompetitive situation; competition seems counter to a social constructivist perspective. Competition among group members fosters extrinsic motivation and individual achievement, which leads to limited engagement in discourse. Competition between groups may foster high levels of group engagement and discourse but hampers a favorable climate for a truly cooperative activity. We did not include a situation in which a reward structure was included for these same reasons and also because it can affect motivation negatively (Damon & Phelps, 1989; Webb, 1982).

The second scenario demonstrates a condition where student roles are to help one another solve problems and complete the assigned task, which is to construct a group booklet. As a group project, each child has ownership over a part of the text but has some investment in the completed booklet as well. In this situation, the group has joint authority. They make decisions as a group and as individuals. Although all members of the group might be consulted regarding a question, such as when Roberto and Juan are uncertain about which information to include about the extinction of dinosaurs, final decisions rest with the author of the particular piece.

Because equality and mutuality are usually high in such groups (Damon & Phelps, 1989), each student shares responsibility for the group roles as well as for her or his own text. Although they seek outside sources for information, they also talk to one another to gain ideas and to solve problems. Therefore, interaction patterns may vary but will be high because the children are working together throughout all of the writing stages (Saunders, 1989). Each child is seen as an equal; no single individual is the knowledgeable other. Instead, each child is perceived as capable of helping the others.

Peer Collaboration
Within the same classroom, pairs of students arranged in partners of their choice must create a single text that represents both students' ideas. Juan and Charlie are seated in a corner with their notebook pads and notes that each has taken from yesterday's visit to the museum. First, both boys look over their notes to select a topic and decide which genre they will use for the piece they will compose together. Juan describes the gazelle he has seen in one of the cases and the food that the gazelle eats. Charlie is interested in describing the various insects he has seen on his way to the museum. After describing their experience and what they liked and did not like about the museum trip, the boys ask each other what they will write about. Neither is interested in changing to the other's topic. After discussing other alternative topics, the boys agree that they will write about Bengal tigers and include the kinds and amount of food they eat.

Charlie suggests they include the places where the tigers live. Because neither of the boys took notes about the Bengal tiger, Charlie suggests they look in a book in the classroom that contains information about various animals and their habitats. Juan mentions that they should make a list divided into sections about "what tigers eat," "where tigers live," and "descriptions and size of tigers."

On the second day of the writing assignment, Juan and Charlie are back in their partnership ready to write their first draft. Initially, Juan writes down the sentences they both construct, and then Charlie takes over when Juan's arm gets tired. The students take turns writing sentences, asking each other questions, making suggestions for wording, and helping with spelling. They decide together how the paper will be organized and decide that the description of the tigers will begin the paper. Throughout the composing process, the boys continually ask each other questions. For instance, Juan asks Charlie when tigers attack humans and then Charlie asks Juan how to spell *habitat*.

As the boys continue to write about the Bengal tigers, Juan comments that the tigers may become extinct because there are so few of them, and the jungle is being continually cut down to build more and more houses for humans. Charlie becomes interested in this idea and suggests they really develop the issue of extinction and relate it to some of the ideas they have been discussing in class. Using what they know about tigers from other sources, the boys begin to make predictions about how a tiger in the future would have to adapt to the changing environment to survive. They brainstorm some possible changes in the size of the tiger, its habitat, and the food it would eat in a more populated area. They continue to write together, providing ideas and descriptions of the tiger's changing appearance and habitat.

Toward the end of class Juan reads the piece aloud to Charlie, who says the paper is no longer about the museum trip but about tigers presently and in the future. After discussing this issue, they decide they like what they have written, but it no longer fits what the teacher had assigned. The boys tell Ms. Brooks their problem. She recommends the students read their piece aloud to the whole class and ask the other students for their responses and suggestions about how to connect it to the trip.

On the third day, Juan reads the story to the whole class, and Charlie explains their concern about the lack of relationship between their work about the tiger and the class trip. They ask for suggestions to solve this problem. Various students provide suggestions ranging from forgetting about the class trip and leaving it the way it is to the idea of including a section that describes how the class field trip inspired the authors to do research on tigers and to make predictions about future habitats. After the group session, Charlie and Juan go back to their corner to consider the suggestions of their peers in order to revise the piece together.

We see here a high degree of collaboration at each phase of the writing process. The task is to create one paper for which both boys provide input. There is equality in authority and ownership over the text. No individual child is perceived as more knowledgeable. Also, both boys are working closely together at all stages of the writing process so there is a high amount of interaction (Saunders, 1989). Damon and Phelps (1989) would say there is a high degree of both equality and mutuality. Juan and Charlie are of equal status and have chosen to work together, each contributing ideas, concepts, and skills to the process. Although they start with different interests, they are able to find an intellectual space where they can work together and transform the knowledge they have to create something new.

At the planning stage, Juan and Charlie disagree about topic selection and genre, each bringing his own experiences, understanding of the assignment, and interest to the situation. Yet they find a mutual space where they can both contribute knowledge and find more information about tigers. During the drafting stage, they construct a text together by composing sentences, providing details, and engaging in ongoing dialogue with one another. Other students contribute during the response and revision stage by suggesting how to resolve the problem of relating the information about tigers to the field trip.

Because the writing process was collaborative, the end product was significantly different from a piece that either partner would have written alone. The learning process was also collaborative, because it took place during the performance of "mutual tasks in which the partners work together to produce something that neither could have produced alone" (Forman & Cazden, 1986, p. 329). The final piece of writing also reflected the input from the total group. Charlie's and Juan's thinking about the relationship between the trip and the tigers was changed by the responses of the group, even though their final piece did not specifically reflect any one response by a class member.

It is through their discourse that the students achieve this high degree of collaboration. Throughout the process of writing, both boys contribute ideas, make suggestions, and compose text. The two students actually construct new knowledge through their predictions about how tigers might adapt to their future environments. During their dialogue, the students talk through their understandings of concepts related to the adaptation of the tiger, and they achieve "socially justified belief" (Bruffee, 1984; Rorty, 1983). The students provide an audience for one another, generate details, locate promising topics, and provide each other with moral support in a way that is consistent with Gebhardt's (1980) ideal of collaborative groups.

Comparisons of Peer Interactions

The next section compares and contrasts the three types of peer interactions in terms of the social constructivist aspects of conception of knowledge, zone of proximal development, and discourse (see Table 1.2).

Conception of Knowledge

Each of the three types of peer interaction embodies a slightly different conception of knowledge. In peer tutoring, one member of the team is perceived as a

Table 1.2. *Features of social constructivist theory*

	Peer tutoring	Cooperative learning	Peer collaboration
Conceptions of knowledge	Unidirectional Transmission	Multidirectional Transmission/ transformation Consensually formed	Bidirectional Transformation Consensually formed
Zone of proximal development		Fluid and dynamic	Fluid and dynamic
	Tutor aids tutee in transfer of control	No focus on transfer of control	No focus on transfer of control
Discourse	Unidirectional	Uni- and multidirectional	Bidirectional

knowledgeable other. The use of this model presupposes that knowledge is passed from one individual to another in a unidirectional manner. The goal of the situation is the transmission of the identified skill from the knowledgeable other to the novice. Peer tutoring is assumed to be a method whereby the novice can gain proficiency in a skill. Webb (1989) has identified six conditions for effective transmission of knowledge in the peer-tutoring situation. To be effective, the tutor must provide help that is relevant, appropriately elaborated, timely, and understandable to the target student, as well as provide an opportunity to use the new information. The final condition is that the target student take advantage of the opportunity to use the new information. These six conditions assume considerable knowledge on the part of the tutor because five of the six conditions depend on the tutor's ability. Only the final one places responsibility on the other learner.

This model represents a social constructivist perspective because it acknowledges the benefits of a knowledgeable other. This knowledgeable individual helps provide the structures for the other, less-advanced learner. The peer tutor model is more of a knowledge transmission model than the other two approaches because knowledge is passed from one individual to another. Through the process of articulating her knowledge, the tutor expands her own knowledge. However, the tutee has little role in shaping the knowledge.

The cooperative learning scenario presented here relates a situation that more closely approximates a social constructivist view than some other cooperative groups might. As mentioned above, these groups can vary along five dimensions (Slavin, 1980). Because the group described here was interdependent in relation to the task and placed in a noncompetitive environment, the students were encouraged to interact more. As a result, each was seen as a possible source of knowledge. Even though the group went to outside sources to gather information, they also turned to one another for assistance. Each child within a cooperative group is perceived as "knowing" (Damon & Phelps, 1989) and there is a recognition that knowledge is reached through some discussion and consensus. This supports a social constructivist viewpoint of knowledge being consensually formed through interaction (Bruffee, 1984).

One way in which cooperative groups differ from peer tutoring is that there is no designated knowledgeable other in cooperative groups. All are perceived as potential sources of knowledge depending upon the specific task. In addition, there is no assumption that knowledge will be transmitted only from one to another. Instead of unidirectional flow of knowledge, this model recognizes a multidirectional one.

Our scenario depicting collaboration between two students most closely approximates Bruffee's (1984) conception of socially constructed knowledge. As in the cooperative group, both children see the other as an equal. They construct their paper from what each remembers about the trip to the museum. The children consult outside, published sources; however, when they encounter a problem, they seek help from their peers. Knowledge is something one gains through talking with others. The task is one that each finds challenging, and the product is substantially different from what each would produce alone (Damon & Phelps, 1989).

The collaborative group differs from peer tutoring in that each student is perceived as knowledgeable and capable of contributing to the project. Neither is being instructed by the other. It differs from a cooperative group in that all knowledge is constructed and sought together. If we construct a continuum to compare the relative views about knowledge contained in each of the types of peer interaction, peer tutoring focuses more on transmission of information from one individual to another. At the other end of the social constructivist continuum lies the collaborative model, in which knowledge is negotiated. The cooperative model contains aspects of transmission and negotiation depending on the particular task.

Zone of Proximal Development

Three interrelated key ideas form the basis of Vygotsky's notion of the zone of proximal development: (1) the conception that there is a difference between actual development and potential development, (2) the belief that what can be achieved with the aid of an adult or more knowledgeable peer is substantially different from what can be accomplished alone, and (3) the implicit notion of transference of control from the more knowledgeable other to the learner. These features of the zone of proximal development have implications for the three approaches to peer interaction in relation to a social constructivist theory as articulated by Vygotsky and those like Wertsch (1985) and Cole (1985) who have developed the concept of the zone of proximal development. Cole (1985) focuses on the joint activity in which participants exercise differential responsibility by virtue of having different expertise within the zone.

If we assume that having more ''capable'' peers is essential to the zone of proximal development, then the peer-tutoring model is consistent with the social constructivist view because there is clearly a more knowledgeable other in the peer-tutoring scenario. In peer tutoring there is an assumption that the tutee can be brought to a different level of understanding through interaction with the tutor; this understanding would not be achieved by the tutee working alone. In addition, there is a clear attempt to transfer control of the learning from the tutor to the tutee through bridging procedures outlined by Rogoff (1986).

In contrast, both the peer collaborative and cooperative learning models contain more fluid and dynamic conceptions of the zone of proximal development. Students are constructing knowledge together without an attempt to transfer control from one student to another. For any given task, there is a more capable peer who assists the others in learning a new concept and, thus, helps the other students develop within the zone. However, because the roles of the students shift throughout the process, there is no designated capable peer who always assists others. The case can be made that students can be brought to a different level of knowledge and that something qualitatively different will emerge through their interaction in relation to the tasks in peer collaboration, but there is no focus on transference of control. Expertise and responsibility are continually changing as specific tasks change.

Discourse

Differences in the amount and direction of the discourse characterize each of the three approaches during writing. In the peer-tutoring situation, the discourse tends to be unidirectional: from the more knowledgeable student to the less knowledgeable one. Because of the nature of the task and the differences in expertise, the tutor assumes more of a traditional teacher role and thus dominates the dialogue. Several studies suggest that peer interaction during writing often tends to replicate traditional teacher roles and emphasizes tasks such as editing and evaluating (Freedman, 1987; Graner, 1987). The unidirectional flow of the discourse reflects the purposes of peer tutoring; essentially, the tutor structures the writing process for the less knowledgeable student.

The dialogue may be more limited in scope in the peer-tutoring situation than in collaborative learning settings because of the tasks and the lack of equality in the situation. The dialogue would tend to focus on making specific improvements in the student's draft. The tutor, however, may still gain cognitively through the very activity of explaining to the less knowledgeable student. It is again through the vehicle of discourse that the tutor learns. Webb (1989) found that the level of elaboration that students provided one another through interaction was related to high achievement. Therefore, the dialogue might well be beneficial for both students in a peer-tutoring situation.

In contrast to peer tutoring, peer collaboration is bidirectional, with a continual flow of discourse between the two students. The nature of the task of constructing a story together requires continual, lengthy dialogue. The nature of the dialogue changes as the task develops and changes.

The discourse in cooperative learning is at times unidirectional, for instance, when one student is explaining certain ideas to others and is assuming the role of the expert, but the flow is multidirectional when students are weighing alternatives and making decisions as a group. The nature of the dialogue is dependent upon the particular situation; however, the tendency is for students to report to one another what each has done. Individual ownership of ideas diminishes in collaborative learning.

The three approaches to peer interaction in writing all emphasize discourse among students; dialogue as a vehicle for internalizing the social world is a fundamental tenet of social constructivist theory. The theory implies that more opportunities for dialogue, as well as the quality of the dialogue, will allow internalization to occur. Although collaborative learning may provide more opportunities for students to engage in discourse, the quality will depend on the specific context and is not necessarily a function of the type of group interaction.

What becomes clear after analyzing the three approaches to peer interaction in writing is the interdependency of roles, interactive structures, and tasks, which, in turn, are related to conceptions of knowledge, the zone of proximal development, and discourse. Peer tutoring, cooperative learning, and peer collaboration serve different functions and have different interaction patterns to serve those functions. One type of interaction is not necessarily better than another type of interaction; rather, the appropriateness of each depends on the knowledge of the individuals, the purposes of instruction, and the nature of the specific task in relation to the broader goals of writing within the curriculum.

Broader goals of writing instruction include both transmission and transformation of knowledge; both goals are important and consistent with social constructivist theory. Social constructivist theory assumes that students need to learn the norms, knowledge, and skills of the culture and that students should be part of the process of creating something new because knowledge is dynamic. Writing instruction can incorporate both goals by equipping students with knowledge and skills to participate in the larger culture while encouraging students to go beyond the information and contribute to the production of knowledge. Peer tutoring is more aligned with transmission goals because the tutor is helping the tutee to acquire the knowledge and skills necessary for participating in literate culture. Peer collaboration is more aligned with goals of knowledge transformation because the students work together to create something new. Students need opportunities to participate in all of these activities to learn the tools necessary to communicate with others within the culture as well as to be active in producing new knowledge to change the existing society.

Future Directions

Future research needs to bring together the strands of discourse, peer interaction, and writing. Future research should focus on establishing the links between different types of peer interaction during writing and student learning. Investigation of student learning could examine improvements in students' texts as well as changes in students' discourse as a measure of what students have internalized from the social interactions. Both sociolinguistic and process-product studies can contribute to our understanding of the complex relationships among peer interactions and learning. Precedence for analysis of the discourse between the teacher and students exists in the literature (Edwards and Mercer, 1987), and a rationale for the importance of discourse among peers can be found in Cazden (1988). Future studies need to build on Daiute's studies (1989) of what occurs during the discourse surrounding student writing. Continued research linking peer interaction with the texts students produce will also be of major importance in assessing the value of peer interaction.

Conclusion

We have presented the fundamental assumptions of the social constructivist framework in order to analyze three different types of peer interactions during writing tasks. Peer tutoring, cooperative learning, and collaborative learning differ along the dimensions of knowledge, the zone of proximal development, and discourse. Each of these types of peer interaction can be viewed as falling along a continuum from transmission to transformation of knowledge, from more static roles to dynamic and fluid roles of the knowledgeable other, and from unidirectional to multidirectional types of discourse. The types of interactions and the tasks in which students are engaged interrelate in complex ways that require further research to investigate the nature of those relationships; this research could be used to develop models of writing and peer interaction for improved classroom instruction.

References

Bruffee, K. A. (1984). Collaborative learning and the "Conversation of mankind." *College English, 46*(7), 635–652.
    (1986). Social construction, language, and the authority of knowledge: A bibliographical essay. *College English, 48*(8), 773–790.
Bruner, J. S. (1985). Vygotsky: A historical and conceptual perspective. In J. V. Wertsch (Ed.), *Culture, communication, and cognition: Vygotskian perspectives* (pp. 21–34). Cambridge: Cambridge University Press.
Carr, E., & Allen, J. (1987, December). *Peer teaching and learning during writing time in kindergarten.* Paper presented at the National Reading Conference, St. Petersburg, FL.
Cazden, C. B. (1988). *Classroom discourse: The language of teaching and learning.* Portsmouth, NH: Heinemann.
Cole, M. (1985). The zone of proximal development: Where culture and cognition create each other. In J. V. Wertsch (Ed.), *Culture, communication, and cognition: Vygotskian perspectives* (pp. 146–161). Cambridge: Cambridge University Press.
Dahl, K. (1988). Peer conferences as social contexts for learning about revision. In J. Readence (Ed.), *Dialogues in literacy research* (pp. 307–315). Chicago: 37th Yearbook of the National Reading Conference.
Daiute, C. (1989). Play as thought: Thinking strategies of young writers. *Harvard Educational Review, 59*(1), 1–23.
Damon, W., & Phelps, E. (1989). Critical distinctions among three approaches to peer education. *International Journal of Educational Research, 58*(2), 9–19.
DiPardo, A., & Freedman, S. W. (1988). Peer response groups in the writing classroom: Theoretic foundations and new directions. *Review of Educational Research, 58*(2), 119–149.
Edwards, D., & Mercer, N. (1987). *Common knowledge.* New York: Methuen.
Fitzgerald, J., & Stamm, C. (1990). Effects of group conferences on first-grader's revisions of writing. *Written Communication, 7*(1), 96–135.
Forman, E. A., & Cazden, C. B. (1986). Exploring Vygotskian perspectives in education: The cognitive value of peer interaction. In J. V. Wertsch (Ed.), *Culture, communication, and cognition: Vygotskian perspectives* (pp. 323–347). Cambridge: Cambridge University Press.
Freedman, S. W. (1987). *Response to student writing* (Research Rep. No. 23). Urbana, IL: National Council of Teachers of English.
Freedman, S. W., Dyson, A. H., Flower, L., & Chafe, W. (1987). *Research in writing: Past, present and future* (Tech. Rep. No. 1). Berkeley, CA: Center for the Study of Writing.
Gebhardt, R. (1980). Teamwork and feedback: Broadening the base of collaborative writing. *College English, 42*(1), 69–74.
Gere, A. R., & Abbott, R. D. (1985). Talking about writing: The language of writing groups. *Research in the Teaching of English, 19*(4), 362–385.
Gere, A. R., & Stevens, R. (1985). The language of writing groups: How oral response shapes revision. In S. W. Freedman (Ed.), *The acquisition of written language: Response and revision* (pp. 85–105). Norwood, NJ: Ablex.

Graner, M. (1987). Revision workshops: An alternative to peer editing groups. *English Journal, 76*(3), 40–45.

Harré, R. (1984). *Personal being: A theory for individual psychology.* Cambridge: Harvard University Press.

Hayes, J. R., & Flower, L. S. (1980). Identifying the organization of writing processes. In L. W. Gregg & E. R. Steinberg (Eds.), *Cognitive processes in writing* (pp. 3–30). Hillsdale, NJ: Erlbaum.

Heap, J. L. (1986). *Collaborative practices during computer writing in a first grade classroom.* Paper presented at the annual meeting of the American Educational Research Association, San Francisco.

Kuhn, T. (1962). *The structure of scientific revolutions.* Chicago: University of Chicago Press.

Mead, G. H. (1934). *Mind, self, and society from the standpoint of a social behaviorist.* Chicago: University of Chicago Press.

Nystrand, M. (1986). Learning to write by talking about writing: A summary of research on intensive peer review in expository writing at the University of Wisconsin–Madison. In M. Nystrand (Ed.), *The structure of written communication* (pp. 79–211). Orlando, FL: Academic Press.

Nystrand, M., & Brandt, D. (1989). Response to writing as a context for learning to write. In C. M. Anson (Ed.), *Writing and response: Theory, practice, and research* (pp. 209–230). Urbana, IL: National Council of Teachers of English.

O'Donnell, A., Dansereau, D., Rocklin, T., Lambiotte, J., Hythecker, V., & Larson, C. (1985). Cooperative writing: Direct effects and transfer. *Written Communication, 2*(3), 307–315.

Rogoff, B. (1986). Adult assistance of children's learning. In T. E. Raphael (Ed.), *Contexts of school based literacy* (pp. 27–40). New York: Random House.

Rorty, R. (1983). *Philosophy and the mirror of nature.* Princeton, NJ: Princeton University Press.

Saunders, W. M. (1989). Collaborative writing tasks and peer interaction. *International Journal of Educational Research, 13*(1), 101–112.

Slavin, R. E. (1980). Cooperative learning. *Review of Educational Research, 50*(2), 315–342.

Vygotsky, L. S. (1978). *Mind in society: The development of higher psychological processes.* Cambridge: Harvard University Press.

(1986). *Thought and language.* Cambridge: MIT Press.

Webb, N. M. (1982). Student interaction and learning in small groups. *Review of Educational Research, 52*(3), 421–445.

(1989). Student interaction and learning in small groups. *International Journal of Educational Research, 13*(1), 21–31.

Wertsch, J. V. (1985). *Vygotsky and the social formation of mind.* Cambridge: Harvard University Press.

Williams, M. (1989) Vygotsky's social theory of mind. *Harvard Educational Review, 59*(10), 108–126.

Wittgenstein, L. (1953). *Philosophical investigations.* (G. E. M. Anscomb, Trans.). Oxford, England: Blackwell & Mott.

2   Cooperative Problem Solving:
A Link to Inner Speech

Barbara L. Bershon

As individuals verbally exchange ideas during a collaborative task, they create opportunities to use a vocabulary that directs and controls problem-solving behavior. Over time, vocabulary used during problem solving becomes internalized into what Vygotsky (1934/1962) defines as inner speech. He believes that inner speech then becomes part of a repertoire of cognitive skills. Other cognitive theorists (Dewey, 1964; Mead, 1934) agree with Soviet psychologists (Levina, 1981; Luria, 1961, 1981; Vygotsky, 1934/1962, 1978, 1981) that cognition develops not in an isolated internal process but in a process that internalizes social interactions.

Cooperative problem solving is a learning situation rich with the social interaction important to inner speech and cognitive development. Such situations allow an individual to (1) guide task involvement and (2) develop a vocabulary of three types of speech: social, egocentric, and inner. This chapter explores Vygotsky's theory of inner speech from its incipient form as social dialogue through its transformation as egocentric language to its final form as verbal thought. It then presents research that suggests a link between cooperative problem solving and the development of inner speech. Finally, it considers the implications that cooperative problem solving and its production of inner speech may have for classroom learning.

Development of Inner Speech

According to Vygotsky, the development of verbal thought that often accompanies cooperative problem solving progresses from social dialogue to egocentric language to its culmination in children's use of inner speech while engaged in

The author acknowledges the gracious assistance of Principal Nancy Perkins and the teachers, students, and parents of Chevy Chase Elementary School, Maryland. Appreciation also goes to Alice Kreindler, Joyce Schwartz, and Laura Seaman for their conscientious coding of the data; and special thanks to Hannah Fein for her editorial assistance.

36

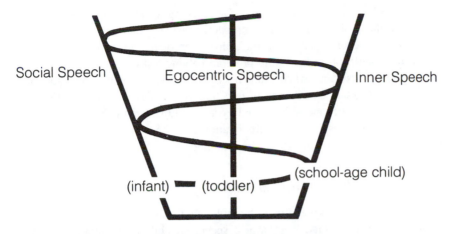

Figure 2.1. Spiral development of speech used to guide problem solving.

task solution. Vygotsky (1978, p. 56) reasons, however, that the development of speech used to mediate problem solving occurs not on a linear continuum but rather in a spiral passing through the same point at each new revolution while advancing to a higher level.

Figure 2.1 shows the spiral-like development of speech used to guide problem solving. Speech used for problem solving begins during social encounters involving communication and mutual regulation between children and adults or among children of varying capabilities. In this way, children build a lexicon of regulatory vocabulary that enables them to produce egocentric language to direct, control, and plan their activities during problem solving. Finally, children internalize this language as inner speech, developing a vocabulary that they can draw on during task involvement to direct their actions.

The development of inner speech is thus a recursive process that repeatedly entails the occurrence of social dialogue and the production of egocentric language. As children develop cognitively, the social speech used in a new problem-solving task includes the mediating speech they have internalized during previous task involvement. Communication and mutual regulation among individuals working together on a problem-solving task begin again with social speech, but now with an enriched lexicon of mediating speech that was previously internalized. Stated simply when confronting new, collaborative problem-solving tasks, individuals use social speech. As an understanding of the new information develops during social encounters through the comprehension of the meanings of new words, individuals direct their behavior with overt, egocentric language while attempting the task. Finally, individuals can accomplish the task by mentally carrying out the planning, directing, and controlling of the behavior needed to succeed with the use of inner speech. On reaching the end of one level of the spiral, when the skills needed to accomplish the task are internalized, these new cognitions then become part of an individual's problem-solving repertoire that can be used when confronting future problem-solving tasks.

As Cole (1985) explains, when children's intrapsychological skills (inner speech) increase, children attain a new level of possibilities for social interaction. Wertsch (1985), Wertsch and Stone (1985), and Forman and Cazden (1985) also assert that there are social aspects of internalization and that language has a role in mediating both social and individual functioning.

Social Dialogue and Egocentric Language

The primary function of speech in both children and adults involves communication through social contact. The earliest speech of children is thus essentially social. Luria (1981) and Bruner (1978) describe how both verbal communication and nonverbal actions between parent and child lay the foundation of children's cognitive development. Luria explained that when a mother asked her infant to "get the ball," she drew the child's attention to the ball while also organizing the child's motor act. When Bruner reported how verbal and nonverbal interactions between mother and child were the basis for children's cognitive development, he defined four domains in which both prelinguistic and verbal communication occurred: (1) affiliating, that is, social interaction between mother and child; (2) indicating, that is, the mother's attempt to direct the child's attention to the task at hand; (3) requesting, that is, the mother's use of communication to obtain services, objects, and cooperation from the child; and (4) generating possibilities, that is, pretending, imagining, and engaging in make-believe. Bruner described how these four communication functions allow children to acquire language during social problem solving with their parents (see Table 2.1).

During these social encounters with adults, children develop their first self-regulating skills. Levina (1981) also proposes that as children begin to understand others' speech they become acquainted with the fact that speech allows them both to separate the environment into objects and to direct and control actions, further suggesting that self-directed acts have their origins in children's early verbal communication with adults.

Egocentric speech emerges when children transfer the language developed during social, collaborative encounters they experience with adults to directing and controlling their own behavior through speech directed toward themselves. Levina (1981, p. 291) contends that young children initially label their ongoing actions because they want to ensure that these actions are comprehensible to others.

Levina (1981) and Luria (1981) explain that subsequently egocentric language occurs in the absence of other people. At this point in toddler speech (i.e., overt

Table 2.1. *Social dialogue: communication through social context*

Affiliating	Social interaction between parent and child, e.g., taking turns, acknowledging presence
Indicating	Parent's direction of the child's attention to the task at hand, e.g., pointing to a picture in a book
Requesting	Parent's use of communication to obtain services, objects, and cooperation from the child, e.g., asking the child to get the ball
Generating possibilities	Parent's communication about imaginary things, e.g., role playing, referring to events that have not occurred

speech used to direct and control behavior), Luria (1981) states that children tend first to describe the setting and to state the difficulty they are confronting before they begin to plan a possible solution. Levina explains that these types of verbal directions that accompany actions are precursors to verbal planning that precedes action. For example, when 4-year-olds selected 5 square blocks from an assortment of various shaped blocks, they counted aloud while performing the task. One child said, "Five square blocks. I gotta count because I don't know how many five is." Another child started counting, "one, two . . . where's another? . . . I find four, I mean five." She counted the five blocks one more time after she put them in a pile.

In his research Vygotsky (1978) reports that children's egocentric speech not only accompanied the task but also played a specific role in task solution. In this regard, he explained that children's speech and action were part of one and the same complex psychological function, directed toward the solution of the problem at hand. In fact, Vygotsky believes that the more complex the action demanded by the situation, and the less direct the solution, the greater the importance played by speech in task solution.

Inner Speech

Vygotsky (1978) describes how the greatest change in children's capacity to use language as a problem-solving tool occurs when egocentric speech (which has previously been used to address an adult) is turned inward. Instead of appealing to adults, children appeal to themselves. Vygotsky thus describes how language takes on an *intra*personal function in addition to an *inter*personal use.

At first children's intrapersonal use of speech occurs overtly in the form of egocentric language, as described above. But over time, the speech used to direct and control problem solving disappears. This type of speech at first becomes fragmentary and appears only in the form of reduced and disconnected links and is sometimes replaced by whispering. Luria (1961) maintains that this type of speech gradually becomes an abbreviated "internal speech," which he believes is an invariable part of thinking.

Vygotsky (1934/1962, p. 133) explains that in their function, egocentric speech and inner speech are similar. Both types of speech do not merely accompany children's activities; they serve mental orientation and conscious understanding; they help in overcoming difficulties; they are speech for the self, intimately and usefully connected with a child's thinking. Vygotsky reasons that the result of the development of egocentric speech is that it becomes inner speech.

Levina (1981) provides evidence supporting her belief that egocentric speech develops into inner speech when she reports that in studies with pictograms older children (8 to 10 years of age) perform the task silently, whereas 5- and 6-year-olds perform the task aloud. She believes that the older children carry out their verbal planning internally – in the form of inner speech planning. Levina also reports that at the intermediate stage between using egocentric and inner speech children are inclined to reason silently, yet they often revert to planning through external speech.

A Study of Elementary Students' Reported Inner Speech During Cooperative Problem Solving

Soviet Psychologists (Levina, 1981; Luria, 1961, 1981; Vygotsky, 1934/1962, 1978, 1981) hypothesize that at about age 7 or 8 children begin to use inner speech along with egocentric speech during problem solving. In their studies, however, no attempts are made to directly elicit children's inner speech.

To provide such evidence Bershon (1988) created a cooperative problem-solving environment designed to generate inner speech and measure its use. Bershon grouped 96 third- through sixth-grade students (48 boys and 48 girls) into four-person, same-gender groups to create three configurations of ability: (1) medium–high (2 medium-ability and 2 high-ability students), (2) all medium (4 medium-ability students), and (3) medium–low (2 medium-ability and 2 low-ability students). She modeled these groupings after a study by Webb (1985) that reported increased amounts of verbal interaction (i.e., helping behaviors among heterogeneous-ability groups as opposed to homogeneous-ability groups).

Giving and receiving help during task engagement involves the type of social dialogue that Vygotsky (1934/1962) posits is used in developing inner speech. Each group was asked to work cooperatively as they build a Lego-blocks model as quickly as possible. This task entailed a manipulative activity modeled after the Lego-blocks construction of Sharan, Raviv, Kussel, and Hertz-Lazarowitz

(1984) and was designed around Vygotsky's (1934/1962, pp. 46–47) notions that children use external signs and external operations (e.g., manipulative tasks) to help internalize overt speech.

Cooperative Problem-Solving Task

Each group constructed a model using 100 small interconnecting Lego blocks. Before the students began working on the Lego construction, the experimenter read instructions adapted from Sharan et al. (pp. 102–103). Students were told to use the Lego pieces in the middle of the table to build an exact copy of the Lego model at the end of the table. They were told to do this in two parts. First, the group had up to 15 minutes to plan how to build the model. Students in the various groups took from 1 to 15 minutes, with an average of 4.5 minutes, to plan the construction. Next, they had a building period. The instructions emphasized that students were to work together during the planning and building of the model. All groups were given enough time to successfully complete the construction, and all successfully completed it. The various groups took from 16 to 90 minutes, with an average of 47.5 minutes, to construct the Lego model. All groups were videotaped during their construction phase.

Spontaneous Overt Social/Egocentric Speech Used During Cooperative Problem Solving

As Vygotsky (1934/1962, 1978) would have predicted, when students were experiencing difficulty with the Lego construction, that is, when they said things like "this is impossible" or "I bet there's a trick," they also engaged in much verbal collaboration as they attempted to find the appropriate Lego pieces. A group of third-grade girls illustrate the use of social/egocentric speech when having a difficult time constructing a Lego boat dock. The following dialogue is abbreviated from a taped session:

DOROTHY: Now where's the other one?
RACHEL: It's over here somewhere. There should be another white little thing.
KATIE: Okay, find another white one of these – another white one.
LAURA: Yeah, like this.
DOROTHY: Hey, wait a minute. There should be another one of these.
RACHEL: There should be another one of these for us. See, look. Look, we need these and there's only one. Did you use one of the white things down there somewhere?
LAURA: No, no we didn't.
RACHEL: Well, where is it, then?
DOROTHY: Probably on the floor.
RACHEL: Well, I don't see it.

KATIE: Let me see. You might have used one by mistake. Let me see. You
    need 1-2 and you have 1-2.
RACHEL: Oh, we used one down here but. . . .
DOROTHY: Yeah, but we're supposed to.
LAURA: Well, you might have used two of these.
DOROTHY: The boat here is the exact same except for this.
RACHEL: Here, let's see, let's match them up.

In this study, as Soviet psychologists (Levina, 1981; Luria, 1961, 1981; Vygotsky 1934/1962, 1978, 1981) found in their studies too, it was difficult to
distinguish social speech from egocentric speech, in the spontaneous communication expressed by the girls as they worked on the task.

Elicitation and Measurement of Inner Speech

Bershon used two different interview procedures to elicit "verbal thoughts" students had while building the model. The method of elicitation was of particular
interest because previous researchers who have provided evidence of students'
cognitive engagement during problem solving did not consider how the methods
used to elicit students' thoughts might have affected their verbal reports (Ames,
1984; Diener & Dweck, 1978; Peterson & Swing, 1982; Peterson, Swing, Stark,
& Waas, 1984, Rohrkemper & Bershon, 1984). Bershon used stimulated recall
interview procedures, modified from ones used by Peterson and Swing (1982)
and Peterson et al. (1984). The playing and pausing of the videotapes were either
student controlled or interviewer controlled.

Following the construction task the four girls were individually asked to report
the verbal thoughts they had had while building the model. Each girl watched a
videotape of the Lego project to stimulate her recall of these thoughts. These
interviews were videotaped, as well. Students were randomly assigned to either
an interviewer-controlled interview procedure or a student-controlled interview
procedure.

In the interviewer-controlled procedure students were shown segments of the
videotape of the Lego construction and asked to report what they thought about
or said to themselves during five designated times: (1) before instructions were
read, (2) after instructions were given, (3) after the planning time, (4) during an
easy part and during a difficult part of the construction, and (5) upon successful
completion of the project. Even though the videotape was fast-forwarded between segments, the tape moved slowly enough so that students could see the
action and thus keep their train of thought.

In the student-controlled procedure students were told to stop the videotape of
the Lego construction whenever they remembered saying anything to themselves
or thinking anything special. Students were also told that they could fast-forward

the tape if there were long periods of time when they were not saying anyth
to themselves. The students who participated in the student-controlled intervie
procedure tended to stop the tape during the same time segments that were use
in the interviewer-controlled procedure. Both interviews took about 30 minutes.

Results

The examples of types of reported inner speech statements provide suggestive
evidence of the cognitions that some researchers assert influence task performance (e.g., Bandura, 1977a, 1977b, 1989; Bershon & Rohrkemper, 1986; Corno
& Rohrkemper, 1985; Graham, 1988; Pressley, Heisel, McCormick, & Nakamura, 1982; Rohrkemper & Corno, 1988; Schunk, 1984; Weiner, 1979). These
cognitions include (1) task-related inner speech (e.g., "which piece do I need
now?"); (2) self-related inner speech (e.g., "I was kind of worried that we
would not get it right"); (3) other-related inner speech (e.g., "they were right");
and (4) off-task statements (e.g., "I was wondering if math was over yet").

The 96 third- through sixth-grade students who participated in Bershon's study
reported 903 inner speech statements, of which 35% were task related, 51% were
self related, 8% were other related, and 6% were off-task. Most verbal thoughts
(86%) fell into two categories: task focused and self directed.

Task-focused speech included (1) general cognitive strategy statements ("trying
to figure out what we did wrong"); (2) self-instruction statements ("I'm going
to take charge"); (3) self-questions ("where could this piece be?"); (4) compar-
ison/retrieval statements ("something looked wrong"); (5) organization/selectiv-
ity ("I was going over everything to make sure what was right and wrong"); (6)
repetitive rehearsals ("I remembered the rules"); and (7) general heuristics ("I
was really concentrating").

Self-directed speech included (1) positive and negative efficacy statements
("we're right on track" or "we're not going to do it"); (2) attributional statements, including (*a*) ability attributions ("I'm good/not good at this"), (*b*) effort
attributions ("come on, we've got to start working"), (*c*) task attributions ("this
is/isn't hard"), (*d*) luck/hope attributions ("I hope we have this right"); (3)
positive and negative affective statements ("I was happy we did that," "I was
worried that we would not get it right"); and (4) self-monitoring statements ("I
think I was right," "I didn't understand what to do").

Students reported more inner speech statements during the construction phase
(Time 4) than during other time periods (see Figure 2.2). They also reported
more inner speech $F(4, 91) = 21.57, p < .001$, when they were having a difficult
time than when they were having an easy time with the project. In addition, the
interview procedure affected students' total reported inner speech, $F(1, 95) = 9.99$,
$p < .01$. Students who participated in the student-controlled interview procedure

Interview procedure

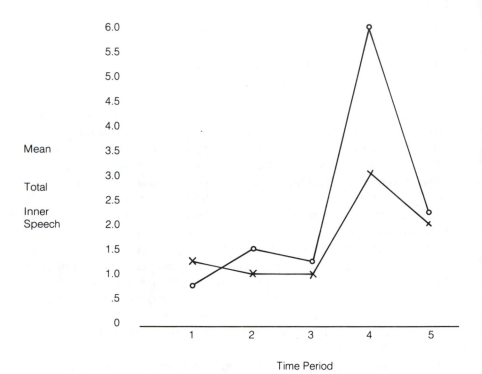

Time Period

Figure 2.2. Mean total inner speech reported in two interview procedures at five times during a problem-solving task (Time 1 = before instructions; Time 2 = after instructions; Time 3 = following planning; Time 4 = during construction; Time 5 = upon successful completion).

reported more inner speech, $M = 11.46$, sd = 5.54, than students who participated in the interviewer-controlled interview procedure, $M = 8.35$, sd = 5.75.

Four examples of reported inner speech elicited by the two videotape stimulated recall procedures are presented here. These reported speech statements all occurred during construction (Time 4), when the children were experiencing difficulty. The type of interview procedure is listed before each excerpt; the type of cognitive strategy statement is listed after.

KATIE (*interviewer-controlled interview procedure*)
Well, I was thinking about if we might have used that piece for our part that we were building on, and maybe they and we didn't notice it, or they used that piece. (*general cognitive strategy statement*)

RACHEL (*student-controlled interview procedure*)
I was just thinking, there's a piece missing, there's a piece missing. Look on the floor, there might be something down there. There might be something mixed in on the table or something. (*general cognitive strategy statement; self-instruction statement*)

This is another part where I was thinking something to myself. I was looking very closely at the boat and I realized that right here that we put one tiny piece here but it was supposed to be a square, and I said to myself, "Oh, see this is the way it was done. Oh, oh, it's supposed to be at the other spot." (*self-instruction statement*)

I was saying to myself: "Let's see, which piece do I need now? Oh, I need to put it here. Okay, this piece should go right here." (*self-question statement; self-instruction statement*)

DOROTHY (*interviewer-controlled interview procedure*)
I was kind of like worried that we would not get it right 'cause the other one . . . I thought that you were supposed to use it on another part and we just used it on the house. (*negative self-efficacy statement; self-monitoring statement*)

LAURA (*student-controlled interview procedure*)
[I was thinking] about how some pieces were missing and where could we find them? (*general cognitive strategy statement*)

I remember thinking "Why, it was one in the back." I was wondering how it could be out in the front and the back and then I realized that it was longer in the front than it was supposed to be in the back. (*self-monitoring statement; comparison/retrieval statement*)

Conclusions and Implications

Bershon's reports of inner speech are consistent with the theory of Vygotsky and his colleagues regarding the occurrence of inner speech and its use as a cognitive tool for solving problems. The types of inner speech statements the students reported are also consistent with studies suggesting that cognitions can influence task performance (e.g., Bandura, 1977a, 1977b, 1989; Bershon & Rohrkemper, 1986; Corno & Rohrkemper, 1985; Graham, 1988; Pressley, Heisel, McCormick, & Nakamura, 1982; Rohrkemper & Corno, 1988; Schunk, 1984; Weiner, 1979).

The students' internal verbalizations are also compatible with Luria's (1981) and Corno's (1988) hypotheses concerning the volitional and self-regulatory function of students' cognitive engagement. Corno notes that while engaged in regulated learning students use "task completion volitional strategies" and "task management volitional strategies." She believes that these types of inner speech statements are used "to mobilize and maintain self-regulatory strategies."

Although children have opportunities during collaborative encounters to develop a strategy that can be used to direct and control their problem solving, this process should not be left to chance. For students to effectively use this lexicon of inner speech systematically, they need to become aware of their task-directed and self-directed thoughts. This awareness could begin in classrooms among teachers and students or among students working in a group while they are engaged in cooperative problem solving.

To facilitate this awareness, Marshall (1988) proposed that classrooms should be thought of as places of learning as opposed to workplaces. In such learning environments a teacher's role would expand from that of "manager" and "facilitator" to that of "collaborator" actively participating in the learning process. Thus, teachers would ask questions that would result in high-level elaborative responses as described by Webb (Chapter 5, this volume). Marshall (1988) has begun to define differences between learning-oriented and work-oriented teachers. Along this line, it may be helpful for investigators to begin to study the differences in the social speech patterns of learning-oriented versus work-oriented teachers, facilitating the development of teacher-student as well as student-student collaboration.

Because Vygotsky (1978) proposes that it is during cooperative problem solving that learning occurs, educators and researchers should explore students' use of social, egocentric, and inner speech during cooperative learning in various subject areas. To strengthen the theoretical link between types of social speech and task performance, it is suggested that future researchers investigate the role and mechanisms of inner speech in directing behavior. Stimulating students' recall of their inner speech while engaged in problem solving and comparing that speech to their task performance could provide some baseline data concerning students' self-regulating speech. Over time, researchers could discover whether students use inner speech productively, and, if so, how to enhance its use.

References

Ames, C. (1984). Achievement attributions and self-instruction under competitive and individualistic goal structures. *Journal of Educational Psychology, 76,* 478–487.

Bandura, A. (1977a). Self-efficacy: Toward a unifying theory of behavioral change. *Psychological Review, 84,* 191–215.

(1977b). *Social learning theory.* Englewood Cliffs, NJ: Prentice-Hall.

(1989). Human agency in social cognitive theory. *American Psychologist, 44,* 1175–1184.

Bershon, B. (1988, April). *Requesting elementary students to report inner speech used during a cooperative problem-solving task.* Paper presented at the annual meeting of the American Educational Research Association, New Orleans.

Bershon, B., & Rohrkemper, M. (1986, April). *Elementary students' perceptions and management of classroom resources.* Paper presented at the annual meeting of the American Educational Research Association, San Francisco.

Bruner, J. S. (1978). Acquiring the uses of language. *Canadian Journal of Psychology, 32,* 204–218.

Cole, M. (1985). The zone of proximal development: Where culture and cognition create each other. In J. V. Wertsch (Ed.), *Culture, communication, and cognition: Vygotskian perspectives* (pp. 146–161), New York: Cambridge University Press.

Corno, L. (1988, April). *Volitional strategies in classroom tasks.* Paper presented at the annual meeting of the American Educational Research Association, New Orleans.

Corno, L., & Rohrkemper, M. (1985). The intrinsic motivation to learn in classrooms. In C. Ames and R. Ames (Eds.), *Research on motivation in education: The classroom milieu.* (pp. 53–90). Orlando, FL: Academic Press.

Dewey, J. (1964). *John Dewey on education: Selected writings* (R. D. Archambault, Ed.). New York: Random House.

Diener, C., & Dweck, C. (1978). An analysis of learned helplessness: Continuous changes in performance, strategy, and achievement cognitions following failure. *Journal of Personality and Social Psychology, 31,* 451–462.

Forman, E. A., & Cazden, C. B. (1985). Exploring Vygotskian perspectives in education: The cognitive value of peer interaction. In J. V. Wertsch (Ed.), *Culture, communication, and cognition: Vygotskian perspectives* (pp. 323–347). New York: Cambridge University Press.

Graham, S. (1988). Can attribution theory tell us something about motivation in blacks? *Educational Psychologist, 23,* 3–21.

Levina, R. E. (1981). L. S. Vygotsky's ideas about the planning and function of speech in children. In J. V. Wertsch (Ed.), *The concept of activity in Soviet psychology* (pp. 279–299). Armonk, NY: M. E. Sharpe.

Luria, A. R. (1961). *Speech and the regulation of behavior.* New York: Liveright Publishing.

(1981). *Language and cognition.* New York: John Wiley & Sons.

Marshall, H. H. (1988). Work or learning: Implications of classroom metaphors. *Educational Researcher, 17,* 9–16.

Mead, G. H. (1934). *Mind, self, and society.* Chicago: University of Chicago Press.

Peterson, P., & Swing, S. (1982). Beyond time on task: Students' reports of their thought processes during classroom instruction. *Elementary School Journal, 82,* 481–491.

Peterson, P., Swing, S., Stark, K., & Waas, G. (1984). Students' cognitions and time on task during mathematics instruction. *American Educational Research Journal, 21,* 487–515.

Pressley, M., Heisel, B., McCormick, C., & Nakamura, G. (1982). Memory strategy instruction with children. In C. Brainard & M. Pressley (Eds.), *Verbal processes in children* (pp. 82–101). New York: Springer-Verlag.

Rohrkemper, M., & Bershon, B. (1984). Elementary school students' reports of causes and effects of problem difficulty in mathematics. *Elementary School Journal, 85,* 127–147.

Rohrkemper, M., & Corno, L. (1988). Success and failure on classroom tasks: Adaptive learning and classroom teaching. *Elementary School Journal, 88,* 297–312.

Schunk, D. (1984). Self-efficacy perspective on achievement behavior. *Educational Psychologist, 19,* 48–57.

Sharan, S., Raviv, S., Kussel, P., & Hertz-Lazarowitz, R. (1984). Cooperative and competitive behavior. In S. Sharan (Ed.), *Cooperative learning in classrooms: Research in desegregated schools* (pp. 73–106). Hillsdale, NJ: Erlbaum.

Vygotsky, L. S. (1962). *Thought and language.* Cambridge: MIT Press. (Originally published in Russian, 1934)

(1978). *Mind in society: The development of higher psychological processes* (M. Cole, V. John-Steiner, S. Scribner, & E. Souberman, Eds.). Cambridge: Harvard University Press.

(1981). The genesis of higher mental functions. In J. V. Wertsch (Ed.), *The concept of activity in Soviet psychology* (pp. 144–188). Armonk, NY: M. E. Sharpe.

Webb, N. (1985). Student interaction and learning in small groups: A research summary. In R. Slavin, S. Sharan, S. Kagan, R. Hertz-Lazarowitz, C. Webb, & R. Schumck (Eds.), *Learning to cooperate, cooperating to learn* (pp. 147–172). New York: Plenum Press.

Weiner, B. (1979). A theory of motivation for some classroom experiences. *Journal of Educational Psychology, 71*, 3–25.

Wertsch, J. V. (1985). *Vygotsky and the social formation of mind.* Cambridge, MA: Harvard University Press.

Wertsch, J. V., & Stone, C. A. (1985). The concept of internalization in Vygotsky's account of the genesis of higher mental functions. In J. V. Wertsch (Ed.), *Culture, communication, and cognition: Vygotskian perspectives* (pp. 162–179). New York: Cambridge University Press.

3 Children's Instrumental Help-Seeking: Its Role in the Social Acquisition and Construction of Knowledge

Sharon Nelson-Le Gall

There is a long-standing tradition, both within the American behavioral science literature and the American popular or folk literature, to emphasize individualism, self-sufficiency, and autonomy as signs of well-being, maturity, and competence. These traditional notions of the overwhelming value of autonomous functioning and individual problem solving are keenly illustrated by the predominantly individualistic and competitively structured American school system – a system so structured despite the extensive research documenting that cooperative and collaborative learning groups enhance complex problem solving, social cohesion, and personal well-being more than do individualistic and competitive environments (Damon, 1984; Johnson & Johnson, 1975; Palincsar & Brown, 1984).

The mythical ideal of the value of independence and of autonomous functioning as the norm for healthy development is beginning to be tempered. Over the past decade, there has been renewed appreciation of the role that social interaction, including experience with peers, plays in knowledge acquisition and cognitive performance. It is acknowledged across the variety of disciplines concerned with human development and educational processes that the study of cognition and learning requires explicit consideration of the social context in which the acquisition and utilization of knowledge takes place.

Classrooms, even traditionally structured classrooms, are intensely social places. Hence the social context is of interest in understanding learning contexts because of the social interactions that children experience in the classroom. Social interactions can have but little influence on the child's thinking and competency of task performance, however, if the child does not actively participate in the construction of the knowledge and understanding that is to be gained from the task. Active participation in learning groups depends, at least in part, on the social-cognitive knowledge and skills possessed by the individual participants. Social-cognitive knowledge and skill in helping interactions is critical for effective participation in learning groups. A related type of social-cognitive knowledge that contributes to learners' effective participation in cooperative groups is the rec-

49

ognition that other individuals, peers as well as adults, can be used as potential resources to aid and supplement learning. In accordance with this knowledge, skill in obtaining and utilizing help from others takes on special importance in a cooperative learning context.

This chapter examines social-cognitive, cognitive-motivational, and situational factors influencing children's effectiveness in using other children as learning resources. Its purpose is to illustrate how, with effective help-seeking behavior, the dual developmental needs for autonomy and social support can be served in learning and problem-solving situations. First a brief, critical overview of extant theories of help-seeking behavior will be presented. The bases of the reconceptualization of help-seeking as a general learning and problem-solving strategy that can be identified in the developmental psychological literature will be highlighted. This overview is presented as background to the integrative review of empirical studies of children's active use of others in the learning situation that follows.

Conceptualizing Help-Seeking as an Adaptive Learning Skill

Most investigators have based their analyses of help-seeking on the values of individualistic Western cultures. Such analyses typically point out the inconsistency of seeking help with the values of self-reliance, independent achievement, and competitiveness that are characteristically emphasized in the socialization goals of such cultures. Indeed, help-seeking was often viewed as an index of dependence in early studies of socialization and personality development (e.g., Beller, 1955). Help-seeking, as an indicator of dependency, was seen as the outcome of insufficient development and faulty socialization if it was displayed beyond very early childhood. Thus, help-seeking has taken on connotations of immaturity, passivity, and even incompetence. Not surprisingly, much of the early theoretical and experimental work from the social psychology and developmental psychology literatures on help-seeking behavior (see DePaulo, Nadler, & Fisher, 1983, for detailed reviews of these literatures) tended to focus on negative interpersonal and intrapersonal consequences of seeking help (e.g., indebtedness, embarrassment, perceptions of dependency), while neglecting the more instrumental functions of help-seeking for skill acquisition and proficiency.

Viewing help-seeking as incompatible with achievement tends to overlook the costs of not seeking necessary help from others for the acquisition and mastery of skills. For example, in the achievement motivation literature, individuals who tend to persist at tasks tend to be viewed as highly achievement oriented (e.g., Feather, 1962). Solitary persistence, however, may not always lead to task proficiency and may even be maladaptive (e.g., Diener & Dweck, 1978), as in the case of students who continue to work at a task without help despite prolonged lack of success and the availability of more productive alternative strategies. For these students, task persistence may function merely as a means of forestalling judgments of failure. When independence in performing the task becomes more important or more salient as a goal than does achieving proficiency, the development of skills necessary for competence in the task domain may be compromised. Proficient task activity provides its own feedback and rewards. Independence, in contrast, may or may not entail proficiency. Consideration of the adaptive functions of help-seeking is particularly important for a more complete understanding of knowledge acquisition and task proficiency.

Although the need for autonomy and the need for social support have often been polarized in theoretical and empirical considerations of human development, recent views emphasize the dual need for social support and autonomy as a basic requirement for development (e.g., Bryant, 1989). Accordingly, instrumental help-seeking as a manifestation of this dual need can be viewed as a phenomenon that will vary with developmental and contextual constraints and opportunities. Help-seeking then can be expected to be an adaptive behavior in learning and achievement contexts throughout the life span (e.g., R. Ames, 1983; Murphy, 1962; Nelson-Le Gall, 1981; Nelson-Le Gall, Gumerman, & Scott-Jones, 1983).

This view is reflected in the recent reconceptualizations of help-seeking behavior by R. Ames (1983) and Nelson-Le Gall (1981, 1985) that emphasize the individual's value priorities and goals related to achievement. The major contribution of the achievement-related view of help-seeking is its focus on the costs of not seeking help and importantly in its treatment of help-seeking as a part of an ongoing process rather than as a dichotomous (i.e., help-seeking – no help seeking) decision. Within this perspective the role of help-seeker is not a static one; nor is it always occupied by the same learners in a group. Individuals in a learning group may move in and out of this role during the course of work on a task such that donors of help become recipients and vice-versa. This achievement-related view of help-seeking identifies it as a critical process variable in didactic (teacher-learner) interactions and in collaborative (doer-doer) interactions in learning groups.

The conceptualization of help-seeking as an adaptive general learning skill is compatible with currently influential theories of mental development and learning (e.g., Brown, Bransford, Ferrara, & Campione, 1983; Brown & Reeve, 1987; Vygotsky, 1978). In Vygotsky's view, knowledge and understanding have their roots in social interactions with more mature learners who plan, direct, monitor, and evaluate the child's task activity. Mental functions are thought to develop first on a social level as children interact with adults or more highly skilled peers, who serve as supportive, knowledgeable others. After interacting with others in learning situations, children gradually internalize the supportive other role and begin to perform these regulatory behaviors for themselves. When children are able and willing to take the initiative to gain the assistance of more mature and expert others, they can participate, in a supportive social context, in the interrogatory process that mature learners employ to construct the relevant contextual knowledge for task solution. Instrumental help-seeking, thus, may serve as a mechanism of transition from a state of other-regulation in problem solving to that of self-regulation.

Recognition of the importance of the social context in the construction, transmission, and utilization of knowledge is also evident in the work of cultural anthropologists (e.g., D'Andrade, 1981). D'Andrade notes that fundamental concepts about the world and its organization, such as what objects are and how they are to be interpreted, are learned by individuals through a process of "guided discovery." According to D'Andrade, people appear to be much better at learning through this process, which is both self-initiated and other-dependent, than at learning on their own.

Learning and understanding are not merely individual processes supported by the social context; rather they are the result of a continuous, dynamic negotiation between the individual and the social setting in which the individual's activity takes place. Both the individual and the social context are active and constructive in producing learning and understanding. Effective learning in groups should occur when the social environment that is provided by adults and other children constrains the information and tasks available to a child to that structured to fit the child's current understanding and cognitive abilities. Furthermore, the nature of the constraints changes as children gain understanding and skill (e.g., Levin & Kareev, 1980; Rogoff & Gardner, 1984; Wood, Bruner, & Ross, 1976; Wood & Middleton, 1975). Indeed, children depend on such socially imposed constraints when seeking help in the form of input and feedback from others in situations where they are aware of their lack of understanding. However, children also take responsibility for structuring and using that support as necessary.

This conceptualization of active co-constraining between the individual and the social environment is characteristic of achievement-related perspectives on help-seeking. In achievement-related frameworks, personal characteristics of the individual help-seeker, such as perceived competence and mastery orientation (e.g., R. Ames, 1983; Harter, 1982), and situational characteristics of the task setting are used to predict and explain help-seeking. For example, a distinction between help-seeking that is dependency-oriented and help-seeking that is mastery-oriented has been drawn by Nelson-Le Gall (1985).

Dependency-oriented help-seeking refers to those instances in which individuals allow someone else to solve a problem or attain a goal on their behalf without their active participation in the solution of the problem. Learners seeking help with problems within and beyond their current level of competence who are willing to relinquish involvement in and responsibility for problem solving and who appear to be more interested in the product or successful outcome rather than in the processes or means of achieving the outcome can be viewed as dependency oriented. Thus, the behavior of help-seekers who continually rely on others to provide more help than is needed and who do not participate in the task in a way that allows them to acquire some of the more skillful helper's understanding of the problem and its solution can be characterized as dependency oriented (Nelson-Le Gall, 1981; Rogoff & Gardner, 1984). This sort of help-seeking is properly considered antithetical to achievement (cf. Winterbottom, 1958).

Mastery-oriented help-seeking, in contrast, is likely to be instrumental to skill acquisition and refers to those instances in which the help requested appears to be focused on learning successful processes of problem solution and is limited to the amount and type needed to allow learners to solve similar problems in the future for themselves. Learners with effective instrumental help-seeking skills are able to refuse help when they can perform a task by themselves and, yet, can obtain help when it is needed. This type of help-seeking represents competent, coping behavior. Whether as the less skilled novice in the interaction or as an equally competent collaborator, learners seeking master-oriented help mediate their learning and problem solving by taking the initiative to question, suggest, observe, and imitate.

Social-Cognitive and Cognitive-Motivational Correlates of Help-Seeking

The effective use of help-seeking as a problem-solving activity requires a fair amount of cognitive and social sophistication on the part of the learner. Consider that in order to seek help effectively, individuals must become aware of the need for help. Once aware of the need for help, individuals must be motivated to assume responsibility for overcoming these obstacles, and to try to do so in ways that increase their competence in dealing with such obstacles (i.e., must request instrumental, effective help that is appropriately timed). The individual must identify potential helpers who can provide needed resources. The individual seeking help must implement and monitor strategies for engaging the targeted person's help. There are two options available to individuals, should they find that their efforts to obtain help from another person are not totally successful. One option is to keep trying to get help from the helper initially chosen, either by continuing with the same strategy or by changing it. The other option is to approach other potential helpers. Finally, the individual has some reaction or evaluative response to the help-seeking episode. Help seekers' reactions may focus on the success or failure of the help-seeking attempt, including the helpfulness of the persons approached, the adequacy of the help obtained, and the appropriateness

and effectiveness of their own help-seeking activity. These judgments may influence future help-seeking behavior. Children's functioning with respect to each
of the component processes depends in part on their metacognitive knowledge
and processing (cf. Brown et al., 1983; Flavell, 1977) of (1) the characteristics
of the help-seeker (PERSON variables), (2) the characteristics of the target helper
and nature of the problem for which help is required (TASK variables), and (3)
the suitability of the means employed to gain the targeted helper's assistance
(STRATEGY variables).

Reasons why children may not seek help appropriately (i.e., seek instrumental
help when it is needed) can be found both in personal characteristics of the child
and in situational constraints on behavior. Effective help-seeking depends on
accuracy and depth of self-knowledge and self-evaluation. For example, the metacognitive processing factors of PERSON, TASK, and STRATEGY variables (cf.
Flavell, 1977) are very likely to be affected by the developmental level and
expertise of the learner; it is, therefore, easy to imagine that appropriate help-
seeking behavior might be inefficient in younger learners and those with less
expertise in the task domain. Effective help-seeking may also be a function of
developmental and individual differences in achievement-related values and goals,
such as independence, mastery, and demonstration of competence (R. Ames,
1983; Dweck & Elliott, 1983; Nicholls, 1984). An examination of some of these
important individual differences and content-related influences follows.

Self-Knowledge, Self-Evaluation, and Effective Help-Seeking

Awareness of the Need for Help.   Seeking help is an intentional act and therefore is contingent on the individual becoming aware of the need for help (i.e.,
knowing that his or her own available resources are not sufficient to reach a
goal). Determination of the need for help may be made by the individual or by
others. An incorrect answer or lack of progress after diligent attempts to solve a
problem might indicate to children or to someone else concerned with their performance that seeking help is necessary (Nelson-Le Gall & Scott-Jones, 1985).
Individuals' knowledge about the compatibility between themselves as learners
and the learning situation plays an important role in effective problem solving
(Brown, 1978). If individuals have some awareness of the complexity of the task
and can monitor their progress on the task well enough to detect a problem, they
are in a relatively good position to utilize help-seeking as an alternative strategy
in response to anticipated difficulties or to recover easily from difficulties encountered.

Accuracy in assessing one's knowledge state may vary with the degree of
background knowledge or familiarity with the task and with the difficulty of the
task (Brown, 1978; Chi, 1978; Flammer, Kaiser, & Mueller-Bouquet, 1981;

Miyake & Norman, 1979; Pressley, Levin, Ghatala, & Ahmad, 1987). There is an increase with age in children's ability to identify conditions (e.g., ambiguous task instructions, task difficulty) that can result in a need for help (e.g., Markman, 1977, 1979; Nicholls, 1984). Age differences have also been reported in children's ability to assess their knowledge states (e.g., Bisanz, Vesonder, & Voss, 1978; Kreutzer, Leonard, & Flavell, 1975) and, therefore, the need for help (e.g., Nelson-Le Gall, 1987; Nelson-Le Gall, Kratzer, Jones, & DeCooke, 1990). The failure of younger children to detect a problem may be due to insensitivity to internally generated signs that a problem exists or to setting a higher criterion for when they will attend to possible problems. Young children who are in general less knowledgeable and less skilled than others may as a consequence be more often confused and thus have a higher threshold for confusion or ambiguity; or it may be that they ignore contradictions and difficulties so as to avoid having to ask for help (Markman, 1980).

Young children may not always be aware that they need help, or at least they do not always verbally express their awareness of this need. Young children often indicate verbally that they have understood when they have not, or they give the impression that they have understood ambiguous or incomplete information by not asking for clarification or additional information (Ironsmith & Whitehurst, 1978). Nevertheless, children may express a need for help nonverbally (e.g., Hudson, Forman, & Brion-Meisels, 1982), and others may interpret these nonverbal cues as bids for help.

In classroom learning groups children's contributions to their peers can be expected to change across early and middle childhood as their cognitive and metacognitive skills change. An awareness of conflicting viewpoints appears to be necessary in collaborative groups to engender the type of peer transactions (e.g., arguments, justifications, explanations, counterarguments) that foster cognitive growth (Brown & Palincsar, 1989). Such awareness is not to be taken for granted in young and less knowledgeable learners, because they may not accurately represent their own or the other's knowledge state, let alone the match or mismatch between their viewpoints. In this case conflict, like confusion, may be tolerated and alternative positions may be joined through pseudoconsensus.

Decision to Seek Help. It might be assumed that awareness of the inadequacy of one's knowledge and skill would be sufficiently motivating to cause a person to seek help (e.g., Markman, 1979; Nash & Torrance, 1974). Once aware of the need for help, however, an individual must also take responsibility for alleviation of the problem and task completion. Very young children, for example, often perceive a need for help but fail to actively seek help because they believe it is the adult's responsibility to determine that help is needed and to offer assistance (Gumerman, 1982).

Research on help-seeking in adults indicates that there are costs perceived to be associated with asking for and accepting help, such as loss of perceived competence or diminished credit or reward for a successful outcome, which may deter the individual from attempting to obtain assistance (e.g., DePaulo & Fisher, 1980). These costs must be outweighed by perceived benefits (e.g., avoiding task failure, increasing or mastering task skills) if help-seeking is to occur. Certain individual differences such as achievement goal orientation (Dweck, 1988), intellectual self-esteem, and preferences for challenge and independent mastery (Harter, 1981) may influence the perception and weighing of these costs and benefits. Thus, the decision to seek help may be affected not only by the need for help but also by the achievement orientation and goals that characterize the help-seeker in a given problem context. These orientations appear to influence the judgment of the relative benefits and costs associated with seeking help (R. Ames, 1983; Nelson-Le Gall, 1990; Nelson-Le Gall, DeCooke, & Jones, 1989; Nelson-Le Gall & Jones, 1990).

It has been suggested (R. Ames, 1983; Murphy, 1962; Nelson-Le Gall, 1981) that help-seeking may serve multiple purposes. The child's primary goal in seeking help may be merely task completion, with comprehension or proficiency as an objective, or the child's primary goal could be to avoid criticism from an agent of evaluation. Alternatively, help may be sought to increase the child's competence in current and future learning tasks. These distinctions map onto distinctions made by achievement motivation theorists, who describe individual differences in children's achievement goals and orientations as indicators of how children will cope with difficulty in learning and problem solving (Dweck & Elliott, 1983; Harter, 1981; Nicholls, 1984). Children whose achievement orientation can be said to be mastery oriented will usually adopt learning goals (Dweck & Elliott, 1983), show a preference for challenge, exhibit curiosity and interest in problem solving and learning contexts, and strive toward independent mastery in their undertakings (Harter, 1981). These children focus their attention on mastery of tasks and do not tend to be concerned with explaining their errors or failures, which they see as a natural and useful source of feedback in the learning process (e.g., C. Ames & Archer, 1988; Elliott & Dweck, 1988). When they do make causal attributions about their task failures, mastery-oriented children attribute poor performance to insufficient effort (Diener & Dweck, (1978), a personal characteristic over which they have control. Mastery-oriented children will tend to have high perceived cognitive competence and, thus, be more likely to view help-seeking as a relevant and viable achievement strategy than children who are not mastery oriented (e.g., Nelson-Le Gall, 1990).

In the context of help-seeking, striving for independent mastery does not mean that cooperative or collaborative problem-solving efforts are shunned. Rather the mastery-oriented help-seeker is concerned with being able to share in and, later, construct independently of the helper the more advanced or effective solution to the problem. This emphasis is clearly evident in the nature of the help sought by the help-seeker. Mastery-oriented help-seekers tend to request elaborated answers and explanations more often than simple answers when they confront difficulty and confusion in problem-solving and learning situations (e.g., Nelson-Le Gall & Jones, 1990). For example, Nelson-Le Gall and Jones (1990) examined the type of help sought by third- and fifth-grade average-achieving students while they performed an academic vocabulary task in a laboratory simulation. A measure of intrinsic orientation to mastery and learning in academic achievement settings was independently obtained for each child observed. Students characterized by high intrinsic orientation to mastery showed a clear preference for help that allowed them to figure out solutions for themselves as opposed to help that directly supplied a ready-made solution. In contrast, students characterized by low intrinsic orientation to mastery showed no clear preference for one type of help over the other. It is important to note that these differences in motivational orientation were only evident in cases where the students perceived themselves to have given incorrect initial answers to the problems presented in the task. Hence, it appears to be the adoption of mastery goals in the face of failure that underlies the tendency to prefer instrumental or knowledge-extending help.

The tendency to make and convey distinctions among types of help is important for effective use of help-seeking in learning situations, and research is needed to examine the acquisition and development of this skill. Unfortunately many of the studies reported in the literature investigating the influence of help-receiving and help-seeking on academic performance and learning do not consistently distinguish between the type of help sought or even differentiate between help received that is solicited and help received that is unsolicited (see Nelson-Le Gall, 1985, for a more detailed review). When no distinction is made, there is generally no relationship found between receiving help and achievement (e.g., Peterson, Janicki, & Swing, 1981). When distinctions are made, receiving help has been shown to be effective only when the help is in response to expressed student need, in which case the type of help sought has been shown to be related to achievement outcomes (e.g., Webb, 1983), such that effective explanations are more likely to lead to positive achievement outcomes than are ineffective explanations or nonexplanatory help (see Chapter 5).

The mastery-oriented use of help-seeking also takes advantage of discourse skills for requesting information and giving explanations (see Cooper, Marquis, & Ayers-Lopez, 1982; Cooper, Marquis, & Edward, 1986). With increasing age and advanced levels of task-related skill, children's exchange of information in group learning situations becomes more effective. This increase in effectiveness is due to greater skill in providing effective explanations to and requesting effective explanations from peers. The skills that children are acquiring that characterize effective requests are the ability to convey directness, task relatedness, specificity, and sincerity (Peterson, Wilkinson, Spinelli, & Swing, 1984). Children learn to differentiate effective requests from ineffective requests on the basis of the differential feedback and response they receive contingent on the quality of their requests. Hence, inasmuch as requests for elaborated answers, explanations, and justifications help to make the understandings of both the help-seeker and the helper overt, concrete, and explicit, all members of a cooperative learning group may benefit from the occurrence of mastery-oriented help-seeking.

Situational Constraints and Effective Help-Seeking

The use of others as learning resources cannot be predicted solely on the basis of knowing that an individual has detected a subjectively felt need for help and desires to seek help by asking for task-related information or intervention. In addition to these person-related influences on help-seeking, context-related factors must be considered. Aspects of the social context of the learning group, such as the patterns of interpersonal relationship in the group, the availability of various "qualified" or preferred helpers, and classroom norms, may influence the presence and nature of help-seeking and information exchange that occurs in a learning group.

The nature of the social relationship between potential helpers and the help-seeker is an important contextual factor to consider. According to Hinde's (1976) multilevel framework for analyzing social relationships, it is important to distinguish between interactions, relationships, and groups. Interactions are viewed as patterns of communication that develop between individuals who may or may not be friends or even familiar to one another. In contrast, relationships are characterized by enduring bonds, histories of interactions, and commitments. Groups, carrying with them normative standards for conduct, influence the nature of both the interactions and the relationships of members of the group.

At the level of interactions, skill in negotiating roles that are mutually acceptable in the learning group is critical. For example it is necessary to recognize that a peer may have other (perhaps competing) ideas, interests, goals, or activities and that these must be considered when communicating and negotiating in helping exchanges. At the level of relationships, skill in repairing breakdowns in shared viewpoints and resolving conflict is important. At this level, it is what is being asked of whom that determines the effectiveness of the didactic or collaborative exchange. At the group level, the larger social context, such as the presence of teachers and other peers, influences the interactions occurring between members of a learning group.

An examination of the influence of constraints imposed by the social context on help-seeking follows. Specifically, characteristics of the potential helper and social norms operating at the classroom level will be closely examined. This discussion illustrates how the social context of learning in groups can moderate the impact of person-related factors.

Helper Characteristics. It is important for children to know and to act on the knowledge that all persons do not bring equal credentials to the role of helper for any given problem for which help is sought. Such matching of helpers and help-seekers is important in learning situations because the help-seeker and the helper may need to renegotiate their ways of viewing the task and the interaction before helping can proceed effectively. Children seem to be aware that the extent to which the help-seeker and the helper hold a shared definition of the problem and their roles in the helping exchange can facilitate or impede their attempts to use their peers as resources (e.g., DeCooke & Nelson-Le Gall, 1989; Ladd & Oden, 1979). For example, DeCooke and Nelson-Le Gall (1989) found that the famil-iarity of help-seekers with their targeted helpers influenced both help-seekers' success and the social status of help-seekers in the classroom. Increased famil-iarity with peer norms concerning help exchanges was cited as the likely mech-anism underlying these effects. Indeed, Ladd and Oden (1979) found that among elementary school children, knowledge about peer norms for giving and seeking help was positively associated with status in the peer group.

An important helper characteristic is the perceived trustworthiness of the helper. There are two important dimensions to trustworthiness to consider in this regard: the previous manner of giving help (i.e., whether the helper was perceived to be critical or supportive) and the helper's previous effectiveness (i.e., whether the helper's response to the request for assistance was beneficial to the help-seeker's problem solving and learning) (e.g., DePaulo, Brown & Greenberg, 1983). Stu-dents are more likely to prefer peer helpers who are supportive and give instru-mental help and whose help has been effective in facilitating learning in the past (Barnett, Darcie, Holland, & Kobasigawa, 1982; Nelson-Le Gall & Gumerman, 1984). This suggests that children will prefer to seek out other children who they perceive to be competent, especially those competent peers with whom they are also friends and/or who have some role obligation to help (e.g., Kratzer & Nelson-Le Gall, 1990; Nelson-Le Gall & DeCooke, 1987).

Classroom Norms, Teacher Behavior, and Help-Seeking. Other students, a readily available source of help, may be ignored by a student seeking help be-cause of explicit or implicit classroom norms (supported by teachers and students alike) that discourage cooperative work by associating it with cheating. Consider the social norms for students' behavior in traditional classrooms in general and how these norms support or detract from appropriate task-related help-seeking. Relatively few children attend schools that regularly encourage peer interactions as a major means of learning. Moreover, with increasing grade level in school, children are likely to encounter classroom learning situations in which competition and independent performance are increasingly normative (Eccles et al., 1984). It is likely, therefore, that unless children begin elementary school in classrooms that emphasize the social sharing of cognitive learning activities, children will come to cooperative learning groups with perceptions that collaborating with and assisting peers in classroom learning activities are not "normal" behaviors for students.

Socialization into the student role for most students will involve assuming a task-oriented role in which performance is evaluated systematically with regard to normative progress and preestablished standards of excellence. As such it is normal that students will vary in their status within that role as a function of their performance. Within this context the attention of the students, as well as the teachers, is drawn to these status variations, making competition and social comparison common events. As a result, students seeking help in the traditional classroom are concerned about the perceived costs of seeking help, such as receiving unfriendly or uncooperative reactions from targeted helpers (e.g., "Weren't you paying attention?"); appearing dependent, unskillful, or incompetent; and experiencing unfavorable social comparisons (Newman & Goldin, 1990; van der Miej, 1988). These perceived costs tend to discourage students from considering help-seeking as a means of coping with learning tasks.

Although students perceive psychological costs of seeking help from others in the classroom, these perceived risks may be moderated by the teacher's instructional behavior and by classroom task organization. The presence of norms discouraging learning in contexts other than adult teacher–student didactic interactions or those that foster individualistic and competitive achievement may account for students' failure to seek help from their peers and even from their teachers. Support for this idea comes from the substantial literature on peer tutoring (Allen, 1976, 1983) and the literature on social interactive behaviors in the classroom (see Chapter 4).

It has been demonstrated that when help-seeking from peers becomes institutionalized – that is, it takes place in formal school-based peer-tutoring programs in which one student is assigned by the teacher to function in the didactic (teacher) role vis-à-vis another student – psychological costs of help-seeking are perceived to increase for the tutee (e.g., Allen, 1983; Rosen, Powell, & Schubot, 1978). These psychological costs become particularly salient when a tutee has a younger or same-age child as tutor. In such arrangements, the achieved role of tutor is perceived by the tutee to be incongruent with the age identity of the tutor and to violate social normative expectations about teaching-learning relationships.

If, however, classroom norms support and encourage active and interactive learning by students as part of the natural learning activity, such as can occur in the context of cooperative and helping exchanges among peers, then the perceived costs of help-seeking may be lessened. For example, Hertz-Lazarowitz (Chapter 4) reports that as teacher centrality in the classroom instructional process decreases and the legitimization of peer interaction in learning increases, there is a corresponding dramatic increase in cooperation, help-giving, and help-seeking behaviors among students.

Summary

In summary, these two types of influences – personal characteristics of the student and contextual characteristics of the learning setting – do not act in isolation of one another; they must be considered together. Social and cognitive processes are interdigitated in the activity of a learning group. Social competence, as an aspect of the individual learner and as a characteristic of the group of classroom peers, may constrain the acquisition and/or display of knowledge mediated by help-seeking. Academic competence, as a feature of the individual learner and as a characteristic of peer and teacher resources in a classroom, may moderate the effectiveness of the help-seeking and help-giving that occurs.

As suggested by Cooper and Cooper (1984), children's effectiveness in using their peers as learning resources may be directly related to certain cognitive capabilities and limitations. The impact of children's cognitive capabilities and limitations is moderated by the social context in which these skills are displayed. For example, the desire for elaborated explanations of a phenomenon is dependent on experience with it (Ginsburg & Opper, 1980). Moreover, children may not request such explanations because they do not often encounter them or because the reactions they receive from others are not differentiated by the type of request made.

In addition, children may fail to utilize skills already in their repertoire because of limitations in their processing capacity. These limitations, however, are more evident in some social contexts than in others. It may be difficult to elicit adequate explanations in certain situations (e.g., from unfamiliar peers) because more processing capacity must be allocated to maintaining and managing the social dimensions of the interaction. Hence, children may appear to be more effective in their learning exchanges with friends because their history of interaction and their commitment to the relationship have allowed the routinization of interactional strategies. This high level of familiarity with the helper means less effort need be devoted to negotiating and maintaining mutually acceptable roles in the learning interaction and to interpreting cues for understanding and misunderstanding in the course of information exchange. Effectiveness in using peers as resources for learning is also a result of being aware that it is important to seek out explanations, justifications, and demonstrations. Finally, effectiveness in using others as resources in learning groups is influenced by the prevalent norms in the learning context that support and encourage willingness to cooperate, share, and explain rather than to attack, interfere, or withdraw.

Implications of Cooperative Learning Structures for Instrumental Help-Seeking

Socially mediated learning as it occurs in everyday, real-life experiences tends to capitalize on children's natural curiosity and desire to find out about the world around them. Acquiring knowledge and new skills becomes the responsibility of each individual in the role of "student," and making use of the social environment is an integral part of the understanding process. These features of learning should be captured in cooperative learning groups to maximize their effectiveness. To illustrate, consider how classroom organizational and activity structures can promote effective social sharing of responsibility for learning in general and instrumental help-seeking in particular.

Task Activity Structures and Socially Shared Responsibility for Learning

There are several cognitive, motivational, and affective aspects of socially shared responsibility for acquiring and utilizing knowledge that serve to enhance learning and achievement (Brown & Palincsar, 1989). The processes that mediate the effectiveness of learning in group contexts over learning in solitary contexts include the provision of opportunities for exposure to new ideas and to external sources of monitoring and evaluation of the student's own, often inadequate, conceptions (Larson et al., 1985). Learning in a group provides occasions for modeling effective thinking strategies. Thinkers with more skill can demonstrate desirable ways of attacking problems, analyzing texts, and constructing arguments. This process can reveal the problem solver's inspection, mental activities that are normally hidden. Through observing and questioning and through discussion with other group members, the student can become aware of mental processes that might otherwise have remained entirely implicit.

Yet, if all that students did was to watch more skilled thinkers perform, they would not substantially improve their own thinking. There is, apparently, something about performing in social settings, as well as watching others perform, that seems to be important. One effect of "thinking aloud" in a social setting is that it becomes possible for others – peers or an instructor – to critique and shape one's performance, something that cannot be done effectively if only the results but not the process of thought are visible. It also seems likely that the social setting can provide a kind of scaffolding for an individual learner's initially limited performance. Instead of practicing small bits of thinking in isolation so that the significance of each bit is not visible, a group solves a problem or analyzes an argument together. In this way, extreme novices can participate in actually solving the problem and can, if things go well, eventually take over all or most of the work themselves, with a developed appreciation and understanding of how individual elements in the process contribute to the whole.

Yet another function of the social setting for practicing thinking skills may be what many would call motivational. Through encouragement from the group to try new, more active approaches and through social support and social reward for even partially successful efforts, individual students in a group come to think of themselves as capable of engaging in interpretation. The public setting also lends social status and validation to what can perhaps best be called the disposition to participate in meaning construction activities.

For young children, cooperation is often equated with helping. Indeed, helping behaviors are often evident in cooperative situations and are at least implicit in many forms of cooperative learning approaches that have been widely adopted by schools such as Jigsaw, Teams Games Tournaments (TGT), and Student Teams Achievement Divisions (STAD) (e.g., Aronson et al., 1978; Slavin, 1983). Some researchers in this area propose that students' helping of one another is a motivational component of cooperative learning structures and that it mediates learning and achievement. Researchers (e.g., Johnson, Falk, Martino, & Purdie, 1976) have found that children evaluate the sharing of information differently depending on the goal and task structures of the work groups. Help-seeking, particularly the seeking of information, is valued more positively than volunteering information in cooperative work conditions; these evaluations are reversed, however, in competitive work conditions. It appears, then, that helping behavior is an important process variable that is implicated in cooperative structures.

Task Activity Structures and Help-Seeking

It must be recognized that aspects of the instructional organization and procedures of classrooms may encourage or discourage appropriate help-seeking behavior. My colleagues and I (Nelson-Le Gall & DeCooke, 1987; Nelson-Le Gall & Glor-Scheib, 1985, 1986) have conducted extensive observations of elementary school students during their mathematics classes. We found that in addition to normative expectations about teacher-student roles, there are certain instructional formats that teachers utilize in classrooms that can promote or impede help-seeking during learning activities.

Consider, for example, that teachers usually allow for questions from students after lecturing to the whole class to introduce new material or while the students are engaged in seatwork (i.e., working individually on exercises in the math workbooks). At these times, the teacher is usually the only "legitimate" helper.

To seek help when a problem is detected during these task activity structures, students must risk appearing inattentive or stupid at work or, at best, must be willing to wait passively until the teacher finds time for them.

In our classroom observations we found that students spent most of their mathematics instruction time in whole-class or individual seatwork activities. However, students in need of help were most likely to seek help by asking questions and requesting explanations when in small cooperative learning groups. In small cooperative learning groups, students may consult, question, explain, and monitor one another, multiplying the number of helpers and learning opportunities available. Because these exchanges occur among students, whether at homogeneous ability levels or heterogeneous ability levels, the students involved may be more likely to discuss, challenge, and request justifications of explanations and responses.

Conclusions

Instrumental help-seeking can and should be promoted as a general learning skill in classroom groups because it allows students to participate more effectively in socially mediated learning experiences. It is important to underscore that help should be actively sought out and not be offered without being solicited. The study of this type of active, help-seeking behavior concerned with extending knowledge and understanding draws attention to the reality that learners actively construct and practice academic as well as social knowledge in the context of classroom learning. Learners can be seen to facilitate or constrain the effects of the group in their attempts to choose when and how to involve others in their construction of knowledge. Learners contribute to the impact of the group context on their learning outcomes by their attempts to choose partners who provide them with different kinds of experience, information, demands, and supports. Importantly, they do so while attending to and negotiating the many layers and nuances of classrooms and schools as social contexts.

A task for scholars concerned with understanding learning in groups then is to build and test a conceptual model in which the reciprocal influences of individuals and learning groups can be captured as an integral determinant of theoretically relevant learning outcomes. Another important task is to investigate what learners know about learning groups as social contexts. For example, what features or dimensions of learning groups as social contexts are salient? What features of the learning group and its activities are encoded and interpreted, and by whom? How do learners' representations of these learning groups change with age and experience, and how do their representations affect the influence of this context? How do individual learners in learning groups evaluate or interpret the particular events that occur in these contexts, including both their own roles/activities and the roles/activities of other participants? How do individual learners develop a sense of personal competence in the context of outcomes experienced as produced by the learning group? It is crucial, then, as we recognize and attempt to model the mechanisms underlying the effects of learning in cooperative learning groups that we consider the role of factors operating at the level of the group as well as the constraints imposed by individuals involved in the group and the individuals' own understanding of such contexts.

References

Allen, V. (1976). The helping relationship and socialization of children: Some perspectives on tutoring. In V. Allen (Ed.), *Children as teachers*. New York: Academic Press.

    (1983). Reactions to help in peer tutoring: Roles and social identities. In A. Nadler, J. Fisher, & B. DePaulo (Eds.), *New directions in helping: Vol. 3. Applied research in help-seeking and reactions to aid* (pp. 213–232). New York: Academic Press.

Ames, C., & Archer, J. (1988). Achievement goals in the classroom: Students' learning strategies and motivation processes. *Journal of Educational Psychology, 80*, 260–267.

Ames, R. (1983). Help-seeking and achievement orientation: Perspectives from attribution theory. In B. DePaulo, A. Nadler, & J. Fisher (Eds.), *New directions in helping: Vol. 2. Help-seeking* (pp. 165–186). New York: Academic Press.

Aronson, E., Stephan, C., Sikes, J., Blaney, N., & Snapp, M. (1978). *The Jigsaw classroom*. Beverly Hills, CA: Sage.

Barnett, K., Darcie, G., Holland, C., & Kobasigawa, A. (1982). Children's cognitions about effective helping. *Developmental Psychology, 18*, 267–277.

Beller, E. (1955). Dependency and independence in young children. *Journal of Genetic Psychology, 87*, 23–35.

Bisanz, G., Vesonder, G., & Voss, J. (1978). Knowledge of one's own responding and the relation of such knowledge to learning. *Journal of Experimental Child Psychology, 25*, 116–128.

Brown, A. (1978). Knowing when, where, and how to remember: A problem of metacognition. In R. Glaser (Ed.), *Advances of instructional psychology* (pp. 77–165). Hillsdale, NJ: Erlbaum.

Brown, A., Bransford, J., Ferrara, R., & Campione, J. (1983). Learning, remembering, and understanding. In P. Mussen (Ed.), *Handbook of child psychology: Vol. 3. Cognitive development* (pp. 77–166). New York: Wiley.

Brown, A., & Palincsar, A. (1989). Guided, cooperative learning and individual knowledge acquisition. In L. Resnick (Ed.), *Knowing, learning, and instruction* (pp. 393–451). Hillsdale, NJ: Erlbaum.

Brown, A., & Reeve, R. (1987). Bandwidths of competence: The role of supportive contexts in learning and development. In L. Liben & D. Feldman (Eds.), *Development and learning: Conflict or congruence?* (pp. 173–222). Hillsdale NJ: Erlbaum.

Bryant, B. (1989). The need for social support in relation to the need for autonomy. In D. Beele (Ed.), *Children's social networks and social supports* (pp. 322–351). New York: Wiley.

Chi, M. (1978). Knowledge structures and memory development. In R. Siegler (Ed.), *Children's thinking: What develops?* (pp. 73–96). Hillsdale, NJ: Erlbaum.

Cooper, C., & Cooper, R. (1984). Skill in peer learning discourse: What develops? In

S. Kuczaj (Ed.), *Discourse development* (pp. 77–97). New York: Springer-Verlag.

Cooper, C., Marquis, A., & Ayers-Lopez, S. (1982). Peer learning in the classroom: Tracing developmental patterns and consequences of children's spontaneous interactions. In L. Wilkinson (Ed.), *Communicating in the classroom* (pp. 69–84). New York: Academic Press.

Cooper, C., Marquis, A., & Edward, D. (1986). Four perspectives on peer learning among elementary school children. In E. Mueller & C. Cooper (Eds.), *Process and outcomes in peer relationships* (pp. 269–300). New York: Academic Press.

Damon, W. (1984). Peer education: The untapped potential. *Journal of Applied Developmental Psychology, 5*, 331–343.

D'Andrade, R. (1981). The cultural part of cognition. *Cognitive Science, 5*, 179–195.

DeCooke, P., & Nelson-Le Gall, S. (1989). The effects of familiarity on the success of children's help seeking. *Journal of Applied Developmental Psychology, 10*, 195–208.

DePaulo, B., Brown, P., & Greenberg, J. (1983). The effects of help on task performance in achievement contexts, In J. Fisher, A. Nadler, & B. DePaulo (Eds.), *New directions in helping: Vol. 1. Recipient reactions to aid* (pp. 223–249). New York: Academic Press.

DePaulo, B., & Fisher, J. (1980). The costs of asking for help. *Basic and Applied Social Psychology, 7*, 23–35.

DePaulo, B., Nadler, A., & Fisher, J. (Eds.). (1983). *New directions in helping: Vol. 2. Help-seeking*. New York: Academic Press.

Diener, C., & Dweck, C. (1978). An analysis of learned helplessness: Continuous changes in performance, strategy, and achievement cognitions following failure. *Journal of Personality and Social Psychology, 39*, 940–952.

Dweck, C. (1988). Motivation. In R. Glaser & A. Lesgold (Eds.), *Handbook of psychology and education* (pp. 187–239). Hillsdale, NJ: Erlbaum.

Dweck, C., & Elliott, E. (1983). Achievement motivation. In P. Mussen (ed.), *Handbook of child psychology: Vol. 4. Socialization, personality and social development* (pp. 643–692). New York: Wiley.

Eccles, J., Midgley, C., & Adler, T. (1984). Grade-related changes in the school environment: Effects on achievement motivation. In J. Nicholls (Ed.), *Advances in motivation and achievement* (Vol. 3, pp. 283–331). New York: JAI Press.

Elliott, E., & Dweck, C. (1988). Goals: An approach to motivation and achievement. *Journal of Personality and Social Psychology, 54*, 5–12.

Feather, N. (1962). The study of persistence. *Psychological Bulletin, 59*, 94–114.

Flammer, A., Kaiser, H., & Mueller-Bouquet, P. (1981). Predicting what questions people ask. *Psychological Research, 43*, 421–429.

Flavell, J. (1977). *Cognitive development*. Englewood Cliffs, NJ: Prentice-Hall.

Ginsburg, H., & Opper, S. (1980). *Piaget's theory of intellectual development: An introduction*. Englewood Cliffs, NJ: Prentice-Hall.

Gumerman, R. (1982). *Young children's help seeking and its implications for the training of professionals in early education*. Unpublished doctoral dissertation, University of Pittsburgh, Pittsburgh, PA.

Harter, S. (1981). A model of intrinsic mastery motivation in children: Individual differences and developmental change. In W. A. Collins (Ed.), *Minnesota symposia on child psychology* (Vol. 14, pp. 215–255). Hillsdale, NJ: Erlbaum.

Hinde, R. (1976). On describing relationships. *Journal of Child Psychology and Psychiatry, 17*, 1–19.

Hudson, L., Forman, E., & Brion-Meisels, S. (1982). Role taking as a predictor of prosocial behavior in cross-age tutors. *Child Development, 53*, 1320–1329.

Ironsmith, M., & Whitehurst, G. (1978). The development of listener abilities in communication: How children deal with ambiguous information. *Child Development, 49,* 348–352.

Johnson, D., Falk, D., Martino, L., & Purdie, S. (1976). The evaluation of persons seeking and volunteering information under cooperative and competitive conditions. *Journal of Psychology, 92,* 161–165.

Johnson, D., & Johnson, R. (1975). *Learning together and alone: Cooperation, competition, and individualization.* Englewood Cliffs, NJ: Prentice-Hall.

Kratzer, L., & Nelson-Le Gall, S. (1990). Understanding the competencies and limitations of wheelchair-bound peers as helper: Developmental changes in early childhood. *Journal of Applied Developmental Psychology, 11,* 69–85.

Kreutzer, M., Leonard, C., & Flavell, J. (1975). An interview study of children's knowledge about memory. *Monographs of the Society for Research in Child Development, 40*(1, Serial No. 159).

Ladd, G., & Oden, S. (1979). The relationship between peer acceptance and children's ideas about helpfulness. *Child Development, 50,* 402–408.

Larson, C., Dansereau, D., O'Donnell, A., Hythecker, V., Lambiotte, J., & Rocklin, T. (1985). Effects of metacognitive and elaborative activity on cooperative learning and transfer. *Contemporary Educational Psychology, 10,* 342–348.

Levin, J., & Kareev, Y. (1980). Problem-solving in everyday situations. *Quarterly Newsletter of the Laboratory of Comparative Human Cognition, 2,* 47–52.

Markman, E. (1977). Realizing that you don't understand: A preliminary investigation. *Child Development, 48,* 986–992.

(1979). Realizing that you don't understand: Elementary school children's awareness of inconsistencies. *Child Development, 50,* 643–655.

(1980, October). *Comprehension monitoring: Developmental and educational issues.* Paper presented at the NIE-LRDC Conference on Thinking and Learning Skills, University of Pittsburgh.

Miyake, N., & Norman, D. (1979). To ask a question, one must know enough to know what is not known. *Journal of Verbal Learning and Verbal Behavior, 18,* 357–364.

Murphy, L. (1962). *The widening world of childhood.* New York: Basic Books.

Nash, W., & Torrance, E. (1974). Creative reading and the questioning abilities of young children. *Journal of Creative Behavior, 8,* 15–19.

Nelson-Le Gall, S. (1981). Help-seeking: An understudied problem-solving skill in children. *Developmental Review, 1,* 224–246.

(1985). Help-seeking behavior in learning. In E. Gordon (Ed.), *Review or research in education* (Vol. 12, pp. 55–90). Washington, DC: American Educational Research Association.

(1987). Necessary and unnecessary help-seeking in children. *Journal of Genetic Psychology, 148,* 53–62.

(1990). Academic achievement orientation and help-seeking behavior in early adolescent girls. *Journal of Early Adolescence, 10,* 176–190.

Nelson-Le Gall, S., & DeCooke, P. (1987). Same-sex and cross-sex help exchanges in the classroom. *Journal of Educational Psychology, 148,* 67–71.

Nelson-Le Gall, S., DeCooke, P. & Jones, E. (1989). Children's self-perceptions of competence and help-seeking. *Journal of Genetic Psychology, 150,* 457–459.

Nelson-Le Gall, S., & Glor-Scheib, S. (1985). Help-seeking in elementary classrooms: An observational study. *Contemporary Educational Psychology, 10,* 58–71.

(1986). Academic help-seeking and peer relations in school. *Contemporary Educational Psychology, 11,* 187–193.

Nelson-Le Gall, S., & Gumerman, R. (1984). Children's perceptions of helpers and helper motivation. *Journal of Applied Developmental Psychology, 5*, 1–12.

Nelson-Le Gall, S., Gumerman, R., & Scott-Jones, D. (1983). Instrumental help-seeking and everyday problem-solving: A developmental perspective. In B. DePaulo, A. Nadler, & J. Fisher (Eds.), *New directions in helping: Vol. 2. Help-seeking* (pp. 265–283). New York: Academic Press.

Nelson-Le Gall, S., & Jones, E. (1990). Cognitive-motivational influences on children's help-seeking. *Child Development, 61*, 581–589.

Nelson-Le Gall, S., Kratzer, L., Jones, E., & DeCooke, P. (1990). Children's self-assessment of performance and task-related help seeking. *Journal of Experimental Child Psychology, 49*, 245–263.

Nelson-Le Gall, S., & Scott-Jones, D. (1985). Teachers' and young children's perceptions of appropriate work strategies. *Child Study Journal, 15*, 29–42.

Newman, R., & Goldin, L. (1990). Children's reluctance to seek help with schoolwork. *Journal of Educational Psychology, 82*, 71–80.

Nicholls, J. (1984). Achievement motivation: Conceptions of ability, subjective experience, task choice and performance. *Psychological Review, 91*, 328–346.

Palincsar, A., & Brown, A. (1984). Reciprocal teaching of comprehension-fostering and comprehension-monitoring activities. *Cognition and Instruction, 1*, 117–175.

Peterson, P., Janicki, T., & Swing, S. (1981). Ability x treatment interaction effects on children's learning in large-group and small-group approaches. *American Educational Research Journal, 18*, 453–473.

Peterson, P., Wilkinson, L., Spinelli, F., & Swing, S. (1984). Merging the process-product and the sociolinguistic paradigms: Research on small-group process. In P. Peterson, L. Wilkinson, & M. Hallinan (Eds.), *The social context of instruction: Group organization and group process* (pp. 125–152). Orlando, FL: Academic Press.

Pressley, M., Levin, J., Ghatala, E., & Ahmad, M. (1987). Test monitoring in young grade children. *Journal of Experimental Child Psychology, 43*, 96–111.

Rogoff, B., & Gardner, W. (1984). Adult guidance of cognitive development. In B. Rogoff & J. Lave (Eds.), *Everyday cognition: Its development in social context* (pp. 95–116). Cambridge: Harvard University Press.

Rosen, S., Powell, E., & Schubot, D. (1978). Competence and tutorial role as status variables affecting peer-tutoring outcomes in public school settings. *Journal of Educational Psychology, 20*, 602–612.

Slavin, R. (1983). *Cooperative learning*. New York: Longman.

van der Miej, H. (1988). Constraints on question-asking in classrooms. *Journal of Educational Psychology, 80*, 401–405.

Vygotsky, L. (1978). *Mind in society: The development of higher psychological processes*. Cambridge: Harvard University Press.

Webb, N. (1983). Predicting learning from student interaction: Defining the interaction variables. *Educational Psychologist, 18*, 33–41.

Winterbottom, M. (1958). The relationship of need for achievement to learning experiences in independence and mastery. In J. Atkinson (Ed.), *Motives in fantasy, action, and society* (pp. 453–478). Princeton, NJ: Van Nostrand.

Wood, D., Bruner, J., & Ross, G. (1976). The role of tutoring in problem solving. *Journal of Child Psychology and Psychiatry, 17*, 89–100.

Wood, D., & Middleton, D. (1975). A study of assisted problem-solving. *British Journal of Psychology, 66*, 181–191.

Part II

**Social Skills and Classroom Factors
Influencing Peer Interactions**

4 Understanding Interactive Behaviors: Looking at Six Mirrors of the Classroom

Rachel Hertz-Lazarowitz

Introduction

The question What are students doing when they are engaged in academic work in the classroom? seems an obvious question with ready-made answers. Many verbs describe student behavior in the classroom: They learn, study, listen to the teacher. They write, read, and do seatwork. They ask and answer questions, chat, daydream, and wait for the bell to ring. There is a universal rhythm of "life in the classroom," described in numerous qualitative and quantitative accounts (Hertz-Lazarowitz, 1984; Jackson, 1968).

Historically, classroom research focused on teacher behavior. The general assumption in the 1960s and 1970s was that teachers should practice a great variety of instructional behaviors to keep students alert, interested, and engaged in academic work (Flanders, 1970). In the late seventies, the focus of research and observation shifted to student behavior. This shift was intensified by *Looking in Classrooms,* an influential book by Good and Brophy (1973). Soon after that, the field of student behavior became interdisciplinary; linguists and sociolinguists joined psychologists and educators to supplement descriptive-phenom-

This chapter is the result of 10 years of collaborative work with colleagues and students. I wish to express my thanks to Professors Shlomo Sharan and Paul Hare. In the late 1970s, we worked together on the initial formulation of the classroom integrative model (Sharan, Hertz-Lazarowitz, & Hare, 1981), and for the next decade I conducted research on the model. From 1988 to 1990, I continued my work on it with Joan Davidson from Royal High School in Simi Valley, California. Each collaboration enriched my conception and the implications of the model.

The research of my graduate students contributed to the development of the model. Shahar Hana studied teacher behavior in different contexts. Ditza Maskit worked on understanding student behavior in cooperative contexts. Ina Fuchs co-authored a book with me on cooperation in the classroom (1987) in which the metaphor of mirrors in relation to learning task structures and student behavior was elaborated. An earlier draft of the chapter was read by Dr. Tamar Zelniker; her helpful comments, clarification, and editing are all highly valued. Haggai Kupermintz helped with most of the data analysis of the studies conducted since 1985. I would like to thank Eduardo Calderón for preparing the figures. Parts of this chapter were prepared during my sabbatical year in the Department of Psychology at the University of Southern California (1988).

enological methods, mainly to analyze communication in different classroom settings (Cazden, 1986; Everston & Green, 1986; Wilkinson, 1982).

Most of the research was conducted in traditional classrooms. In this context, teaching is expository-frontal. The "classroom" was considered to be a room, with one teacher and 30 to 40 students, who were treated as one collective group. In such a setting, students are usually perceived by teachers and by researchers of the classroom as a passive audience.

Recently, researchers have increasingly perceived the classroom as a complex social and academic system. Its main components are the physical organization of the room, the structure of the learning task, the instructional and communicative patterns of the teacher, and the social and academic behaviors of the students (Sharan & Hertz-Lazarowitz, 1980). Student social and academic behaviors are the *outcome* of the pattern in which other dimensions of the classroom function, implying that student behavior can be either passive or active, depending on the specific classroom context (Hertz-Lazarowitz, 1984; 1989a; Hertz-Lazarowitz, Fuchs, Eisenberg, & Sharabany, 1989).

Two main theoretical frameworks contribute to the legitimization and value of pupils as active participants: social-constructivist theory (Vygotsky, 1978) and the social psychology of contact (Allport, 1954) and cooperation (Deutch, 1949). Cooperative learning (DeVries and Edwards, 1973; Sharan and Hertz-Lazarowitz, 1980) combines these theoretical frameworks into practical instruction (Sharan, 1990; Slavin, 1989).

Investigators of the classroom, however, have paid only limited attention to student behavior as a factor that influences the complex social learning environment. The few notable exceptions (Getzel & Thelen, 1960; Thelen, 1981) highlight that neglect. Moreover, most theory and research on the classroom is unidimensional, focusing on the effects of one or another set of variables to the exclusion of others.

In this chapter I describe a model that takes into consideration the richness and complexity of the classroom and its relation to student behavior. The model proposes that the dimensions of (1) physical organization, (2) learning task structure, and (3) teacher instructional and (4) communicative behaviors are interrelated and function simultaneously in each classroom. Only by studying these four dimensions can one predict the behaviors that will be observed in the 5th and 6th dimensions, student academic and social behavior in the classroom.

Each of the model's six dimensions, termed *mirrors,* contains five components of increasing complexity. The model can be analyzed vertically by examining levels within each dimension, or horizontally by examining a given level of complexity across all dimensions. Following the description of the model, I present a taxonomy of student behavior. Together the model and the taxonomy served as a theoretical framework for an observational research program. Tex studies that used this conceptual framework are described and discussed in the third section of the chapter. They were conducted in different countries with diverse cultures and social contexts and examined three distinct classroom contexts: traditional, nontraditional, and cooperative. A final section summarizes the chapter and poses questions for future research.

Mirrors of the Classroom: An Integrative Model

The model consists of six interrelated mirrors: physical organization of the classroom, the learning task, teacher's instructional behavior, teacher's communicative behavior, student's academic behavior, and student's social behavior (see Figure 4.1). I use the metaphor "mirrors" to express the view that the dimensions that characterize the classroom setting are interrelated; structures and activities in one dimension are reflected in each dimension. The relationships can range from maximum coordination and harmony to minimum coordination and disharmony. When the classroom is functioning on similar levels of complexity in each of the dimensions, it is perceived as "harmonious." It is suggested that when this harmony takes place at a high level of complexity, student academic and social behaviors become more interactive and result in a higher level of thinking.

Looking in the Mirrors of Traditional and Cooperative Classrooms

Comparison of a traditional, expository classroom with a cooperative classroom will illustrate and clarify the mirrors of the model. The traditional classroom is usually perceived as a single social system, "the class as a whole." Its structure maximizes the isolation of students from one another by seating arrangements such as individual desks in rows. The teacher is the center of activity. He or she controls all communication networks and presents knowledge to pupils (the teacher's mirrors). The learning task is structured as individualistic or competitive (Johnson & Johnson, 1975). Cooperation is not usually required or even tolerated in means, processes, or outcomes of learning. Lessons (task mirror) are presented via a whole-group format and the task is structured so that each pupil is expected to complete it on his or her own by referring to printed sources of information (Bossert, 1979).

In such a classroom, pupils are expected to listen and to respond to the teacher only when called on to do so. Student-student interactions are minimal, and each student looks after himself or herself (student's mirrors). This classroom func-

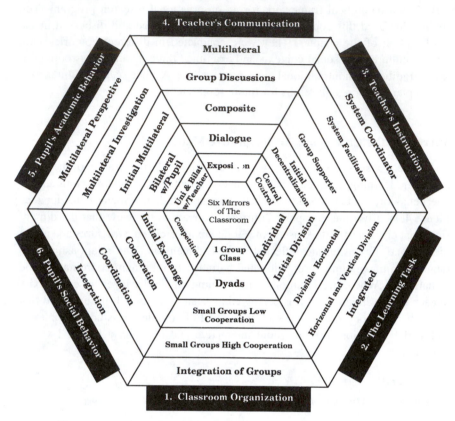

Figure 4.1. Six mirrors of the classroom.

tions harmoniously at the first level of complexity of each of the mirrors in the
model.

The outer levels of the model relate to a classroom that works in complete
cooperation, such as the one that uses the Group Investigation method (Sharan
& Hertz-Lazarowitz, 1980). In such a classroom the same six dimensions exist,
but in different forms. The class functions as a set of small groups, or "group of
groups," more typical of a complex social system (Mirror 1). The learning task
is of a divisible and/or investigative nature. It deals with multifaceted problems
rather than with unitary tasks that can be solved by a single correct answer (Mirror 2). The teacher offers guidance to develop the skills that pupils need as
members of relatively autonomous groups and acts as a learning facilitator or
resource rather than as a dispenser of information (Mirrors 3 and 4). As a result,
pupils must rely on and develop their social interactive and cognitive skills to

Figure 4.2. Classroom organization.

carry out their learning task. They exchange information, generate ideas, and participate in active information gathering as well as in multilateral communication networks. They take on various social roles in the learning process: leaders, planners, investigators, and so on. Their behaviors will follow the social-constructivist approach to learning rather than the passive-receptive approach typical of the former example (Mirrors 5 and 6).

These two short descriptions present the basic characteristics of the integrative model. They emphasize that the context of instruction, communication, and the learning task within the specific organization of the classroom are interrelated in a systematic way and cannot be separated when observing and studying interaction. The following sections will present each dimension in some detail. As indicated, each mirror contains five components of increasing levels of complexity.

1. Physical Organization of the Classroom

Every classroom functions, first and foremost, as an organization of some kind. This organization is determined primarily, though not exclusively, by the teacher. Sometimes, classroom organization is dictated by circumstances beyond the teacher's control, including school policy or even physical features of the room. In taking a closer look at Mirror 1, we see that the classroom structural organization ranges from a one-group class to a classroom consisting of a group of groups (Figure 4.2).

The classroom can be organized as a centralized system with the teacher as

Figure 4.3. The learning task.

the main figure and with the students forming a single large group (Level 1). This organization is generally referred to as the traditional classroom. On the other end of the continuum, the classroom can be a decentralized organization with many smaller units (groups) operating simultaneously. This organization is a group of groups (Level 5).

Going from Level 1 to Level 5, the organization of the classroom becomes more complex and more flexible in terms of workspace assigned to teachers and students for learning activities, and the degree of cooperation increases among group members and between groups. As classroom organization becomes more complex, there is a concomitant increase in interaction, cooperation, and helping among individuals and groups. The *quality* of those interactions is dependent on the levels of other dimensions of the classroom. The frequency of interactions is affected to a great extent by the classroom's physical organization.

2. The Learning Task

Very often, teachers perceive the learning task as the single most important component of classroom activity. Completion of learning tasks is the object of the classroom's production process. Students are well aware of the fact that they are evaluated and graded by the teacher on the degree of successful completion of the tasks. Structurally, learning tasks vary in levels of complexity, determined by the pattern of division of the task and integration of the learning products (Figure 4.3). As depicted in Mirror 2 of the model, the least complex level is the unitary task, where every pupil must individually complete the same task in its entirety. At the next level of complexity, a task is shared among two or more individual students. In horizontal learning, the task is divided into subtasks and each of its components is assigned to different individuals in the group. Once the initial learning has been completed, the different components are combined. Each subsequent level incorporates the level just below it. In the vertical structure, there is an additional elaboration of the horizontal structure that cuts across tasks, such as, for example, the identification of differences or similarities among tasks. Finally, in the fifth level of complexity, the integrated task, all information is integrated to form a cohesive whole or, alternatively, becomes the basis of yet a higher level question to be integrated with existing answers (Hertz-Lazarowitz & Fuchs, 1987).

For example, if a classroom is studying Native American tribes and their task is to learn about different dance rituals, in the horizontal task each group member will study one of the dance rituals of one tribe. Later, each group member will contribute his or her part to the group product, a summary report of the dancing rituals of all of the tribes studied. In the vertical task structure, all group members will identify and discuss similarities and differences in the dance rituals of all tribes that were identified in the original task. The group product at this level will be an integrative task in which the members will use critical thinking skills in a give-and-take social interaction to develop theories or hypotheses regarding the causes underlying the identified similarities and differences in tribal rituals.

3. Teacher's Instructional Behavior

Mirror 3 in the model depicts the behaviors of the teacher as an instructional leader (Figure 4.4). The levels of complexity vary from centralization of the teacher's role, in which the teacher's main pattern of instruction is lecturing and fully controlling students' responses, to a decentralized style, wherein decision-making processes are distributed among groups of students. The latter style presents the teacher as a facilitator for students' learning and interaction rather than as the central focus of classroom life and the primary source of knowledge. The teacher thus is the guide on the side, not the sage on the stage (Hertz-Lazarowitz & Shachar, 1990).

4. Teacher's Communicative Behavior

Related to the teacher's behavior as an instructor is his or her behavior as communicator and organizer of communication networks in the classroom (Figure 4.5). The communication mirror is defined in patterns developed by Thew (1975) and elaborated in Hertz-Lazarowitz and Davidson (1990). Teacher communication networks range from expository unilateral lectures to bilateral and multilat-

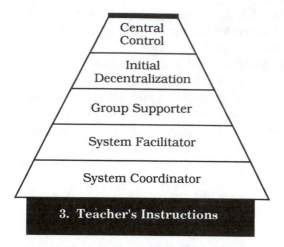

Figure 4.4. Teacher's instruction.

Figure 4.5. Teacher's communication.

eral systems existing on several levels: teacher to individual, teacher to small group, teacher to whole class, and teacher as facilitator of communication among and between groups.

In the most complex pattern of organization of communication, teachers focus on encouraging communication among students and between groups, usually by facilitating planning, investigation, and reports. Teachers determine pathways of

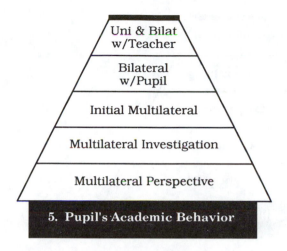

Figure 4.6. Pupil's academic behavior.

communication in the classroom by introducing composite, coordinated, and integrated networks of communication.

5. *Student's Academic Behavior*

The two mirrors of student behavior, social and academic, are closely interrelated. The more differentiated the social organization of the classroom, the more complex they become. Academic skills range from simple and passive, such as listening or interacting only with the textbook and/or the teacher, to highly complex, where evaluative and creative academic skills are necessary to synthesize several sources of information (Figure 4.6). The use of complex academic skills usually occurs within an interactive learning context. In high cooperation the edges of these two mirrors blur. Because the dimensions of student social and academic behaviors are the focus of my own research, these mirrors are further elaborated in the later sections of the chapter.

6. *Student's Social Behavior*

Social skills are needed to play the role of a student and a learner. One categorization of these skills relates them to individualistic, competitive, and cooperative goal structures (Johnson & Johnson, 1975, 1989). In the mirror model, levels of complexity range from noninteractive to interactive behaviors, and later to cooperative and integrative behaviors (Figure 4.7). The least complex social behavior is when the student functions as an isolated individual member. Isola-

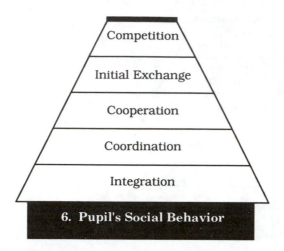

Figure 4.7. Pupil's social behavior.

tion can be perceived as "you swim, I swim" (individualistic) or as "I swim, you sink" (competitive) where student success implies the failure of other class-mates. Social skills of both individualistic and competitive modes are less com-plex compared with those necessary to facilitate learning that requires interaction between students. Academic exchange in cooperative learning calls for a give-and-take type of social skill, for the distribution of resources, and simultaneous attention to and consideration of all group members' ideas. Learning tasks in-clude three stages: input, process, and outcomes. Students' level of cooperation can range from low to high, based on the actual interactive behavior that takes place in each of these stages. Hertz-Lazarowitz (1989a) defines low cooperation as interacting only in the input stage, for sharing resources. High cooperation includes student interaction while producing a product. For example, a task where students are required to write a group story can be performed at either a low or a high level of cooperation. If a student writes his or her own story, and then combines it mechanically into a group story, this is considered low level. If students engage in discussions, clarifications, and feedback to rewrite the group story, this is high-level cooperation. Being a member of a highly cooperative team calls for complex social skills such as participation, taking turns, relating to others' contributions, and reflecting on the content and form of one's own interactive behaviors as well as on that of others. In the mirror these are labeled as gradually progressing from coordination to integration (see also Hertz-Lazarowitz & Fuchs, 1987; Hertz-Lazarowitz & Davidson, 1990; Sharan & Hertz-Lazarowitz, 1978).

Integrating the Mirrors of the Model

There are several ways to integrate the information of this model. We can first view each mirror separately, looking from the center outward. This vertical arrangement suggests a continuum of complexity, with the outward activities being on the most highly sophisticated levels. Furthermore, this model suggests that the teachers should gradually progress outward step by step rather than skipping over levels or carrying out the process too rapidly.

If we look at the task mirror, the second level is initial division, and the third level is divisible horizontal. The assumption is that initial division is more complex than the individual task and less complex than divisible horizontal. To illustrate, for initial division, teachers might structure tasks for dyads and ask them to work mainly as individuals. The element of cooperation is introduced in this level by adding activities such as mutual checking – comparing or listening to each other's answers. This level requires the student to exhibit social skills such as listening to each other and exchanging simple feedback. Academically, they are asked to compare or check for accuracy, usually with a ready-made teacher answer sheet. The STAD (Student Teams Achievement Divisions) method frequently uses this task structure (Slavin, Sharan, Kagan, Hertz-Lazarowitz, Webb, & Schmuck, 1985).

When the teacher assigns learning tasks that are divisible horizontal, each member of the group (usually three to five students) is responsible for one part of the content, and the group works toward a combined product. The Jigsaw method (Aronson, Stephan, Sikes, Blaney, & Snapp, 1978) uses this structure. At this level, students are required to engage in more complex social and academic behaviors and thus need more complex skills. Usually the time allotted for the cooperative process increases, and in the social behavior dimension students attentively listen, take turns in participation, keep a time schedule, perform social roles, and relate to each other.

Academic behavior in such tasks is cognitively more complex than in individual tasks. Students need to progress from simple recall of information to more complex information processing and critical thinking skills such as teaching each other, summarizing different opinions, and combining information. The change in the contextual mode of the classroom should occur simultaneously in all the mirrors, following the stages proposed. The model contains a developmental sequence and proposes that both teacher and pupils must master skills at each level before proceeding to the next.

We can also view the chart horizontally, looking in a circular fashion around the mirrors. Implicit in the idea that the mirrors are interrelated is that different activities in the classroom should be linked with their compatible levels from the other mirrors for maximum efficiency and best results. Within a given period or day in the classroom, the teacher can successfully design different activities structured at different levels. It is important that within each activity the levels of all mirrors are in harmony. For example, if the teacher structures a whole group task and uses an expository-frontal instructional style, all other mirrors should function at the same level as the communicative and instructional style chosen by the teacher for that activity. If the teacher structures the task at the fifth level as an integrative investigation, he or she should likewise ensure that structures are in place to facilitate the same high level of functioning in all other mirrors (e.g., seating arrangements conducive to small group discussion, allowing a higher sound level so as not to inhibit verbal exchanges, and so forth). The teacher thus becomes the architect of the classroom, attempting to best match the learning task to his or her preferred role as instructor and communicator within a given organization. This process will determine the context of the classroom.

The research conducted in Israel focused on the impact of the first four mirrors – classroom organization, tasks, teacher communication, and teacher instructions – on student behavior in the academic and social dimensions. The model served as a framework to describe traditional and cooperative classroom contexts. The dimensions of student behaviors served as the dependent variables in the research program. An operationalized system of observable categories of behavior was needed, and a four-cluster taxonomy was developed for this purpose.

Four Clusters of Student Learning in the Classroom

Student behavior can be described on two axes: on-task versus off-task and interactive versus noninteractive. This 2×2 taxonomy encompasses the full range of student behaviors. A major body of research studies on-task seatwork behaviors (Anderson, 1984; Karweit & Slavin, 1982). In the current conceptualization, these behaviors are defined as on-task, noninteractive behaviors. Cooperation, helping, and peer instruction are defined as on-task and interactive. Disruptive behaviors such as discipline problems, chatting, or fighting are interactive, off-task behaviors. Withdrawal and daydreaming are off-task, noninteractive behaviors.

All student classroom activity falls within this four-cluster conceptualization. The clusters studied and observed during the past two decades reflected the educational ideology of the era. "Time-on-task" research flourished in the late seventies. It put disproportional emphasis on intrapersonal processes and was based on the erroneous assumption that the more students engage in solitary time on a task, the better their academic outcome. In fact, research in both the United States and Israel documents that time on a task is not highly correlated with academic achievement (Hertz-Lazarowitz, 1984). Often, such behaviors are low-level busy work, such as filling in worksheets, which does not contribute substantially to cognitive development (Anderson, 1984; Karweit & Slavin, 1982).

More recently, the focus of study has shifted from time on task in a noninteractive mode to on-task, interactive behaviors. This shift to student-student interaction was influenced by the theories presented earlier and was followed by an impressive body of research on peer interaction in learning (Brown & Palincsar,1989; Damon & Phelps, 1989; Dansereau, 1988; Johnson & Johnson, 1989; Sharan & Shachar, 1988; Slavin, 1989). Most of this research, however, focused on specific behaviors (e.g., helping), which occur in low frequencies in the learning context (see Chapter 5), and omitted the full spectrum of student behaviors within distinct learning contexts (Hertz-Lazarowitz, 1989b).

Because clusters are interdependent and because interactive and noninteractive on-task behaviors complement each other, research has to account for changes in quantity and quality in these two interactive clusters. Studying isolated categories of behavior may distort our understanding of the full array of student behaviors. For example, helping interactions are quite rare in the classroom (Hertz-Lazarowitz, 1983), and their correlation with academic achievement is not consistent (Webb, 1989). Helping interactions differ in their cognitive-academic characteristics partly as a function of the learning task. It is proposed that correlations of specific behavior with academic outcomes might be stronger if additional student on-task interaction behaviors were included in the analysis. Studies conducted in a contextual framework that presents data on the full repertoire of student behaviors might produce higher correlation between process-interaction and outcome behaviors.

The Research Program and Methodology

From 1983 to 1989, 10 studies were guided by the mirror model of the classroom. In each, the full range of behaviors for *all* the students in a given classroom for the lesson observed were coded during naturalistic classroom observations. The dependent variables were student behaviors. Independent variables were aspects of one or more of the model's mirrors.

The six behavior categories observed are presented in Table 4.1. Based on the four-cluster taxonomy, solitary on-task and off-task behaviors are noninteractive, whereas cooperation, helping, and teacher-student interactions are interactive, on-task behaviors. Interactive, off-task behaviors were also observed.

Cooperation and helping were further elaborated to include task-related elements. Low and high cooperation were defined based on whether it occurred in one or more components of task performance. These components include input, process, and outcome activities (Hertz-Lazarowitz & Fuchs, 1987; Sharan & Hertz-Lazarowitz, 1989a,b; Steiner, 1972). Cooperation was defined as high when

Table 4.1. *Student-behaviors in the classroom (six basic categories)*

Behavior category	Definition and examples
Noninteractive	
On-task	Pupil is engaged in the formal activity of the lesson (reads, writes, watches films, listens to teacher or student)
Off-task	Pupil is engaged in an activity that is off-task (reads a comic book, daydreams)
Interactive	
On-task: cooperation	Pupil is on-task cooperating with a peer, in means, process, or product of learning (two or more build a cell model from clay, two or more read and discuss a text)
On-task: helping	One pupil helps another pupil who asked for help with an on-task activity (shows how to do an experiment, explains instructions)
On-task: teacher-student	Verbal interaction between teacher and student that is related to learning activity
Off-task: social event	Pupil is engaged in verbal exchange unrelated to the learning activity (talks about a party or TV show)

it occurred between students in the process component and in one or both of the other components. Helping was coded in regard to the initiator of the act, following Hertz-Lazarowitz (1983) and Eisenberg, Cameron, and Trayon (1984). Distinctions were made regarding the importance of voluntary (initiated by the student) versus imposed (designed by the teacher) help (for examples see Table 4.2). The verbal content of cooperative and helping interaction was transcribed and analyzed later for its level of reasoning according to Bloom's (1956) taxonomy of informative, applicative, and evaluative levels of thinking. In this way levels of reasoning were coded within categories of cooperation and helping (Hertz-Lazarowitz, 1989a; Hertz-Lazarowitz, Baird, Webb, & Lazarowitz, 1984). Table 4.2 presents the definitions of these behaviors.

The studies were conducted within three main types of classrooms: traditional, nontraditional (but not cooperative), and cooperative. The procedure used an elaborated version of Altman's (1973) method of instantaneous sampling procedure, which was initially developed to observe young children in natural play. It included a short observation of the student (child) and the recording of behavior on a precoded set of categories. The large number of observations ensured a representative sample of student behavior.

In the studies observing traditional instruction, most of the seating arrange-

Table 4.2. *Cooperation and helping*

	Description and examples
Cooperation	
Low cooperation (simple)	Cooperation in means (resources) or product, without cooperating in the process (students use common books or other materials in their learning activity, or they work individually on a task and then combine their products)
High cooperation (complex)	Cooperation in the process of activity, usually cooperating in a long-term process to create a cooperative product (students are engaged in a temporally extended process of working together, such as building a clay model of a cell, where planning and executing the model are carried out in a constant interactive manner)
Helping	
Student initiated	Help is performed as result of a voluntary act of the student-helper or as a response to a request from a peer
Teacher initiated	Help is imposed by the teacher or by the task instruction
Cognitive characteristics	
Informative	Exchange of information between pupils (related to "what?")
Applicative	Extending information to application, such as solving the problem, performing an experiment, giving broader examples (related to "how?")
Evaluative	Making generalizations or judgments, creating new solutions, examining current data (related to "why?")

ments were by rows. In each lesson, three cycles were conducted; each cycle included 15 to 18 students and lasted 10 minutes. Thus 45 to 54 segments of behavior, per lesson, were coded. The observer approached the target student and observed him or her, coded the category of behavior, and then proceeded to the next student in the row. Within each row starting points were randomly selected for first or last student observed. When students were interacting, the observer listened to the content of their interaction and coded the categories and the cognitive level. Last, transcripts of sample interactions between students were taken (a detailed description of the procedure and an example of the observational form are presented in Hertz-Lazarowitz et al., 1984).

In the second phase of the research, when we observed nontraditional classrooms such as learning centers (Hertz-Lazarowitz, 1984) and active classrooms (Hertz-Lazarowitz, Fuchs, Eisenberg, & Sharabany, 1989) the instrument was redesigned for group observation. In these classrooms, the observation began a few minutes after the beginning of the lesson. A target group of five to six pupils was randomly selected, and although the observer followed the same basic procedure, more time was allocated for recording students' verbal interactions. Thus, the observation included the precoded category-based procedure and an open observation. (See Hertz-Lazarowitz, Fuchs, Eisenberg, & Sharabany, 1989, for a full description of the method.)

The third phase of the research observed classrooms that used cooperative learning. In this research, more detailed categories were defined and analyzed to examine unique aspects of cooperative interaction (Maskit, 1986; Maskit & Hertz-Lazarowitz, 1986, 1989a, 1989b). In all studies, the physical arrangement of the classroom, the content area of the lesson, and the students' learning task were carefully described. The research attempted to clarify four issues. Do students exhibit universal behavior in the classroom? Do students' on-task, interactive behaviors in cooperative classrooms have unique features? Is student behavior sensitive to cultural variability? Which classroom dimensions are most powerful in producing interactive behaviors?

Student Behavior in Traditional Classroom Contexts

We studied traditional classrooms first because they are the most prevalent type in Western schools today. Two studies observed elementary (Hertz-Lazarowitz, 1983) and high school students in Utah (Hertz-Lazarowitz et al., 1984). Another study observed elementary school students in Israel, studying schools from distinct demographic (Jewish, Arab, and Druze) and geographic sectors (city, villages, and kibbutzim). (Table 4.3 presents a summary of all the studies presented in this chapter.) The naturalistic observation procedures described earlier were conducted including the independent variables of the physical organization of the classroom, task content area, instructional method (within the traditional context), sociocultural background, and age (grade level).

Our specific aims were to develop useful measures for a general description of student behaviors in traditional classrooms. Such baseline measures were necessary for further examination of the model. We needed to assess whether interactive behaviors are indeed those that are most sensitive to classroom contexts. If so, even instructional variation within traditional contexts (such as lecture vs. whole-class discussion, laboratory work) should affect interactive behavior. We needed to determine whether behaviors remain stable across age (grade levels) and cultural background. Our results show that the four-cluster conceptualization is valid and describes what students do in the classroom. Furthermore, in tradi-

Table 4.3. *Summary of studies (chronological)*

Study: Hertz-Lazarowitz, 1983
Sample: Elementary school (United States), 450 subjects
Context: Traditional instruction
Independent variables: Age: first through sixth grades
Dependent variables: Student behaviors, cognitive level of interaction, what children think about helping in the classroom
Findings: No clear developmental trend. Half of behaviors noninteractive. Helping and cooperation rare. Low levels of cognition. Conflicting norms about help and cooperation in the classroom.

Study: Hertz-Lazarowitz, 1984
Sample: Elementary school (Israel), two fourth-grade classrooms (70 subjects)
Context: Learning centers
Independent variables: Analyzing tasks in three dimensions: cognitive, social, and structure (unitary, division, coordinate)
Dependent variables: Teacher-planned task activities vs. student actual-task activities
Findings: Because teacher involvement in the process of task completion was minimal, students simplified assigned tasks. They used fewer critical thinking and integrative skills, and more lower-level procedural skills.

Study: Hertz-Lazarowitz, Baird, Webb, & Lazarowitz (1984)
Sample: High school (United States), 30 classrooms
Context: Traditional
Independent variables: Subject matter and instructional variation
Dependent variables: Student behaviors and cognitive level of cooperation and help
Findings: Subject matter (especially biology) and variation in instructional methods drastically affect interactive behaviors of students compared with other behaviors. Teacher centrality reduces interactive, on-task and increases interactive, off-task behaviors, whereas less centralization (laboratory) increases on-task interaction. Cooperation and help are more sensitive to instructional variations than other behaviors.

Study: Maskit, 1986; Maskit & Hertz-Lazarowitz, 1986, 1989a, 1989b
Sample: 93 adult students
Context: Cooperative learning
Independent variables: Group size, sex, group composition, and time (these variables are not discussed here; see Maskit & Hertz-Lazarowitz, 1986)
Dependent variables: Student behavior and attitudes toward and evaluation of cooperative learning
Findings: Six factors emerged: Two were universal general factors and four were cooperative interactive. The universal general factors were negatively correlated with the cooperative interactive factors. Stability across time in behaviors was observed.

Study: Lazarowitz, Hertz- Lazarowitz, Baird, & Bowlden, 1988
Sample: 113 high school students learning biology; two units: the cell and plants
Context: Individual mastery vs. Jigsaw investigative
Independent variable: Mode of instruction
Dependent variables: Academic achievement, on-task behavior, and maintenance of on-task behaviors over time
Findings: Higher achievement for the Jigsaw investigative group in the cell unit, which required more inquiry activities. Higher achievement for individual mastery in the

Table 4.3. *(cont.)*

plants unit, which required more information learning. Increase in and maintenance of on-task behavior for the Jigsaw investigation method.

Study: Hertz-Lazarowitz, Fuchs, Eisenberg, & Sharabany, 1989
Sample: Elementary school, 65 students in third grade
Context: Traditional and active learning
Independent variables: Socialization setting: kibbutz vs. city; instructional mode: active vs. traditional
Dependent variables: Prosocial reasoning, student behavior, cooperation, and helping
Findings: Students exhibit different behaviors in the two classroom contexts. In an active classroom, on-task behavior is more interactive and cooperative. Instruction affects behavior more than socialization.

Study: Hertz-Lazarowitz, 1989a
Sample: 752 students (Israel), third through eighth grades
Context: traditional with variations
Independent variable: Task structure
Dependent variables: Student behaviors, cooperation and helping, cognitive level of interaction
Findings: High-cooperative learning tasks produce explanations and elaborations at a high cognitive level. Low-cooperative tasks produce interaction only on the informative level.

Study: Maskit & Hertz-Lazarowitz, 1989b
Sample: 93 adult students
Context: Cooperative
Independent variable: Experience in cooperative learning
Dependent variables: Attitudes and evaluations of cooperative learning
Findings: Positive evaluation and attitudes. Efficacy and enjoyment of cooperative learning increased within time of learning.

Study: Calderón, Tinajero, & Hertz-Lazarowitz, 1990; Hertz-Lazarowitz, 1989
Sample: 8 classrooms (El-Paso, Tx), second and fourth grades, bilingual
Context: Traditional, in transition to cooperative CIRC
Independent variable: Observation of the six mirrors of the classroom
Dependent variables: Student and teacher behavior
Findings: For the initial observation most of the classrooms were organized to maximize isolation and noninteractive learning. Learning tasks were either collective or paper-pencil, individual, unitary tasks. Teachers' instruction was lecturing or assigning individual tasks. Teachers' communication was mostly to the whole class, with simple questions to a few students. Students' behavior was filling in worksheets or passive listening – on-task, noninteractive. Individual variation observed among teachers. A year later a change in the mirrors of the classroom had taken place. As a result, students' behavior became more interactive.

Study: Hertz-Lazarowitz & Shahar, 1990
Sample: 27 elementary school teachers, traditional and cooperative instruction
Context: Traditional vs. Group Investigation
Independent variables: Instructional mode, grade taught, teacher seniority, attitudes toward cooperative learning

Table 4.3. *(cont.)*

Dependent variables: Categories of teachers' verbal behavior

Findings: Teachers' instructional behavior changed significantly. They reduced formal and rigid verbal behavior used in traditional instruction and increased formal and interactive verbal behavior in Group Investigation. The classroom context of instruction explained more of the variance in teachers' behavior than seniority, grade, and attitude.

---

tional contexts, similar frequencies of behaviors were found regardless of sociocultural factors (Hertz-Lazarowitz, 1989).

Six major findings resulted. *On-task noninteractive behavior* is by far the most dominant in the traditional classroom. About 50% to 75% of observed behavior fell into this cluster. With increasing age, however, its frequency decreases. *On-task, interactive behavior* in the form of cooperation and helping also naturally occurs in traditional classrooms. Though relatively rare, 10% to 18% of observed behavior, it was stable across grade level (age). Most on-task interactions were of short duration and were performed in an "underground" way, because the teacher provided no legitimization of them. As one child put it, "The teacher says we should help each other, but she then tells us to be quiet. How can you help your friend without talking?"

Off-task, interactive behavior is the second most frequent behavior. Social event interactive behavior constitutes 15% to 30% of the total behavior observed. Its share increases with age up through high school students. *Off-task, noninteractive* behavior is the most difficult cluster to code. Differentiating between listening and daydreaming is usually not possible. We could reliably code only about 5% of such behaviors. Thus, a small part of on-task, noninteractive behavior is confounded with off-task, noninteractive behavior.

Finally, *teacher-student interaction* was coded when one-to-one interaction between student and teacher took place but not when the teacher talked to the whole class. It accounted for only 7% to 8% of our observations.

These findings suggest a general rule for traditional contexts: *One third of behaviors are interactive, and half of them are off-task.* It seems that students engage in such behavior because they *need* peer interaction in the learning process for their own cognitive and social development. If the context is highly noninteractive, students will look for legitimized and nonlegitimized avenues for interactions. In classrooms that are mainly noninteractive, as students progress in age and grade level (from first to twelfth), they increase their social interactive behavior. This off-task interaction is perceived by teachers as an indication of growing discipline problems. For the students, however, it helps to fulfill their need for interaction. If interaction is not channeled into legitimate academic processes, it emerges as social events.

The level of cognitive reasoning within interactions was also analyzed. When high school students were cooperating in the learning task, 80% of their verbal interaction concerned explanation, clarification, and guidance, which are categorized as applicative levels of reasoning (Bloom, 1956). In contrast, when helping, 75% of the interactions concerned information exchange, that is, mainly answering "what" questions, which merely provide information without further explanation or elaboration. In the elementary school, children balanced cooperative interactions between informative (47%) and applicative (48%). Help interaction in the elementary school was mostly informative (70%). In general, within the limited frequency with which interactive, on-task behavior occurs in traditional contexts, cooperation produces higher reasoning levels than does helping.

To test the sensitivity of the interactive, on-task cluster of behaviors to minor variation in instructional procedures, we observed traditional classrooms that varied in five of their specific methods: expository-lecture teaching, lectures with follow-up questions, lectures with some group work, lectures with individual seatwork, and lectures followed by laboratory activities. Variations in instruction affected student interactive behavior. As teacher centrality was reduced, the frequency of cooperation and help between students increased significantly. For example, in the science classes observed, the teacher asked the student to build a cell model out of clay. Each pair of students had one lump of clay. The task was entirely open to the students' decision as to *how* to perform it, because the teacher did not give specific instructions. Students could engage in a competitive process (one taking *all* the clay), an individualistic process (dividing the clay and each doing his or her own cell), or a cooperative one (working together). We observed that when the lecture was followed by the laboratory activities, the teacher became less central and did not forbid interaction. As a result, a high frequency of complex cooperation and voluntary helping took place. Indeed, the 1984 study indicated that cooperation was most frequent in science lessons that integrated some laboratory activities. Helping was most frequent in labs and, surprisingly, also in nonlab individual seatwork when teachers do not lecture and assume a less central role. In this circumstance, when teachers assigned noncollective tasks, students interacted to perform their tasks. We concluded that cooperation and helping are very sensitive to instructional variation (see Table 4.3).

Student Behavior in Nontraditional Classroom Contexts

The classrooms most commonly termed less traditional are those that use either individualized instruction or active learning. In nontraditional classrooms at least 30% of instruction is nonfrontal. In Israel there is a formal network of schools that define themselves as active schools and share certain characteristics with progressive education. Active classrooms are characterized by a rich learning environment, with multilevel learning tasks and various organizational settings, such as individual seatwork, learning centers, group work, and short lectures by the teachers.

In many Israeli elementary schools, although teachers follow the central state-wide curricula, they alter the classroom structure from traditional to active, according to the content area and students' needs (Harrison, Strauss, & Glaubman, 1981; Hertz-Lazarowitz, 1984; Hertz-Lazarowitz, Fuchs, Eisenberg, and Sharabany, 1989; Klein & Eshel, 1980). Therefore, one can observe and study the *same* teachers and the same pupils in different classroom contexts. This enables the researcher to fully control variation in teacher style and student academic proficiency, and thereby maximize the measurement of contextual dimensions on student interaction.

In the study conducted by Hertz-Lazarowitz, Fuchs, Eisenberg, and Sharabany (1989), the same children in third grade with the same teachers were observed during two types of instruction: traditional and active. Classrooms were chosen in two socialization contexts: a kibbutz and a city school (see Fuchs, Eisenberg, Hertz-Lazarowitz, & Sharabany, 1986 and Eisenberg, Hertz-Lazarowitz, & Fuchs, 1990, for a description of kibbutz–city differences). The instructional mode had the strongest effect on student behavior. In the traditional classroom, students primarily displayed on-task, noninteractive behavior. In the active context, the same students more than doubled their on-task, interactive behavior, mainly showing more cooperation and helping. Nevertheless, the overall percentage of on-task behavior remained equal to that found under traditional instruction. Whereas in the traditional classroom on-task behavior was mostly noninteractive, in the active classroom, 50% of on-task behavior was interactive. Thus, in the active classroom children significantly change the nature and quality of their own on-task behavior. Instead of doing their work alone, they work together. The instruction factor contributed significantly more to this effect than did the socialization factor of whether the school was within a kibbutz or a city.

In a study of second- and fourth-grade bilingual classrooms in Texas, the same teachers and same children were observed over several months from the beginning to the end of the school year. Even in small classrooms with less than 20 students, the teacher's organization of the classroom and instruction were the most crucial factors affecting student behavior. In one classroom, children ($N = 9$) were seated in a "dining room" setting, with the teacher at the head of the table, in front of the blackboard. Over 60 words were presented on the blackboard, and the teacher very skillfully led a highly interactive sequence of language enrichment dialogue. Her students interacted very frequently with her, responding to her many questions, clarifications, and examples. The data showed a high frequency of teacher-student interaction and on-task, noninteractive behaviors, but no student-student, on-task interaction. A few months later, the same teacher, after being introduced to some cooperative active structures, was observed again. This time her students were seated in pairs by their desks. After a 10- to 15-min lecture, in which the teacher presented the story and the vocabulary, she assigned learning tasks to *pairs* of students. Although the children continued to refer to the teacher and seek her interactive behavior, their on-task, interactive behaviors increased, and they cooperated and helped each other frequently (Calderon, Tinajero, & Hertz-Lazarowitz, 1990; Hertz-Lazarowitz, 1989b) (see Table 4.3 for a summary).

When the teacher introduces either active learning or cooperative structure into a nontraditional classroom, it alters and redesigns the classroom's mirrors. Interactive behavior among students is stimulated by the reduction of the teacher's centrality and by legitimizing verbal exchanges among students. In the beginning of such restructuring, on-task interactions are simple, both in their linguistic structure and in their cognitive elaboration. To promote more elaborate student interactions, teachers must design the learning task appropriately and train students how to engage in high-level, complex verbal interaction.

Student Behavior in Cooperative Classroom Contexts

Some cooperative methods, despite a cooperative reward or goal structure, primarily induce on-task, noninteractive behavior. Moreover, in some methods, elements of competitiveness are more salient than elements of cooperation. My own concept of cooperative learning emphasizes the importance of a high frequency of interaction among students. These interactions should take place in the context of a cooperative goal (task) structure and within a cooperative interactive process. For example, in the Group Investigation model developed and tested by Sharan and Hertz-Lazarowitz (1980) and further described by Hertz-Lazarowitz and Fuchs (1987), we omitted external reward structures and proposed that internal motivation and involvement of students in challenging and interesting learning tasks would have the motivational potency to increase academic achievement. Complex processes of cooperative interaction are instrumental in achieving this outcome. (Similar viewpoints are expressed by Cohen, 1986, and Damon & Phelps, 1989.)

Studies conducted in Israel support this assumption (Hertz-Lazarowitz & Sharan, 1984; Sharan & Hertz-Lazarowitz, 1980; Sharan, Kussel, & Hertz-Lazarowitz, 1984; Sharan & Shachar, 1988). Furthermore, although task interdependence (cooperative interaction) augments the degree to which cooperative team learning promotes intergroup acceptance in ethnically heterogeneous classrooms, reward structures that are interdependent (team grades) or external (publicized performance) do not (Miller & Davidson-Podgorny, 1987). In the Group Investigation method, students, with the assistance of the teacher, plan together what topic to study and determine why and how to study it. In such a context, students interact in order to take charge of their own learning. They decide on the division of work among themselves, plan their learning tasks, and assign them on the basis of self-interest by self-selection processes. The Group Investigation learning process incorporates unitary, divisible, and combined learning tasks to produce a group product. When each group presents its project and teaches it to the other groups, an integration of the different subtopics of the theme is achieved. Thus, in the mirrors model of the classroom, Group Investigation is one of the most sophisticated contexts.

An important step in our research was to observe groups in cooperative contexts to describe the nature of cooperative interaction. Maskit (1986) developed a cooperative method called the Circle, in which four cooperative elements – selection, specialization, sharing, and group production – are introduced *after* teacher presentation of a general background and after each member reads the *same* story, poem, or essay. In the cooperative phase of the lesson, several learning tasks are presented to the group. In a process of negotiation, each student selects the specific learning task he or she will undertake, then specializes in it, and after that presents it. The group then discusses each presentation. In the final stage, the group combines, by mutual discussion and group consensus, individual outcomes and integrates them into a group product. This method incorporates elements of the Jigsaw (Aronson et al., 1978) and Group Investigation (Sharan & Hertz-Lazarowitz, 1980), but it differs from them in the wholeness-unitary element of the content (same content for all group members) and the self-selection of the task to specialize in.

After adult students learning Hebrew literature at an evening school were introduced to the Circle and practiced it for a few weeks, trained observers entered the classroom and coded their behavior. Each group was observed six times, for a period of 30 to 40 min. In a factor analysis of the observational data, based on 13 categories of behaviors, six factors with loadings of .40 or more emerged. Four factors involved interactive cooperative behaviors, and two factors involved mostly noninteractive behaviors. The latter were labeled universal general learning. The cooperative learning factors correlated positively and significantly with each other and negatively and significantly with universal general learning. Within cooperative learning, the following factors emerged: Group Maintenance, Group Consensus, Integration, and Helping. Within universal general learning, the two factors were Listening and On-Task Solitary.

On the basis of the emerging factors, we concluded that even within the cooperative learning context, solitary on-task behaviors are very frequent and, thus, universal and general to all learning modes. Apparently, the cooperative context is characterized by the addition of interactive and cooperative behaviors. In the cooperative context, universal-general behaviors were frequent in student behavior (50%). However, cooperative behaviors were almost as frequent (45%).

A close look at the four factors of cooperative learning suggests that students work on social aspects such as group maintenance and group regulation while they engage in academic interactions. They also shift between interactive and noninteractive modes of learning. It may be that in order to combine the noninteractive and the cooperative interactive behaviors, students have to develop this set of group regulation and group maintenance behaviors. Students regulate their shift from solitary to interactive modes of learning by using specific transitional behaviors such as calling for group attention to the task and forming specific organizational strategies. These behaviors are completed prior to engaging in higher levels of cooperative interaction, such as exchanging ideas, seeking agreements, and reaching conclusions. The success of the group depends on harmony and the management of the transitional, regulative, and cooperative functions that students must take upon themselves.

The significant negative correlation between the universal general behaviors and the cooperative behaviors ($-.52$) suggests that these behaviors can be viewed as distinct and qualitatively different. Both types of behavior, however, are very frequent in the cooperative context of learning. In contrast, off-task, interactive behaviors (social events) were very rare, implying that legitimization of interaction within the learning context reduces the need of students to interact outside it (see Table 4.3).

When teachers first shift their instructional style from traditional direct teaching or supervising individual seatwork to a more interactive and cooperative mode of instruction, they experience a dramatic change in role definition. It must be recast from taking charge of *teaching* to taking charge of *learning*. When teachers perceive that their role is to place children together in order to learn in an interactive and communicative fashion, they must simultaneously relinquish their role as expositors of content. Instead, they become facilitators of the acquisition of knowledge by teaching their students how to become active and interactive learners.

In previous years, when teachers predominantly adopted the "front and center" mode of classroom instruction, numerous studies consistently showed that the teacher provides most of the *talk* in the classroom. The countermovement of "increased pupil talk" that captured the educational milieu for more than a decade did not result in significant change in the domain (mirror) of classroom communication. One can hardly expect that changing one mirror, without altering others, will bring about a change.

To document this interdependency between dimensions, we observed a group of 27 elementary teachers who participated in a year-long project of in-service training in Group Investigation (Sharan & Hertz-Lazarowitz, 1980). included 30 hours of workshops, lectures, and experiential hands-or It focused on restructuring the physical organization of the classroo turing the learning task, and enhancing students' interactive communic; they were learning.

Teachers gradually implemented the Group Investigation method of ......pera- tive learning in their classrooms. They agreed to be observed and audiotaped three times during the year. From the tape-recorded data we identified 20 differ- ent categories of verbal behaviors, such as lecturing (presenting content), asking yes-or-no questions, instructing, disciplining, praising, encouraging student ini- tiative, giving feedback. Durations of use of these categories were converted to percentages of teachers' verbal communication within each observation session.

Comparison of teachers' verbal behavior in October and May of the same year showed that they produced the *same amount of talk* at each point in time. The nature of their verbal interaction, however, changed drastically. They shifted from a style of presenting content, giving instruction, asking short questions, and disciplining to one of supplying *direct help* to students on their part of the group task, providing feedback on task performance, facilitating communication among students, praising individuals, and encouraging pupil initiative. They changed their method of organizing and communicating learning activities in the classroom. In the beginning they were mainly figures of central control with expository roles, utilizing unilateral communication networks or bilateral com- munication techniques by asking short questions. They devoted a great deal of their "verbal time" to discipline. As they adopted the Group Investigation method, they became system facilitators and increased their use of multilateral commu- nication networks (they had verbal exchanges with the whole class, with small groups, and with individuals and also facilitated interactive communication among learners).

The categories of teacher verbal behavior were factor analyzed. Four factors emerged: Feedback on Task Performance, Intimate-Personal Interaction, Cen- tralized Communication, and Rigid-Authoritarian Interaction. The first two fac- tors were student oriented, whereas the latter two were teacher oriented. The former were significantly more frequently used in the cooperative context, and the latter were most frequent in the traditional context (Hertz-Lazarowitz & Shachar, 1990). It seems that small group teaching "brings out" of the teacher more student-focused conduct in the form of intimate, personalized, and prosocial be- havior.

Additional teacher variables were examined as predictors of their verbal be- havior. Socioeconomic status, number of years in teaching, grade level, and educational attitudes explained less variance in their verbal behavior than did the instructional mode (Hertz-Lazarowitz & Shachar, 1990) (see Table 4.3).

The explanation for these results is that the intensive training in Group Investigation increased teachers' skills. They learned to redesign the classroom as a complex organization that tolerated subsystems, that is, groups working in the classroom. They also learned to restructure the learning task. In group investigation the learning task is divided into subtopics between groups and into subunits within groups (Sharan & Hertz-Lazarowitz, 1980). Thus, it engages children in a new cluster of activities and makes them, to a substantial degree, responsible for planning and carrying out their learning. In such a context, where work assignments are differentiated, yet coordinated and integrated, teachers must adopt new instructional and communicational behaviors. The purposeful change in the mirrors of organization and task structure brought about changes in the mirrors of teacher behavior to bring them into harmony with the classroom context.

Summary and Directions for Future Research

The integrative model contributes to the development of a theory of the classroom by providing a system for conceptualizing its various dimensions simultaneously. An observational schedule that studies the classroom in this way challenges prior approaches that focus on isolated dimensions. Future work may find new important dimensions that should be integrated into the model or may elaborate on existing structures within the dimensions. One of the areas that calls for extensive research is the dimension of the learning task, which until now was the least researched one (Bossert, 1979). The model provides teachers and researchers with a developmental sequence of how to progress from a traditional classroom to an active, interactive one and finally to a cooperative one. By using the same dimensions in various types of classrooms, teachers are offered a pathway to cooperative organization of learning and teaching (Hertz-Lazarowitz & Davidson, 1990). It is important for teachers to see that when they progress to new stages, and thus create a new context, the former contexts are not excluded. Even in the cooperative context, the teacher makes use of noncooperative structures. However, in the nontraditional classrooms, teachers as well as students are learning within complex structures of organization, tasks, and instruction.

The sequence suggested here was based on practical work and initial findings in change projects, which is a schoolwide transition from traditionally structured to cooperatively structured learning. It stemmed from questioning teachers about the significance of different dimensions in the classroom, and their interdependence. Teachers' practical thinking about how to implement interactive and cooperative learning in their classrooms, as well as analysis of the trial-and-error implementation efforts, contributed to the model. The future research challenge is to test the model and to find which dimensions are the easiest to modify and under what conditions.

The notion of the harmony between coordinated stages in each mirror underwent very little experimental testing. Learning task structures and their effect on other dimensions are special challenges for experimentation. Students' behavior was the mirror most researched in the studies presented here. The studies reported were basically concerned with describing and measuring that process variable. They followed the input-process paradigm, which is rare in research.

Several assumptions that directed the program of study were confirmed. The assumption that student behavior is affected by the structures of the various dimensions was supported (Hertz-Lazarowitz et al., 1984). We confirmed that interactive, on-task behaviors in the forms of cooperation and helping are the most sensitive to contextual dimensions (Hertz-Lazarowitz, 1989b). The assumption that changes should take place in more than one dimension and in coordinated stages was also supported experimentally. For example, when only physical organization is changed, students are less interactive than if the physical organization and the task are changed simultaneously. Changing only the physical organization also results in more off-task interactions. On the other hand, changing the physical organization and introducing initial divisible tasks is a powerful combination for increasing on-task interaction. The changes in the mirrors of organization, task, and teacher behavior were so powerful in making children's behavior interactive that they overcame such profound variables as socialization (kibbutz, city) and the personalities of the children themselves (Hertz-Lazarowitz, Fuchs, Eisenberg, & Sharabany, 1989).

The research on teacher behavior emphasizes the changes teachers have to make, specifically in the areas of their centrality and the amount of talking they do to the whole class. Many teachers disturb children's interactions within groups in order to communicate with them as "a class." In such a setting, disharmony between mirrors takes place, and the potential for quality interaction is reduced.

The specific contributions of each stage within each mirror were not studied here or elsewhere. Future research should systematically manipulate not only mirrors but the stages within them.

One danger inherent in the implementation of the model is the creation of low-level, irrelevant interaction. Solitary, on-task behavior often consists of non-meaningful busywork. Interaction in its negative sense can become what I have labeled elsewhere as "ritual interaction" – children interact a lot, but when analyzed, the interaction is found to be of a procedural and repetitive nature (Hertz-Lazarowitz, 1984).

The conceptualization and observational findings that student behavior can be operationalized on the axes of interactive versus noninteractive and on-task versus off-task are important contributions to research and practice. The model helps clarify the different educational practices within and between approaches. Cooperative learning, collaborative learning, active learning, and reciprocal teaching share the view that children's overt interactive behavior is the most powerful tool for cognitive, social, and affective development. Other techniques, such as mastery learning, direct teaching, and individualized learning, hold that noninteractive behaviors are the most powerful for learning and development. The finding that all classroom contexts generate interactive and noninteractive behaviors but that these behaviors differ in frequency and quality enables all instructional contexts to be included in one conceptual organizing system and to be ordered on a continuum. The terminology offered addresses the differences in levels of cooperation. It also elaborates forms of helping. It is hoped such work will connect types of interaction in different learning contexts and thus encourage testing the impact of interactive versus noninteractive behavior on outcomes.

The observational studies of cooperative contexts show that noninteractive behaviors in learning are very frequent even there. The uniqueness of cooperative contexts is in the additional behaviors that students have to perform. Based on the factor analysis of student behaviors, it was possible to identify groups of behaviors and the relations among them. In addition to the interactive and noninteractive on-task behaviors, a set of behaviors termed transitional was identified. Making the transition from noninteraction to interaction in a cooperative context is not simple. It requires reciprocal social and cognitive behaviors. Students need to regulate their own behavior as well as that of the other members of the group to move back and forth from solitary to interactive work. They must also try to maintain themselves and their group on-task (Lazarowitz, Hertz-Lazarowitz, Baird, & Bowlden, 1988). Last, in high-level cooperation, where the product is a group one, they need to be engaged in the production phase. The factor analysis suggests that the behaviors involved in cooperative learning go far beyond a simple conceptualization that differentiates between social and cognitive skills. The factor analysis conducted in the Maskit study suggests that groups of behaviors support each other. I assume that meta-sociocognitive behaviors take place in cooperative learning and that the two cannot be separated. More studies are required to verify this.

Two directions are suggested for future research. First, the contextual dimensions of the classroom should not be neglected. It is impossible to understand, interpret, or generalize if the full story of what is going on in the classroom is lacking. The second suggestion is to include the full repertoire of student behavior in each study as a background to the specific behaviors being examined. Correlating isolated behaviors to outcomes will not broaden our understanding of the anatomy of cooperative interaction. We must understand the *process* variables before we can precisely relate process to outcome.

References

Allport, G. W. (1954). *The nature of prejudice*. Cambridge, MA: Addison-Wesley.

Altman, J. V. (1973). Observational study of behavior: Sampling methods. *Behavior, 49*, 227–267.

Anderson, L. M. (1984). The environment of instruction: The function of seatwork in a commercially developed curriculum. In G. G. Duffy, L. Roehler, & J. Mason (Eds.), *Comprehensive instruction: Perspectives and suggestions* (pp. 93–103). New York: Longman.

Aronson, E., Stephan, C., Sikes, J., Blaney, N., & Snapp, M. (1978). *The Jigsaw classroom*. Beverly Hills, CA: Sage.

Bloom, B. S. (1956). *The taxonomy of educational objectives: The classification of educational goals*. London: Longman.

Bossert, S. T. (1979). *Tasks and social relationships in the classroom*. New York: Cambridge University Press.

Brown, A. L., & Palincsar, A. S. (1989). Guided, cooperative learning and individual knowledge acquisition. In L. Resnick (Ed.), *Knowing, learning and instruction* (pp. 393–451). Hillsdale, NJ: Erlbaum.

Calderón, M., Tinajero, J., & Hertz-Lazarowitz, R. (1990, April). *Promoting student interaction for biliteracy development: Bilingual Cooperative Integrated Reading and Composition (CIRC)*. Paper presented at the American Educational Research Association (AERA) meeting, Baltimore.

Cazden, C. B. (1986). Classroom discourse. In M. Wittrock (Ed.), *Handbook of research on teaching* (pp. 432–463). (3rd ed.). New York: Macmillan.

Cohen, E. (1986). *Designing groupwork: Strategies for the heterogeneous classroom*. New York: Teachers College Press.

Damon, W., & Phelps, E. (1989). Critical distinctions among three methods of peer education. *International Journal of Educational Research, 58*(2), 9–19.

Dansereau, D. F. (1988). Cooperative learning strategies. In C. E. Weinstein, E. T. Goetz, & P. A. Alexander (Eds.), *Learning and study strategies: Issues in assessment, instruction, and evaluation*. New York: Academic Press.

Deutch, M. (1949). A theory of competition and cooperation. *Human Relations, 2*, 129–151.

DeVries, D. L., & Edwards, K. J. (1973). Learning games and student teams: Their effect on classroom process. *American Educational Journal, 10*, 307–318.

Eisenberg, N., Cameron, E., & Trayon, K. (1984). Prosocial behavior in the preschool years: Methodological and conceptual issues. In E. Staub, D. Bar-Tal, J. Karylowsky, & J. Reykowsky (Eds.), *Development and maintenance of prosocial behavior* (pp. 101–117). New York: Plenum Press.

Eisenberg, N., Hertz-Lazarowitz, R., & Fuchs, I. (1990). Prosocial moral judgment in Israeli kibbutz and city children: A longitudinal study. *Merrill Palmer Quarterly, 36*(2), 273–285.

Everston, C. M., & Green, J. L. (1986). Observation as inquiry and method. In M. C. Wittrock (Ed.), *Handbook of research on teaching* (3rd ed.). New York: Macmillan.

Flanders, N. A. (1970). *Analyzing teacher behavior*. Reading, MA: Addison-Wesley.

Fuchs, I., Eisenberg, N., Hertz-Lazarowitz, R., & Sharabany, R. (1986). Kibbutz, Israeli city and American children's moral reasoning about prosocial conflicts. *Merrill Palmer Quarterly, 32*(1), 37–49.

Getzel, J., & Thelen, H. (1960). The classroom as a unique social system. In *59th yearbook of the National Society for the Study of Education* (pp. 53–81). Chicago: University of Chicago Press.

Good, T. & Brophy, J. (1973). *Looking in classrooms*. New York: Harper & Row.

Harrison, J., Strauss, H., & Glaubman, R. (1981). The impact of open and traditional classrooms on achievement and creativity: The Israeli case. *Elementary School Journal, 82*, 27–35.

Hertz-Lazarowitz, R. (1983). Prosocial behavior in the classroom. *Academic Psychology Bulletin, 5*, 319–333.

(1984). *Learning in the active classroom: Research findings, conceptual clarifications, and suggestions for action*. Jerusalem: Ministry of Education and Culture. (In Hebrew.)

(1989a). Cooperation and helping in the classroom: A contextual approach. *International Journal of Research in Education, 13*(1), 113–119.

(1989b). *Observations in experimental and control classrooms* before *implementation of the CIRC* in El Paso Report No. 1. University of California, Santa Barbara.

Hertz-Lazarowitz, R., Baird, H., Webb, C., & Lazarowitz, R. (1984). Student-student interaction in science classrooms: A naturalistic study. *Science Education, 68*, 603–619.

Hertz-Lazarowitz, R., & Davidson, J. (1992). *Six mirrors of the classroom: A pathway to cooperative learning*. El Paso, TX: MTTI.

Hertz-Lazarowitz, R., & Fuchs, I. (1987). *Cooperative learning in the classroom*. Haifa: Ach Publishing. (In Hebrew.)

Hertz-Lazarowitz, R., Fuchs, I., Eisenberg, N., & Sharabany, R. (1989). Student interactive and non-interactive behavior in the classroom: A comparison between two types of classroom in the city and the kibbutz in Israel, *Contemporary Educational Psychology, 14*, 22–32.

Hertz-Lazarowitz, R., & Shachar, H. (1990). Teacher verbal behavior in cooperative and whole-class instruction. In S. Sharan (Ed.), *Cooperative learning: Theory and research* (pp. 77–94). New York: Praeger.

Hertz-Lazarowitz, R., & Sharan, S. (1984). Enhancing prosocial behavior through cooperative learning in the classroom. In E. Staub, D. Bar-Tal, J. Karylowski, & J. Reykowski (Eds.), *Development and maintenance of prosocial behavior: International perspectives*. New York: Plenum.

Jackson, P. (1968). *Life in the classroom*. New York: Holt, Rinehart & Winston.

Johnson, D. W., & Johnson, R. T. (1975). *Learning together and alone: Cooperation, competition and individualization*. Englewood Cliffs, NJ: Prentice-Hall.

(1989). *Cooperation and competition: Theory and research*. Edina, MN: Interaction Book Co.

Karweit, N., & Slavin, R. E. (1982). Time on task: Issues of timing, sampling, and definitions. *Journal of Educational Psychology, 74*, 844–851.

Klein, Z., & Eshel, Y. (1980). The open classroom in cross-cultural perspective: A research note. *Sociology of Education, 53*, 114–121.

Lazarowitz, R., Hertz-Lazarowitz, R., Baird, J. H., & Bowlden, V. (1988). Academic achievement and on-task behavior of high school biology students instructed in a cooperative investigative small group. *Science Education, 72*,(4), 475–487.

Maskit, D. (1986). *Cooperative teaching and learning in adult learning*. Unpublished master's thesis, University of Haifa, School of Education. (In Hebrew.)

Maskit, D., & Hertz-Lazarowitz, R. (1986, July). *Internal group learning dynamics: An observational study in adults' cooperative learning*. Paper presented at the 21st International Congress of Applied Psychology (ICAP), Jerusalem, Israel.

(1989a). Adults learning in cooperation: Attitudes and evaluation. *Studies in Educational Administration and Organization, 15*, 97–119. (In Hebrew.)

(1989b). Cooperative learning: What is in the black box? *Studies in Education, 51/52,* 189–207. (In Hebrew.)

Miller, N., & Davidson-Podgorny, G. (1987). Theoretical models of intergroup relations and the use of cooperative teams as an intervention for desegregated settings. In C. Hendrick (Ed.), *Group processes and intergroup relations* (pp. 41–67). Newbury Park, CA: Sage Publications.

Sharan, S. (1990). *Cooperative learning: Theory and research.* New York: Praeger.

Sharan, S., & Hertz-Lazarowitz, R. (1978). *Cooperation and communication in schools.* Tel Aviv: Schocken Publishing House. (In Hebrew.)

(1980). A group investigation method of cooperative learning in the classroom. In S. Sharan, P. Hare, C. Webb, & R. Hertz-Lazarowitz (Eds.), *Cooperation in education* (pp. 14–46). Provo, UT: Brigham Young University Press.

Sharan, S., Hertz-Lazarowitz, R., & Hare, P. (1981). The classroom: A structural analysis. In S. Sharan & R. Hertz-Lazarowitz (Eds.), *Changing schools: The Small Group Teaching Project in Israel* (pp. 21–53). Tel Aviv: Ramot. 21–53. (In Hebrew.)

Sharan, S., & Shachar, H. (1988). *Language and learning in the cooperative classroom.* New York: Springer.

Sharan, S., Kussel, P., Hertz-Lazarowitz, R., Bejarano, Y., Raviv, S., Sharan, Y. (1984). *Cooperative learning in the classroom: Research in desegregated schools.* Hillsdale, NJ: Erlbaum.

Slavin, R. E. (1983). *Cooperative learning.* New York: Longman.

(Ed.). (1989). *School and classroom organization.* Hillsdale, NJ: Erlbaum.

Slavin, R., Sharan, S., Kagan, S., Hertz-Lazarowitz, R., Webb, N., & Schmuck, R. (Eds.). (1985). *Learning to cooperate, cooperating to learn.* New York: Plenum Press.

Steiner, I. (1972). *Group process and productivity.* New York: Academic Press.

Thelen, H. A. (1981). *The classroom society: The construction of educational experience.* London: Croom, Helm, Halsted.

Thew, D. (1975). The classroom social organization category system. *Classroom Interaction Newsletter, 11,* 18–24.

Webb, N. M. (1989). Peer-interaction and learning in small groups. *International Journal of Educational Research, 13*(1), 21–31.

Wilkinson, L. C. (Ed.). (1982). *Communicating in the classroom.* New York: Academic Press.

Vygotsky, L. S. (1978). *Mind in society: The development of higher psychological processes.* Cambridge: Harvard University Press.

5   Testing a Theoretical Model of Student Interaction and Learning in Small Groups

Noreen M. Webb

Although cooperative learning and other kinds of peer-based small-group instruction are flourishing in classrooms around the world, researchers are just beginning to identify and understand the dynamics that influence learning in these settings. Some of the internal dynamics of small-group learning approaches seem to be beneficial for learning; others are not. The purpose of this chapter is to describe a theoretical model of student interaction and learning in small groups and to clarify some aspects that have not been tested previously.

The kinds of task-related verbal interaction that may influence learning in small groups are discussed first. The relationships between peer interaction and learning that have been found in empirical research and the theoretical bases for the findings are then reviewed. From the theoretical and empirical work reviewed, several components of a model of peer interaction and learning in small groups are described. The chapter then uses data from a study of learning in small groups to test several predictions of the model that have not been tested previously as well as to replicate previous findings. The purpose of the theoretical and empirical analyses presented here is to clarify important features of group interaction that may be amenable to change in order to maximize the learning of students within groups.

Theoretical Rationale and Review of Research

Because the opportunity to share resources and knowledge is one of the most commonly cited advantages of peer-based learning, much of the literature on the relationship between peer interaction and learning in small groups focuses on help-giving and help-receiving within the group. This section, therefore, provides a theoretical rationale for when different kinds of help given and received are likely to be effective for learning and when they are not, and describes rele-

I would like to thank Carol Hodgson, Weichang Li, Janet Sutton Heyman, and Wai-Yan Tam for their help in coding transcripts during preliminary analyses.

vant findings from empirical research. Because not all students in small groups participate in helping relationships, this section also discusses the experiences of students who do not give help, receive help, or give any indication that they need help.

Receiving Help

A primary motivation for the use of cooperative small groups is that students can help other students who are having difficulty learning or understanding the material. Students may express their need for help in a variety of ways. Asking for explanations ("How do you solve this one?" and "Can you explain how to do it?") and making mistakes are probably the clearest indications of a need for help. Most students who ask how to solve a problem (or declare that they don't understand what to do) or who make mistakes likely have some major misunderstanding or lack of understanding of the material that can only be remedied with elaborated help. Students may also ask for specific information (e.g., "What is 4 times 15?" "Did you get 10.5 for Number 2?" and "You add them first before dividing, right?"). These questions also reflect a need for help but probably indicate less serious difficulty.

Requests for help and errors cannot always be interpreted literally, of course. Not all requests for help reflect an underlying need for help. Students may ask for help to get attention, for example. And some requests for help may not accurately express a student's need for help. Students may ask for specific information when they really need extended help, or they may ask for help when they are simply seeking confirmation that their own work is correct. Furthermore, errors may be careless and not due to a major misunderstanding. Only by considering the full context of a cooperative group's interaction is it possible to accurately interpret students' need for help from their behavior.

When students do need help, whether the help they receive will ultimately lead to their learning the material probably depends on several variables: (1) the timeliness of the help offered, (2) the relevance of the help to a student's need for help, (3) the amount of detail or elaboration in the help given, (4) whether the help is understood by the person who needs it, and (5) whether the student who receives help has an opportunity to use the help to solve the problem and uses that opportunity (Vedder, 1985). To be effective for learning, help must be timely, relevant, of sufficient elaboration, understood by the recipient, and applied by the recipient to the problem at hand.

It is hypothesized here that failure to meet even one of the above conditions may make help ineffective for the recipient. If the help offered is not timely and the target student no longer remembers his or her area of difficulty, the help will be of little use. If the help is not relevant to a student's need for help or contains insufficient detail (e.g., includes the correct answer to a problem but not any details about how to solve it, as will be discussed later in this section), the target student will not be able to correct his or her difficulty. If the target student does not understand the help, he or she will not be able to use it to correct misconceptions about the material. Even if the target student understands the help and it is timely, relevant, and has sufficient detail, it will be effective only if the target student actually applies it. Students can say that they understand each others' explanations, and may well believe it themselves, but they may not understand the explanations well enough to solve the problem or complete the work for themselves.

Students working in cooperative small groups are in a good position to satisfy at least some of these conditions for effective help. When students are working together on the same material, they can provide immediate help when someone has difficulty. Furthermore, because students working together may all be learning the material for the first time, they may understand better than the teacher or other adults the specific difficulties that their peers are having (Vedder, 1985). Consequently, they have the potential for offering each other explanations that pinpoint exactly the areas of difficulty. Moreover, students can make explanations more understandable by using language that is familiar to other students (Noddings, 1985).

The final condition for effective help, actually applying the help received, is more subtle than the others. Anecdotal observations suggest that students often "help" by doing the work for another student (Shavelson, Webb, Stasz, & McArthur, 1988; Vedder, 1985); such help may prevent the target student from trying to correct his or her misunderstanding or lack of understanding. Without attempting to use the help to correct their misunderstandings, target students (as well as the rest of the group) may not realize that they still do not understand the material.

This sequence of necessary conditions for help received to be effective for learning is shown in Figure 5.1. When students need help, this sequence of experiences is one pathway to a positive learning outcome. The other pathway to a positive learning outcome occurs when students provide their own help; that is, they answer their own questions or correct their own errors without help from others in the group. Such behavior likely indicates that such students have corrected their misunderstanding or lack of understanding. Alternatively, it is possible that these students understood the material all along but were asking for help for some other reason, such as to get attention or reinforcement from the group or to show off. In either case, one would expect a positive learning outcome.

Receiving Different Kinds of Help and Achievement: Global Empirical Results. Most of the empirical studies investigating the relationship between learning

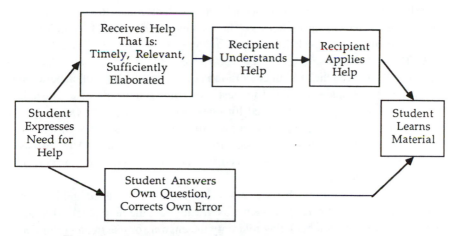

Figure 5.1. Sequences of experiences leading to positive learning outcomes for students who express a need for help.

outcomes and receiving different kinds of help have not taken into account the underlying need for help being expressed. The major distinction in help received in these studies is between explanations (e.g., detailed descriptions of how to solve a problem) and other kinds of information (e.g., only the answer to a problem or a yes/no response to a question). In 12 studies examining the relationship between receiving explanations and achievement in small groups, only 25% of the correlations reported were positive and statistically significant; the remainder were not significant (Peterson & Janicki, 1979; Peterson, Janicki, & Swing, 1981; Peterson & Swing, 1985; Peterson, Wilkinson, Spinelli, & Swing, 1984; Roeders, 1987; Swing & Peterson, 1982; Webb, 1980a, 1982b, 1984a, 1984b; Webb, Ender, & Lewis, 1986; Webb & Kenderski, 1984, 1985). It is possible that the positive correlations occurred when the help given satisfied the conditions for effective help, and that the other correlations occurred when the help provided did not satisfy all the conditions for effective help.

Similarly, studies examining the relationship between receiving nonelaborated help (e.g., information, the answer to a problem, a yes/no response to a question) and achievement reported mixed results. Most correlations (59%) were nonsignificant, only 7% were positive, and 33% were negative (Peterson & Swing, 1985; Peterson et al., 1984; Roeders, 1987; Swing & Peterson, 1982; Webb, 1982b, 1984a, 1984b; Webb et al., 1986; Webb & Kenderski, 1984, 1985). As before, it is possible that most of the help received in these studies did not satisfy the conditions for effective help.

Receiving Help and Achievement: Empirical Results Taking into Account the Need for Help. Some studies examining the relationship between receiving help and achievement have taken into account the student's need for help. These studies investigated the match between the amount of help needed (as indicated by the kind of request for help) and the amount of help received (see Webb, 1989). These studies, then, represent a test of one of the conditions for effective help: a match between the level of elaboration needed and the level of elaboration received. In these studies, general requests for help, statements of confusion, and errors were interpreted as a need for elaborated help (e.g., an explanation instead of a brief response). Requests for information and questions seeking yes/ no responses were interpreted as a need for less elaborated help. The various matches and mismatches between the need for help and help received were then correlated with achievement.

In the first type of mismatch between level of elaboration needed and level of elaboration received, the need for help was greater than the help received (e.g., asking for an explanation but being told only the answer, or making an error and being told only that one's answer was incorrect without being told why). Receiving inadequate help was uniformly negatively related to achievement: Of 17 correlations between receiving inadequate help and achievement, 76% were negative and statistically significant (Webb, 1982a, 1982b, 1984a; Webb & Cullian, 1983; Webb & Kenderski, 1984, 1985). This set of results is not surprising. It is unlikely that most students can figure out how to solve the problem from only the correct answer (the common kind of group response to questions) or from being told only that one's answer is wrong. Furthermore, asking for an explanation and receiving only minimal information (or, worse, no response at all) may be frustrating to students, may serve as negative reinforcement for asking questions, and, consequently, may cause students to expend less effort to learn the material.

The other type of mismatch, giving more elaboration than was needed, rarely occurred. The mismatches in this direction were so infrequent that they could not be analyzed.

When the level of elaboration of the help received matched the need for help (e.g., asking for and receiving an explanation), the results were mixed. Of 15 correlations between adequate help and achievement, only 20% were positive; the majority (73%) were not significantly different from zero (Webb, 1982b, 1984a, 1984b; Webb & Kenderski, 1984, 1985; Webb et al., 1986). A likely explanation for the lack of significant findings is that although the level of elaboration in the help received may have been adequate, other conditions for help to be effective may not have been met (e.g., students may not have used the help they received to try to solve the problem).

No Expression of Need for Help

Some students do not make errors or ask questions, so it is difficult to [ ] need for help. Some of these students understand the material and d[ ] help; they either observe the group's discussion without participatin[ ] work by themselves. These students have no difficulty with the ma____ial and would be expected to show positive learning outcomes.

Other students who do not express a need for help have some difficulty with the material and really do need help. They may not realize that they do not understand, or even if they do realize it, they may not ask for help for fear of appearing stupid, may not know what question to ask, or may not know who to ask (Nelson-Le Gall, 1981, 1985; Nelson-Le Gall, Gumerman, & Scott-Jones, 1983). Students who are afraid of asking for help are likely to be insecure and nonassertive; confident and assertive students are more likely to seek help when they need it.

When students need help but do not ask for it, they can learn the material in one of two ways. They can answer their own unasked question or correct their own unannounced error by obtaining information from other resources such as the textbook or other classroom materials. Students who can learn this way must have at least moderately high ability and some skills in the curriculum area being studied.

The other way to learn in a small group without receiving help from others is by observing group interaction and learning from it. Students may internalize other students' problem-solving strategies or information they did not know (Damon, 1984; Damon & Phelps, 1989; Forman, 1989; Forman & Cazden, 1985; Gall & Gall, 1976; Heap, 1986; Rubin, 1983; Slavin, 1977; Vygotsky, 1981; Wertsch, 1979), notice discrepancies with other students' work and look for new information to resolve them (Johnson & Johnson, 1979; Mugny & Doise, 1978; Perret-Clermont, 1980; Weinstein & Bearison, 1985), or build on the work of others to complete the problem (Riel, 1983; Palincsar, 1986; Palincsar & Brown, 1984; Palincsar, Stevens, & Gavelek, 1989). Whether students can learn by observing group interaction probably depends on two factors: the richness of the group's discussion and whether the student assimilates and applies the discussion. First, a student is more likely to learn by watching group interaction when group members give clear, systematic explanations than when they merely exchange answers to problems. Second, the student must assimilate the group's interaction and use it to correct his or her misconception or lack of understanding. Just as it is possible for a student receiving help to listen to an explanation without applying it (as described in the previous section), it is possible for a student observing group interaction to listen to the group without assimilating what has been heard and without applying it to the problem at hand. Student

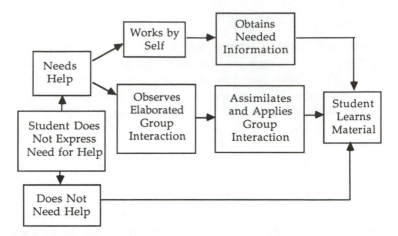

Figure 5.2. Sequences of experiences leading to positive learning outcomes for students who do not express a need for help.

ability level is probably also a mediating variable in this process. A student must have sufficient ability to be able to assimilate the group's discussion and apply it to the area of difficulty.

The hypothesized sequences of experiences leading to successful learning outcomes for students who do not express a need for help are portrayed in Figure 5.2. These sequences have not been tested empirically. The only study to examine the learning outcomes of students who do not ask for help found simply that a lack of participation led to poor performance (Webb, 1980b).

Giving Help

Past studies have also examined the impact of the kind of help given on the learning of the help-giver. Again, the main distinction has been between explanations and other kinds of help (e.g., yes/no answers to questions, simple information, giving the answer to a problem without any further description).

Giving explanations may have important benefits for the giver as well as potential benefits for the receiver. Over a decade ago, Bargh and Schul (1980) proposed that the processes of clarifying, organizing, and reorganizing material, which are part of formulating and giving explanations, increase one's own understanding. And, indeed, perhaps the most consistent finding in previous studies is that giving explanations is positively associated with achievement, even after controlling for ability or previous achievement (Peterson & Janicki, 1979; Peterson et al., 1981; Peterson & Swing, 1985; Roeders, 1987; Swing & Peterson,

1982; Webb, 1980a, 1982b, 1984c; 1985; Webb et al., 1986; Webb & Kenderski, 1984).

Giving other kinds of help (e.g., information, yes/no responses to questions, pointing out that someone has made an error without explaining what it is), on the other hand, probably involves little or no reorganization or clarification of material and would be expected to have fewer benefits for the help-giver. Consistent with this prediction, empirical studies typically report no significant relationship between the frequency of giving nonexplanatory help and achievement (Peterson & Swing, 1985; Peterson et al., 1984; Swing & Peterson, 1982; Webb, 1980a, 1982b, 1984a, 1984c; Webb & Kenderski, 1984), with only a few exceptions (Roeders, 1987; Webb, 1984c).

It is hypothesized here, then, that giving explanations has a positive impact on learning and that giving other kinds of information and responses has a weak or no impact on learning. Being able to state the correct answer during group work is probably a positive indicator of learning in most cases and is an important follow-up to receiving help (as described earlier), but the number of times students state the correct answer is unlikely to have any impact on their understanding.

Tests of the Model of Student Interaction and Learning

The results of the previous studies cannot be used to fully test the relationships hypothesized for at least two reasons. First, previous studies have not examined extensive sequences of verbal interaction in the group. They have treated behavior in isolation, such as investigating the relationship between receiving information and achievement without considering the kind of request for help that elicited the information. Or, they may have considered sequences of requests for help and responses but have not examined whether students who received help subsequently used it to try to solve the problem.

Second, the vast majority of studies correlated the frequency of each behavior with a composite achievement measure. This makes it difficult to isolate the effects of any particular behavior. For example, a student may ask for and receive information for some aspects of the material and fail to receive requested help for other aspects of the material. Positive effects of the first behavior and negative effects of the second behavior may cancel out, leaving the student with middling overall achievement. Because a student may have different experiences in group interaction for different aspects of the material, it is important to examine the relationship between behavior and achievement for each one.

To remedy the drawbacks just described, a study was conducted to test the following three hypotheses: (1) Receiving an adequate level of help and applying the help received are both necessary conditions for learning, (2) students who do not express a need for help are more likely to learn the material if they have higher ability than if they have lower ability, and (3) giving explanations will be more likely to lead to learning than giving non-elaborated help. In testing these hypotheses, each student's behavior with respect to a particular component of the material is linked to that student's learning outcomes for that component only, yielding more straightforward and unambiguous results.

Description of the Study

The hypotheses were tested using data on the verbal interaction and achievement of five mixed-ability groups of eleventh-grade students learning novel mathematical problems. Each group had one high-ability student, one low-ability student, and two medium-ability students.

Students worked in small groups to learn how to solve problems involving arithmetic series. The analyses reported here focus on four major components of this work: drawing a geometric array representing a particular arithmetic series, determining the first term in the arithmetic series, determining the second term, and determining the difference between terms in the series. Students were instructed to help each other learn how to solve the problems so that all students would perform well on the achievement test. Immediately after group work, students completed a test on the material individually, without help from anyone or the materials (called the immediate test). One week later, they completed another test, also individually (called the delayed test). All group interaction was tape-recorded and transcribed.

To test the hypotheses, the following kinds of verbal interaction were coded. First, the levels of elaboration of the help requested and the help received were coded to determine the match or mismatch between the need for help and help received. Requests for explanation ("Why is d [equal to] 3?" "Wait, how did you get that?" "What are we supposed to do?"), statements of confusion or misunderstanding (e.g., "I don't get it"; "I'll never be able to do this"), and errors were interpreted as indicators that a student needed an elaborated response (i.e., an explanation). Specific requests for information ("What is [the definition of] a again?" "Is it 3 or 4?") and yes/no questions (e.g., "Did you get 4 for this part?" "That's 4, then?") were taken as indicators that a student needed a less elaborated response (e.g., a specific answer, yes or no).

The help received was categorized as explanations (high-level elaboration) or information (low-level elaboration). Explanations consisted of step-by-step descriptions of how to solve a problem or part of one. Information consisted of the answer, yes/no responses to questions, or details related to managing the task (e.g., which problem they should work on first). These same categories applied to the help-giver: explanations versus information.

Next, the level of elaboration of each sequence of help requested and help received was categorized as a match (i.e, a student received the level of elaboration requested) or a mismatch (i.e., a student received less elaborated help than requested).

Then, for all instances of receiving help, the follow-up behavior of the target student was coded. Students' verbalization after receiving help was coded in two categories: verbalizing the work (typically, giving the correct answer to a problem or giving an explanation) and not saying anything. The former was used as evidence that the student applied the help received; the latter was used as evidence that the student did not apply the help received (at least not overtly). In the event that a student received more than one kind of response to a question or error (e.g., students sometimes asked for help, did not receive it, asked again, and received it; or students made an error and did not receive an explanation the first time but received an explanation the second time they made the same error), the final response was the one coded.

An additional category of codes for students who indicated a need for help was whether they answered their own question or corrected their own error without assistance from the group.

The final category of interaction concerned whether students participated in group interaction. Some students did not verbalize any work on one or more components of the task.

Tests of the Hypotheses

Receiving Help: Adequacy of the Level of Elaboration and Applying the Help Received.   The five conditions for effective helping outlined early in this chapter are considered to be necessary conditions; that is, all of them must be met for the help received to promote learning. Previous research has examined only one of them systematically: the adequacy of the level of elaboration. This section presents a test of an additional condition: whether students receiving help apply that help to solve the problem.

The other three conditions for effective explanations could not be tested here because (1) it was difficult to decide whether help received was timely or untimely without specific feedback from students, (2) there was no variability in the relevance of help received (all help seemed to be relevant to the need for help expressed), and (3) it was not always possible to ascertain whether target students understood the help they received. To accurately determine whether students understood the help received and considered it timely, it would be necessary to use some method of eliciting students' thoughts and reactions, such as stimulated recall (e.g., students are shown a videotape of their group's interaction and are asked to describe what they were thinking or feeling at various points).

Analysis of the sequences of interaction in the groups analyzed here showed that about half satisfied neither of the two conditions tested here and about half satisfied both. That is, students who received inadequate help tended not to apply the help to solve the problem. Students who did receive adequate help nearly always applied that help to solve the problem correctly.

Among students who expressed a need for help, failure to meet the conditions for effective help often led to successful performance on the immediate posttest (10 out of 15 sequences of interaction, or 67%) but rarely led to successful performance on the delayed test (3 out of 15, or 20%). For the sequences of interaction that met the conditions for effective help tested here (receiving adequate help and applying the help received), the majority led to successful performance on both the immediate posttest and the delayed test (8 out of 13 on both tests, or 62%). Because the delayed test is probably a more accurate measure of learning than the immediate test, these results support the hypothesis that an adequate level of elaboration and applying the help received to solve the problem are necessary conditions for learning. The fact that students who received adequate help and applied the help they received did not always learn the material suggests that these two conditions, although necessary, are not sufficient for learning.

No Expression of a Need for Help.   A substantial number of students, all of them of medium or low ability, did not say anything aloud about some of the components of the material during group work. Whether the silent students learned the material depended on their ability level. Whereas both medium-ability and low-ability students who were silent on some components tended to show successful performance on the immediate posttest (10 out of 11 for medium-ability students, or 91%; and 10 out of 12 for low-ability students, or 83%), only medium-ability students showed successful performance on the delayed test. On the delayed test, the rate of successful performance for silent medium-ability students was 82%, but for silent low-ability students, it was only 25%.

What do these results mean? There are at least three explanations for the different learning outcomes for silent students of medium and low ability, corresponding to the three sequences of experiences leading to a positive learning outcome in Figure 5.2. The first concerns whether students needed help. Silent low-ability students may have been more likely than silent medium-ability students to need help. The second explanation concerns whether silent students were doing the work on their own without contributing to group interaction. Medium-ability students working on their own would be more likely to learn the material than low-ability students working on their own. Third, if silent students were observing group interaction, medium-ability students would be more likely than low-ability students to be able to assimilate the group's discussion and apply it to correct their misunderstanding or improve their understanding.

An additional explanation for these results comes from a sequence of behavior that is purposively omitted from Figure 5.2 because it is unlikely to lead to a positive learning outcome: not attending to the task. It is possible for silent students to be off-task. In this study, low-ability students may have been more likely than medium-ability students to be off-task.

The audiotapes used in this study to collect information on group interaction do not provide enough information to determine whether quiet students needed help, whether they were doing the work by themselves, whether they were observing group interaction, or whether they were paying no attention to the task. Videotapes would help distinguish between students who were working by themselves, students who were observing group interaction, and students who were off-task. Direct feedback from students, from interviews or stimulated recall, would help determine whether silent students did or did not need help.

Clearly, silent students of low ability had difficulty learning and remembering the material, as indicated by their poor performance on the delayed test. If they had difficulty, why didn't they ask questions? Nelson-Le Gall's model of help-seeking (Nelson-Le Gall, 1981, 1985; Nelson-Le Gall et al., 1983) offers several possible explanations. First, they may not have recognized that they did not understand the material. It is possible to understand someone else's solution to a problem without being able to solve it by yourself. Second, even if they knew they did not understand the material, they may have been afraid to ask for help. Interviewing students would help show why these students did not participate in group interaction.

Giving Help: Explanations Versus Other Help.   Some students, most with high or medium ability, gave help on one or more components of the material. There was no difference between high-ability and medium-ability students in their rates of giving explanations. Furthermore, the proportions of giving explanations versus giving other kinds of help were also similar among high-ability and medium-ability students (about half of the help given consisted of explanations; the other half consisted of information or brief responses). So there was no need to take ability into account in the analysis of help-giving. When students gave explanations, they nearly always showed proficiency on the achievement tests (13 out of 14 on the immediate posttest, or 93%; 12 out of 14 on the delayed test, or 86%). Giving other kinds of information (typically, the answer to a problem without any elaboration) also led to positive learning outcomes, but less often (12 out of 15 on the immediate posttest, or 80%; 9 out of 15 on the delayed test, or 60%). These results lend some support to the hypothesis that giving elaborated help is more beneficial for learning than giving information.

Conclusions

The tests of the hypotheses about the relationships between group interaction and learning presented here generally support the predictions made. First, when students indicated a need for help, receiving adequate help and applying that help to solve the problem tended to lead to successful test performance; failing to meet these conditions tended not to lead to successful test performance. Second, the effects of not participating in group discussions (whether observing group interaction or working on their own) seemed to depend on students' ability level. Higher ability students were more likely than lower ability students to learn the material without overtly participating in group interaction. Third, giving elaborated help led to successful test performance more often than giving nonelaborated help.

These results show that it is important for researchers investigating the internal dynamics of cooperative groups to distinguish between sequences of behavior that occur in a group rather than to consider a student's behavior in isolation. The kind of help a student needs, the kind of help received, and whether the student applies the help received are all important predictors of learning outcomes.

These findings have several implications for classroom practice. Students should be encouraged or trained to give sufficiently elaborated help to others. When others experience difficulty, students should give explanations rather than only the answer to a problem or other nonelaborated information. This will likely benefit the help-giver as well as the help-receiver. Conversely, when students experience difficulty, they should ask teammates for explanations and persist until they receive them. Importantly, they should use the help they receive to attempt the work themselves to make sure that they understand it. After they have resolved their misunderstanding, explaining the work to other students may help them solidify their learning even more. Encouraging results on the feasibility of training students to give explanations comes from a study by Swing and Peterson (1982). Swing and Peterson significantly increased the frequency of explaining among students in small groups with a combination of direct instruction, role play, practice, and feedback.

An indirect way to increase explaining in groups may be to use a cooperative reward structure, in which students are rewarded on the basis of the achievement of all group members. Group rewards are thought to increase students' accountability for teammates' learning and have been shown to promote helping behavior in general (Johnson, Johnson, & Stanne, 1985, 1986; Sharan, 1980; Slavin, 1977, 1980, 1983, 1987). If students feel responsible for each other's learning, they may be more inclined to give each other high-quality help. Whether such positive effects of group rewards would occur, and whether they would counterbalance possible negative effects on group functioning, such as frustration with (or even animosity toward) low-achieving group members, remains to be investigated empirically. Clearly, the effects of group rewards on a wide range of group dynamics variables need to be examined, not only helping behavior.

Another indirect way of increasing explaining in groups may be to design tasks to require giving (and asking for) explanations. For example, the Jigsaw method of cooperative learning (Aronson et al., 1978) assigns students to expert roles in which they teach unique information to their teammates. Even in the absence of specific roles for students, requiring students to explain portions of the material to each other has been shown to increase recall (Lambiotte et al., 1987) and may produce more explaining than would occur in the absence of these instructions. Another way of modifying the task to increase the frequency and level of explanations is to require students to ask each other questions. King (1990) found that guided reciprocal peer questioning, in which students were trained how to ask each other high-quality questions, yielded more explanations than other small-group discussion methods.

Still another indirect way to shape group interaction is to manipulate the composition of the group. Previous research has shown that the frequency of explaining and providing adequate help to others may depend on the group's composition. For example, more explaining has been found in homogeneous groups of medium-ability students than in heterogeneous groups with a wide range of ability (see Webb, 1982c). Furthermore, students of a particular ability level may behave differently in different kinds of groups; for example, medium-ability students give more explanations and are more likely to receive needed help in relatively homogeneous groups than in heterogeneous groups (Webb, 1980b, 1982c; Webb & Kenderski, 1984). The ratio of girls to boys in a group may also influence the incidence of explaining. In one study, girls were more likely to receive explanations when they asked for help or made errors in groups with equal numbers of girls and boys than in groups with more boys than girls or more girls than boys (Webb, 1984b). Teachers may unwittingly promote certain patterns of interaction through their assignment of students to groups. Explicitly taking into account group composition may be a fairly straightforward way to increase the incidence of adequate levels of help in small groups.

Although some of the relationships between peer interaction and learning outcomes reported here are straightforward and have clear implications for practice, other results can be clarified only with further research. One major unanswered question is the nature of explanations that are likely to be most understandable to students. This chapter hypothesizes that receiving help will benefit the recipient only if the help is understood. But what constitutes understandable help? Students may understand help better when it builds on what they already know, when multiple symbolic representations are used in an explanation (e.g., numbers, diagrams, pictures), or when it incorporates specific examples (see Shavelson et al. 1988). Future research needs to examine what kinds of help seem to be most understandable to students and when students might need different kinds of help, and it should systematically test the effectiveness of different kinds of help. This information would provide the foundation for training students to give optimal help.

Another major unanswered question concerns the experience of students who do not participate in group interaction. In the findings discussed in this chapter, being quiet did not seem to pose a problem for medium-ability students. Most of them solved the problems successfully on the achievement tests. For students of low ability, on the other hand, being quiet was definitely a problem, particularly for long-term retention. Several questions immediately arise. Were quiet medium-ability students able to learn from group work in ways that quiet low-ability students could not? Or were quiet medium-ability students able to figure out the work by themselves? What accounted for quiet low-ability students' success in the short term but failure to remember how to solve the problems in the long term? Would encouraging low-ability students to participate actively in group discussions improve their performance? To help answer these questions, future studies should include stimulated recall procedures to obtain information about what students are thinking and understanding at different points in group interaction. Such information will help guide recommendations for how students should interact in small groups to maximize their learning.

Clearly, understanding the effects of cooperative learning on achievement depends on understanding the internal dynamics of cooperative groups. Understanding how different patterns of group interaction influence students' learning permits the next step in cooperative learning research and practice: developing and testing instructional methods that will promote beneficial peer interaction that in turn will maximize the learning of all students in the group.

References

Aronson, E., Stephan, C., Sikes, J., Blaney, N., & Snapp, M. (1978). *The Jigsaw classroom*. Beverly Hills, CA: Sage.

Bargh, J. A., & Schul, Y. (1980). On the cognitive benefits of teaching. *Journal of Educational Psychology, 72*, 593–604.

Damon, W. (1984). Peer education: The untapped potential. *Journal of Applied Developmental Psychology, 5*, 331–343.

Damon, W., & Phelps, E. (1989). Critical distinctions among three methods of peer education. *International Journal of Educational Research, 13*, 9–19.

Forman, E. (1989). The role of peer interaction in the social construction of mathematical knowledge. *International Journal of Educational Research, 13*, 55–70.

Forman, E., & Cazden, C. (1985). Exploring Vygotskian perspectives in education: The cognitive value of peer interaction. In J. Wertsch (Ed.), *Culture, communication, and cognition: Vygotskian perspectives* (pp. 323–347). New York: Cambridge University Press.

Gall, M. D., & Gall, J. P. (1976). The discussion method. In N. L. Gage (Ed.), *The psychology of teaching methods* (pp. 166–216). Chicago: University of Chicago Press.

Heap, J. L. (1986, April). *Collaborative practices during computer writing in a first grade classroom.* Paper presented at the annual meeting of the American Educational Research Association, San Francisco, CA.

Johnson, D. W., & Johnson, R. T. (1979). Conflict in the classroom: Controversy and learning. *Review of Educational Research, 49,* 51–70.

Johnson, D. W., Johnson, R. T., & Stanne, M. B. (1985). Effects of cooperative, competitive, and individualistic goal structures on computer-assisted instruction. *Journal of Educational Psychology, 77,* 668–678.

_____ (1986). Comparison of computer-assisted cooperative, competitive, and individualistic learning. *American Educational Research Journal, 23,* 383–392.

King, A. (1990). Enhancing peer interaction and learning in the classroom through reciprocal questioning. *American Educational Research Journal, 27,* 664–687.

Lambiotte, J. G., Dansereau, D. F., O'Donnell, A. M., Young, M. D., Skaggs, L. P., Hall, R. H., & Rocklin, T. R. (1987). Manipulating cooperative scripts for teaching and learning. *Journal of Educational Psychology, 79,* 424–430.

Mugny, G., & Doise, W. (1978) Socio-cognitive conflict and structure of individual and collective performances. *European Journal of Social Psychology, 8,* 181–192.

Nelson-Le Gall, S. (1981). Help-seeking: An understudied problem-solving skill in children. *Developmental Review, 1,* 224–246.

_____ (1985). Help-seeking behavior in learning. *Review of Educational Research, 12,* 55–90.

Nelson-Le Gall, S., Gumerman, R. A., & Scott-Jones, D. (1983). Instrumental help-seeking and everyday problem-solving: A developmental perspective. *New Directions in Helping, 2,* 265–282.

Noddings, N. (1985). Small groups as a setting for research on mathematical problem solving. In E. A. Silver (Ed.), *Teaching and learning mathematical problem solving* (pp. 345–359). Hillsdale, NJ: Erlbaum.

Palincsar, A. S. (1986). The role of dialogue in providing scaffolded instruction. *Educational Psychologist, 21,* 73–98.

Palincsar, A. S., & Brown, A. L. (1984). Reciprocal teaching of comprehension-fostering and comprehension-monitoring activities. *Cognition and Instruction, 1,* 117–175.

Palincsar, A. S., Stevens, D. D., & Gavelek, J. R. (1989). Collaborating in the interest of collaborative learning. *International Journal of Educational Research, 13,* 41–53.

Perret-Clermont, A. N. (1980). *Social interaction and cognitive development in children.* European Monographs in Social Psychology, No. 19. New York: Academic Press.

Peterson, P. L., & Janicki, T. C. (1979). Individual characteristics and children's learning in large-group and small-group approaches. *Journal of Educational Psychology, 71,* 677–687.

Peterson, P. L., Janicki, T. C., & Swing, S. R. (1981). Ability × treatment interaction effects on children's learning in large-group and small-group approaches. *American Educational Research Journal, 18,* 453–473.

Peterson, P. L., & Swing, S. R. (1985). Students' cognitions as mediators of the effectiveness of small-group learning. *Journal of Educational Psychology, 77,* 299–312.

Peterson, P. L., Wilkinson, L. C., Spinelli, F., & Swing, S. R. (1984). Merging the

process-product and the sociolinguistic paradigm: Research on small-group processes. In P. L. Peterson, L. C. Wilkinson, & M. Hallinan (Eds,), *The social
context of instruction* (pp. 126–152). Orlando: Academic Press.

Riel, M. (1983). Education and ecstasy: Computer chronicles of students writing together. *Quarterly Newsletter of the Laboratory of Comparative Human Cognition,
5,* 59–67.

Roeders, P. (1987, September). *Training LOGO programming in school efficiently: Effects and processes in collaborative learning.* Paper presented at the Second European Conference for Research on Learning and Instruction, Tubingen, West Germany.

Rubin, A. (1983). The computer confronts language arts: Cans and shoulds for education.
In A. C. Wilkinson (Ed.), *Classroom computers and cognitive science* (pp. 201–
217). New York: Academic Press.

Sharan, S. (1980). Cooperative learning in small groups: Recent methods and effects on
achievement, attitudes, and ethnic relations. *Review of Educational Research, 50,*
241–272.

Shavelson, R. J., Webb, N. M., Stasz, C., & McArthur, D. (1988). Teaching mathematical problem solving: Insights from teachers and tutors. In R. Charles & E.
Silver (Eds.), *Teaching and assessing mathematical problem solving: A research
agenda.* Hillsdale, NJ: Erlbaum.

Slavin, R. E. (1977). Classroom reward structure: An analytical and practical review.
Review of Educational Research, 47, 633–650.

    (1980). Cooperative learning. *Review of Educational Research, 50,* 315–342.

    (1983). *Cooperative learning.* New York: Longman.

    (1987). Developmental and motivational perspectives on cooperative learning: A rec-
onciliation. *Child Development, 58,* 1161–1167.

Swing, S. R., & Peterson, P. L. (1982). The relationship of student ability and small-
group interaction to student achievement. *American Educational Research Journal, 19,* 259–274.

Vedder, P. (1985). *Cooperative learning: A study on processes and effects of cooperation
between primary school children.* Westerhaven Groningen, Netherlands: Rijkuni-
versiteit Groningen.

Vygotsky, L. S. (1981). The genesis of higher mental functioning. In J. V. Wertsch
(Ed.), *The concept of activity in Soviet psychology.* Armonk, NY: Sharpe.

Webb, N. M. (1980a). An analysis of group interaction and mathematical errors in heterogeneous ability groups. *British Journal of Educational Psychology, 50,* 266–
276.

    (1980b). A process-outcome analysis of learning in group and individual settings.
Educational Psychologist, 15, 69–83.

    (1982a). Group composition, group interaction and achievement in cooperative small
groups. *Journal of Educational Psychology, 74,* 475–484.

    (1982b). Peer interaction and learning in cooperative small groups. *Journal of Edu-
cational Psychology, 74,* 642–655.

    (1982c). Student interaction and learning in small groups. *Review of Educational Re-
search, 52,* 421–445.

    (1984a). Microcomputer learning in small groups: Cognitive requirements and group
processes. *Journal of Educational Psychology, 76,* 1076–1088.

    (1984b). Sex differences in interaction and achievement in cooperative small groups.
Journal of Educational Psychology, 76, 33–34.

    (1984c). Stability of small group interaction and achievement over time. *Journal of
Educational Psychology, 76,* 211–224.

(1989). Peer interaction and learning in small groups. *International Journal of Educational Research, 13*, 21–39.

Webb, N. M., & Cullian, L. K. (1983). Group interaction as a mediator between student and group characteristics and achievement: Stability over time. *American Educational Research Journal, 20*, 411–424.

Webb, N. M., Ender, P., & Lewis, S. (1986). Problem-solving strategies and group processes in small groups learning computer programming. *American Educational Research Journal, 23*, 243–261.

Webb, N. M., & Kenderski, C. M. (1984). Student interaction and learning in small groups and whole class settings. In P. L. Peterson, L. C. Wilkinson, & M. Hallinan (Eds.), *The social context of instruction: Group organization and group processes* (pp. 153–170). New York: Academic Press.

(1985). Gender differences in small-group interaction and achievement in high- and low-achieving classes. In L. C. Wilkinson & C. B. Marrett (Eds.), *Gender differences in classroom interaction* (pp. 209–236). New York: Academic Press.

Weinstein, B. D., & Bearison, D. J. (1985). Social interaction, social observation, and cognitive development in young children. *European Journal of Social Psychology, 15*, 333–343.

Wertsch, J. V. (1979). From social interaction to higher psychological processes. *Human Development, 22*, 1–22.

6   Scripted Cooperation in Student Dyads: A Method for Analyzing and Enhancing Academic Learning and Performance

Angela M. O'Donnell and Donald F. Dansereau

Cooperative learning is a widely used instructional technique. Evidence of its widespread appeal can be found in the growing number of cooperative learning organizations, the inclusion of information about cooperative learning in introductory educational psychology texts (e.g., Woolfolk, 1990), and the publication of books such as this. Research on cooperative learning to date has focused largely on successfully demonstrating the efficacy of cooperative learning in comparison to competitive or individualistic efforts on a variety of measures of academic achievement and social attitudes (Johnson, Maruyama, Johnson, Nelson, & Skon, 1981; Johnson & Johnson, 1989; Slavin, 1980, 1983). Despite the volume of research on cooperative learning, it remains unclear as to *why* or *how* it works. This is unfortunate in that its improvement and appropriate use depends on a clear understanding of its critical elements.

A number of factors contribute to the difficulty of identifying critical elements of cooperative learning. First, many different techniques are couched under the beguilingly simple umbrella term *cooperative learning*. For example, important distinctions are drawn between peer-tutoring, peer collaboration, and cooperative learning (Damon & Phelps, 1989), although these techniques are often grouped together as "cooperative learning" techniques. Cooperative learning techniques can vary widely in the size of the cooperative group, individual accountability of the members, the extent of externally imposed structures, the tasks performed, and whether or not between-group competition is employed (Slavin, 1983).

Second, much cooperative learning research to date was conducted as field research in regular classrooms with relatively loose experimental controls. Diverse

The research reported here was supported in part by Army Research Institute Grant No. MDA903-84-C-0323. The views, opinions, and findings contained here are those of the authors and should not be construed as an official Department of the Army position, policy, or decision.

This material is based on work supported in part by the National Science Foundation under Grant No. MDR8751369. The government has certain rights in this material. Any opinions, findings, and conclusions or recommendations expressed in this material are those of the authors and do not necessarily reflect the views of the National Science Foundation.

subject matter was taught to a variety of age-groups using different cooperative learning techniques (Johnson & Johnson, 1989; Slavin, 1980, 1983). The inherent variability of the contexts in which cooperative learning was implemented makes it very difficult to identify critical components of the techniques. Finally, although a number of theoretical frameworks guide the research on cooperative learning (see Slavin, 1987b), little work has been conducted on an analysis or manipulation of the processes engaged in by cooperating students. Rather, the predominant focus of the research has involved the assessment of goals and outcomes of cooperative experiences.

Efforts made to diagnose the critical components of cooperative learning have followed one of three approaches: (1) comparing the characteristics of the existing cooperative learning systems (e.g., Slavin, 1983); (2) analyzing student activities in detail during cooperative episodes (e.g., Webb, 1982b); and (3) manipulating variables that influence cooperative activities (e.g., Dansereau, 1988). Slavin (1983) reviewed a series of studies that examined the effects of cooperative learning on achievement to identify factors that distinguish between successful and unsuccessful techniques. Two primary attributes characterized the successful use of cooperative learning: the use of group rewards and the inclusion of a mechanism to ensure individual accountability. However, little information is available on how these factors affect the information processing and interpersonal interaction patterns of the participating individuals. Slavin's level of analysis of the effective components of cooperative learning is necessarily a very global one as a result of the variety of educational settings, differing age-groups, duration of cooperative learning episodes, and diversity of subject matter used in the studies surveyed.

A separate body of literature focused on a more microlevel approach to identifying how small problem-solving groups work (Webb, 1982a, 1982b). Analyzing the relationship of the interactions within these groups to achievement was the primary focus of this research. Variables found to be related to positive achievement outcomes included "giving and receiving highly elaborated explanations" (Webb, 1988a, 1988b). Variables that influenced the kind of interactions that occurred in a group included characteristics of the group (e.g., size, composition) and characteristics of participating individuals (e.g., ability). The research was conducted with unstructured groups, however, and although important interaction variables were identified, it is unlikely that all participants in such groups had the opportunity to engage in appropriate activities. The third approach to understanding cooperative learning – by manipulating relevant variables (Dansereau, 1988) – has received the least emphasis. The remainder of this chapter will describe our efforts to examine experimentally the critical elements of cooperative learning.

Table 6.1. *Prototypical script*

1. Both partners read the first section of the text.
2. Partner A reiterates the information without looking at the text.
3. Partner B provides feedback, without looking at the text.
4. Both partners elaborate on the information (e.g., develop images, relate the information to prior knowledge).
5. Both partners read the second section of the text.
6. Partners A and B switch roles for the second section.
7. A and B continue in this manner until they have completed the passage.

An Approach to the Analysis of Cooperative Learning: Scripted Cooperation

The problems inherent in attempting to analyze the underlying mechanisms of cooperative learning within the fluid context of regular instruction pose serious threats to the internal validity of research on cooperative learning. As a consequence, we focused our research and development efforts on its analysis in a more controlled context. The resultant cooperative learning system is known as *Scripted Cooperation* (Dansereau, O'Donnell, & Lambiotte, 1988). This context is laboratory based and involves college students working together in structured dyads to master an academic or technical task.

Unlike other cooperative learning techniques, the processing activities of the dyad members are specified, or scripted. *Script* is used here in the same way it is used in the theater. The roles and the nature and timing of the activities of the participants are specified. Scripted Cooperation differs from peer-tutoring approaches in that participants in a dyad are equal with respect to the task at hand; that is, neither partner is assumed to be an expert on the material. There are two primary reasons for the directive nature of the scripting. First, it is clear from our extensive research with college students that a great many students lack necessary learning skills. As a consequence, when left entirely to their own devices to select methods of studying, they may not choose appropriate strategies. This problem is exacerbated when both members of a dyad have such difficulty. Scripting the activities in which the dyad engages provides a method of training students in the use of effective skills and thus provides an opportunity for learning transferable skills. Second, the use of directive scripts allows us to selectively activate a variety of cognitive and metacognitive activities.

Although the same basic script can be applied to a variety of tasks (e.g., writing, performance of concrete procedures), we will use a text-processing task to illustrate how a prototypical script is used (see Table 6.1). The text is first broken down (by the experimenter/instructor or by cooperating students) into a number of sections. Both partners read the first section of the text and then put the material away. One partner then plays the role of "recaller" and recalls all the information he or she can remember. The other partner plays the role of "listener/detector" and listens carefully, attempting to detect errors or omissions in the recall. Both partners then share ideas about how to elaborate on the information to make it memorable. Examples of elaborative activities include developing analogies with other information and generating images. Participants then proceed to the second section of the text, switching roles at the end of it. They proceed in this manner until they have completed the entire text, alternating between the two roles.

The script is designed to facilitate a number of potentially effective activities that have emerged from research findings in cognitive and educational psychology, such as oral summarization (Ross & DiVesta, 1976; Yager, Johnson, & Johnson, 1985), metacognitive activities (Baker & Brown, 1984), elaborative activities (Reder, 1980), cross-modeling/imitation of strategies (Bandura, 1971), and the use of multiple passes through the material (Dansereau, 1985).

The use of a laboratory-based approach allowed us to provide appropriate experimental controls for cooperative learning groups and to control the actual implementation of the cooperative learning technique under investigation. It is likely that with appropriate tailoring the principles of cooperative learning that emerge from investigations in this context can be profitably applied in other, less controlled contexts and can be tailored according to specific situational constraints.

Dyads were selected as the operative social unit for a number of reasons. First, dyads are the smallest possible social unit. As the size of the cooperative group increases, it becomes progressively more difficult to identify the successful components of cooperative learning. Second, the use of larger groups may, in some instances, promote the formation of coalitions, thus encouraging competition rather than cooperation (Peterson & Janicki, 1979). A third concern is that the use of larger groups may overload the participants as they cope with the information inputs from a variety of sources. The problem of cognitive overload is likely to be especially important for less able or less skilled students. Fourth, the use of larger groups may encourage social loafing (Latane, Willliams, & Harkins, 1979) or passivity (O'Donnell et al., 1986) on the part of the learners.

One advantage of our use of college students in the analysis of cooperative learning is the reduction of developmental variability of the participants, which might be found with younger students. Previous investigations have used a wide variety of age-groups. Children do not necessarily collaborate easily (Palincsar, Stevens, & Gavelek, 1989). Thus, the ability of students at various developmental stages to actually implement cooperative learning techniques as intended by researchers may be limited by inappropriate models of cooperation or lack of experience. Efforts to identify important elements of cooperative learning by making comparisons across studies that use populations of various ages are complicated by developmental differences in component cognitive and social skills.

In summary, our approach to the analysis of cooperative learning has been to use structured dyads composed of college students in a laboratory-based program of research. The systematic analysis of cooperative learning in this controlled context allows us to identify some important principles underlying successful cooperative learning.

A Framework for Understanding Cooperative Learning

One of the problems associated with much of the research on cooperative learning is the lack of an overall framework within which to describe the learner, couch the goals of the instructional/learning episodes, and evaluate the outcomes from such episodes. Dansereau (1986) developed a framework for cooperative task performance that addresses these difficulties and can be used to describe cooperative learning research in general and our own particular research program in particular. The purpose of this framework is to tentatively delineate some important variables that are likely to influence effective cooperative learning and to indicate how such a framework can guide the analysis of the separate and interactive effects of these variables.

The basic framework used to describe cooperative learning is presented in Figure 6.1. A number of classes of variables are expected to influence the group interactions in a cooperative learning experience, resulting in a variety of outcomes. Important influences on such interactions include the goals and incentives of the group, the nature of the task, the individual differences of the group members, and the script or organization of the group in performing the task. Other influences on outcomes could include the follow-up activities engaged in by the group. Although a directionality of influence is indicated in Figure 6.1, this is not intended to indicate causality. As we describe later, the influences of each of these classes of variables interact in complex ways with other classes of variables.

The central feature of this framework is the group interactions that occur during cooperative learning. Group interactions involve complex combinations of the cognitive/motor (C), affective (A), metacognitive (M), and social (S) activities of the learners involved. These activities will be referred to as CAMS. Cognitive/motor activities include comprehension, recall, and skilled performance. Affective activities include motivation, anxiety, and concentration. Metacognitive activities include comprehension and performance monitoring, error detection and correction, and awareness of performance levels. Social activities include awareness of and effective communication with others in the cooperative

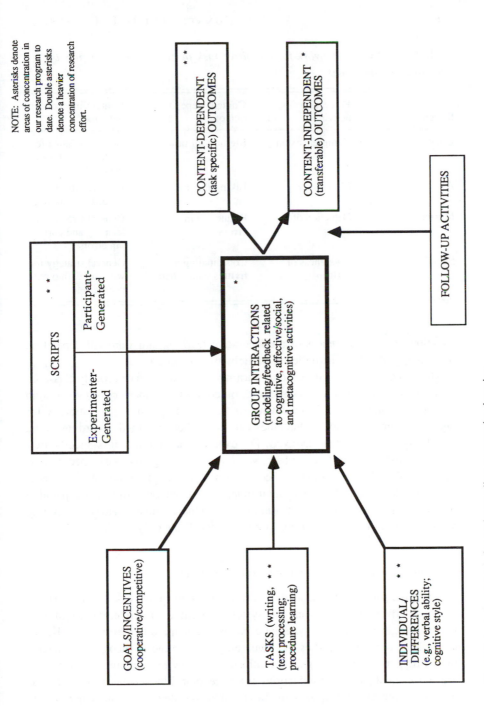

NOTE: Asterisks denote areas of concentration in our research program to date. Double asterisks denote a heavier concentration of research effort.

SCRIPTS **

Experimenter-Generated | Participant-Generated

CONTENT-DEPENDENT (task specific) OUTCOMES **

CONTENT-INDEPENDENT (transferable) OUTCOMES *

FOLLOW-UP ACTIVITIES

GROUP INTERACTIONS (modeling/feedback related to cognitive, affective/social, and metacognitive activities) *

GOALS/INCENTIVES (cooperative/competitive)

TASKS (writing, ** (text processing; procedure learning)

INDIVIDUAL/ DIFFERENCES ** (e.g., verbal ability; cognitive style)

Figure 6.1. A framework for understanding cooperative learning.

Table 6.2. *CAMS framework for cognitive task performance: Examples of activities and outcomes*

System	Processing activity	Content-dependent outcome	Content-independent outcome
Cognitive	Comprehension	Memory of task	General schema for dealing with type of material
Affective	Motivation	Liking the task	Positive attitude toward related task
Metacognitive	Detection of errors	Reduction in errors	General strategy for locating and correcting errors
Social	Awareness of partner	Coordinating activities with others	General strategy for working with other people

situation. The effectiveness of a cooperative learning situation will depend on the synergy of CAMS activities of participating members.

The outcomes from a cooperative learning experience can be broadly classified into content-dependent, or task-specific, outcomes (e.g., mastery of two-column subtraction) and content-independent, or transferable, skills (e.g., strategy for checking comprehension). Outcomes can be further classified according to the CAMS system or system involved. For example, a cognitive task-specific outcome involves memory of the task, whereas a metacognitive task-specific outcome involves knowing how to check for errors in the performance of the task. An example of an affective content-independent outcome from a cooperative learning experience might be learning some generalizable strategy for coping with frustration in the face of difficult tasks (see Table 6.2).

Influences on Group Interactions and Outcomes

Cooperative performance depends on a synergy between the CAMS of all participants. An overemphasis on any one system (cognitive, affective, metacognitive, or social) can disrupt this synergetic balance and inhibit performance. If, for example, a participant places too much emphasis on the metacognitive system, the participant's ability to generate information may be impaired. Writers who are too critical of their productions often become blocked because of excess activity in the monitoring system. In our analysis, there are four major factors that influence the intertwining of the CAMS activities in cooperative groups and, as a consequence, the effectiveness of cooperation (see Figure 6.1). These factors are the goals/incentive conditions of the task, the task itself, individual differences of the learners, and the cooperative script. These factors and their interactions influence which CAMS activities are prevalent in a cooperative situation and which outcomes will result. The follow-up activities engaged in by the learners also influence the outcomes. In the following pages, we will describe how each of these factors might affect the group interactions and outcomes. In later sections, we will describe empirical findings from our research program that have specifically addressed the influence of some of these factors.

The Goals/Incentive Conditions of the Task

The goals of cooperative groups can be classified as content dependent (i.e., task specific) or content independent (i.e., transferable skills). Mastery of the content is a content-dependent goal for a text-processing task, whereas the acquisition of strategies for coping with anxiety or frustration is a content-independent goal for the same task. Within the domain of current cooperative learning practices, content-independent goals are rarely present. Such goals can potentially be attained through the use of Scripted Cooperation because it provides the opportunity for participants to acquire content-independent CAMS knowledge and skills by reflection, observational learning, practice, and/or feedback.

Much of the research on cooperative learning to date focused on issues related to the incentive conditions of the task. For example, the efficacy of cooperation in comparison to competitive and individualistic goal structures has been repeatedly demonstrated (see Johnson et al., 1981). Additional issues that have received attention include the provision of extrinsic group reward as a component of effective cooperative learning. According to Slavin (1980, 1987b), there is little evidence that cooperative learning works in the absence of extrinsic reward, an assertion that has recently been challenged (Damon & Phelps, 1989). Further research on the specific contribution of goal/incentive structures to the resultant efficacy of cooperative learning is warranted.

Task Characteristics

Task characteristics include difficulty of the task, the specific nature of the materials used, the sequence of actions to be completed, and the amenability of the task to cooperative performance. The nature, difficulty, and duration of the task will strongly influence the type and amount of processing required and will, consequently, partially determine the kind of outcomes that result. For example, the cooperative performance of an easy task (e.g., a low-demand, low-consequence task performed without time pressure or distractions) will most likely be successfully completed by relatively smooth, automatic processing by group members. Such processing will most likely result in a content-dependent outcome but provide little opportunity for the observation and modeling of CAMS (e.g., planning) processes that are likely to be necessary for achieving content-independent outcomes. Moderately difficult tasks are most likely to produce both content-dependent and content-independent outcomes. Such tasks will disrupt habitual processing to some degree and by doing so are likely to make more CAMS processes available for observation.

Tasks also differ in the extent to which props for memory, observation of participants' CAMS processes, and communication between members of cooperative groups are intrinsic to the task. For example, the availability of equipment in tasks that require the performance of concrete procedures provides participants with props that serve the functions described earlier. Participants use the equipment as aids to their explanations, and actions performed with the equipment by members of the group provide the other members with an overt, observable record of their partners' comprehension of the task. The availability of pictures, graphs, and figures in other tasks also provides participants with props that guide their explanations and direct attention to important points. These kinds of tasks are markedly different from those involving text-processing of expository or narrative texts, which do not have the immediately available and observable aids to memory and communication characteristic of more technical tasks.

The Individual Differences among Members

The mixture of information-processing strengths, weaknesses, preferences, and styles of group members of a cooperative unit plays a crucial role in determining outcomes. The development of transferable, content-independent CAMS skills may be inhibited if the opportunities and motivation for observational learning are restricted by the smooth, effortless processing of highly competent members. Opportunities for observational learning can be smothered by the size and composition of a cooperative group. When the target task has a low level of task interdependence (i.e., any of the participants can complete the task), larger groups improve the probability that one individual will have the necessary skills to complete the task (Steiner, 1972). In such a situation, other members of the group receive few benefits. They do not acquire the specific skill of completing the task nor do they learn anything about the process involved in the successful completion of the task.

Motivation to engage in observational learning may suffer as a result of perceived or actual competency differences in the group. If the skill differences among members of the group are too great, the less skilled members may be unable to internalize the observed behaviors successfully due to the lack of appropriate knowledge and skill bases in which to integrate new information. New users of computer systems, for example, who are given a rapid demonstration of the computer's capabilities often cannot benefit from such a demonstration because they do not have the necessary knowledge structures to encode the information. Perhaps what they need to know is how to turn the computer on. Such experiences also lessen motivation for engaging in such tasks.

The Cooperative Script

The cooperative script is the mechanism that guides the interaction of cooperating groups as they complete the designated task. Cooperative scripts can be participant generated, imposed by an outside agent (e.g., instructor), or involve some blending of the two. These scripts vary along a number of dimensions (e.g., the degree of specification of the group activities, the amount of interaction permitted or encouraged, the nature of the interaction, the degree of equality of the roles played, and the permanence of the roles played).

The nature of the script in interaction with the individual characteristics of the participants and the nature of the task will determine the outcomes of the group interaction. Performance groups that use scripts that allow group members with task-relevant expertise to dominate and control the group's activities are more likely to lead to the successful completion of the task but with few content-independent outcomes. Scripts that maximize the opportunities for observational learning from self and others may provide the most fruitful context for acquiring content-independent CAMS skills. In this regard, imposed scripts that encourage a high degree of interaction and role changing may be more effective than participant-generated scripts that typically place people in familiar and comfortable roles that maintain habitual ways of responding to a task or group situations.

Follow-up Activities

The outcomes emerging from cooperative task performance, especially content-independent outcomes, may be enhanced by postgroup reprocessing of the group interactions. This may be accomplished via videotape analysis, discussion, stimulated recall, or other procedures. It is likely that the objectives/goals given to participants in their reprocessing of the interactions facilitate outcomes that are different from those resulting from the original group participation. For example, participants can be told to reexamine the content-dependent CAMS processes, content-independent CAMS processes, or both. Reprocessing that focuses on goals not presented in the initial task instructions may have the greater utility. Such activities could be particularly valuable under conditions in which the participants are likely to be overloaded during the interactions (e.g., high rates of processing, multiple sources of information, personality conflicts).

Although follow-up activities generally have been considered to be necessary for the success of experiential learning episodes (e.g., Cooper & Levine, 1978), there has been very little systematic examination of their impact on the transfer of cooperative group outcomes to subsequent individual outcomes. We have not yet addressed the possible effects of such activities in our own research program.

Empirical Findings

Using variants of the prototypical script (see Table 6.1), we conducted a series of experiments to determine the effects of the factors previously described (e.g., goals, individual differences, tasks, scripts) on content-dependent and content-independent outcomes. We focused particularly on the effects of scripts and the interaction of scripts with tasks and individual differences. The experiments typically compare the performance of dyads using experimenter-provided scripts with participants using self-generated scripts, and with individuals performing in a number of control conditions. Participants usually receive 1 hour of instruction and practice with the scripts and then study text materials for approximately 40 min per passage. Participants are often given an individual learning task to assess content-independent transfer. A variety of individual-difference measures are administered, and participants take free- and cued-recall tests after a delay of approximately 5 days. The report presented here of the findings from our research program is illustrative rather than exhaustive.

Effects of Scripts

Scripts for cooperation can vary according to the degree of participant control (e.g., participant generated vs. experimenter generated; fixed roles vs. alternating roles), major differences in the scripts (e.g., cooperative teaching vs. cooperative learning; Lambiotte et al., 1987), or more subtle differences that arise from the differential emphasis on the precise activities or substrategies they contain (e.g., the inclusion of planning, an emphasis on metacognition).

Participant-Generated Versus Experimenter-Generated Scripts. Students who use Scripted Cooperation (the use of an imposed script) consistently outperform those who work alone, on both initial acquisition of material (Larson, Dansereau, O'Donnell, Hythecker, Lambiotte, & Rocklin, 1985) and transfer to individual study (McDonald, Larson, Dansereau, & Spurlin, 1985). Scripted Cooperation is also more effective than participant-generated scripts (Larson et al.,

1986). The benefits of imposed scripts have been found in a variety of task domains such as text-processing of expository and descriptive prose (Spurlin, Dansereau, Larson, & Brooks, 1984), performance of concrete procedures (O'Donnell, Dansereau, Hythecker, et al., 1988; O'Donnell, Dansereau, Rocklin, et al., 1988), and text-processing of technical texts (Hall et al., 1988).

Imposed scripts are not always superior to participant-generated scripts. The latter may be useful in producing content-dependent outcomes if they capitalize on task-relevant expertise of members of the cooperative unit. For example, participants in one experiment (O'Donnell, Dansereau, Rocklin, et al., 1988) were required to perform a concrete procedure. Immediate performance of the task by cooperating dyads that generated their own scripts was better than performance by those who used imposed scripts. The reverse was true on a delayed-performance task. When a single performance of a task is required, it seems more efficient to allow participants to take advantage of the available expertise in the group, although this goal is rarely found in educational settings. Because participant-generated scripts typically allow people to select information-processing roles with which they are comfortable and familiar, they do not provide significant opportunities for acquiring content-independent CAMS skills. A moderate to strong level of disruption in habitual processing appears to be necessary (Dansereau, 1988) for the development of an expanded repertoire of knowledge and skills. Evidence of how an unfamiliar task can disrupt the habitual processing of individuals comes from research on concrete procedures (O'Donnell, Dansereau, Rocklin, et al., 1988). Participants frequently made self-derogatory statements (e.g., 'I'm no good at this'') and generated more observable affect in the situation than might be expected on more familiar tasks (e.g., an individual text-processing task).

Differences in the relative efficacy of the two kinds of scripts may show up on some CAMS outcomes and not on others. Supporting evidence for this notion comes from an experiment that compared the effects of exposure to either participant- or experimenter-generated scripts on transfer to a second, unscripted cooperative experience (O'Donnell, Dansereau, Hall, et al., 1987). Students who generated their own scripts for learning achieved as well as those students who used experimenter scripts (content-dependent outcome). Significant differences, however, were found on a measure of attitudes toward the partner after the second cooperative experience, with those who had used their own scripts in both cooperative experiences expressing more negative attitudes toward their new partners (content-independent outcome) than those students whose initial cooperative experience had been with an experimenter-provided script. This difference in expressed attitude toward the partners would be likely to seriously affect the motivation and achievement of an ongoing cooperative group.

Adapting Scripts. Although we have generally found the prototypical script to be successful, we have also found that modifications to it are often necessary. Factors such as task differences, the individual differences of participants, and desired outcomes are among those that have necessitated adaptations to the prototypical script. We have used the CAMS framework as the basis for adapting the prototypical script when such adaptations are necessary.

The activities included in the prototypical dyadic cooperative script tap into all four systems of the CAMS framework. The activities engaged in by the cooperating dyad include reading, overt verbalization, detection of errors, and elaboration of information. Cognitive systems are activated by the necessity to read, comprehend, recall, and elaborate on the information. The metacognitive system is explicitly involved by the requirement to detect errors and omissions. Sharing the task of mastering the target material, alternating roles, and the interactions involved in sharing feedback and working together tap the affective and social system and provide opportunities for modulating the affective states of the learners. If, for example, a learner experiences anxiety when playing the role of recaller, such a learner is likely to experience a release from anxiety when it is his or her opportunity to play the role of listener. Modifications of this script can amplify the activation of a particular CAMS system or activity. In one experiment (Larson, Dansereau, O'Donnell, et al., 1985), we compared the effects of scripts that amplified metacognitive activities (i.e., detecting errors) with those that amplified cognitive activities (i.e., efforts toward deeper processing through elaboration). The metacognitive script led to significantly better content-dependent outcomes, whereas the cognitive/elaborative script led to significantly better content-independent transfer.

Script and Task Interactions. To determine the generality and limitations of our basic scripts, we have conducted experiments employing a variety of tasks. We found that modifications to the basic scripts are necessary as a result of the nature of the tasks. In one set of experiments, for example, we examined the relationship between scripted cooperation and the learning of technical material, which typically consists of structural and functional information (declarative information) about a piece of equipment and a set of procedures for operating or troubleshooting the equipment. The prototypical dyadic script was effective for both content-dependent and content-independent outcomes in the learning of structural/functional material (Lambiotte et al., 1986; Larson et al., 1986) but not with procedural information (O'Donnell, Dansereau, Rocklin, Lambiotte, Hythecker, Larson, & Young, 1985). However, when the recaller role was expanded to a performer role with the individual performing simulated movements or actual movements with the equipment, both content-dependent and content-independent outcomes were enhanced.

Individual Differences and Scripted Cooperation

In our research we have found that individual differences in cognitive ability, cognitive style, and personality affect the success of Scripted Cooperation. Students who receive higher scores on a measure of social orientation perform better in cooperative dyads than in individual study conditions, whereas the reverse is true for those with low scores on this measure (Hall et al., 1988). Informal interviews with students who have little or no experience in working cooperatively on academic tasks indicate that these students experience a great deal of anxiety in working with others (O'Donnell & Adenwalla, 1991). Thus, it appears that not all students immediately profit from cooperative learning or are ready to engage in it.

In most of our experiments we created dyads by randomly assigning same-sex pairs of students. Responses to postexperimental questionnaires and examination of within-cell variances clearly indicate that some pairings are more successful than others. Pairs of students who were heterogeneous on measures of verbal aptitude and cognitive style were more effective than homogeneous pairings (Larson, Dansereau, Goetz, & Young, 1985; Larson et al., 1984).

Under some conditions, the efficacy of a particular script also interacts with the individual differences of the members of cooperating dyads. In learning to perform a concrete procedure (O'Donnell, Dansereau, & Rocklin, 1991), field-dependent participants performed best when they used a script that provided some cognitive and social support to their learning by allowing them to refer to their partners or their instructions for assistance. In contrast, field-independent students performed best when using a script that required them to plan prior to performance but did not allow access to their partners or to the instructional materials.

Individual differences also interact with the nature of the task to be performed. For example, in one experiment that focused on how students reviewed two related sets of information, students with low verbal ability performed better when they were directed to compare/contrast the two sets of material, whereas high–verbal ability students performed best when they were simply directed to review the material (Young et al., 1987). In addition, the differences found between the performance of high– and low–verbal ability participants were less dramatic on the performance of a concrete procedure than on the recall of procedural information (O'Donnell, Dansereau, Rocklin, et al., 1987).

Scripted Cooperation: Emerging Principles

A number of principles of scripted cooperation can be identified, based on research findings gleaned from over 10 years of systematic research. Although our research was conducted in laboratory settings at the college level, the emerging principles can be readily applied in other school settings. Many of them are consistent with current practices in cooperative learning. However, the combination of the principles makes an important contribution to the systematic use of cooperative learning as an instructional tool for *both* content-dependent and content-independent outcomes. The principles that emerged can be used, not only with dyads, but also with larger groups. The use of larger groups will require modification in the distribution and kind of activities included.

First, active processing on the part of all participants involved in a cooperative episode is necessary. When we have manipulated the degree of activity of the participants (O'Donnell et al., 1986; Spurlin et al., 1984; Spurlin, Dansereau, O'Donnell, & Brooks, 1988), participants who were relatively passive performed worse than those who were active. Appropriate scripting of the cooperative experience is an effective method for stimulating active involvement. Such scripting provides opportunities for interaction, observational learning, and modeling. Careful scripting of such activities also builds in opportunity and time for reflection, which is also positively related to achievement outcomes (Meichenbaum & Goodman, 1971). Another method of maintaining involvement is to use very small groups. Webb (1988a) noted that dyads promote the highest degree of interaction and that greater interaction is associated with improvements in achievement. The larger the group, the more important it becomes to maintain the activity level of all participants.

A second principle that has emerged from our research is that cooperation among peers is better than individual efforts. Cooperating dyads performed better than individuals in the acquisition of descriptive (Spurlin et al., 1984) and technical information (Hall et al., 1988; Larson et al., 1986). In addition, cooperating dyads wrote more communicative instructions than individuals (O'Donnell, Dansereau, Rocklin, Lambiotte, Hythecker, & Larson, 1985) and outperformed individuals on the immediate and delayed performance of a procedure (O'Donnell, Dansereau, Hythecker, et al., 1988). Furthermore, the initial benefits that accrued as a result of a brief cooperative training experience persisted over relatively long intervals (O'Donnell, Dansereau, Hythecker, et al., 1988; O'Donnell, Dansereau, Lambiotte, et al., 1988). Individuals exposed to a dyadic learning experience also successfully transferred their skills to subsequent individually performed tasks (McDonald et al., 1985). These findings are consistent with those of other cooperative learning research. We have added to this previous knowledge base by demonstrating the efficacy of cooperation among peers in situations that are well controlled and that do not have any explicit reward structure associated with performance in cooperative dyads. The scripting of the activities of the cooperating individuals may be enough to maintain interest and motivation during the short-term analyses of cooperative learning that we have conducted. It may be that other types of motivation are necessary for younger learners or for long-term use. However, it is worth noting that at least in our limited arena, cooperative learning was more effective than individual efforts even without the explicit use of extrinsic rewards.

Third, externally imposed scripts are generally more effective than participant-generated scripts. Clear advantages for the externally provided scripts were found on acquisition of both descriptive (McDonald et al., 1985; Spurlin et al., 1984) and technical information (Larson et al., 1986; O'Donnell, Dansereau, Hythecker, et al., 1988) and on the immediate and delayed performance of relatively complex concrete procedures (O'Donnell, Dansereau, Hall, et al., 1991). The provision of scripts also promotes positive affect toward the task at hand (Lambiotte et al., 1986). As discussed previously, participant-generated scripts can be effective for content-dependent outcomes. The participant-generated scripts are likely to allow people to maintain habitual ways of processing information and comfortable ways of interacting. These kinds of mechanisms do not facilitate the kinds of deep processing necessary for the retention of information or acquisition of transferable skills.

Although grouping by ability has a long tradition as a method of organizing instruction, an accumulating body of research suggests that the supposed positive benefits associated with this technique are more imaginary than real (Slavin, 1987a). The empirical evidence from our research is consistent with other findings that argue for the benefits of heterogeneous grouping. Within our cooperative learning paradigm, dyads who are heterogeneous with respect to ability or cognitive style outperform dyads who are homogeneous with respect to these characteristics (Larson, Dansereau, Goetz, & Young, 1985; Larson et al., 1984). The performance of high-ability individuals in heterogeneous groups does not appear to suffer and that of lower ability students is certainly improved. Among the possible factors that contribute to the efficacy of heterogeneous dyads is that more skills are available for observation and modeling by the lower ability student. High-ability students in homogeneous problem-solving groups tend to assume that everyone can master the material (Webb, 1988a, 1988b). In such situations, fewer of the CAMS activities engaged in by learners are explicit and available for observation or modeling.

Finally, tailoring the imposed script to the individual characteristics of participants (ability, experience, personality) is more effective than the detailed prescription of interaction and process behaviors. The interactions of individual differences in ability and style with aspects of the task, and so forth, have already been described in this chapter. A second aspect of the tailoring process relates to the task-relevant skills or experiences that participants have prior to the task. Participants who engage in cooperative learning experiences will require the opportunity to integrate newly acquired skills with previous knowledge and skills.

For example, O'Donnell et al. (1986) examined the impact of strategy prescription on transfer from cooperative experiences to individual learning. Those who were directed to adapt elements of the script that they found useful into their own study methods and use the combination to study individually performed better on the transfer task than those who were directed to continue using the prescribed script.

General Boundary Conditions of Imposed Scripts

Although the use of imposed scripts in dyadic cooperative learning is generally successful, certain kinds of scripts have failed. These failures generally have occurred when the script has led to a high degree of passivity on the part of one or more of the learners (O'Donnell et al., 1986; Spurlin et al., 1984), or the script has been too detailed and explicit about the prescribed activities (Hythecker et al., 1986). In the first instance, social loafing (Latane et al., 1979) may lead to poor performance, and in the second case, information-processing overload (Hythecker et al., 1986; O'Donnell et al., 1986) and a high degree of incongruence of the script with personal aptitudes and styles may create problems (Dansereau, 1988). Problems also arise when the script has resulted in poor motivation (O'Donnell, Dansereau, Hythecker, et al., 1988) or debilitating affective states (O'Donnell, 1986). It appears that the most effective script is one that encourages active processing of the information by the participants, promotes positive affect, and is flexible enough to permit the participants to tailor the roles they play to exploit their own processing strengths.

Further Development of Scripted Cooperation

Findings from our research program have provided us with evidence that the preliminary conceptual framework we described earlier is a useful tool to describe how cooperative learning works, to examine the impact of a variety of influences on the processes and outcomes from cooperative learning, and to adapt scripts as necessary. We have found that Scripted Cooperation not only is a useful vehicle for analyzing the process of cooperative learning but is also an effective tool for the immediate acquisition of information and transferable skills.

A number of important issues remain to be addressed in the analysis of cooperative learning as we conceive it. We will describe only two of these. First, the experimentation we have conducted to date has involved only very brief periods of training on the use of Scripted Cooperation, and outcomes from such training have been assessed after relatively brief delays (e.g., 5 to 7 days). Recent findings (e.g., O'Donnell, Dansereau, Hythecker, et al., 1988; O'Donnell, Dansereau, Hall, et al., 1991) show some promising indications that effects engendered by a cooperative experience are maintained over 3- to 6-week intervals. However, we have not assessed the long-term effects of Scripted Cooperation. Of particular interest in such an assessment would be the acquisition of transferable skills or an expanded repertoire of learning strategies.

A second important issue relates to the degree to which content-independent skills can be acquired as a result of cooperative learning experiences. Our research to date has only touched on this issue. Although we have found evidence of students acquiring such skills, the potential use of cooperative learning as a vehicle for the specific training of such skills has yet to be explored. It is still unclear to what extent students actually profit from one another's learning. We have hypothesized that those same factors that affect the combined outcomes from Scripted Cooperation will also influence participants' reception of CAMS information and hence their acquisition of transferable skills. The explicitness, rate, and redundancy of CAMS information generated will strongly influence the degree to which it is encoded and subsequently employed by an observing partner. If an individual's CAMS skills are too similar or too dissimilar to those presented by a partner, it is expected that very little meaningful acquisition will occur. A moderate level of discrepancy would be expected to produce the highest degree of acquisition.

Videotaped analyses can inform us about the amount of time spent on various activities, the nature of the information generated, and how the emphasis in type of generated information can change over time. However, we cannot know how much of the generated information is actually received or interpreted by the observer in the dyad. To assist us in exploring this issue, we have developed a method for measuring subjective reactions to cooperative experiences that holds some promise in assisting us to establish what is actually received by or reflected upon by participant members of student dyads. This method is called subjective graphing (see Figure 6.2).

Upon completion of a training episode, participants are asked to graph the fluctuations in their feelings, motivation, perceptions, and so forth, over the time course of the cooperative experience. Using this method, we have been able to identify how subjective reactions to a cooperative experience changed over time. The subjective graph in Figure 6.2 is one student's actual response to a particular experimental situation. The use of subjective graphs appears to have enormous potential for providing an important window on the receptive processes of the learners engaged in a cooperative experience and on the possible acquisition of transferable skills. In addition, the use of follow-up activities or reprocessing of the cooperative interchange may be of critical importance to the acquisition of transferable skills.

Building on the information already accumulated on the nature and effects of cooperative learning, the continued exploration of the operation of cooperative

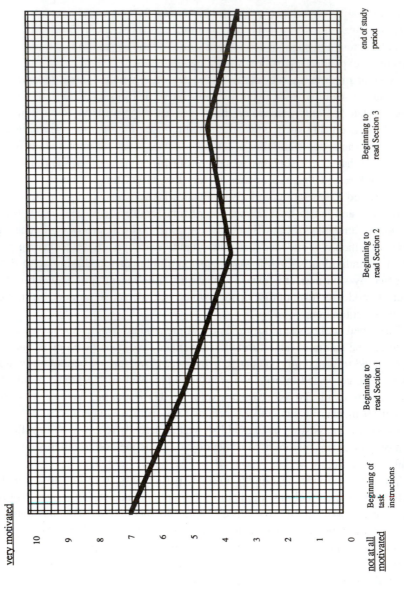

Figure 6.2. Example of a subjective graph.

learning over time and the receptive processes involved in learning from cooperation will allow us to elaborate a theory of cooperation. Such a theory would then allow us to predict outcomes from specific cooperative learning situations and to design instructional programs to produce desired outcomes.

References

Baker, L., & Brown, A. L. (1984). Metacognitive skills and reading. In P. D. Pearson (Ed.), *Handbook of reading research* (pp. 353–394). New York: Longman.

Bandura, A. (1971). *Psychological modeling: Conflicting theories.* Chicago: Aldine-Atherton.

Cooper, C. L., & Levine, N. (1978). Implicit values in experiential learning groups: Their functional and dysfunctional consequences. In C. L. Cooper & C. P. Alderfer (Eds.), *Advances in experiential social processes* (Vol. 1). New York: John Wiley & Sons.

Damon, W., & Phelps, E. (1989). Critical dimensions among three approaches to peer education. *International Journal of Educational Research, 13,* 9–20.

Dansereau, D. F. (1985). Learning strategy research. In J. W. Segal, S. F. Chipman, & R. Glaser (Eds.), *Thinking and learning skills: Vol. 1. Relating instruction to research* (pp. 209–239). Hillsdale, NJ: Erlbaum.

(1986, April). *Dyadic cooperative learning and performance strategies.* Paper presented at the annual meeting of the American Educational Research Association, San Francisco, CA.

(1988). Cooperative learning strategies. In C. E. Weinstein, E. T. Goetz, & P. A. Alexander (Eds.), *Learning and study strategies: Issues in assessment, instruction, and evaluation* (pp. 103–120). Orlando, FL: Academic Press.

Dansereau, D. F., O'Donnell, A. M., & Lambiotte, J. G. (1988, April). *Concept maps and scripted peer cooperation: Interactive tools for improving science and technical education.* Paper presented at the annual meeting of the American Educational Research Association, New Orleans, LA.

Hall, R. H., Rocklin, T. R., Dansereau, D. F., Skaggs, L. P., O'Donnell, A. M., Lambiotte, J. G., & Young, M. D. (1988). The role of individual differences in the cooperative learning of technical material. *Journal of Educational Psychology, 80,* 172–178.

Hythecker, V. I., Dansereau, D. F., Rocklin, T. R., O'Donnell, A. M., Young, M. D., & Lambiotte, J. G. (1986, April). *The development and evaluation of a modified procedure learning strategy.* Paper presented at the annual meeting of the Southwestern Psychological Association, Fort Worth, TX.

Johnson, D. W., & Johnson, R. T. (1989). *Cooperation and competition: Theory and practice.* Edina, MN: Interaction Book Co.

Johnson, D. W., Maruyama, G., Johnson, R., Nelson, D., & Skon, L. (1981). Effects of cooperative, competitive, and individualistic goal structures on achievement: A meta-analysis. *Psychological Bulletin, 89,* 47–62.

Lambiotte, J. G., Dansereau, D. F., Hythecker, V. I., O'Donnell, A. M., Young, M. D., & Rocklin, T. R. (1986, April). *Technical learning strategies: Acquisition of structural and functional information.* Paper presented at the annual meeting of the Southwestern Psychological Association, Fort Worth, TX.

Lambiotte, J. G., Dansereau, D. F., O'Donnell, A. M., Young, M. D., Skaggs, L. P.,

Hall, R. H., & Rocklin, T. R. (1987). Manipulating cooperative scripts for teaching and learning. *Journal of Educational Psychology, 79*, 424–430.

Larson, C. O., Dansereau, D. F., Goetz, E. T., & Young, M. D. (1985, February). *Cognitive style and cooperative learning: Transfer of effects*. Paper presented at the annual meeting of the Southwest Educational Research Association, Austin, TX.

Larson, C. O., Dansereau, D. F., Hythecker, V. I., O'Donnell, A. M., Young, M. D., Lambiotte, J. G., & Rocklin, T. R. (1986). Technical training: An application of a strategy for learning structural and functional information. *Contemporary Educational Psychology, 11*, 217–228.

Larson, C. O., Dansereau, D. F., O'Donnell, A. M., Hythecker, V. I., Lambiotte, J. G., & Rocklin, T. R. (1984). Verbal ability and cooperative learning: Transfer of effects. *Journal of Reading Behavior, 16*, 289–295.

(1985). Effects of metacognitive and elaborative activity on cooperative learning and transfer. *Contemporary Educational Psychology, 10*, 342–348.

Latane, B., Williams, K., & Harkins, S. (1979). Many hands make light the work: Causes and consequences of social loafing. *Journal of Personality and Social Psychology, 37*, 822–832.

McDonald, B. A., Larson, C. O., Dansereau, D. F., & Spurlin, J. E. (1985). Cooperative learning: Impact on acquisition of knowledge and skills. *Contemporary Educational Psychology, 10*, 369–377.

Meichenbaum, D. H., & Goodman, J. (1971). Training impulsive children to talk to themselves: A means of developing self-control. *Journal of Abnormal Psychology, 77*(2), 115–126.

O'Donnell, A. M. (1986). *Cooperative procedural learning: The effects of prompting and planning activities*. Doctoral dissertation, Texas Christian University, Fort Worth, TX.

O'Donnell, A. M., & Adenwalla, D. (1991). Using cooperative learning and concept maps with deaf college students. In D. S. Martin (Ed.), *Advances in cognition, education, and deafness*. Washington, DC: Gallaudet University Press.

O'Donnell, A. M., Dansereau, D. F., Hall, R. H., & Rocklin, T. R. (1987). Cognitive, social/affective, and metacognitive outcomes of scripted cooperative learning. *Journal of Educational Psychology, 79*, 431–437.

O'Donnell, A. M., Dansereau, D. F., Hall, R. H., Skaggs, L., Hythecker, V. I., Peel, J., & Rewey, K. (1991). Learning concrete procedures: The effects of processing strategies and cooperative learning. *Journal of Educational Psychology, 82*, 171–177.

O'Donnell, A. M., Dansereau, D. F., Hythecker, V. I., Hall, R. H., Skaggs, L. P., Lambiotte, J. G., & Young, M. D. (1988). Cooperative procedural learning: The effects of prompting and pre- vs. distributed planning activities. *Journal of Educational Psychology, 80*, 161–171.

O'Donnell, A. M., Dansereau, D. F., Hythecker, V. I., Larson, C. O., Rocklin, T. R., Lambiotte, J. G., & Young, M. D. (1986). Effects of monitoring on cooperative learning. *Journal of Experimental Education, 54*, 169–173.

O'Donnell, A. M., Dansereau, D. F., & Rocklin, T. R. (1991). Individual differences in the cooperative learning of concrete procedures. *Learning and Individual Differences, 3*, 149–162.

O'Donnell, A. M., Dansereau, D. F., Rocklin, T. R., Hythecker, V. I., Hall, R. H., Young, M. D., Skaggs, L. P., & Lambiotte, J. G. (1987, April). *The role of individual differences in procedure/skill acquisition*. Paper presented at the annual meeting of the American Educational Research Association, Washington, DC.

(1988). Promoting functional literacy through cooperative learning. *Journal of Reading Behavior, 20,* 339–356.

O'Donnell, A. M., Dansereau, D. F., Rocklin, T. R., Lambiotte, J. G., Hythecker, V. I., & Larson, C. O. (1985). Cooperative writing: Direct effects and transfer. *Written Communication, 2,* 307–315.

O'Donnell, A. M., Dansereau, D. F., Rocklin, T. R., Lambiotte, J. G., Hythecker, V. I., Larson, C. O., & Young, M. D. (1985). Effects of elaboration frequency on cooperative learning. *Journal of Educational Psychology, 77,* 572–580.

Palincsar, A., Stevens, D. D., & Gavelek, J. R. (1989). Collaborating in the interest of collaborative learning. *International Journal of Educational Research, 13,* 41–53.

Peterson, P. L., & Janicki, T. C. (1979). Individual characteristics and children's learning in large-group and small-group approaches. *Journal of Educational Psychology, 71,* 677–687.

Reder, L. (1980). The role of elaboration in the comprehension and retention of prose: A critical review. *Review of Educational Research, 49,* 5–53.

Ross, S. M., & DiVesta, F. J. (1976). Oral summary as a review strategy for enhancing recall of textual material. *Journal of Educational Psychology, 68,* 689–695.

Slavin, R. E. (1980). Cooperative learning. *Review of Educational Research, 50,* 315–342.

(1983). When does cooperative learning increase student achievement? *Psychological Bulletin, 94,* 429–445.

(1987a). Ability grouping: A best-evidence synthesis. *Review of Educational Research, 57,* 293–336.

(1987b). Developmental and motivational perspectives on cooperative learning: A reconciliation. *Child Development, 58,* 1161–1167.

Spurlin, J. E., Dansereau, D. F., Larson, C. O., & Brooks, L. W. (1984). Cooperative learning strategies in processing descriptive text: Effects of role and activity level of the learner. *Cognition and Instruction, 1,* 451–463.

Spurlin, J. E., Dansereau, D. F., O'Donnell, A. M., & Brooks, L. W. (1988). Text processing: Effects of summarization frequency on performance. *Journal of Experimental Education, 56,* 199–202.

Steiner, I.D. (1972). *Group processes and productivity.* New York: Academic Press.

Webb, N. M. (1982a). Peer interaction and learning in cooperative small groups. *Journal of Educational Psychology, 74,* 642–655.

(1982b). Student interaction and learning in small groups. *Review of Educational Research, 52,* 421–445.

(1988a, April). *Peer interactions and learning in small groups.* Paper presented at the annual meeting of the American Educational Research Association, New Orleans, LA.

(1988b, April). *Small group problem-solving: Peer interaction and learning.* Paper presented at the annual meeting of the American Educational Research Association, New Orleans, LA.

Woolfolk, A. E. (1990). *Educational psychology* (4th ed.). Englewood Cliffs, NJ: Prentice-Hall.

Yager, S., Johnson, D. W., & Johnson, R. T. (1985). Oral discussion, group-to-individual transfer, and achievement in cooperative learning groups. *Journal of Educational Psychology, 77,* 60–66.

Young, M. D., Dansereau, D. F., O'Donnell, A. M., Hythecker, V. I., Lambiotte, J. G., Skaggs, L. P., Hall, R. H., & Rocklin, T. R. (1987, April). *Effects of cooperative compare/contrast and review strategies on the acquisition of technical information.* Paper presented at the annual meeting of the American Educational Research Association, Washington, DC.

Part III

The Effects of Task and Reward Structure on Academic Achievement

7   When and Why Does Cooperative Learning Increase Achievement? Theoretical and Empirical Perspectives

Robert E. Slavin

"Class," said Ms. Cooper, "it's now time for you to start your team practice. I've given you each a blank outline map of Europe. I'd like you to work with your teammates to make sure that you and everyone else in your team can recognize the major countries. You'll have the rest of the period to study your maps together. Tomorrow I'll give you a quiz on this material, and any teams that get an average of 90% or better will get Superteam certificates and will be able to go to recess first. Do a good job of explaining to each other; remember, you won't be able to help each other on the quiz, so everyone in your team has to be able to fill out the map correctly. Are there any questions? You may begin work."

Ms. Cooper's sixth-grade class is studying a unit on the geography of Europe using Student Teams Achievement Divisions (STAD) (Slavin, 1986), one form of cooperative learning. She has taught a lesson on the major countries of Europe and is now giving instructions to the teams on how they are to work together. The teams consist of four to five students who are heterogeneous in performance level, sex, and ethnicity. They remain together for about 6 weeks, and then students are assigned to new teams according to the same criteria.

The instructions Ms. Cooper gives her class seem simple and straightforward enough. Yet she is making profound changes in two of the most important elements of classroom organization: *task structure* and *incentive structure*. Task structure refers to the ways in which the teacher (or students themselves) set up activities designed to result in student learning. Most classrooms use *independent task structures,* in which students are expected to work by themselves, listen to the teacher, or respond to the teacher (Bossert, 1977; Sirotnik, 1982). Yet Ms. Cooper has set up a *cooperative task structure,* in which students are encouraged to work together to help one another learn.

Ms. Cooper is also significantly altering the classroom incentive structure.

This chapter was written under a grant from the Office of Educational Research and Improvement, U.S. Department of Education (No. OERI-R-117-90002). However, any opinions expressed are those of the author and do not represent OERI policy.

145

Most classrooms use a *competitive incentive* structure, in which students compete for a limited number of good grades, the teacher's praise and attention, or other rewards. Other classes may use an *individualistic incentive structure,* in which students earn a particular grade if they achieve at a given, preestablished level (e.g., 90% is an "A" regardless of how many students score at this level). However, Ms. Cooper has set up a *cooperative incentive structure,* in which students can earn certificates and a little extra recess time based on the average score achieved by all members of a heterogeneous team. The particular cooperative incentive structure used by Ms. Cooper emphasizes *individual accountability,* in that the group's success depends on the learning of each group member, as demonstrated on a quiz taken without teammate help. In this situation, the only way the team can succeed is if every member of the group can independently fill out the outline map, so the most effective practice strategy is for students to explain to each other, quiz each other, and continue to work with each other until every team member has the skill. In a cooperative incentive structure lacking individual accountability, students might be rewarded based on the quality of a single worksheet, test, project, or other product.

Although there is a growing consensus among researchers about the positive effects of cooperative learning on student achievement as well as a rapidly growing number of educators using cooperative learning at all levels of schooling and in many subject areas, there is still a great deal of confusion and disagreement about *why* cooperative learning methods affect achievement and, even more important, *under what conditions* cooperative learning has these effects. Researchers investigating cooperative learning effects on achievement have often operated in isolation from one another, almost on parallel tracks, and often describe theoretical mechanisms held to explain achievement effects of cooperative learning that are totally different from the mechanisms assumed by others. In particular, there are researchers who emphasize the changes in incentive structure brought about by certain forms of cooperative learning, whereas others hold that changes in task structure are all that is required to enhance learning. The problem is that applications of cooperative learning typically change many aspects of both incentive and task structures, so disentangling which is responsible for which outcomes can be difficult.

This chapter discusses theories to account for the achievement effects of cooperative learning and examines the empirical data from classroom experiments that inform these theories.

Effects of Cooperation: Laboratory Research

The issue of cooperative versus competitive incentive structures is one of the oldest themes in social psychology (this section is adapted from Slavin, 1983a).

Research on this topic was already well developed by the 1920s (Maller, 1929). However, until recently this research was done in brief studies either in social psychological laboratories or, more commonly, in contrived field settings that resemble the laboratory. In this chapter, studies that were implemented over periods of less than 2 weeks in any setting are referred to as laboratory studies. Although these brief studies tend to be too limited in external validity to be useful as evaluations of cooperative learning methods for use in classrooms, they have provided much of the theoretical basis on which the practical cooperative learning programs and research on these programs are based. This chapter does not presume to review the hundreds of laboratory studies on cooperation and competition but summarizes the major findings relevant to building the theoretical base from which research on practical cooperative learning methods derives its conceptual framework.

Effects of Cooperation on Performance

Despite the many studies conducted to determine the effects of cooperation on performance, these effects are still rather poorly understood. Four reviews completely disagreed on the direction of the effects. D. W. Johnson and R. T. Johnson (1974) summarized the research by stating that cooperation is better than competition or individualization for all but the most concrete, repetitive tasks. In a later meta-analysis, D. W. Johnson, Maruyama, R. Johnson, Nelson, and Skon (1981) suggested that the evidence supporting cooperative incentive structures over competitive and individualistic ones in increasing productivity is so strong that further research on this comparison is unnecessary. However, Michaels (1977) reviewed much of the same literature and concluded that competition is usually better than cooperation for most tasks. Slavin (1977) held that over the brief duration of a laboratory study, cooperation is more effective in increasing performance when coordination of efforts is vital to effective functioning, whereas competition is at least as effective as cooperation when coordination of efforts is not so important. Because most tasks of practical importance (including learning) do not *require* coordination of efforts between two or more individuals, this conclusion was closer to that of Michaels (1977) than to those of D. W. Johnson and R. T. Johnson (1974) or D. W. Johnson et al. (1981). However, Slavin (1977) held that over longer periods, growth of social pressures favoring performance in cooperative groups makes cooperation more effective. A similar conclusion was reached by Miller and Hamblin (1963), who postulated that cooperative reward structures were most effective for interdependent (cooperative) task structures but least effective for independent tasks.

To understand the controversy over the laboratory evidence concerning the effects of cooperative incentive structures on performance, it is important to have a causal model linking cooperative incentive structures with enhanced performance. The following sections develop such a model.

Does Help Help?

The most obvious effect of a cooperative incentive structure should be to get individuals to help one another. This is so apparent that most studies have not measured it, but those that have done so have always found more helping under a cooperative incentive than under an individual or competitive one (Deutsch, 1949a; Slavin, 1980; Johnson & Johnson, 1981). It is obvious that for many tasks, such as carrying heavy loads, taking tests, or solving difficult problems, helping is likely to lead to a better group product. However, although it appears likely that cooperative incentives increase helping among group members, it is not so clear that helping per se always increases performance. Two similar studies illustrate the distinction. Klugman (1944) had small groups of children do arithmetic problems under a cooperative contingency in which the groups received rewards based on the number of problems they could do accurately, with no time limit. He contrasted this condition with one in which children worked for individual rewards based on the number of problems they could work correctly. The group under the cooperative condition got significantly more problems right. In a similar study, DeCharms (1957) found exactly the opposite relationship; the children who worked independently got more correct answers on the arithmetic problems than did those working under the cooperative incentive. There was a critical difference between the studies; Klugman (1944) allowed the children unlimited time, but DeCharms (1957) set a time limit and told his subjects to concentrate on speed. In the Klugman study, students were able to pool their knowledge to improve the performance of all group members; in the DeCharms study, helping was of little value and might have even slowed the subjects down.

   Thus, although it is clear that under certain conditions cooperative incentives lead to increased helping behavior, *the degree to which help is valuable for performance depends on the task and outcome measure.* Most of the tasks used in the laboratory research on cooperation, competition, and individualization on which cooperation produces the highest performance are problem-solving tasks on which two (or more) heads are obviously better than one. For example, Miller and Hamblin (1963) gave each of four subjects 3 unique numbers between 1 and 13. The task was to find the missing number. Since the four subjects had 12 numbers between them, they only had to share their numbers to find the missing one, and they did share more readily when they received a group reward based on how fast they could find the answer than when they were in competition to find the answer first, where sharing would simply help others to win. Literally dozens of studies have shown that two or more individuals working together can figure out a maze or a concept underlying a set of numbers or words faster than can individuals working alone (e.g., Lemke, Randle, & Robertshaw, 1969; Gurnee, 1968; Laughlin, McGlynn, Anderson, & Jacobson, 1968). When two or more individuals take a test together, they do better than when they work separately (e.g., Laughlin & H. Johnson, 1966; D. W. Johnson & R. T. Johnson, 1979). Many studies have shown that two or more individuals can solve problems of various kinds better when they work in groups than when they work independently (e.g., Deutsch, 1949a; Hammond & Goldman, 1961; Thorndike, 1938).

On the kinds of tasks used in the studies cited above, groups *obviously* score better than individuals. In the problem-solving studies, groups would have outscored individuals even if more able group members solved the problems by themselves, because the less able group members would have still been assigned the group score. As early as the 1930s, Thorndike (1938) considered the superiority of group to individual problem solving to have been proved and proposed that further research go beyond that rather obvious finding to explore what kinds of tasks groups do best. In fact, in many of the studies cited above, it was assumed at the beginning that groups would outperform individuals, and some issue beyond group versus individual problem solving was the focus of research.

A few studies examined the reasons that groups did better on problem-solving tasks and concluded that they did better simply because they pooled the problem-solving abilities of their members. Faust (1959), Marquart (1955), and Ryack (1965) compared groups that really worked together with ''nominal'' groups. The nominal group scores were created by randomly assigning subjects who had actually worked alone to artificial ''groups'' and crediting all ''group'' members with having solved a problem if any one of them solved the problem. In all three studies, the real groups had much higher scores than the individuals, but not than the nominal groups, suggesting that the real groups had high scores not because of their interaction or motivation but because if any individual could solve the problem their teammates would get credit for it, regardless of their own participation or learning.

Another category of tasks where cooperation is obviously more efficient than competition is when competition is likely to disrupt performance. The classic example is the Mintz (1951) experiment, in which the task was for several individuals to pull cones on strings out of a milk bottle whose neck would permit only one cone to be withdrawn at a time. Under cooperative instructions (get all the cones out as quickly as possible), the individuals arranged to take turns and quickly got all the cones out, but under noncooperative instructions (get your own cone out as quickly as possible), the traffic jam at the mouth of the bottle increased everyone's time. In another study, Graziano, French, Brownell, and

Hartup (1976) gave children stacks of blocks. The children were assigned to groups of three. In a cooperative condition, the children built a tower together and were rewarded based on the total number of blocks in the tower. In a non-cooperative condition, children also built a single tower, but they were rewarded based on the number of their *own* blocks they could get into the tower. In the condition in which children were trying to get their own blocks into the tower, the towers fell more often and ultimately included fewer blocks than in the condition in which children were concerned only with increasing the total number of blocks in the tower.

When hindering is a likely outcome of a cooperative task or reward structure, and cooperative instructions or rewards remove the hindering, cooperation will, of course, improve group performance. Many studies comparing cooperation and competition are of this type (e.g., Crombag, 1966; Raven & Eachus, 1963).

Group Productivity versus Individual Learning

The kind of performance of interest in this chapter bears little relationship to building towers of blocks, pulling cones out of bottles, or even problem solving in the sense studied in the experiments just discussed. *Learning* is a completely individual outcome that may or may not be improved by cooperation, but it is clearly not obviously improved by cooperation the way problem-solving perfor-mance of the kind described earlier is. Leonard Bernstein and I could write a brilliant concerto together, about twice as good as the average of the concerto he could write and the one I could write working separately (I can barely read music). But how much would we *learn* from working cooperatively? I doubt that Leonard Bernstein would learn much about writing concertos from me, and I might do better to take a course on music than to start by watching a composer write a concerto. The point of this example is to illustrate that *learning is com-pletely different from "group" productivity.* It may well be that working in a group under certain circumstances does increase the learning of the individuals in that group more than would working under other arrangements, but a measure of group productivity provides no evidence one way or the other on this; only an individual learning measure that cannot be influenced by group member help can indicate which incentive or task structure is best. Learning takes place only be-tween the ears of the learner. If a group produces a beautiful lab report, but only a few students really contributed to it, it is unlikely that the group as a whole learned more than they might have learned had they each had to write their own (perhaps less beautiful) lab reports under an individualistic or competitive incen-tive structure. In fact, what often happens in cooperative groups that produce a single report, worksheet, or other group product is that the most able group members simply do the work or give the answers to their teammates, which may be the most efficient strategy for group productivity but is a poor strategy for individual learning. There are several studies in which productivity measures were at variance with learning outcomes. Haines and McKeachie (1967) found that psychology students in large discussion groups covered more questions under cooperative incentives than under competitive ones, but the groups did not differ on exams they took by themselves. Smith, Madden, and Sobel (1957) found more ideas expressed in a cooperative discussion group than in a competitively structured group, but there were no differences in recall of the material discussed. D. W. Johnson, R. T. Johnson, J. Johnson, and Anderson (1976) and D. W. Johnson, R. T. Johnson, and Scott (1978) found that students who worked cooperatively and then took a test on which they could help each other performed much better than did students who worked alone and took the tests by themselves. However, when the tests were given to the cooperative students individually, they did no better than the individual students in one study (D. W. Johnson et al., 1976) and worse than the individual students in the other (D. W. Johnson et al., 1978).

Because it makes sense only at the individual level, learning is a performance measure that resembles "means-independent" tasks studied in many social psychological laboratory studies. In these studies, the evidence does not clearly favor cooperative incentives (Miller & Hamblin, 1963). The DeCharms (1957) study in which subjects could do little to help one another found no differences between cooperative and competitive incentives. When differences favoring cooperative incentive structures are found on tasks on which helping is forbidden or useless, it is usually because a cooperative incentive is being compared with no incentive at all. Hurlock (1927) found that students worked more arithmetic problems when they worked in teams trying to "beat" another team than when they simply were asked to work problems by themselves with no incentive. However, when both groups received some reward, cooperative and competitive incentive structures tended to produce equal performance (e.g., Seta, Paulus, & Schkade, 1976) or competition actually exceeded cooperation in effect on performance (e.g., Bruning, Sommer, and Jones, 1966; Scott & Cherrington, 1974; Weinstein & Holzbach, 1972).

In their meta-analysis entitled "Effects of Cooperative, Competitive, and Individualistic Goal Structures on Achievement," D. W. Johnson and colleagues (1981) reviewed 122 studies. They concluded that "the overall effects stand as strong evidence for the superiority of cooperation in promoting achievement and productivity. . . . Given the general dissatisfaction with the level of competence achieved by students in the public school system, educators may wish to considerably increase the use of cooperative learning procedures to promote higher student achievement" (p. 58). This unequivocal conclusion, based on a substantial difference in effect size favoring cooperative over individualistic and competitive incentive structures, would appear to make the cautions discussed in this chapter concerning the effects of cooperation on learning irrelevant. However, despite the title, only about 40 of the 122 studies reviewed involved comparisons of cooperative and competitive or individualistic methods with *individual achievement* as a dependent variable (see Slavin, 1984). Most of the studies compared group productivity with individual productivity on tasks on which group productivity was obviously more effective, such as jointly solving mazes, number problems, scrambled words, and so on. In one study, the dependent variable was scores in a card game, in which cooperating individuals could share cards to get a higher score (Workie, 1974). One (Bjorkland, Johnson, & Krotee, 1980) involved golf performance, and another (Martino & Johnson, 1979) involved swimming and compared the number of swimming skills gained by two learning-disabled students who learned cooperatively with the number gained by two who learned individualistically. Many of the studies involved building block towers, manipulating apparatus, judging weights, and other tasks minimally related to school achievement (e.g., Gordon, 1924; Graziano et al., 1976; Raven & Eachus, 1963). Of the studies that did involve achievement, many simply found that two or more students who take a test together do better than students who work alone (e.g., Garibaldi, 1979; Hudgins, 1960; D. W. Johnson & R. T. Johnson, 1979; D. W. Johnson et al., 1976; D. W. Johnson et al., 1978; D. W. Johnson, R. Johnson, & Skon, 1979; Laughlin & Bitz, 1975; Laughlin, Branch, & Johnson, 1969). Thus, the net direction of the effects of cooperative, competitive, and individualistic incentive and task structures per se on individual learning is not resolved by the Johnson et al. (1981) meta-analysis (Slavin, 1984).

The purpose of the foregoing discussion was to illustrate the observation that the evidence of the laboratory and brief field studies is inconclusive with respect to the effects of helping on individual learning. Clearly, studies of group productivity or other studies in which working together is obviously more effective than working separately add little to an understanding of how different task structures affect individual learning, and such studies dominate the social psychological laboratory literature on cooperation, competition, and individualization. Because individual learning is an individual task, the most relevant literature for a theory of cooperation and learning would be the studies of other individual tasks that tend to find equal or greater performance under competitive and individualistic conditions than under cooperative conditions. However, learning is not just like typing or coding, either. For certain kinds of learning, discussion under cooperative conditions may improve subsequent individual achievement. For example, discussion of text improves student recall of the text content more than reviewing the text alone (Dansereau, 1985; Slavin & Tanner, 1979). Engaging in controversy over social studies materials apparently improves recall of important concepts (D. W. Johnson & R. T. Johnson, 1979), as does controversy among pairs of nonconservers on Piagetian conservation tasks (Ames & Murray, 1982). Thus,

studying in small groups may in itself be more effective than solitary s
some learning tasks, but at this point the laboratory research on this is *l*

Group Norms

Helping between group members is not the only means by which cooperative
incentive (as opposed to task) structures might influence individual performance.
Another mediating variable that could link cooperative incentive structures to
increased performance is group member support for whatever helps the group to
be rewarded or group norms favoring performance. For example, in Ms. Cooper's class, students encourage one another to learn the geography of Europe
because the group's success depends on the individual learning of all group
members. These norms are central to Deutsch's (1949b) theory of cooperation
and competition, and in his study of cooperating discussion groups he docu-
mented their occurrence (Deutsch, 1949a). Thomas (1957) also found that cooperative incentives led to peer norms favoring the performance of tasks that
help the group to be rewarded. Slavin (1975) and Slavin, DeVries, and Hulten
(1975) found that students in cooperative groups who gained in academic performance also gained in sociometric status in cooperative groups, whereas they lost
status in competitive groups. Hulten and DeVries (1976), Madden and Slavin
(1983), and Slavin (1978) found that students who had worked in cooperative
learning groups were significantly more likely than control students to agree that
their classmates wanted them to do their best. These findings indicate that peer
norms do come to favor achievement as a consequence of cooperative incentive
structures.

If group member norms support performance of tasks that help the group to
succeed, it seems logical that this would improve performance on the part of
group members. Coleman (1961) found that in schools in which academic
achievement helped a student to be accepted by the "leading crowd," the bright-
est students turned their attention more toward doing well academically than they
did in schools in which achievement was not so well esteemed by the peer group.
Student support for academic goals was also found by Brookover, Beady, Flood,
Schweitzer, and Wisenbaker (1979) to be a strong predictor of student achievement, controlling for student background factors. Thus, the evidence supports a
conclusion that group member helping on a group task and group member norms
supporting performance are consequences of cooperative incentive structures and,
under certain circumstances, may increase performance, including learning.

Diffusion of Responsibility

Although the effects of group tasks and group norms favoring achievement are
likely to have positive or, at worst, neutral effects on performance, there is one

effect of cooperative incentives whose net impact is probably to *decrease* performance. This is the problem of diffusion of responsibility. In a cooperative group, it is often possible for individuals to be rewarded even if they themselves made little contribution to the group, or for individuals to fail to be rewarded even though they have done their utmost (Slavin, 1977). Laboratory science groups in which a single lab report is produced are good examples of this problem; some students always seem to find a way to get others to do the work. For this reason, studies in which a single product is made by a group are the most likely to show significantly greater gains in individual learning for competitive or individualistic groups than for cooperative ones (D. W. Johnson et al., 1978; Julian & Perry, 1967). Diffusion of responsibility is highest when group members can substitute for one another in performing the group task. When this is possible, some students are likely to do the minimum, hoping that their teammates will pick up the slack. In theory, diffusion of responsibility should be a very serious problem in cooperative incentive and task structures. According to expectancy theory (Atkinson & Birch, 1978; Kukla, 1972), given a reward of a certain value, motivation is related to the difference between the probability that individuals will be successful if they do their best minus the probability that they will be successful if they do not do their best (Slavin, 1978, 1980). In a cooperative incentive structure, especially one involving a large group, the chances that any group member's extraordinary efforts will make a difference in the group's success is far less than would be the case in an individualistic or a fair competitive structure, where extraordinary effort is more likely to pay off (Slavin, 1977, 1978).

Because cooperative incentive structures are common in adult life (if not in classrooms), societies have worked out many ways to deal with the inherent problem of diffusion of responsibility. These include repeated exhortations to group members about the virtues of cooperation or of doing whatever helps the group to be rewarded. The pep talk before the game is an example of this, as are special televised appeals by the president to conserve energy or to do anything that may not be in an individual's best interests but is in the nation's best interest (a nation is a cooperative incentive and task structure). Another way that groups combat diffusion of responsibility is to have interpersonal sanctions for doing whatever helps the group: Teammates cheer each other on and express norms in favor of practicing and doing one's best. If a girl on a swimming team decides to skip practice or miss an important meet, her teammates are likely to be upset with her (much in contrast to the situation in a classroom, in which skipping school may be tolerated or even encouraged by peers). If group members' performances are visible to the other group members, they are likely to administer a very contingent reward and punishment system to ensure that group members are all doing their best.

In summary, individuals placed under a cooperative incentive are likely to

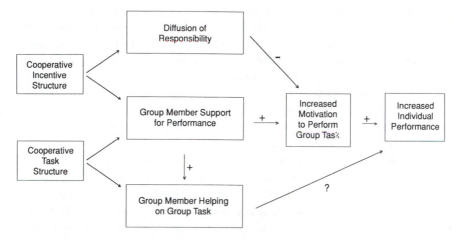

Figure 7.1. Simple theoretical model of effects of cooperative incentive and task structures on performance. From Slavin (1983a). Reprinted with permission.

encourage one another to do whatever helps the group to succeed and to help one another with the group task. Cooperative incentive structures are also likely to increase diffusion of responsibility, because each group member's own rewards are no longer dependent on his or her own efforts alone. The effect of group member encouragement on performance is probably positive, but the effect of helping may or may not be positive, depending on the kind of task involved. The effect of diffusion of responsibility is to reduce the chances that additional effort will be rewarded and thus is likely to reduce performance. Cooperative task structures are hypothesized to increase performance by increasing helping among group members and by influencing group members to encourage one another to perform the group task.

A model of how cooperative incentive and task structures might affect performance is depicted in Figure 7.1 (from Slavin, 1983a). Again, there is only one route by which cooperative incentive structures may be definitely assumed to enhance individual motivation and thus individual performance, the route through group member support for performance. Group members' helping one another may or may not improve individual performance, depending on what the task and outcome measures are. Diffusion of responsibility, which increases as group size increases, is hypothesized to have a negative effect on individual motivation (and thus performance).

What is implied in Figure 7.1 is not, of course, that the net effect of cooperative incentive and task structures on individual performance is zero. What it is meant to convey is that the net effect depends on whether the cooperative incentive and task structures are designed to maximize the positive effects and minimize the negative ones. For example, all of the ways (described earlier) that group members use to reduce the effects of diffusion of responsibility essentially involve accentuating group member support for performance (or negative sanctions for nonperformance). In structuring a group task to increase individual performance, there are many ways to activate group support for performance. Making group member contributions visible and quantifiable makes it possible for group members to accurately identify contributing and noncontributing members. This may be done by making the group reward depend on the sum of the members' individual performances (as in a wrestling or a chess team) or by giving each member a unique subtask (as in an assembly line). Increasing the value of group rewards is likely to increase motivation to apply interpersonal sanctions to motivate members' efforts. The impact of helping can also be influenced by restructuring the task to improve performance under cooperative conditions. This is likely to be the case whenever the group's goal is to produce some product, as in problem-solving tasks or projects. However, when the goal is not a group product but is an individual outcome (such as learning), helping can be made more effective, for example, by training group members in effective tutoring methods or by providing materials that lend themselves to peer learning (see, e.g., Slavin, Leavey, & Madden, 1984). Making the group goal and means of achieving it as clear as possible may also focus group members' efforts on effective helping. Certain learning tasks, such as comprehending technical material (Dansereau, 1985) or acquiring conservation principles (Murray, 1982), seem to lend themselves to cooperative task structures and may not require group rewards at all.

Seen in the light of the model outlined in Figure 7.1, the results of the laboratory research are no longer inconsistent. As noted earlier in this chapter, when positive effects of cooperative incentive and task structures on performance are found in brief experiments (e.g., Klugman, 1944; Slavin & Tanner, 1979), the tasks involved have tended to be ones where helping is likely to improve performance and group members can easily monitor and thereby reinforce each others' performance. Where competitive or individualistic incentives have produced greater performance, the tasks have tended to be ones on which helping is unlikely to make much difference (e.g., DeCharms, 1957) or individual group members' contributions are difficult to observe or reinforce and individuals may easily substitute for one another in performing the group task (e.g., D. W. Johnson et al., 1978; Julian & Perry, 1967).

Actually, as noted earlier, brief laboratory or field-based laboratory studies are inherently biased against cooperative incentive and task structures. Diffusion of responsibility can occur from the first minutes a group is together. Helping strategies and especially group member support and norms favoring performance are likely to take time to develop. However, although the laboratory research on cooperative incentive and task structures has not produced performance effects that are unambiguous in general direction, it can support an understanding of the conditions under which positive or negative results are likely to be seen.

Alternative Perspectives on Cooperative Learning

The theory outlined in the preceding section is an example of a *motivational* perspective on the achievement of cooperative learning, in that it emphasizes the potential effects of cooperative incentive structures (as opposed to task structures). However, there are several quite different perspectives on cooperative learning. The following sections (adapted from Slavin, 1989) expand on the motivational perspectives and review alternative perspectives, summarize the empirical support for each, and present an integrative theory of cooperative learning and achievement.

Motivational Perspectives

Motivational perspectives on cooperative learning focus primarily on the reward or goal structures under which students operate (see Slavin, 1977, 1983a). From a motivationalist perspective (e.g., D. W. Johnson et al., 1981; Slavin, 1983a), cooperative incentive structures create a situation in which the only way group members can attain their own personal goals is if the group is successful. Therefore, to meet their personal goals, group members must both help their teammates to do whatever helps the group to succeed and, perhaps even more important, encourage them to exert maximum efforts. In other words, rewarding groups based on group performance (or the sum of individual performances) creates an interpersonal reward structure in which group members will give or withhold social reinforcers (e.g., praise, encouragement) in response to teammates' task-relative efforts (Slavin, 1983a). One intervention that uses cooperative goal structures is the group contingency (Slavin, 1987), in which group rewards are given based on group members' behaviors. The theory underlying group contingencies does not require that group members be able to actually help one another or work together. The fact that outcomes are dependent on one another's behavior is enough to motivate students to engage in behaviors that help the group to be rewarded, because the group incentive induces students to encourage goal-directed behaviors among their teammates (Slavin, 1983a). A substantial literature in the behavior modification tradition has found that group contingencies can be very effective at improving students' appropriate behaviors and achievement (Hayes, 1976; Litow & Pumroy, 1975).

The motivationalist critique of traditional classroom organization holds that the competitive grading and informal reward system of the classroom creates peer norms opposing academic efforts (Coleman, 1961). Because one student's success decreases the chances that others will succeed, students are likely to express norms reflecting that high achievement is for "nerds" or teachers' pets. Such work restriction norms are familiar in industry, where the "rate buster" is scorned by his or her fellow workers (Vroom, 1969). However, by having students work together toward a common goal, they may be motivated to express norms favoring academic achievement, to reinforce one another for academic efforts.

Not surprisingly, motivational theorists incorporate group rewards into their cooperative learning methods. In methods developed by my colleagues and myself at Johns Hopkins University (Slavin, 1986) students can earn certificates or other recognition if their average team scores on quizzes or other individual assignments exceed a preestablished criterion. Methods developed by D. W. and R. T. Johnson (1986b) and their colleagues at the University of Minnesota often give students grades based on group performance, which is defined in several different ways. The theoretical rationale for these group rewards is that if students value the success of the group, they will encourage and help one another to achieve, much in contrast to the situation in the traditional, competitive classroom.

Evidence from practical applications of cooperative learning in elementary and secondary schools supports the motivational position that group rewards are essential to the effectiveness of cooperative learning, with one critical qualification. Use of group goals or group rewards enhances the achievement outcomes of cooperative learning if and only if the group rewards are based on the individual learning of all group members (Slavin, 1983a, 1990). Most often, this means that team scores are computed based on average scores on quizzes that all teammates take individually, without teammate help. For example, in STAD (Slavin, 1986) students work in mixed-ability teams to learn material initially presented by the teacher. Following this, students take individual quizzes on the material, and the teams may earn certificates based on the degree to which team members have improved their own past records. The only way the team can succeed is to ensure that all team members have learned, so the team members' activities focus on explaining concepts to one another, helping one another practice, and encouraging one another to achieve. In contrast, if group rewards are given based on a single group product (e.g., the team completes one worksheet or solves one problem), there is little incentive for group members to explain concepts to one another, and one or two group members may do all the work (Slavin, 1983b).

A recent review of 68 studies of cooperative learning in elementary and secondary schools that lasted at least 4 weeks compared achievement gains in cooperative learning and control groups. Of 43 studies of cooperative learning methods that provided group rewards based on the sum of group members' individual learning, nearly all found positive effects on achievement (Slavin, 1990). The median effect size for the 32 studies from which effect sizes could be computed was .30 (30% of a standard deviation separated cooperative learning and control treatments). In contrast, studies of methods that rewarded groups based on a single group product or that provided no group rewards found few positive effects. Comparisons within studies found similar patterns; group goals based on the sum of individual learning performances were necessary to the instructional effectiveness of the cooperative learning models (e.g., Huber, Bogatzki, & Winter, 1982).

Social Cohesion Perspectives

One theoretical perspective somewhat related to the motivational viewpoint holds that the effects of cooperative learning on achievement are strongly mediated by the cohesiveness of the group, in essence that students will help one another learn because they care about one another and want one another to succeed. This perspective is similar to the motivational perspective in that it emphasizes primarily motivational rather than cognitive explanations for the instructional effectiveness of cooperative learning. However, motivational theorists hold that students help each other learn because it is in their own interests to do so. Social cohesion theorists, in contrast, emphasize the idea that students help group members learn because they care about the group. A hallmark of the social cohesion perspective is an emphasis on team-building activities in preparation for cooperative learning and on processing or group self-evaluation during and after group activities. Social cohesion theorists tend to downplay or reject the influence of group incentives and individual accountability held by motivationalist researchers to be essential. For example, Cohen (1986, pp. 69–70) states that "if the task is challenging and interesting, and if students are sufficiently prepared for skills in group process, students will experience the process of groupwork itself as highly rewarding. . . . [N]ever grade or evaluate students on their individual contributions to the group product." Cohen's work as well as that of Sharan and Hertz-Lazarowitz (1980) and Aronson (Aronson, Blaney, Stephan, Sikes, & Snapp, 1978) and their colleagues is based more on social cohesiveness theories. Cohen, Aronson, and Sharan all use forms of cooperative learning in which students take on individual roles within the group, which Slavin (1983a) calls "task specialization" methods. In Aronson's Jigsaw method, students study material on one of four or five topics distributed among the group members. Th~~~~ ~eet in "expert groups" to share information on their topics with membe teams who had the same topic and then take turns presenting their team. In the Sharan and Hertz-Lazarowitz Group Investigation me take on topics within a unit studied by the class as a whole and subdivide each topic into tasks distributed among members of the group. Each student investigates his or her subtopic individually and ultimately presents their findings to the class as a whole. Cohen's adaptation of DeAvila and Duncan's (1980) Finding Out/Descubrimiento program has students take different roles in discovery-oriented science activities.

One main purpose of the task specialization used in Jigsaw, Group Investigation, and Finding Out/Descubrimiento is to create interdependence among group members. In the methods of D. W. Johnson and R. T. Johnson, a somewhat similar form of interdependence is created by having students take on roles as "checker," "recorder," "observer," and so on. The idea is that if students value their teammates (as a result of team-building and other cohesiveness-building activities) and are dependent on one another, they are likely to encourage and help one another to succeed. The Johnson and Johnson (1986b) work straddles the social cohesion and motivationalist perspectives described in this chapter; while their models do use group goals and group incentives, their theoretical writings emphasize development of group cohesion through team building, group self-evaluation, and other means more characteristic of social cohesion theorists.

The achievement outcomes of cooperative learning methods using task specialization are unclear. Research on Jigsaw has not generally found positive effects of this method on student achievement (Slavin, 1990). One problem with this method is that students have limited exposure to material other than that which they studied themselves, so learning gains on their own topics may be offset by losses on their teammates' topics. In contrast, there is evidence that when it is well implemented, Group Investigation can significantly increase student achievement (Sharan & Shachar, 1988). In studies of at least 4 weeks' duration, the Johnson and Johnson (1986b) methods have not been found to increase achievement more than individualistic methods unless they incorporate group rewards (in this case, group grades) based on the average of group members' individual quiz scores (Slavin, 1990).

Research on practical classroom applications of methods based on social cohesion theories provides inconsistent support for the proposition that building cohesiveness among students through team building alone (i.e., without group incentives) will enhance student achievement. There is some evidence that group processing activities such as reflection at the end of each class period on the group's activities can enhance the achievement effects of cooperative learning (Yager, R. T. Johnson, D. W. Johnson, & Snider, 1986). On the other hand an Israeli study found that team-building activities had no effect on the achievement outcomes of Jigsaw (Rich, Amir, & Slavin, 1986).

In general, methods that emphasize team building and group process but do not provide specific group rewards based on the learning of all group members are no more effective than traditional instruction in increasing achievement (Slavin,

1990). One major exception is Group Investigation (Sharan & Hertz-Lazarowitz, 1980; Sharan & Shachar, 1988). However, in this method groups are evaluated based on their group products, which are composed of unique contributions made by each group member. Thus, this method may be using a form of the group goals and individual accountability held by motivationalist theories to be essential to the instructional effectiveness of cooperative learning.

Cognitive Perspectives

The major alternatives to the motivationalist and social cohesiveness perspectives on cooperative learning, both of which focus primarily on group norms and interpersonal influence, are the cognitive perspectives, which contend that interactions among students will in themselves increase student achievement for reasons that have to do with mental processing of information rather than with motivations. Cooperative methods developed by cognitive theorists involve neither the group goals that are the cornerstone of the motivationalist methods nor the emphasis on building group cohesiveness characteristic of the social cohesion methods. However, there are several quite different cognitive perspectives.

Developmental Perspective. One widely researched set of cognitive theories is the developmental perspective (e.g., Damon, 1984; Murray, 1982). The fundamental assumption of the developmental perspective on cooperative learning is that interaction among children while performing appropriate tasks facilitates learning of critical concepts. Vygotsky (1978, p. 86) defines the zone of proximal development as "the distance between the actual developmental level as determined by independent problem solving and the level of potential development as determined through problem solving under adult guidance *or in collaboration with more capable peers*" (emphasis added). In his view, collaborative activity among children promotes growth because children of similar ages are likely to be operating within one another's proximal zones of development, modeling in the collaborating group behaviors more advanced than those they could perform as individuals. Vygotsky (1978, p. 86) described the influence of collaborative activity on learning as follows: "Functions are first formed in the collective in the form of relations among children and then become mental functions for the individual. . . . Research shows that reflection is spawned from argument."

Similarly, Piaget (1926) held that social-arbitrary knowledge – language, values, rules, morality, and symbol systems – can only be learned in interactions with others. Peer interaction is also important in logical-mathematical thought in disequilibrating the child's egocentric conceptualizing and providing feedback to the child about the validity of logical constructions.

There is a great deal of empirical support for the idea that peer interaction can help nonconservers become conservers. Many studies have shown that when conservers and nonconservers of about the same age work collaboratively on tasks requiring conservation, the nonconservers generally develop and maintain conservation concepts (Bell, Grossen, & Perret-Clermont, 1985; Murray, 1982; Perret-Clermont, 1980). In fact, a few studies (e.g., Ames & Murray, 1982; Mugny & Doise, 1978) have found that pairs of disagreeing nonconservers who had to come to consensus on conservation problems both gained in conservation. The importance of peers operating in one another's proximal zones of development was demonstrated by Kuhn (1972), who found that a small difference in cognitive level between a child and a social model was more conducive to cognitive growth than a larger difference.

On the basis of these and other findings, many Piagetians (e.g., Damon, 1984; Murray, 1982; Wadsworth, 1984) have called for an increased use of cooperative activities in schools. They argue that interaction among students on learning tasks will lead *in itself* to improved student achievement. Students will learn from one another because in their discussions of the content, cognitive conflicts will arise, inadequate reasoning will be exposed, disequilibration will occur, and higher quality understandings will emerge.

From the developmental perspective, the effects of cooperative learning on student achievement would be largely or entirely due to the use of cooperative *tasks*. In this view, the opportunity for students to discuss, argue, and present their own and hear one another's viewpoints is the critical element of cooperative learning with respect to student achievement. For example, Damon (1984, p. 335) integrates Piagetian, Vygotskian, and Sullivanian perspectives on peer collaboration to propose a "conceptual foundation for a peer-based plan of education":

1. Through mutual feedback and debate, peers motivate one another to abandon misconceptions and search for better solutions.
2. The experience of peer communication can help a child master social processes, such as participation and argumentation, and cognitive processes, such as verification and criticism.
3. Collaboration between peers can provide a forum for discovery learning and can encourage creative thinking.
4. Peer interaction can introduce children to the process of generating ideas.

However, Damon (1984, p. 337) explicitly rejects the use of "extrinsic incentives as part of the group learning situation," arguing that "there is no compelling reason to believe that such inducements are an important ingredient in peer learning."

One category of practical cooperative methods closely related to the developmental perspective is group discovery methods in mathematics, such as Burns's

(1981) Groups of Four method. In these techniques, students work in small groups to solve complex problems with relatively little teacher guidance. They are expected to discover mathematical principles by working with unit blocks, manipulatives, diagrams, and other concrete aids.

The theory underlying the presumed contribution of the group format is that in the exploration of opposing perceptions and ideas, higher order understandings will emerge; also, students operating within one another's proximal zones of development will model higher quality solutions for one another. However, studies of group discovery methods such as Groups of Four (Burns, 1981) find few achievement benefits for them in comparison to traditional expository teaching (Davidson, 1985; L. C. Johnson, 1985; L. C. Johnson & Waxman, 1985).

Despite considerable support from theoretical and laboratory research, practical cooperative learning methods based on developmental or discovery theories have yet to demonstrate their instructional effectiveness outside of the laboratory. However, it is likely that the cognitive processes described by developmental theorists are important as mediating variables to explain the effects of group goals and group tasks on student achievement (Slavin, 1987, 1990). This possibility is explored in the last section.

Cognitive Elaboration Perspective. A cognitive perspective on cooperative learning quite different from the developmental viewpoint is one that might be called the cognitive elaboration perspective. Research in cognitive psychology has long held that if information is to be retained in memory and related to information already in memory, the learner must engage in some sort of cognitive restructuring, or elaboration, of the material (Wittrock, 1978). One of the most effective means of elaboration is explaining the material to someone else. Research on peer tutoring has long found achievement benefits for the tutor as well as the tutee (Devin-Sheehan, Feldman, & Allen, 1976). More recently, Dansereau and his colleagues at Texas Christian University have found in an impressive series of brief studies that college students working on structured "cooperative scripts" can learn technical material or procedures far better than can students working alone (Dansereau, 1985; also see Chapter 6 in this volume). In this method, students take roles as recaller and listener. They read a section of text, and then the recaller summarizes the information while the listener corrects any errors, fills in any omitted material, and helps think of ways both students can remember the main ideas. On the next section, the students switch roles. Dansereau (1985) found in a series of studies that although both the recaller and the listener learned more than did students working alone, the recaller learned more. This mirrors both the peer-tutoring findings and the findings of Webb (1985; also see Chapter 5 in this volume), who discovered that the students who gained the most from cooperative activities were those who provided elaborated explanations to others. In this research as well as in Dansereau's, students who received elaborated explanations learned more than those who worked alone, but not as much as those who served as explainers.

One practical use of the cognitive elaboration potential of cooperative learning is in writing process models (Graves, 1983), in which students work in peer response groups or form partnerships to help one another draft, revise, and edit compositions. Such models have been found to be effective in improving creative writing (Hillocks, 1984), and a writing process model emphasizing use of peer response groups is part of the Cooperative Integrated Reading and Composition (CIRC) program (Stevens, Madden, Slavin, & Farnish, 1987), which has been found to increase student writing achievement. Part of the theory behind the use of peer response groups is that if students learn to evaluate others' writing, they will become better writers themselves, a variant of the cognitive elaboration explanation. However, it is unclear at present how much of the effectiveness of writing process models can be ascribed to the use of cooperative peer response groups as opposed to other factors (such as the revision process itself).

One interesting development in recent years that relates to the cognitive elaboration perspective on cooperative learning is Reciprocal Teaching (Palincsar & Brown, 1984), a method for teaching reading comprehensive skills. In this technique, students are taught to formulate questions for one another around narrative or expository texts. In doing so, they must process the material themselves and learn how to focus in on the essential elements of the reading passages. Studies of Reciprocal Teaching have generally supported its effects on student achievement (Palincsar, 1987).

Practice Perspective.   One perspective on cooperative learning that has rarely been articulated is one based on the idea that cooperative learning increases opportunities to practice or rehearse material to proficiency. Direct instruction theorists (e.g., Brophy, 1979) hold that opportunities to practice are critical determinants of instructional effectiveness. At least one theorist, Rosenshine (Rosenshine & Stevens, 1986), accounts for the success of cooperative learning largely in these terms. Practice explanations make most sense in connection with the learning of skills or information with high memory demands but few concepts, such as spelling and math facts. In fact, two of the only studies to find positive effects from forms of cooperative learning lacking group rewards or individual accountability are two Dutch studies of pair learning in spelling (Van Oudenhoven, Van Berkum, & Swen-Koopmans, 1987; Van Oudenhoven, Wiersma, & Van Yperen, 1987). In this subject, it may be apparent to students that the opportunity to take turns quizzing one another on spelling lists is simply more effective than trying to study alone, and no incentives may be needed.

Classroom Organization Perspective

One perspective on cooperative learning that has not been identified previously focuses on the ability of students to take responsibility for managing themselves in cooperative groups, freeing the teacher to attend to more essential tasks (such as teaching). For example, in a class using reading groups, students can work with one another on meaningful activities during follow-up time while the teacher is teaching one of the reading groups. This use of cooperative learning is essential to CIRC (Stevens et al., 1987) and Team Assisted Individualization–Mathematics (TAI-Math) (Slavin, 1985). In both of these methods, students work in mixed-ability learning teams while the teacher calls up groups of students at the same performance level for lessons. Back at their desks, the remaining students work together on activities that advance them in the subject. In TAI-Math, they work separately on units, check each other's work, and provide explanations and help. In CIRC, students take turns reading to one another; they locate characters, settings, problems, and problem solutions; they summarize stories to one another; and they practice spelling, vocabulary, decoding, and comprehension skills. Both TAI (Slavin, 1985) and CIRC (Stevens et al., 1987) have been consistently effective in increasing student achievement. The classroom organization aspect of these programs is not directly parallel to the theoretical perspectives described earlier and is not a major theoretical rationale for their effectiveness, but it provides a structure within which motivational, cognitive elaboration, and practice dynamics (among others) can operate.

Use of pairs or peer response groups in writing also takes advantage of the classroom management potential of cooperative learning. By training students to respond to one another's writing, the teacher not only is freed from the impossible burden of responding to several drafts but is also able to spend most of class time communicating with students individually.

Reconciling the Six Perspectives

The six theoretical perspectives discussed here all have well-established rationales, and most have supporting evidence. All are demonstrably "correct" in some circumstances, but none are probably both necessary and sufficient in *all* circumstances. Research in each tradition tends to establish setting conditions favorable to that perspective. For example, most research on cooperative learning models from the motivational and social cohesiveness perspectives takes place in real classrooms over extended periods, as both extrinsic motivation and social cohesion may be assumed to take time to show their effects. In contrast, studies undertaken from the developmental and cognitive elaboration perspectives tend

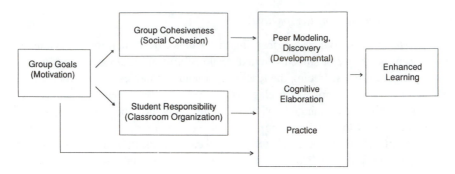

Figure 7.2. Hypothesized relationships among six perspectives on cooperative learning. From Slavin (1989). Reprinted with permission.

to be very short, making issues of motivation moot. These latter paradigms also tend to use pairs, rather than groups of four or more; pairs involve a much simpler social process than larger groups, which may need time to develop ways of working well together. Developmental research almost exclusively uses young children trying to learn conservation tasks, which bear little resemblance to the "social-arbitrary" learning that characterizes most school subjects; cognitive elaboration research mostly involves college students.

However, these alternative perspectives on cooperative learning may be seen as complementary, not contradictory. For example, motivational theorists would not argue that the cognitive theories are unnecessary. Instead, they would argue that motivation drives cognitive process, which in turn produces learning. It is unlikely that over the long haul students would engage in the kind of elaborated explanations found by Webb (1985) to be essential to profiting from cooperative activity if they had no reason to care about their teammates' learning. Similarly, motivational theorists would hold that an intermediate effect of extrinsic incentives must be to build cohesiveness, caring, and prosocial norms among group members, which could in turn affect cognitive processes. One model of the relationships among the six alternative perspectives is diagrammed in Figure 7.2 (from Slavin, 1989).

The process depicted in Figure 7.2 shows how group goals might enhance the learning outcomes of cooperative learning. Provision of group goals based on the individual learning of all group members might affect cognitive processes directly by motivating students to engage in peer modeling, cognitive elaboration, and/or practice with one another. Group goals may also lead to group cohesiveness, increasing caring and concern among group members and making them feel responsible for one another's achievement, thereby motivating students to engage in cognitive processes that enhance learning. Finally, group goals may motivate students to take responsibility for one another independently of the teacher, thereby solving important classroom organization problems and providing increased opportunities for cognitively appropriate learning activities.

From the perspective of the model diagrammed in Figure 7.2, researchers from outside the motivational perspective are attempting to short-circuit the process to intervene directly on mechanisms identified as mediating variables in the full model. For example, social cohesion theorists intervene directly on group cohesiveness by engaging in elaborate team building and group processing training. The Sharan and Shachar (1988) Group Investigation study suggests that this can be done successfully, but it takes a great deal of time and effort. In this study, teachers were trained over the course of a full year, and then teachers and students used cooperative learning for 3 months before the study began. Earlier research on Group Investigation failed to provide a comparable level of preparation of teachers and students, and the achievement results of these studies were less consistently positive (Slavin, 1989).

Cognitive theorists would hold that the cognitive processes that are essential to any theory relating cooperative learning to achievement can be created directly, without the motivational or affective changes discussed by the motivationalist and social cohesion theorists. This may turn out to be accurate for some school tasks, but at present demonstrations of learning effects from direct manipulation of peer cognitive interactions have mostly been limited to very brief durations and to tasks that lend themselves directly to the cognitive processes involved. For example, the Piagetian conservation tasks studied by developmentalists have few practical analogues in the school curriculum. However, the research on Reciprocal Teaching in reading comprehension (Palincsar & Brown, 1984) shows promise as a means of intervening directly on peer cognitive processes, and long-term applications of Dansereau's (1985) cooperative scripts for comprehension of technical material and procedural instructions seem likely to be successful.

Clearly, much work remains to be done to fully develop a theory to account for cooperative learning effects on achievement and to understand the conditions under which each of the several motivational and cognitive perspectives has explanatory value. Each of the perspectives discussed here contributes to a more complex understanding of how cooperative learning affects student achievement. Until recently, researchers have tended to work on parallel tracks, showing little recognition of work being done in other research traditions on issues related to the achievement effects of cooperative learning. It is now time to look beyond usual disciplinary boundaries to consider more broadly how cooperation among students can enhance their learning.

References

Ames, G. J., & Murray, F. B. (1982). When two wrongs make a right: Promoting cognitive change by social conflict. *Developmental Psychology, 18*, 894–897.

Aronson, E., Blaney, N., Stephan, C., Sikes, J., & Snapp, M. (1978). *The Jigsaw classroom*. Beverly Hills, CA: Sage.

Atkinson, J. W., & Birch, D. (1978). *Introduction to motivation* (2nd ed.). New York: Van Nostrand.

Bell, N., Grossen, M., & Perret-Clermont, A.-N. (1985). Socio-cognitive conflict and intellectual growth. In M. Berkowitz (Ed.), *Peer conflict and psychological growth*, (pp. 88–112). San Francisco: Jossey-Bass.

Bjorkland, R., Johnson, R., & Krotee, M. (1980). *Effects of cooperative, competitive, and individualistic goal structures on golf skills*. Unpublished manuscript, University of Minnesota.

Bossert, S. (1977). Tasks, group management, and teacher control behavior: A study of classroom organization and teacher style. *School Review, 85*, 552–565.

Brookover, W., Beady, C., Flood, P., Schweitzer, J., & Wisenbaker, J. (1979). *School social systems and student achievement*. New York: Praeger.

Brophy, J. E. (1979). Teacher behavior and its effects. *Journal of Educational Psychology, 71*, 733–750.

Bruning, J., Sommer, D., & Jones, B. (1966). The motivating effects of cooperation and competition in the means-independent situation. *Journal of Social Psychology, 68*, 269–274.

Burns, M. (1981, September). Groups of four: Solving the management problem. *Learning, 9*, 46–51.

Cohen, E. (1986). *Designing groupwork: Strategies for the heterogeneous classroom*. New York: Teachers College Press.

Coleman, J. (1961). *The adolescent society*. New York: Free Press.

Crombag, H. G. (1966). Cooperation and competition in means-interdependent triads. *Journal of Personality and Social Psychology, 4*, 692–695.

Damon, W. (1984). Peer education: The untapped potential. *Journal of Applied Developmental Psychology, 5*, 331–343.

Dansereau, D. F. (1985). Learning strategy research. In J. Segal S. Chipman, & R. Glaser (Eds.), *Thinking and learning skills: Relating instruction to basic research, Vol. 1*. Hillsdale, NJ: Erlbaum.

Davidson, N. (1985). Small-group learning and teaching in mathematics: A selective review of the research. In R. E. Slavin, S. Sharan, S. Kagan, R. Hertz-Lazarowitz, C. Webb, & R. Schmuck (Eds.), *Learning to cooperate, cooperating to learn* (pp. 211–230). New York: Plenum.

DeAvila, E., & Duncan, S. (1980). *Finding Out/Descdubrimiento*. Corte Madera, CA: Linguametrics Group.

DeCharms, R. (1957). Affiliation motivation and productivity in small groups. *Journal of Abnormal and Social Psychology, 55*, 22–226.

Deutsch, M. (1949a). An experimental study of the effects of cooperation and competition upon group process. *Human Relations, 2*, 199–231.

(1949b). A theory of cooperation and competition. *Human Relations, 2*, 129–152.

Devin-Sheehan, L., Feldman, R., & Allen, V. (1976). Research on children tutoring children: A critical review. *Review of Educational Research, 46*(3), 355–385.

Faust, W. (1959). Group vs. individual problem-solving. *Journal of Abnormal and Social Psychology, 59*, 68–72.

Garibaldi, A. (1979). The effective contributions of cooperative and group goal structures. *Journal of Educational Psychology, 71,* 788–795.

Gordon, K. (1924). Group judgements in the field of lifted weights. *Journal of Experimental Psychology, 7,* 398–400.

Graves, D. (1983). *Writing: Teachers and children at work.* Exeter, NH: Heinemann.

Graziano, W., French, D. Brownell, C., & Hartup, W. (1976). Peer interaction in same- and mixed-age triads in relation to chronological age and incentive condition. *Child Development, 47,* 707–714.

Gurnee, H. (1968). Learning under competitive and collaborative sets. *Journal of Experimental Social Psychology, 4,* 26–34.

Haines, D., & McKeachie, W. (1967). Cooperation versus competitive discussion methods in teaching introductory psychology. *Journal of Educational Psychology, 58,* 386–390.

Hammond, L., & Goldman, M. (1961). Competition and non-competition and its relationship to individual and group productivity. *Sociometry, 24,* 46–60.

Hayes, L. (1976). The use of group contingencies for behavioral control: A review. *Psychological Bulletin, 83,* 628–648.

Hillocks, G. (1984). What works in teaching composition: A meta-analysis of experimental treatment studies. *American Journal of Education, 93.* 133–170.

Huber, G. L., Bogatzki, W., & Winter, M. (1982). *Kooperation als Ziel schulischen Lehrens und Lehrens.* Tubingen, West Germany: Arbeitsbereich Padagogische Psychologie der Universität Tubingen.

Hudgins, B. (1960). Effects of group experience on individual problem solving. *Journal of Educational Psychology, 51,* 37–42.

Hulten, B. H., & DeVries, D. L. (1976). *Team competition and group practice: Effects on student achievement and attitudes* (Report No. 212). Baltimore: Johns Hopkins University, Center for Social Organization of Schools.

Hurlock, E. (1927). Use of group rivalry as an incentive. *Journal of Abnormal and Social Psychology, 22,* 278–290.

Johnson, D. W., & Johnson, R. T. (1974). Instructional structure: Cooperative, competitive or individualistic. *Review of Educational Research, 44,* 213–240.

(1979). Conflict in the classroom: Controversy and learning. *Review of Educational Research, 49,* 51–70.

(1981). Effects of cooperative and individualistic learning experiences on interethnic interaction. *Journal of Educational Psychology, 73,* 444–449.

(1986a). The effect of prolonged implementation of cooperative learning on social support within the classroom. *Journal of Psychology, 119,* 405–411.

(1986b). *Learning together and alone.* (2nd ed.). Englewood Cliffs, NJ: Prentice-Hall.

Johnson, D. W., Johnson, R. T., Johnson, J., & Anderson, D. (1976). The effects of cooperative vs. individualized instruction on student prosocial behavior, attitudes toward learning, and achievement. *Journal of Educational Psychology, 68,* 446–452.

Johnson, D. W., Johnson, R. T., & Scott, L. (1978). The effects of cooperative and individualized instruction on student attitudes and achievement. *Journal of Social Psychology, 104,* 207–216.

Johnson, D. W., Johnson, R., & Skon, L. (1979). Student achievement on different types of tasks under cooperative, competitive, and individualistic conditions. *Contemporary Educational Psychology, 4,* 99–106.

Johnson, D. W., Maruyama, G., Johnson, R., Nelson, D., & Skon, L. (1981). Effects of cooperative, competitive, and individualistic goal structures on achievement: A meta-analysis. *Psychological Bulletin, 89,* 47–62.

Johnson, L. C. (1985). *The effects of the "groups of four" cooperative learning model on student problem-solving achievement in mathematics.* Unpublished doctoral dissertation, University of Houston.

Johnson, L. C. & Waxman, H. C. (1985, March). *Evaluating the effects of the "groups of four" program.* Paper presented at the annual meeting of the American Educational Research Association, Chicago.

Julian, J., & Perry, F. (1967). Cooperation contrasted with intra-group and inter-group competition. *Sociometry, 30,* 79–90.

Klugman, S. (1944). Cooperative versus individual efficiency in problem solving. *Journal of Educational Psychology, 34,* 91–100.

Kuhn, D. (1972). Mechanism of change in the development of cognitive structures. *Child Development, 43,* 833–844.

Kukla, A. (1972). Foundations of an attributional theory of performance. *Psychological Review, 77,* 454–470.

Laughlin, P., & Bitz, D. (1975). Individual versus dyadic performance on a dysjunctive task as a function of initial ability level. *Journal of Personality and Social Psychology, 31,* 487–496.

Laughlin, P., Branch, L., & Johnson, H. (1969). Individual versus triadic performance on a unidimensional complementary task as a function of initial ability level. *Journal of Personality and Social Psychology, 12,* 144–150.

Laughlin, P., & Johnson, H. (1966). Group and individual performance on a complementary task as a function of initial ability level. *Journal of Experimental Social Psychology, 2,* 407–414.

Laughlin, P., McGlynn, R., Anderson, J., & Jacobson, E. (1968). Concept attainment by individuals versus cooperative pairs as a function of memory, sex, and concept rule. *Journal of Personality and Social Psychology, 8,* 410–417.

Lemke, E., Randle, K., & Robertshaw, C. (1969). Effects of degree of initial acquisition, group size and general mental ability on concept learning and transfer. *Journal of Educational Psychology, 60,* 75–78.

Litow, L., & Pumroy, D., (1975). A brief review of classroom group-oriented contingencies. *Journal of Applied Behavior Analysis, 8,* 341–347.

Madden, N. A., & Slavin, R. E. (1983). Effects of cooperative learning on the social acceptance of mainstreamed academically handicapped students. *Journal of Special Education, 17,* 171–182.

Maller, J. (1929). *Cooperation and competition.* New York: Teachers College, Columbia University.

Marquart, D. (1955). Group problem solving. *Journal of Social Psychology, 41,* 103–113.

Martino, L., & Johnson, D. (1979). The effects of cooperative vs. individualistic instruction on interaction between normal-progress and learning-disabled students. *Journal of Social Psychology, 107,* 177–183.

Michaels, J. (1977). Classroom reward structures and academic performance. *Review of Educational Research, 47,*(1), 87–88.

Miller, L., & Hamblin, R. (1963). Interdependence, differential rewarding, and productivity. *American Sociology Review, 28,* 768–778.

Mintz, A. (1951). Non-adaptive group behavior. *Journal of Abnormal and Social Psychology, 46,* 150–159.

Mugny, G., & Doise, W. (1978). Socio-cognitive conflict and structuration of individual and collective performances. *European Journal of Social Psychology, 8,* 181–192.

Murray, F. B. (1982). Teaching through social conflict. *Contemporary Educational Psychology, 7,* 257–271.

Palincsar, A. S. (1987, April). *Reciprocal teaching: Field evaluations in remedial and content area reading.* Paper presented at the annual meeting of the American Educational Research Association, Washington, D.C.

Palincsar, A. S., & Brown, A. L. (1984). Reciprocal teaching of comprehension monitoring activities. *Cognition and Instruction, 2,* 117–175.

Perret-Clermont, A.-N. (1980). *Social interaction and cognitive development in children.* London: Academic Press.

Piaget, J. (1926). *The language and thought of the child.* New York: Harcourt Brace.

Raven, B., & Eachus, H. (1963). Cooperation and competition in means-interdependent triads. *Journal of Abnormal and Social Psychology, 67,* 307–316.

Rich, Y., Amir, Y., & Slavin, R. E. (1986). *Instructional strategies for improving children's cross-ethnic relations.* Ramat Gan, Israel: Bar Ilan University, Institute for the Advancement of Social Integration in the Schools.

Rosenshine, R., & Stevens, R. (1986). Teaching functions. In M. C. Wittrock (Ed.), *Handbook of research on teaching* (3rd ed.), pp. 367–391. New York: Macmillan.

Ryack, B. (1965). A comparison of individual and group learning of nonsense syllables. *Journal of Personality and Social Psychology, 2,* 296–299.

Scott, W., & Cherrington, D. (1974). Effects of competitive, cooperative, and individualistic reinforcement contingencies. *Journal Personality and Social Psychology, 30,* 748–758.

Seta, J., Paulus, P., & Schkade, J. (1976). Effects of group size and proximity under cooperative and competitive conditions. *Journal of Personality and Social Psychology, 34,* 47–53.

Sharan, S., & Hertz-Lazarowitz, R. (1980). A group-investigation method of cooperative learning in the classroom. In S. Sharan, P. Hare, C. Webb, & R. Hertz-Lazarowitz (Eds.), *Cooperation in education.* Provo, UT: Brigham Young University Press.

Sharan, S., & Shachar, H. (1988). *Language and learning in the cooperative classroom.* New York: Springer.

Sirotnik, K. A. (1982, March). *What you see is what you get: A summary of observations in over 1,000 elementary and secondary classrooms.* Paper presented at the annual meeting of the American Educational Research Association, New York.

Slavin, R. E. (1975). *Classroom reward structure: Effects on academic performance, social connectedness, and peer norms.* Unpublished doctoral dissertation, Johns Hopkins University.

(1977). Classroom reward structure: An analytic and practical review. *Review of Educational Research, 47,* 633–650.

(1978). Student teams and comparison among equals: Effects on academic performance and student attitudes. *Journal of Educational Psychology, 70,* 532–538.

(1980). Effects of individual learning expectations on student achievement. *Journal of Educational Psychology, 72,* 520–524.

(1983a). *Cooperative learning.* New York: Longman.

(1983b). When does cooperative learning increase student achievement? *Psychological Bulletin, 94,* 429–445.

(1984). Team assisted individualization: Cooperative learning and individualized instruction in the mainstreamed classroom. *Remedial and Special Education, 5*(6), 33–42.

(1985). Team-Assisted Individualization: Combining cooperative learning and individualized instruction in mathematics. In R. E. Slavin, S. Sharan, S. Kagan,

R. Hertz-Lazarowitz, C. Webb, & R. Schmuck (Eds.), *Learning to cooperate, cooperating to learn* (pp. 177–209). New York: Plenum.

(1986) *Using student team learning: Third edition.* Baltimore, MD.: Center for Social Organization of Schools, The Johns Hopkins University.

(1987). Cooperative learning: Where behavioral and humanistic approaches to classroom motivation meet. *Elementary School Journal, 88,* 9–337.

(1989). Cooperative learning and achievement: Six theoretical perspectives. In C. Ames and M. L. Maehr (Eds.), *Advances in motivation and achievement* (pp. 161–177). Greenwich, CT: JAI Press.

(1990). *Cooperative learning: Theory, research, and practice.* Englewood Cliffs, NJ: Prentice-Hall.

Slavin, R. E., DeVries, D. L., & Hulten, B. H. (1975). Individual vs. team competition: The interpersonal consequences of academic performance (Report No. 188). Baltimore: Johns Hopkins University, Center for Social Organization of Schools.

Slavin, R. E., Leavey, M., & Madden, N. A. (1984). Combining cooperative learning and individualized instruction: Effects on student mathematics achievement, attitudes, and behaviors. *Elementary School Journal, 84,* 409–422.

Slavin, R. E., & Tanner, A. M. (1979). Effects of cooperative reward structures and individual accountability on productivity and learning. *Journal of Educational Research, 72*(5), 294–298.

Smith, A. J., Madden, H. E., & Sobel, R. (1957). Productivity and recall in cooperative and competitive discussion groups. *Journal of Psychology, 43,* 193–204.

Stevens, R. J., Madden, N. A., Slavin, R. E., & Farnish, A. M. (1987). Cooperative Integrated Reading and Composition: Two field experiments. *Reading Research Quarterly, 22,* 433–454.

Thomas, E. J. (1957). Effects of facilitative role interdependence on group functioning. *Human Relations, 10,* 347–366.

Thorndike, R. L. (1938). On what type of task will a group do well? *Journal of Abnormal and Social Psychology, 33,* 409–413.

Van Oudenhoven, J. P., Van Berkum, G., & Swen-Koopmans, T. (1987). Effect of cooperation and shared feedback on spelling achievement. *Journal of Educational Psychology, 79,* 92–94.

Van Oudenhoven, J. P., Wiersma, B., & Van Yperen, N. (1987). Effects of cooperation and feedback by fellow pupils on spelling achievement. *European Journal of Psychology of Education, 2,* 83–91.

Vroom, V. H. (1969). Industrial social psychology. In G. Lindzey & E. Aronson (Eds.), *The handbook of social psychology* (Vol. 5, 2nd ed.). Reading, MA: Addison-Wesley.

Vygotsky, L. S. (1978). *Mind in society* (M. Cole, V. John-Steiner, S. Scribner, & E. Souberman, Eds.). Cambridge: Harvard University Press.

Wadsworth, B. J. (1984). *Piaget's theory of cognitive and affective development* (3rd ed.). New York: Longman.

Webb, N. (1985). Student interaction and learning in small groups: A research summary. In R. E. Slavin, S. Sharan, S. Kagan, R. Hertz-Lazarowitz, C. Webb, & R. Schmuck (Eds.), *Learning to cooperate, cooperating to learn* (pp. 147–172). New York: Plenum.

Weinstein, A. G., & Holzbach, R. L. (1972). *Effects of financial inducement on performance under two task structures.* Proceedings of 80th Annual Convention of the American Psychological Association. Washington, D.C. APA.

Wittrock, M. C. (1978). The cognitive movement in instruction. *Educational Psychologist, 13,* 15–29.

Workie, A. (1974). The relative productivity of cooperation and competition. *Journal of Social Psychology, 92,* 225–230.

Yager, S., Johnson, R. T., Johnson, D. W., & Snider, B. (1986). The impact of group processing on achievement in cooperative learning. *Journal of Social Psychology, 126,* 389–397.

8   Positive Interdependence: Key to Effective Cooperation

David W. Johnson and Roger T. Johnson

Cooperation is not effective under all conditions. The variables mediating cooperation's effectiveness have only been partially empirically demonstrated. One of the key mediating variables is the degree to which participants perceive they are interdependent in that they share a mutual fate and that their success is mutually caused. The purposes of this chapter are to conceptually analyze positive interdependence and to review a systematic series of studies we have conducted over the past few years contrasting the relative impacts of goal, reward, and resource interdependence on such outcomes as achievement and interpersonal attraction. To do so, however, positive interdependence needs to be placed in the context of social interdependence, the outcomes generally promoted by cooperation, and the barriers to implementing cooperative learning successfully.

Definition and Theory of Social Interdependence

Social interdependence exists when the outcomes of individuals are affected by the actions of others (D. W. Johnson & R. T. Johnson, 1989). There are two types of social interdependence: cooperation, which is based on positive interdependence, and competition, which is based on negative interdependence. Social interdependence may be differentiated from dependence and independence. *Social dependence* exists when the outcomes of Person A are affected by Person B's actions, but the reverse is not true. *Social independence* exists when individuals' outcomes are unaffected by each other's actions. The absence of social interdependence and dependence results in individualistic efforts. *Cooperation* is working together to accomplish shared goals. In cooperative situations, the goal attainments of participants are positively correlated: Individuals perceive that they can reach their goals if and only if the other group members also do so (Deutsch, 1949a). Thus, individuals seek outcomes that are beneficial to themselves *and* to all other individuals with whom they are cooperatively linked. *Competition* is working against each other to achieve a goal that only one or a few can attain. In competitive situations, the goals of the separate participants are so linked that there is a negative correlation among their goal attainments; each individual perceives that he or she can reach his or her goal if and only if the other participants cannot attain their goals (Deutsch, 1949). Thus, individuals seek an outcome that is personally beneficial but detrimental to all others in the situation. *Individualistic efforts* exist when individuals work by themselves to accomplish goals unrelated to those of others. In individualistic situations, there is no correlation among participants' goal attainments; individuals perceive that they can reach their goals regardless of whether other individuals attain or do not attain their goals (Deutsch, 1962; D. W. Johnson & R. T. Johnson, 1991).

Deutsch's (1949) original theory has served as a major conceptual structure for this area of inquiry for the past 40 years. His pioneering theory and research evolved from Lewin's (1935, 1948) field theory. Lewin stated that (1) the essence of a group is the interdependence among members (created by common goals), which results in the group being a "dynamic whole" so that a change in the state of any member or subgroup changes the state of any other member or subgroup; and (2) an intrinsic state of tension within group members motivates movement toward the accomplishment of the desired common goals.

Deutsch (1949a, 1962), in his theory of how the tension systems of different people may be interrelated, conceptualized two types of social interdependence (cooperative and competitive) and individualistic efforts as the absence of interdependence. Deutsch's theory was based on two basic continua: one relating to the type of interdependence among the goals of the people involved in a given situation and one relating to the type of actions taken by the people involved. He identified as the ends of one continuum two basic types of goal interdependence: *promotive,* where the goals are positively linked in such a way that the probability of one person obtaining his or her goal is positively correlated with the probability of others obtaining their goals; and *contrient,* where goals are negatively linked in such a way that the probability of one person obtaining his or her goal is negatively correlated with the probability of others obtaining their goals. He identified as the ends of the second continuum two basic types of actions by an individual: *effective,* which improves the person's chances of obtaining his or her goal; and *bungling,* which decreases the person's chances of obtaining his or her goal. He then combined the two continua to posit how they jointly affect three basic social psychological processes: *substitutability, cathexis* (i.e., the investment of psychological energy in objects and events outside oneself), and *inducibility* (i.e., openness to influence). Essentially, in cooperative situations the actions of participants substitute for each other, participants positively cathect to each other's effective actions, and there is high inducibility among participants. In competitive situations the actions of participants do not substitute for each other, participants negatively cathect to each other's effective actions, and inducibility is low.

Based on Deutsch's theorizing, it may be posited that how social interdependence is structured determines how individuals interact within the situation, which, in turn, affects their outcomes (D. W. Johnson, 1970; D. W. Johnson & R. T. Johnson, 1974). The research has focused on numerous outcomes, but the effects of social interdependence may be subsumed under three broad categories (D. W. Johnson & R. T. Johnson, 1989): (1) effort exerted to achieve, (2) quality of relationships among participants, and (3) participants' psychological adjustment and social competence. Within cooperative situations, positive interdependence is structured to create a promotive interaction pattern (which requires social skills), which largely determines participants' efforts to achieve, the quality of relationships, and psychological adjustment. Within competitive situations, negative interdependence is structured to create a contrient interaction pattern, which largely determines the same set of outcomes. Within individualistic situations, no interdependence or dependence is structured, which results in no interaction among participants, which, in turn, largely determines the three outcomes. Two interrelated questions are (1) under what conditions will cooperative, competitive, and individualistic efforts increase the effort to achieve, promote caring and committed relationships, and increase participants' psychological health and well-being, and (2) what variables mediate the effectiveness of cooperative, competitive, and individualistic efforts? In considering these two questions, only cooperation is dealt with in this chapter. To attempt to understand how cooperation works, an overview of all the existing research and the barriers to effective cooperation need to be discussed.

Overview of All the Existing Research

Over the past 20 years we have conducted a program of research that has resulted in over 80 published studies. We have also reviewed all the published and unpublished research conducted over the past 90 years comparing cooperative, competitive and individualistic efforts (see D. W. Johnson & R. T. Johnson, 1989, for a complete review). Over 520 experimental studies and 100 correlational studies have been conducted. These studies have been conducted in different historical periods, with subjects of various ages, with numerous types of tasks, with vastly different subject populations, in different settings, with different operationalizations of the independent variables, and with a wide variety of measures of the dependent variables. Therefore, the overall results have considerable power and generalizability. From the existing research, a number of conclusions may be drawn (D. W. Johnson & R. T. Johnson, 1989).

Under a broad range of conditions, cooperative efforts resulted in higher achievement and greater productivity than did competitive or individualistic efforts (D. W. Johnson & R. T. Johnson, 1989). Over the past 90 years over 378 studies on the relative impact of cooperative, competitive, and individualistic efforts have been conducted. The overall effect size is 0.67 when cooperative and competitive efforts are compared, 0.66 when cooperative and individualistic efforts are compared, and 0.29 when competitive and individualistic efforts are compared. These effect sizes are weighted for the number of findings within each study; for each dependent variable the homogeneity of the effect sizes was tested. Further analyses revealed that the results held constant when group measures of productivity were included as well as individual measures, for short-term as well as long-term studies, and when symbolic as well as tangible rewards were used. Further, increases in requirements for higher-level reasoning, critical thinking, problem solving, creativity, and the application of the learning material to real-world situations resulted in greater increases in the superiority of cooperative over both competitive and individualistic learning.

Not all the research, however, was carefully conducted. The methodological shortcomings found within many research studies may significantly reduce the certainty of the conclusion that cooperative efforts produce higher achievement than do competitive or individualistic efforts. Therefore, we analyzed the results of studies in which individuals were randomly assigned to conditions, in which there was an unambiguous and well-defined control condition, in which teacher and curriculum effects were controlled for, and in which it was verified that the experimental and control conditions were successfully implemented. When only the methodologically high quality studies are included, the effect sizes for the cooperative versus competitive and the cooperative versus individualistic comparisons go up to 0.86 and 0.88 respectively.

If cooperative learning does in fact promote higher achievement than do competitive and individualistic efforts, it would follow that operationalizations of cooperative learning that contained a mixture of cooperative, competitive, and individualistic efforts would produce lower achievement than would ''pure'' operationalizations of cooperative learning. The original Jigsaw procedure (Aronson, Blaney, Stephan, Sikes, & Snapp, 1978), for example, was a combination of resource interdependence (cooperative) and individual reward structures (individualistic). Teams Games Tournaments (DeVries & Edwards, 1974) and Student Teams Achievement Divisions (Slavin, 1980) are a mixture of cooperation and intergroup competition. Team-Assisted-Instruction (Slavin, Leavey, & Madden, 1983) is a mixture of individualistic and cooperative learning. When the results of ''pure'' and ''mixed'' operationalizations of cooperative learning were compared, the effect sizes were 0.70 and 0.37 respectively for the cooperative versus competitive comparison and 0.63 and 0.42 for the cooperative versus individualistic comparison. Pure cooperation consistently produced stronger effects.

Generally, cooperative efforts resulted in greater interpersonal attraction and more social support than did competitive or individualistic efforts (D. W. Johnson & R. Johnson, 1989). Over 180 studies on interpersonal attraction and 106 studies on social support have been conducted. The weighted effect sizes for cooperation versus competition and cooperation versus individualistic efforts were 0.65 and 0.64, respectively. When only the methodologically high quality studies were examined, the effect sizes were 0.77 and 0.67. When pure and mixed operationalizations of cooperation were compared, the effect sizes were 0.75 and 0.48 for the cooperative versus competitive comparison and 0.67 and 0.36 for the cooperative versus individualistic comparison. Similar results were found for social support.

Generally, cooperative efforts resulted in higher self-esteem and greater psychological health than did competitive or individualistic efforts (D. W. Johnson & R. T. Johnson, 1989). Over 79 studies on self-esteem have been conducted. The weighted effect sizes for cooperation versus competition and cooperation versus individualistic efforts were 0.60 and 0.44 respectively. When only the methodologically high quality studies were examined, the effect sizes were 0.68 and 0.45. When pure and mixed operationalizations of cooperation were compared, the effect sizes were 0.78 and 0.33 for the cooperative versus competitive comparison and 0.51 and 0.22 for the cooperative versus individualistic comparison.

There are bidirectional relationships among the outcomes promoted by positive interdependence. Within cooperative situations, efforts to achieve positive interpersonal relationships and psychological health are all reciprocally related (D. W. Johnson & R. Johnson, 1979). Each induces the others.

Barriers to Effective Cooperative Learning

Although the evidence demonstrating the relative effectiveness of cooperation is quite strong, it is evident that cooperation does not always work. Simply placing individuals in groups and telling them to work together does not in and of itself create effective cooperation that results in the above outcomes. There are many ways in which group efforts may go wrong. Less able members sometimes "leave it to George" to complete the group's tasks, thus creating a *free-rider* effect (Kerr & Bruun, 1983) whereby group members expend decreasing amounts of effort and just go through the teamwork motions. At the same time, the more able group members may expend less effort in an attempt to avoid the *sucker effect* of doing all the work (Kerr, 1983). High-ability group members may be deferred to and may take over the important leadership roles in ways that benefit them at the expense of the other group members (the *rich-get-richer* effect). In a learning group, for example, a more able group member may give all the explanations of what is being learned. Because the amount of time spent explaining correlates highly with the amount learned, the more able member learns a great deal while the less able members flounder as a captive audience. The time spent listening in group brainstorming can reduce the amount of time any individual can state their ideas (Hill, 1982; Lamm & Trommsdorff, 1973). Group efforts can be characterized by self-induced helplessness (Langer & Benevento, 1978), diffusion of responsibility and social loafing (Latane, Williams, & Harkins, 1979), ganging up against a task, reactance (Salomon, 1981), dysfunctional divisions of labor ("I'm the thinkist and you're the typist") (Sheingold, Hawkins, & Char, 1984), inappropriate dependence on authority (Webb, Ender, & Lewis, 1986), destructive conflict (Collins, 1970; D. W. Johnson & R. Johnson, 1979), member ineptness caused by a lack of social skills, failure to learn from mistakes, and other patterns of behavior that debilitate group performance.

Essential Components of Cooperation

The numerous barriers to effective cooperative efforts are avoided when cooperation is structured to ensure that the conditions mediating its effectiveness are present. Only under certain conditions are cooperative efforts expected to be more effective than competitive and individualistic efforts (see Figure 8.1). Three of the mediating conditions identified by the research are (D. W. Johnson & R. Johnson, 1989):

1. Clearly perceived positive interdependence that promotes personal responsibility to achieve the group's goals. Inherent in positive interdependence is individual accountability, which exists when the performance of each individual student is assessed and the results are given back to the group and the individual.
2. Considerable promotive, face-to-face interaction. High-level cooperation requires participants to promote each other's success, face-to-face, by helping, explaining, elaborating, encouraging, and supporting each other's efforts to achieve.
3. Frequent use of the relevant interpersonal and small-group skills (this includes frequent and regular processing of how effectively the skills are being used). Placing socially unskilled individuals in a group and telling them to cooperate does not guarantee that they will be able to do so. Persons must be taught the small-group and interpersonal skills required for cooperating and be motivated to use them (D. W. Johnson, 1990, 1991; D. W. Johnson & F. Johnson, 1991). Periodically, groups need to discuss what member actions are helpful and unhelpful and make decisions about what behaviors to continue or change. This is called group processing. Such processing facilitates learning of the social skills, reminds participants to practice the skills, and provides feedback as to how well the skills are being used (D. W. Johnson, R. Johnson, & Holubec, 1990).

Although all three elements are crucial, positive interdependence is commonly assumed to be the most important factor in structuring situations cooperatively. Yet there has been relatively little written about positive interdependence and

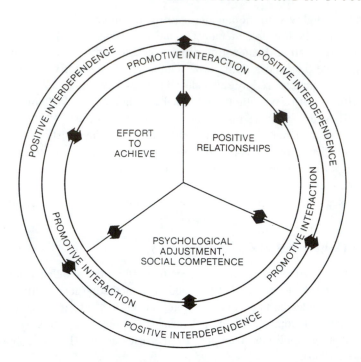

Figure 8.1. Outcomes of cooperative learning. From D. W. Johnson &
R. T. Johnson (1989). Reprinted with permission.

relatively little empirical examination of its nature and the comparative efficacy
of the different ways it may be structured. The rest of this chapter contains a
conceptual analysis of positive interdependence and a review of studies we have
conducted over the past few years contrasting the relative impacts of goal, reward, and resource interdependence on such outcomes as achievement and interpersonal attraction.

Positive Interdependence: A Conceptual Analysis

Positive interdependence exists when individuals perceive that they are linked
with others in such a way that they cannot succeed unless the others do (and vice
versa) and/or that they must coordinate their efforts with the efforts of others to
complete a task. The state of positive interdependence defines whether cooperation is taking place: If individuals do not perceive their mutual fate and/or mutual
causation of each other's success, then the situation is not cooperative.

There are two major categories of positive interdependence: outcome interdependence and means interdependence (Deutsch, 1949a, 1949b; D. W. Johnson

& R. T. Johnson, 1989; Thomas, 1957). How individuals behave in a situation is largely determined by their perceptions of the outcomes desired and the means by which the desired outcomes may be reached. When persons are in a cooperative or competitive situation, they are oriented toward a desired outcome. If there is no outcome interdependence, there is no cooperation or competition. Outcome interdependence includes

1. Goal interdependence (individuals perceive that they can attain their goals if and only if the other individuals with whom they are cooperatively linked attain their goals). Goal interdependence subsumes outside-enemy interdependence (striving to perform higher than other groups) and fantasy interdependence (striving to solve hypothetical problems such as how to deal with being shipwrecked on the moon).
2. Reward interdependence (each group member receives the same reward for successfully completing a joint task).

The means through which the mutual goals or rewards are to be accomplished specify the actions required on the part of group members. Means interdependence includes:

1. Resource interdependence (each member has only a portion of the information, materials, or resources necessary for the task to be completed, and member resources have to be combined for the group to achieve its goal).
2. Role interdependence (each member is assigned complementary and interconnected roles).
3. Task interdependence (a division of labor is created so that the actions of one group member have to be completed if the next group member is to complete his or her responsibilities).

Positive outcome interdependence results in realizing that all group members (D. W. Johnson & R. Johnson, 1989):

1. Share a common fate where they all gain or lose on the basis of the overall performance of group members. One result is a sense of personal responsibility (*a*) for the final outcome and (*b*) to do their share of the work.
2. Are striving for mutual benefit so all members of the group will gain. There is recognition that what helps other group members benefits oneself and what promotes one's own productivity benefits that of the other group members.
3. Have a long-term time perspective so that long-term joint productivity is perceived to be of greater value than short-term personal advantages.
4. Have a shared identity based on group membership. Besides being a separate individual, one is a member of a team. The shared identity binds members together emotionally and creates an expectation for a joint celebration based on mutual respect and appreciation for the success of group members. The experience creates a positive cathexis so that group members like each other. Feelings of success are shared and pride is taken in other members' accomplishments as well as one's own.

Positive means interdependence results in individuals realizing that the performance of group members is mutually caused. Each person views him- or herself as instrumental in the productivity of other group members and views other group members as being instrumental in his or her productivity. Members realize that their efforts are required for the group to succeed (i.e., there can be no free riders) and that their potential contribution to the group is unique (because of their role, resources, or task responsibilities). Each member shares responsibility for other members' productivity (mutual responsibility) and is obligated to other members for support and assistance (mutual obligation). As a result of the mutual causation, cooperative efforts are characterized (1) by positive inducibility in that group members are open to being influenced by each other and (2) by substitutability in that the actions of group members substitute for each other so that if one member of the group has taken the action, there is no need for other members to do so. There is a mutual investment in each other.

Finally, positive interdependence creates motives that enhance and complement each other. Affiliation needs and the desire to be involved in relations with others, for example, may operate directly to increase productivity and psychological health in cooperative situations.

For the past several years we have been conducting a systematic series of studies to illuminate a number of controversies concerning positive interdependence and cooperation. These controversies can be summarized with six questions:

1. Is group membership in and of itself sufficient to produce higher achievement and productivity, or are group membership and positive interdependence required?
2. Is interpersonal interaction sufficient to increase productivity or is positive interdependence required?
3. Is goal or reward interdependence more important in promoting productivity and achievement?
4. Do different types of reward interdependence have different effects on productivity?
5. Is goal or resource interdependence more important in enhancing productivity and achievement?
6. Is positive interdependence strictly a motivational influence on how hard individuals work or does it facilitate the development of new insights and discoveries through promotive interaction?

Positive Interdependence Versus Group Membership

The first question is whether higher productivity and achievement result from positive interdependence or from simply identifying oneself as a member of a group. Deutsch (1962) hypothesizes that an implication of the positive interdependence inherent in cooperative situations is that "responsibility forces" are generated by the knowledge that one's achievement affects the outcomes of teammates and, therefore, individuals will exert more effort to achieve and will expect their teammates to do likewise. On the other hand, perhaps membership in a group and the experience of working together cooperatively result in increased motivation to do well regardless of whether or not one's performance affects the outcomes of teammates.

This issue was not clearly investigated until recently. Hwong conducted a study within which the "responsibility forces" hypothesis was tested against the "group membership" hypothesis (Hwong, Caswell, D. W. Johnson, & R. T. Johnson, 1991). Forty-three college students enrolled in an elementary music education class were randomly assigned to cooperative and individualistic conditions stratifying on the basis of previous musical experiences. The study lasted for 10 weeks (one session per week). Two achievement measures were included. One measure was structured so that the performance of one group member affected the grade received by all other group members. Each group member was expected to complete an assignment, and then the paper of one member was picked at random to be evaluated, and all group members received the resulting grade. Thus, the performance of any member in the group could determine the grade for all group members on the assignment. A second achievement measure was structured so that the performance of any one member did not affect the grades received by the other members. Each group member took a final exam and was given an individual score based on his or her performance. If the responsibility forces hypothesis is valid, higher performance would be expected on the former but not on the latter achievement measure. If the group membership hypothesis is valid, individuals in the cooperative condition would be expected to outperform individuals in the individualistic condition on both measures. The results supported the responsibility forces hypothesis (see Figure 8.2). Students in the cooperative groups outperformed their individualistic peers on the written assignments, but there were no significant differences between the conditions on the final examination. Positive interdependence did tend to make every member feel responsible for working hard to ensure that both they and their teammates were successful. In addition, individuals in the cooperative condition had stronger beliefs that they should study because classmates expected them to. It seems that simply being a member of a cooperative group in and of itself does not promote higher achievement. There has to be clear positive interdependence structured among members' outcomes for the increased effort required for higher achievement to be exerted.

Positive Interdependence Versus Interpersonal Interaction

It may be hypothesized that discussing the material being studied may be the critical variable affecting achievement. Students, for example, can be given individualistic assignments but be allowed to talk to each other about the assign-

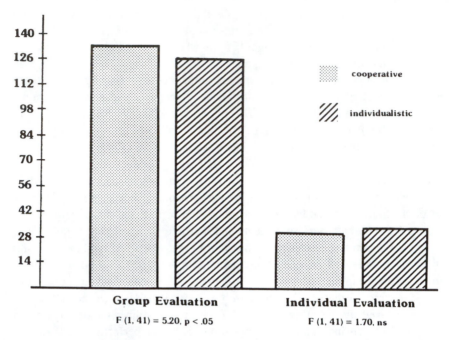

Figure 8.2. Impact of group versus individual evaluation on achievement.
From Hwong, Caswell, D. W. Johnson, & R. T. Johnson (1991). Reprinted
with permission.

ment. The opportunity to discuss assignments may be sufficient to explain the
higher achievement found within cooperative situations.

The second question, therefore, is whether positive interdependence is necessary for achievement to increase or whether a group discussion within an individualistic situation will produce the same results. Recent studies conducted by
Mesch and Lew at Simmons College in Boston tested the individualistic discussion hypotheses (Lew, Mesch, D. W. Johnson, & R. Johnson, 1986a, 1986b;
Mesch, D. W. Johnson, & R. Johnson, 1988; Mesch, Lew, D. W. Johnson, &
R. Johnson, 1986). They conducted four studies, using an A-B-A reversal design. All four studies lasted over 21 weeks. Teachers were thoroughly trained in
how to conduct the conditions, and careful observations of teacher and student
behavior were made twice a week to ensure that the conditions were being implemented correctly. The four studies took place in sixth-grade reading, eighth-
grade foreign language, eighth-grade math, eighth-grade English, eleventh-grade
chemistry, and tenth-grade social studies classes. The conditions included in the
studies were (1) the opportunity to interact with classmates under an individualistic goal and reward structure, (2) group work within positive goal interdepen-

Table 8.1. *Impact of positive interdependence on achievement*

Conditions	Weeks	Means
Study 1: $F(4, 6) = 3.13, p < .05$		
Individualistic	4	67.50
Goal + academic reward	5	73.50
Goal + academic & skills rewards	9	79.58
Goal + academic reward	2	77.50
Goal + academic & skills rewards	3	87.48
Study 2: $F(5, 90) = 15.86, p < .01$		
Individualistic	4	76.14
Goal	3	76.22
Goal + academic reward	4	77.09
Goal + academic & skills rewards	4	86.11
Goal + academic reward	3	89.12
Individualistic	6	82.56
Study 3: $F(5, 125) = 3.53, p < .01$		
Individualistic	4	77.36
Goal	3	80.53
Goal + social skills reward	4	81.87
Goal + academic skills rewards	4	85.03
Goal + social skills reward	3	81.79
Individualistic	3	80.92
Study 4: $F(5, 135) = 10.00, p < .01$		
Individualistic	6	71.09
Goal	6	76.40
Goal + academic reward	4	80.20
Goal	3	77.30
Goal + academic reward	3	85.10
Individualistic	2	80.10

Note: Study 1 (Mesch, Lew, D. W. Johnson, & R. T. Johnson, 1986). *Study 2* (Lew, Mesch, D. W. Johnson, & R. T. Johnson (1986b). *Study 3* (Lew, D. Mesch, D. W. Johnson, & R. T. Johnson (1986a). *Study 4* Mesch, D. W. Johnson, & R. T. Johnson (1988).

dence, (3) group work within positive goal and reward interdependence, and (4) group work within positive goal and reward interdependence with an added reward for engaging in cooperative skills. A repeated ANOVA was used to analyze the data.

Three of the four studies contained the two conditions relevant for our purposes (see Table 8.1): (1) the opportunity to interact with classmates under an individualistic goal and reward structure and (2) group work within positive goal interdependence. In two of the three studies, achievement was higher under pos-

itive goal interdependence than when subjects worked individually but had the
opportunity to interact with others.

Goal Versus Reward Interdependence

There is a basic theoretical disagreement among researchers as to whether positive goal interdependence or positive reward interdependence mediates the relationship between cooperation and achievement. On one side of the controversy
are Deutsch (1962) and D. W. Johnson & R. T. Johnson (1974, 1989), who state
that positive goal interdependence results in a promotive interaction pattern among
individuals, which increases their achievement and productivity. From this perspective, given the perception of positive interdependence, individuals will act
to facilitate each other's goal accomplishment (when they have the collaborative
skills to do so), and increased achievement and productivity will result. On the
other side of the controversy are researchers such as Hayes (1976) and Slavin
(1983), who state that positive reward interdependence largely explains the relationship between cooperation and achievement. From their perspective, individuals will increase their achievement only if there is a specific group contingency reinforcing them for doing so, and they will engage in facilitative behavior
only if there is a specific collaborative-skills contingency reinforcing them for
doing so.

Contrasting the two theoretical positions is complicated by the fact that although it is possible to implement positive goal interdependence without positive
reward interdependence, reward interdependence cannot be implemented without goal interdependence. For group members to be motivated by a group contingency, they must first perceive that their goal accomplishments are positively
interdependent. To contrast the two theoretical positions, cooperative groups with
only positive goal interdependence have to be compared with cooperative groups
with both positive goal and positive reward interdependence.

The studies conducted by Mesch and Lew provide such a test (Lew et al.,
1986a, 1986b; Mesch et al., 1986, 1988). Their findings (see Table 8.1) indicated that although positive goal interdependence is sufficient to produce higher
achievement and productivity than an individualistic structure that allowed talking, the combination of goal and reward interdependence is even more effective.
The impact of the two types of outcome interdependence seems to be additive.

Positive Reward Interdependence: Gain Versus Loss

Two of the types of reward interdependence are working to gain a reward and
working to avoid the loss of a reward. Frank (1984) compared the two types of
positive reward interdependence with each other and with individualistic efforts.

In the "reward" condition, subjects were told that they would receive either $5 or $0, depending on how they did on the task. In the "loss" condition, subjects were given $5 unconditionally and told that they could keep it or lose it, depending on their performance on the task. Research subjects were 160 individuals from fourth-, fifth-, and sixth-grade classes who were randomly assigned to pairs. The study lasted for two class sessions. The task consisted of learning French vocabulary. He found that cooperation promoted higher achievement than did individualistic efforts. There were no significant differences between positive interdependence structured by working to gain a reward or working to avoid the loss of a reward.

Goal Versus Resource Interdependence

Although few research studies have attempted to differentiate between the effects of positive goal interdependence and positive resource interdependence, some distinction may be made theoretically. There are two basic positions, one represented by Deutsch and one represented by Aronson. From the theorizing of Deutsch (1949b, 1962) and D. W. Johnson & R. T. Johnson (1974, 1989), it may be posited that when the cooperative situation is based on positive goal interdependence, individuals will act to promote each other's success out of recognition that they will benefit from doing so. When the cooperative situation is based on positive resource interdependence, however, there is mutual dependence on each other's resources, but individuals benefit only from obtaining resources from each other, not from each other's success. Aronson and his associates (1978) have conducted a set of studies in which they operationalized cooperation through a combination of positive resource interdependence and individual rewards, assuming that positive resource and goal interdependence were interchangeable and nonadditive. Their studies and two major field evaluations by Schaps and his associates (Moskowitz, Malvin, Schaeffer, & Schaps, 1985) indicate that positive resource interdependence with an individualistic reward structure does not increase achievement beyond what would be expected with a competitive or individualistic reward structure alone.

Theoretically, there are at least two reasons for hypothesizing that resource interdependence will not promote higher achievement than individualistic efforts in the absence of positive outcome interdependence. The first is that although positive outcome interdependence creates a situation in which each person benefits from the achievement and productivity of his or her teammates (and, therefore, exerts efforts to promote their success), resource interdependence creates a situation in which each person is dependent on receiving resources from teammates but does not gain from sharing his or her resources. When resource interdependence alone exists within a group, each person will be motivated to have teammates present what they know but will be penalized by presenting what he or she has learned. Every minute a person is presenting his or her resources is a minute that he or she is not obtaining needed resources from others.

Second, positive goal interdependence may promote substitutability among the actions of group members whereas resource interdependence may not. This may be seen in individuals' reactions to less able group members. Within a cooperative situation characterized by positive goal interdependence, when one member cannot do the work, group members will increase their motivation and effort to ensure joint success (because their actions can substitute for the actions of the less capable group member). Within a cooperative situation characterized by resource interdependence, when a member cannot provide his or her part of the required resources, the motivation and effort of the rest of the group members will decrease (because their actions cannot substitute for the actions of the less capable members).

To examine the relative impact of positive goal interdependence and positive resource interdependence on individual achievement and group productivity, D. W. Johnson & R. T. Johnson (1991) conducted a study directly comparing goal and resource interdependence. Sixty-three individuals enrolled in U.S. military history participated in the study. The study lasted for five class sessions of 45 min each. Achievement was measured by quizzes given at the end of Class Sessions 2, 3, and 4 and by a final test given at the end of the study. Students were randomly assigned to conditions and within conditions to groups of three. In the goal interdependence condition individuals studied all the material and were graded on the basis of their total group score. In the resource interdependence condition individuals were given one third of the material to learn and teach to the other two members of their group but were graded on their individual performance on the tests. Both on the quizzes and on the final examination, individuals in the goal interdependence condition performed better than did those in the resource interdependence condition.

D. W. Johnson, R. T. Johnson, Stanne, and Garibaldi (1990) conducted a more complex study comparing goal and resource interdependence on achievement on a computer-assisted problem-solving task. Forty-four black American high school seniors and college freshmen were randomly assigned to conditions, stratifying for ability, sex, and urban/rural background. Four conditions were included in the study: both positive goal and resource interdependence, positive goal interdependence only, positive resource interdependence only, and neither positive goal nor resource interdependence (individualistic). Subjects were involved in a 3-hour computer simulation on the fundamentals of map reading and navigation. Their task was to master technical information on map reading and navigation and apply their knowledge in deciding what actions to take to successfully solve navigational problems, using the computer to record their deci-

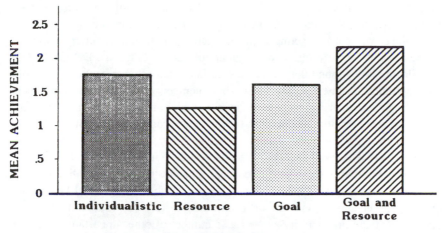

Figure 8.3. Impact of goal and resource interdependence on achievement. From D. W. Johnson, R. T. Johnson, Stanne, & Garibaldi (1990). Reprinted with permission.

sions and give feedback on the consequences of the actions taken. Positive goal interdependence promoted higher individual achievement and group productivity than did no goal interdependence (see Figure 8.3). The combination of positive goal and resource interdependence promoted higher individual achievement and group productivity than did any of the other conditions, indicating that two sources of positive interdependence are more powerful than one. When used in isolation from positive goal interdependence, positive resource interdependence produced the lowest individual achievement and problem-solving success, even lower than individualistic efforts.

Positive Interdependence: Motivational or Promotive?

There is disagreement over whether the positive interdependence found within cooperative situations is strictly a motivational influence that affects how hard individuals work (Slavin, 1983) or instead results in promotive interaction that facilitates new insights and understandings (Deutsch, 1962; D. W. Johnson & R. Johnson, 1974, 1983, 1989). The Delphi method of group decision, for example, requires group members to generate ideas independently, read a summary of the ideas of the other group members, and then vote (D. W. Johnson & F. Johnson, 1991). DeVries and Edwards (1974), Slavin (1983), and Hamblin, Hathaway, and Wordarski (1971) all developed procedures for cooperative learning that assumed that positive reward interdependence is a motivational proce-

dure that encourages individuals to study harder. They do not use the team structure as a way to pool individual skills and ideas. Thus, individuals are told to
work alone, without interacting with their peers or colleagues, but are rewarded
on the basis of the performance of all group members. Hulten and DeVries (1976)
and Slavin (1980) found that group reward increased achievement even without
an opportunity for interaction among group members. In effect, group members
reinforced each other for good performance, which may have created "responsibility forces" resulting in increased efforts and productivity (Deutsch, 1949b;
Thomas, 1957).

Deutsch (1949a, 1962) and D. W. Johnson and R. Johnson (1974, 1983, 1989)
have theorized that positive goal interdependence results in a promotive interaction pattern (within which individuals interact, discuss the material being considered, and encourage and support each other's efforts to produce) that affects
achievement and productivity as well as a number of other important variables.
They and others have developed procedures that use the cooperative structure
primarily as a facilitative procedure to encourage group members to share ideas,
give and receive explanations, compare the material being discussed with previously known information, decide how to structure their efforts, and so forth.

If positive interdependence is strictly motivational, it will not affect cognitive
processing or quality of reasoning strategy. If, on the other hand, positive interdependence results in promotive interaction, increased cognitive processing and
high-level reasoning strategies will be expected. A set of our studies focused on
the relative impact of cooperative, competitive, and individualistic efforts on the
reasoning strategies of category search and retrieval, intersectional classification,
formulating equations from math story problems, formulating strategies for avoiding
repetitions and errors in a spatial reasoning task, concept attainment, problem
solving, language acquisition, sequencing, mathematical reasoning, visual sort-
ing, metaphoric reasoning, and conservation strategies (Gabbert, D. W. Johnson, & R. T. Johnson, 1986; D. W. Johnson & R. T. Johnson, 1981a; D. W.
Johnson, Skon, & R. T. Johnson, 1980; Skon, D. W. Johnson, & R. T. Johnson,
1981). The results indicated that the discussion in cooperative groups promoted
more frequent discovery and development of higher quality cognitive reasoning
strategies than did working alone in competitive and individualistic situations.
Gabbert, D. W. Johnson and R. Johnson (1986) found that on the tasks representing Levels 4 to 6 on Bloom's taxonomy of cognitive instructional objectives
(requiring the use of higher level reasoning strategies) individuals in the cooperative condition achieved higher on the posttest taken individually than did the
individuals in the individualistic condition. The group-to-individual transfer was
especially interesting on a visual discrimination problem-solving task in which
the first-grade students had to manage a number of different attributes at the same
time, a process that is difficult for even college students.

In the categorization and retrieval task used by D. W. Johnson, Skon, and R. T. Johnson (1980) and Skon, D. W. Johnson, and R. T. Johnson (1981), for example, subjects (first-grade students) were required to memorize 12 nouns during the instructional session and to complete several retrieval tasks during the testing session the following day. The 12 nouns were given in random order, and subjects were instructed to (1) put the cards in an order that made sense to them and that would aid memorization and (2) memorize the words. Three of the words were fruits, three were animals, three were clothing, and three were toys. Eight of the nine cooperative groups discovered and used all four categories, and only one subject in the competitive and individualistic conditions did so. Salatas and Flavell (1976) found that even third-grade individuals had difficulty using category search procedures, yet in this study first-grade children were able to do so after discussing the task within cooperative learning groups. Even the most intelligent and gifted participants developed higher quality reasoning strategies in cooperative than in the other two situations (that is, they benefited from collective induction). Also, individuals working cooperatively more frequently reported using higher thought processes than did persons working individualistically (D. W. Johnson & R. T. Johnson, 1981).

These results suggest that the positive interdependence found within cooperative situations goes beyond motivating individuals to work hard and facilitates the development of new insights and understandings through promotive interaction.

Positive Interdependence and Personal Responsibility

In cooperative situations participants share responsibility for the joint outcome or product. Each group member is expected to (1) contribute his or her efforts to accomplish the group's goals and (2) help other group members do likewise. The greater the positive interdependence structured within a cooperative group, the more group members will feel *personally responsible* for contributing their efforts to accomplish the group's goals and the more they will realize that negative sanctions appear for failing to do one's part. The shared responsibility adds the concept of *ought* to members' motivation – one ought to do one's part, pull one's weight, contribute, and satisfy peer norms.

To ensure that all group members perceive the positive interdependence and personally accept the shared responsibility to contribute toward the group's success, individual accountability may need to be highlighted. Increasing the individual accountability will tend to increase members' awareness of their positive interdependence. *Individual accountability* exists when the performance of each individual is assessed and the results are given back to the group and the individual. It is important that group members know that they cannot "hitchhike" on the work of others. Individual accountability may be highlighted by frequently (1) identifying the contributions of each member, (2) assessing who needs more assistance, support, and encouragement in fulfilling their responsibilities, (3) assessing what redundancy, if any, exists among member efforts, and (4) identifying the unique contributions of each group member (because of their role, resources, or task responsibilities).

One of the major obstacles to group effectiveness is social loafing. When groups work on tasks where it is difficult to identify members' contributions, when there is an increased likelihood of redundant efforts, when there is a lack of group cohesiveness, and when there is lessened responsibility for the final outcome, the less some members will try to contribute to goal achievement (Harkins & Petty, 1982; Ingham, Levinger, Graves, & Peckham, 1974; Kerr & Bruun, 1981; Latane et al., 1979; Moede, 1927; Petty, Harkins, Williams, & Latane, 1977; Williams, 1981; Williams, Harkins, & Latane, 1981). Such social loafing can be avoided by clearly structuring positive interdependence so feelings of personal responsibility for the group's final outcome are high, making it clear how much effort each member is contributing, assigning roles to members to ensure a lack of redundancy and a unique contribution by each member, and promoting caring relationships among members. The more group members are provided with information about the level of productivity and helpfulness of each member, the more individually accountable each member will be and the better members will be able to provide support and assistance to each other. The smaller the size of the group, furthermore, the greater the individual accountability.

The personal responsibility felt by members of cooperative groups to work toward mutual benefit provides a motivation for continuing cooperation indefinitely, even if the original group goals are attained or changed. Developing an interest in the welfare of collaborators provides a source of motivational stability that buttresses a cooperative system against the otherwise debilitating effects of changing individual goals. The more group members care about each other, the more stable the group. A mutual interest in each other's welfare is not a necessary condition for cooperation, but caring and committed relationships arise as a consequence of cooperation and then provide a basis for continuing cooperation.

Conclusion

Generally, the results of the research reviewed suggest that interpersonal interaction under an individualistic reward structure and group membership in and of itself are not sufficient to explain the higher achievement typically found in cooperative situations. Positive interdependence must be present. Although there is disagreement as to whether goal or reward interdependence is chief contributor to cooperation's effectiveness, the point is irrelevant because reward interdependence cannot be structured without including goal interdependence and the two types of outcome interdependence seem to be additive. It may not matter whether the participants are working to gain a reward or working to prevent a loss of a reward. Resource interdependence may not be sufficient in and of itself to promote the effectiveness of cooperation; it may have a positive effect only in combination with goal interdependence. Positive interdependence seems to go beyond simply motivating participants to work hard; rather, it creates the conditions for the development of new insights and understandings through promotive interaction. When positive interdependence is clear, participants may tend to feel a sense of personal responsibility to do their fair share of the work.

The results of these studies should not be taken to indicate that the presence of positive interdependence is always good. Positive means interdependence may be constructive only when used in combination with outcome interdependence. The perception of positive interdependence increases participants' inducibility, which, in turn, creates the potential for being exploited and taken advantage of by less committed group members. The positive relationships created by positive interdependence may lead to favoritism in situations where it is not appropriate. Further research is needed to delineate further the conditions under which positive interdependence does and does not contribute to the effectiveness of cooperative efforts.

Importance of Social Interdependence

The research on positive interdependence is in its infancy, but there is little doubt as to its importance. Humans by their nature cooperate with each other. Just as the cheetah survives by speed and hawks survive by their eyesight, humans survive by their ability to ''work together to get the job done.'' There are few things more important to teach our children, adolescents, and young adults than a basic understanding of how cooperative systems function, the desire to promote the success of all collaborators, and the social competencies required to work cooperatively with a wide variety of individuals. Of all the social competencies required to cooperate effectively, those involved with resolving conflicts constructively may be most crucial (D. W. Johnson & R. T. Johnson, 1979, 1991).

We increasingly live in a world characterized by interdependence, pluralism, conflict, and rapid change. There is greater and greater interdependence among individuals, communities, and countries. The major problems faced by individuals (e.g., contamination of the environment, warming of the atmosphere, world hunger, international terrorism, nuclear war) are increasingly ones that cannot be solved by actions taken only at the national level. Cooperation, therefore, must be established among disparate peoples and nations. Conflicts result as individuals, communities, organizations, and countries become more and more vulnerable to each other. How constructively such conflicts are resolved becomes a central issue of how well interdependence is managed.

Although the world and individuals have become more interdependent, many children, adolescents, and young adults have become more isolated, egocentric, self-centered, and alienated (Astin, Green, & Korn, 1987; Astin, Green, Korn, & Schalit, 1986; Conger, 1981). Over the past two decades concern for personal well-being on the part of adolescents and young adults has increased, and concern for the welfare of others (particularly the less advantaged) and society has decreased (Astin et al., 1986, 1987; Conger, 1981). Concern with material values and success in their chosen field of work is much higher among today's high school and college individuals than it was 20 or even 10 years ago. Less than one in six of today's college-bound high school seniors consider "making a contribution to society" or "working to correct social and economic inequities" a very important value. There seems to be a *delusion of individualism* where each person believes he or she is separate and apart from all other individuals and, therefore, the frustration, unhappiness, hunger, despair, and misery of others has no significant bearing on his or her own well-being.

One contributor to the absence of perceived interdependence is that cooperative experiences are absent from the home and school life of most children, adolescents, and young adults. Many, if not most, children, adolescents, and young adults no longer contribute to the family's economic well-being. In most schools 80% to 90% of the day is spent listening to lectures, completing individual worksheets, studying alone, and taking individual tests on Friday. Thus, many children, adolescents, and young adults seem not to have experienced cooperation or to have observed models who demonstrated how to manage interdependence effectively. An increased emphasis on cooperative learning in schools, interdependence within the family, and cooperative teams within organizations may help remedy the situation.

Summary

Cooperation is not effective under all conditions. To understand the conditions under which cooperation is and is not effective, cooperation must be placed within the context of social interdependence. Social interdependence exists when the outcomes of individuals are affected by each other's actions. There are two types of social interdependence: cooperation, which is based on positive interdependence, and competition, which is based on negative interdependence. The absence of interdependence and dependence results in individualistic efforts. The basic premise of social interdependence theory is that how a situation is structured, with positive, negative, or no interdependence, determines how individuals interact with each other (promotively, contriently, or not at all), which, in turn, determines the outcomes participants experience. The numerous outcomes studied over the past 90 years may be divided into the three categories of effort to achieve, quality of interpersonal relationships, and psychological health and social competence.

Over 520 experimental and 100 correlational studies have been conducted on social interdependence over the past nine decades. Generally, the results suggest that achievement and productivity are higher in cooperative than in competitive or individualistic situations, more positive and supportive relationships are fostered by cooperation, and higher self-esteem, social competence, and psychological adjustment tend to result from cooperative experiences. The relationships among these variables are bidirectional. Because each contributes to the presence of the others, they tend to be found together as a gestalt.

Of all the variables that may mediate the effectiveness of cooperation, positive interdependence may be the most important, because its presence largely defines the presence of cooperation. Yet little research has focused on delineating the nature of positive interdependence and the relative efficacy of the various ways it may be structured within a situation. Positive interdependence exists when one perceives that one is linked with others in a way that one cannot succeed unless they do (and vice versa) and/or that one must coordinate one's efforts with the efforts of others to complete a task. There are two major types of positive interdependence: outcome and means.

Six questions concerning the nature of positive interdependence and its impact on achievement have been systematically investigated in a series of research studies. The first question is whether group membership in and of itself is sufficient to produce higher achievement and productivity or whether group membership and positive interdependence are required. The results of Hwong, Casswell, D. W. Johnson, and R. T. Johnson (1991) indicate that positive interdependence is necessary. Knowing that one's performance affects the success of teammates seems to create responsibility forces that increase one's efforts to achieve.

The second question is whether interpersonal interaction is sufficient to increase productivity or whether positive interdependence is required. Mesch and Lew conducted a series of studies in which they investigated whether the relationship between cooperation and achievement was due to the opportunity to interact with peers or to positive goal interdependence. Their results are quite consistent. The individuals achieved higher under positive goal interdependence than when they worked individualistically but had the opportunity to interact with classmates (Lew et al., 1986a, 1986b; Mesch et al., 1986, 1988).

The third question is whether goal or reward interdependence is more important in promoting productivity and achievement. The results of the Mesch and Lew studies indicate that although positive goal interdependence is sufficient to produce higher achievement and productivity than individualistic efforts, the combination of goal and reward interdependence is even more effective. The impact of the two types of outcome interdependence seems to be additive.

The fourth question is whether different types of reward interdependence have different effects on productivity. Frank's study indicates not. Both working to achieve a reward and working to avoid the loss of a reward produced higher achievement than did individualistic efforts.

The fifth question is whether goal or resource interdependence is more important in enhancing productivity and achievement. D. W. Johnson and R. T. Johnson (1991) found goal interdependence promoted higher achievement than did resource interdependence. The study by D. W. Johnson, R. T. Johnson, Stanne, and Garibaldi (1990) indicated that goal interdependence alone increased achievement, but the combination of goal and resource interdependence increased achievement even further, and the use of resource interdependence alone seemed to decrease achievement and lower productivity compared with individualistic efforts.

Finally, there is a question as to whether positive interdependence simply motivates individuals to try harder or facilitates the development of new insights and discoveries through promotive interaction. The latter position is supported by the fact that some studies have found that members of cooperative groups use higher level reasoning strategies more frequently than do individuals working individualistically or competitively.

The constructive effects positive interdependence contributes to cooperative efforts does not mean that it is always advantageous. There are conditions under which positive interdependence may have negative effects on cooperation. Further research is needed to clarify the conditions under which positive interdependence does and does not contribute to cooperation's effectiveness.

References

Aronson, E., Blaney, N., Stephan, C., Sikes, J., & Snapp, M. (1978). *The Jigsaw classroom*. Beverly Hills, CA: Sage.

Astin, A., Green, K., & Korn, W. (1987). *The American freshman: Twenty year trends*. Los Angeles: University of California at Los Angeles, Higher Education Research Institute.

Astin, A., Green, K., Korn, W., & Schalit, M. (1986). *The American freshman: National norms for fall, 1986*. Los Angeles: University of California at Los Angeles, Higher Education Research Institute.

Collins, B. (1970). *Social psychology*. Reading, MA: Addison-Wesley.

Conger, J. (1981). Freedom and commitment: Families, youth, and social change. *American Psychologist, 36*, 1475–1484.

Deutsch, M. (1949a). A theory of cooperation and competition. *Human Relations, 2,* 129–152.

 (1949b). An experimental study of the effects of cooperation and competition upon group processes. *Human Relations, 2,* 199–231.

 (1962). Cooperation and trust: Some theoretical notes. In M. R. Jones (Ed.), *Nebraska symposium on motivation* (pp. 275–319). Lincoln: University of Nebraska Press.

DeVries, D., & Edwards, K. (1974, April). *Cooperation in the classroom: Towards a theory of alternative reward-task classroom structures.* Paper presented at the annual meeting of the American Educational Research Association, Chicago.

Frank, M. (1984). *A comparison between an individual and group goal structure contingency that differed in the behavioral contingency and performance-outcome components.* Unpublished doctoral thesis, University of Minnesota.

Gabbert, B., Johnson, D. W., & Johnson, R. T. (1986). Cooperative learning, group-to-individual transfer, process gain and the acquisition of cognitive reasoning strategies. *Journal of Psychology, 120*(3), 265–278.

Hamblin, R., Hathaway, C., & Wordarski, J. (1971). Group contingencies, peer tutoring, and accelerating academic achievement. In E. Ramp & B. Hopkins (Eds.), *A new direction for education: Behavior analysis.* Lawrence: University of Kansas, Department of Human Development.

Harkins, S., & Petty, R. (1982). The effects of task difficulty and task uniqueness on social loafing. *Journal of Personality and Social Psychology, 43,* 1214–1229.

Hayes, L. (1976). The use of group contingencies for behavioral control: A review. *Psychological Bulletin, 83,* 628–648.

Hill, G. (1982). Group versus individual performance: Are $N + 1$ heads better than one? *Psychological Bulletin, 91,* 517–539.

Hulten, B., & DeVries, D. (1976). *Team competition and group practice: Effects on student achievement and attitudes.* (Report No. 212). Baltimore: Johns Hopkins University, Center for Social Organization of Schools.

Hwong, N., Caswell, A., Johnson, D. W., & Johnson, R. T. (1991). *Effects of cooperative and individualistic learning on prospective elementary teachers' music achievement and attitudes.* Manuscript submitted for publication.

Ingham, A., Levinger, G., Graves, J., & Peckham, V. (1974). The Ringelmann effect: Studies of group size and group performance. *Journal of Personality and Social Psychology, 10,* 371–384.

Johnson, D. W. (1970). *The social psychology of education.* New York: Holt, Rinehart & Winston.

 (1990). *Reaching out: Interpersonal effectiveness and self-actualization* (4th ed.). Englewood Cliffs, NJ: Prentice-Hall.

 (1991). *Human relations and your career: A guide to interpersonal skills* (3rd ed.). Englewood Cliffs, NJ: Prentice-Hall.

Johnson, D. W., & Johnson, F. (1991). *Joining together: Group theory and group skills* (4th ed.). Englewood Cliffs, NJ: Prentice-Hall.

Johnson, D. W., & Johnson, R. T. (1974). Instructional goal structure: Cooperative, competitive, or individualistic. *Review of Educational Research, 44,* 213–240.

 (1979). Conflict in the classroom: Controversy and learning. *Review of Educational Research, 49,* 51–70.

 (1981). Effects of cooperative and individualistic learning experiences on interethnic interaction. *Journal of Educational Psychology, 73*(3), 454–459.

 (1983). Social interdependence and perceived academic and personal support in the classroom. *Journal of Social Psychology, 120,* 77–82.

(1989). *Cooperation and competition: Theory and research.* Edina, MN: Interaction Book Co.

Johnson, D. W., & Johnson, R. T. (1991a). *The effects of different levels of positive interdependence in cooperative learning groups on achievement.* Manuscript submitted for publication.

(1991b). *Learning together and alone: Cooperation, competition, and individualization* (3rd ed.). Englewood Cliffs, NJ: Prentice Hall.

Johnson, D. W., Johnson, R. T., & Holubec, E. (1990). *Circles of learning: Cooperation in the classroom* (rev. ed.). Edina, MN: Interaction Book Co.

Johnson, D. W., Johnson, R. T., Stanne, M., & Garibaldi, A. (1990). Impact of group processing on achievement in cooperative groups. *The Journal of Social Psychology, 130*(4), 507–516.

Johnson, D. W., Skon, L., & Johnson, R. T. (1980). Effects of cooperative, competitive, and individualistic conditions of children's problem-solving performance. *American Education Research Journal, 17*(1), 83–94.

Kerr, N. (1983). The dispensability of member effort and group motivation losses: Free-rider effects. *Journal of Personality and Social Psychology, 44*, 78–94.

Kerr, N., & Bruun, S. (1981). Ringelmann revisited: Alternative explanations for the social loafing effect. *Personality and Social Psychology Bulletin, 7*, 224–231.

(1983). The dispensability of member effort and group motivation losses: Free-rider effects. *Journal of Personality and Social Psychology, 44*, 78–94.

Lamm, H., & Trommsdorff, G. (1973). Group versus individual performance on tasks requiring ideational proficiency (brainstorming): A review. *European Journal of Social Psychology, 3*, 361–388.

Langer, E., & Benevento, A. (1978). Self-induced dependence. *Journal of Personality and Social Psychology, 36*, 886–893.

Latane, B., Williams, K., & Harkins, S. (1979). Many hands make light the work: The causes and consequences of social loafing. *Journal of Personality and Social Psychology, 37*, 822–832.

Lew, M., Mesch, D., Johnson, D. W., & Johnson, R. T. (1986a). Components of cooperative learning: Effects of collaborative skills and academic group contingencies on achievement and mainstreaming. *Contemporary Educational Psychology, 11*, 229–239.

(1986b). Positive interdependence, academic and collaborative-skills group contingencies and isolated students. *American Educational Research Journal, 23*, 476–488.

Lewin, K. (1935). *A dynamic theory of personality.* New York: McGraw-Hill.

(1948). *Resolving social conflicts.* New York: Harper.

Mesch, D., Johnson, D. W., & Johnson, R. T. (1988). Impact of positive interdependence and academic group contingencies on achievement. *Journal of Social Psychology, 128*, 345–352.

Mesch, D., Lew, M., Johnson, D. W., & Johnson, R. T. (1986). Isolated teenagers, cooperative learning and the training of social skills. *Journal of Psychology, 120*, 323–334.

Moede, W. (1927). Die Richtlinien der Leistungs-Psychologie. *Industrielle Psychotechnik, 4*, 193–207.

Moskowitz, J., Malvin, J., Schaeffer, G., & Schaps, E. (1983). Process and outcome evaluation of a cooperative learning strategy. *American Journal of Educational Research, 20*(4), 687–696.

(1985). Evaluation of Jigsaw, a cooperative learning technique. *Contemporary Educational Psychology, 10*, 104–112.

Petty, R., Harkins, S., Williams, K., & Latane, B. (1977). The effects of group size on cognitive effort and evaluation. *Personality and Social Psychology Bulletin, 3,* 575–578.

Salatas, H., & Flavell, J. (1976). Retrieval of recently learned information: Development of strategies and control skills. *Child Development, 47,* 941–948.

Salomon, G. (1981). *Communication and education: Social and psychological interactions.* Beverly Hills: Sage Publications.

Sheingold, K., Hawkins, J., & Char, C. (1984). ''I'm the thinkist, you're the typist'': The interactions of technology and the social life of classrooms. *Journal of Social Issues, 40*(3), 49–61.

Skon, L., Johnson, D. W., & Johnson, R. (1981). Cooperative peer interaction versus individual competition and individualistic efforts: Effects on the acquisition of cognitive reasoning strategies. *Journal of Educational Psychology, 73*(1), 83–92.

Slavin, R. (1980). Cooperative learning. *Review of Educational Research, 50,* 315–342. (1983). *Cooperative learning.* New York: Longman.

Slavin, R., Leavey, M., & Madden, N. (1983). *Combining student teams and individualized instruction in mathematics: An extended evaluation* (Report No. 336). Baltimore: Johns Hopkins University, Center for Social Organization of Schools.

Thomas, D. (1957). Effects of facilitative role interdependence on group functioning. *Human Relations, 10,* 347–366.

Webb, N., Ender, P., & Lewis, S. (1986). Problem-solving strategies and group processes in small groups learning computer programming. *American Educational Research Journal, 23*(2), 243–261.

Williams, K. (1981). *The effects of group cohesiveness on social loafing.* Paper presented at the annual meeting of the Midwestern Psychological Association, Detroit.

Williams, K., Harkins, S., & Latane, B. (1981). Identifiability as a deterrent to social loafing: Two cheering experiments. *Journal of Personality and Social Psychology, 40,* 303–311.

Part IV

Factors Influencing the Promotion of Positive Intergroup Relations

9 Social Categorization and Intergroup Acceptance: Principles for the Design and Development of Cooperative Learning Teams

Norman Miller and Hugh J. Harrington

Rarely are classrooms designed to meet the conditions for effective intergroup contact, as stated by Allport in 1952 to the U.S. Supreme Court. These conditions are equal-status interaction, interaction that is sanctioned and supported by authorities, and interaction that leads to knowledge of participants as individuals (see Harrington & N. Miller, in press, for issues of consensus and controversy). Various techniques, which we refer to collectively as cooperative learning teams (CLT), have been developed to facilitate learning of subject matter in small groups and promotion of interpersonal relationships, particularly when there is cultural diversity in the classroom. Their use in classrooms is usually limited in percentage of classroom time and duration. Despite this limited investment, however, benefits of CLT have been noted both in student achievement and in interpersonal relations (D. W. Johnson, R. Johnson, & Maruyama, 1983).

A number of these techniques, for example, Group Investigation, Jigsaw, Learning Together, Student Teams Achievement Divisions (STAD), and Teams Games Tournaments (TGT), meet most of Allport's conditions. This chapter discusses four general principles for improving on the use of existing CLT approaches to strengthen certain conditions. These principles are (1) the minimization of the salience of social categories when forming teams and during group process, (2) the minimization of threats to identity and self-esteem, (3) the provision of opportunities for the personalization of team members, and (4) the provision of opportunities for the development of interpersonal skills. In the first section, we review our conceptual approach and discuss the role of identity in intergroup relations. In the second section, we focus on the role of the teacher in developing effective learning teams. The next four sections present each principle. In each section we introduce a conceptual framework, provide data that support our recommendations, and describe how the principle could work at its best (or its worst) in the classroom.

Conceptual Orientation: The Role of Identity
in Intergroup Relations

The concept of identity has ebbed and flowed within psychology in general. It played little role in intergroup relations until Tajfel and Turner (1979) began to elaborate social identity theory (SIT). Elsewhere, we have reviewed SIT in comparison with other theories of intergroup relations and presented our departures from its basic tenets (N. Miller & Harrington, 1990b). The basic assumptions of SIT are that people have a basic need to establish and maintain a positive identity, one's identity includes both social and personal components, one's attention can be focused on either social or personal identity in either the perception of others or self-awareness, and orthogonal to this descriptive dimension is an evaluative dimension of identity – the esteem attributed to these characteristics (N. Miller & Harrington, 1990b, p. 52). We present here a complementary look at some important, and often overlooked, properties of identity and types of relationships. We then examine this approach in the context of how we come to know and be known by others (impression formation and impression management) and how we categorize and compare ourselves and others (social categorization and social comparison processes).

Properties of Identity

There are four important properties of identity that help state our perspective. First, identity is *relational;* it is who one is in relation to others. This seems readily apparent with respect to the social components of identity or memberships in groups of persons (e.g., one's gender, ethnicity, age). It also applies to personal characteristics – traits, interests, preferences. Many traits are clearly interpersonal, such as shy, friendly, or humorous. Traits that appear task oriented, for example, competent, persistent, or analytical, are defined comparatively and are meaningful to the extent that they are socially relevant and valued. One is competent compared with one set of others, not with another. Given the premise that persons will seek to enhance self-identity, students who feel less competent than certain others may look toward those who are less competent than themselves to reaffirm their esteem, or they may seek out other characteristics by which they can be valued.

We maintain that in any situation only certain aspects of one's identity will be salient to self and others and that features of the situation help determine which aspects receive attention. A second property of identity, then is that it is *situational*. Identity is better understood, we propose, as fluid and temporal rather than "prepackaged" and stable. In part, this helps us understand why one could behave cooperatively within the classroom, when aspects of social identity are not threatened, yet discriminate on the playground against the same outgroup members if social identity becomes the salient feature of that situation. Behavior toward another on the basis of group membership has been termed *categorical responding* (Brewer & N. Miller, 1984). A number of situational features promote or reduce categorical responding. Elsewhere, we have presented data from 10 studies to support this position (N. Miller & Harrington, 1990a).

A third property of identity is that it is *interactive;* in any situation it emerges and evolves over the course of time. In the contact situation, persons are simultaneously engaged in two processes: impression formation of the other and impression management, or self-presentation. These are described in more detail later in this section. We note here that identity in a situation is not only who we think we are or want to portray ourselves as, but also who others think we are. Impressions develop as persons interact, exchanging verbal and nonverbal information. To establish a positive identity, persons engage in attempts to influence how others perceive them – impression management. As the process is extended in time, identities become negotiated during interaction – attributes are revealed or concealed, accepted or challenged. Neither person can completely control the impression formation and self-presentation processes of the other. This reciprocal, iterative give-and-take is important in another respect. If I am treated by others as a representative of my social group, rather than as a unique individual, then my behavior will reflect it. This creates a self-fulfilling prophecy for the other – I am subjected to categorical responding and respond in kind. The reverse, how I treat others, also operates the same way (Snyder & Swann, 1978).

The fourth important property of identity is that it is *affective;* as it emerges in a situation it is a source of self-esteem – that is, a positive or negative self-evaluation. Identity has emotional significance, and threats to any aspect of it arouse anxiety. Moreover, one's personal identity is, by affective significance, more central than social identity. Nevertheless, people resent attempts by others to categorize them on the basis of social identity (D. M. Taylor & Dubé, 1986), and being categorized on that basis can lower situational self-esteem (Lemyre & Smith, 1985). Therefore, if the salient feature of identity in the situation is one's social category, then people will behave in ways to enhance the in-group's image relative to the outgroup. This bias, we propose, can be reduced only if category salience is reduced, that is, if the relevance of social identity is diminished, and, simultaneously, opportunities to establish a positive personal identity are present. Personal identity is enhanced by recognition of one's unique character and individual contributions. Threats to social identity will undermine these opportunities. In its simplest form, interventions that foster personal relationships can establish the positive affect that is necessary for behaving cooperatively in the learning team.

Identity Relationships

We stated that an important property of identity is that it is relational. There are several noteworthy relationships that exist within the heterogeneous classroom: (1) ingroup to outgroup (the extent to which the groups are assumed to differ or be opposed); (2) oneself to the ingroup (the extent to which situational identity is derived from membership in the ingroup); (3) the other to the outgroup (the extent to which an outgroup member is presumed to represent the outgroup); (4) self to other and other to self (the extent to which self-other similarity is perceived); (5) self to team (the extent to which membership in the team promotes self-esteem); and (6) own team to other teams (the extent to which various classroom teams complement or compete with one another).

We can restate these relationships in terms of two dimensions: similarity and complexity. Elsewhere (N. Miller & Harrington, 1990a), we presented evidence to support the role of ingroup identification, perceived similarity, intragroup complexity, and intrapersonal complexity in mediating intergroup bias. Paralleling the relationships stated earlier, we found that (1) perceived group differences are related to increased bias or ingroup favoritism, (2) increased identification between self and the ingroup is correlated with bias, (3) lack of differentiation between the outgroup other and the outgroup is related to increased bias, (4) increased similarity between self and outgroup other is related to decreased bias, (5) increased satisfaction with one's own team is related to decreased bias, and (6) competitive structures between one team and other teams are related to increased bias. With respect to complexity, we found that (1) increased homogeneity (low complexity) within either the ingroup or the outgroup is related to increased bias, and (2) increased complexity, or personalization, of the outgroup other is related to decreased bias. Stated differently, similarity between members and their respective groups (assimilation) is associated with bias, just as perceived differences between groups or between self and other (contrast) are related to bias. Likewise, homogeneity of groups and low complexity of individuals are associated with bias. As groups become more differentiated and individuals become more personalized (complex), bias decreases.

Impression Formation and Social Categorization

Who the other is, initially, is determined by perceptual features. Attention is typically drawn to social features, and generally, one can identify or form an impression of the gender, ethnic background, age-group, and social status of the other. These are easily recognized features and usually exist within a rich network of associations (imagery, affect, attitudes, assumptions). The process of impression formation is essentially perceptual and descriptive – how to identify someone. A principal dimension of this descriptive process is the target's similarity to the perceiver. Because social features are stable and easily categorized, they can be ascertained with some certainty (same/different). Category labels simplify information processing and serve as a basis for predictions of future behaviors. Personal features, on the other hand, are often relative (more or less than), are "fuzzy" compared with social features, and take longer to discover. There is an evaluative connotation to this descriptive dimension; usually similarity to self or own group is positively evaluated, perhaps because it implies familiarity, which is affectively positive (Zajonc, 1968). In contrast, differences tend to be negatively evaluated. When one attempts to judge how similar a stranger is to self, then, there is little else on which to base such judgment other than social features. A dominant psychological process in impression formation, therefore, is social categorization.

Impression Management and Social Comparison

In contrast, with respect to self, one usually operates from the personal end of the identity dimension, that is, one's uniqueness or distinctiveness. Personal self-definition is based on characteristics that are positive, yet fuzzy and relative. Because identity is intimately related to self-esteem, the process of impression management is more motivational than perceptual, evaluative rather than descriptive. Who the self is, in large part, is defined by comparison to others; even ideals are culturally influenced. A principal dimension of comparison is relative status (better than/worse than). A dominant psychological process in impression management (self-presentation) is competitive social comparison.

What is often overlooked in research on social comparison (cf. D. T. Miller, Turnbull, & McFarland, 1988) is its interactive nature. The process and the outcome of the interaction can be more important to the perceiver than identifying others or comparing them with self. Also overlooked are the situational properties of this process, particularly as they relate to comparison selection. In the classroom, other students are the salient comparison group, irrespective of their similarity to the perceiver. Here we take issue with D. T. Miller et al., who propose that distinctive (social) characteristics are more central to identity. They may be more situationally salient and, therefore, dominate attention; we contend, however, that although they are more relevant to the task of identifying or describing another, they are less relevant to understanding that other. Because persons ordinarily interact with ingroup members, it is the personal features that make a person feel different from other ingroup members that are ordinarily most central to that person's identity.

These two psychological processes, social categorization and social comparison, do not operate independently. Categorization of others makes salient the social dimension of identity and at the same time increases the probability one will process information about self in terms of one's own social category memberships. That is, the salience of an outgroup in a social situation makes the relevant ingroup salient (Wilder & Shapiro, 1984) and determines the individual's situational identity in that context (Allen, Wilder, & Atkinson, 1983). Conversely, when a person's own category membership is relatively unique in a social context, that membership becomes a more salient feature of the person's self-description (McGuire & Padawa-Singer, 1978).

Application: The Role of the Teacher in Developing Effective Learning Teams

The teacher plays a critical role in helping the team set goals, providing resources to the team, offering constructive feedback on their performance, modeling desired behaviors, and establishing the reward system for the class, the teams, and their members. It is important that a teacher's expectations for students be stated clearly – expectations about what behaviors will be met with approval and what the consequences will be for students. To influence behaviors, these consequences need to be valued by students. The criteria for evaluation as well as the process of evaluation need to be made explicit to students. Most important, we believe, is that the teacher be able to demonstrate (model) examples of desired behaviors and outcomes. In this section, we first describe what an effective team would look like and how members of such a team would interact. Then we emphasize the acquisition of team skills for students, which is a gradual and incremental developmental process.

Characteristics of Effective Teams

Cooperation has both task- and person-oriented components that are intertwined. A number of characteristics of effective teams can be identified. First, an effective team has a clear goal or purpose that is shared and valued by each member. The goal must be challenging, yet achievable. Second, during team meetings there needs to be a sense of participation in problem solving and decision making on the part of every member. Effective meetings improve communications and access to information, resolve important issues, and establish actions to be taken. They are not dominated by one or two people but encourage participation from all members. Third, there needs to be sufficient access to resources and support from the external environment (in this case, the teacher), particularly in the form of helping students develop both learning and teamwork skills. Students must be given access to all the information they need for problem solving and they must have the opportunity to learn about all aspects of class projects. Fourth, leadership activities, such as assignment of tasks, feedback on performance, and re ward and recognition, should be perceived as equitable by the team members. Students should have some participation in setting objectives, assigning tasks, scheduling activities, allocating resources, and evaluating outcomes for themselves and for the team. Feedback on performance, which is critical to skills development, is most useful when it is timely, instructive, and positive.

Finally, and perhaps most important, effective teams exhibit group-developed norms for mutual respect, resource sharing, openness to different viewpoints, high performance standards, and shared responsibility for the team outcome. Team members need to feel a sense of belonging; they need to be valued and trusted by other members, and their ideas need to be taken seriously. They must not be made to feel inhibited or self-conscious. Members of effective teams encourage each other to contribute; they express different viewpoints, openly evaluate each other's ideas, and are willing to experiment with ideas and methods. They willingly share information, go out of the way to help each other, help others feel comfortable asking for assistance, change roles or rotate task assignments, and fairly distribute recognition among themselves. Effective teams also have high performance standards; members set high expectations for one another, inspire others to work hard, draw the best out of each other, and help each other to feel responsible for the team's success. It is equally important for teams to foster constructive norms for how error, risk, and disagreement are handled. In effective teams, past mistakes are forgiven, the focus is on how to do it better; people who take risks and fail are encouraged to try again; and disagreements are encouraged and worked out rather than avoided or ignored. Other sections of this chapter will describe how the development of these characteristics can be derailed.

Skill Development

It is not uncommon for the nature of the learning task to focus on information acquisition (language, math, science) rather than skills development (problem solving, communication, interaction). The nature of the learning task is also related to the perceived role of the teacher: as an information provider, learning facilitator, resource provider, stimulus for learning, or role model.

Academic proficiency is important to students to the extent that it is valued by their family, peers, and respected authority figures. Teachers, almost by definition, value academic proficiency; they cannot assume that it is valued by every student. If a student's lack of proficiency is made salient, proficiency may become less valued – situational identity is threatened and efforts will be made to negotiate a different identity (e.g., Steele, 1988; Tesser, 1988). Such an identity might be perceived as "tough" (and therefore to be feared), "popular" (and therefore to be envied), or athletically skilled (and to be admired on the playground). In any event, attempts will be made to create an impression held by others that will restore a student's esteem, by whatever characteristics they can excel at and at the same time count on some other students to value.

Although social comparison is intrinsic to human interaction, to further curtail its negative effects, human and instructional resources routinely can be made available at a level likely to ensure team success. Certainly, a learning team's goal is task oriented. The ability to listen to others and recognize the value of good ideas, however, is critical to team success. The exercise of these skills will depend, in large measure, on the absence of category-based responding. Therefore, it is important to create an environment that not only minimizes the salience of social category memberships but also trains students in interpersonal team skills that serve that same function.

Some cooperative team procedures (D. W. Johnson & F. P. Johnson, 1987) emphasize creating an awareness of the process events that underlie effective team performance, such as listening well to others and taking their perspective, helping rather than rejecting less motivated or less skilled team members, taking responsibility at the group as well as the individual level. When present, these features will promote the cross-category reciprocal self-disclosure processes essential to personalized interaction and, at the same time, impede and disrupt the dysfunctional social comparison and attribution processes that tend to arise when there are obstacles that interfere with completing the team task.

There are two approaches, however, to developing personalized interaction. One is exemplified by human relations training programs that emphasize the general development of sensitivity, receptivity, openness, reciprocity, and so on. From this perspective, the attainment of such skills is the focal point, constituting an independent, substantive team activity. We emphasize instead the direct linking of group process skills to the team's task goals. In this sense, these skills become instrumental. This has the effect of maximizing the quality of the team's task performance and thereby can act to build in reinforcement in terms of the team's outcome. In contrast to an emphasis on more general group process skills, this latter approach might emphasize instead disclosing how one successfully or unsuccessfully approached an aspect of the team task; freely making direct requests for help when one needs it; giving helpful, rather than demeaning, responses to requests for help, in which a team member provides elaborative explanation rather than mere "answer giving"; and providing constructive evaluation of both own and teammates' task performance and of group process behavior. When there are no overriding external constraints on leadership positions, ad hoc teams provide an excellent opportunity to rotate leadership so that minorities and females have the chance to demonstrate and develop their skills and majority members can experience the leadership capabilities of minorities and females.

Principle 1: Minimize the Salience of Social Categories

Students bring with them to the classroom setting the social attitudes and preju-dices of their culture. People use stereotypes to process information about others, exaggerate the differences between social groups and then explain actual differ-ences in a biased manner (Hewstone, 1990), exaggerate the similarity among members of other groups compared with members of their own group (Park & Judd, 1990), expect and interpret behavior in a way that is consistent with these assumptions (e.g., Darley & Gross, 1983; Duncan, 1976; Lord, Ross, & Lepper, 1979), and evaluate members of their own group more favorably and prefer to be with them than with others.

We propose that being on a cooperative team is not sufficient to negate these influences. Situational features within the interaction setting can trigger percep-tual and motivational processes related to these attitudes that will, in turn, shape the nature of the interaction. Identity is so sensitive that the mere categorization of people into mutually exclusive groups on a trivial basis is sufficient to generate intergroup bias (Brewer, 1979). We recognize that characteristics of culture, such as external social status and associated stereotypes, can have significant impact on intergroup relations (Berger & Zelditch, 1985) and that there is little direct control the interventionist (teacher) can have over these external forces. Two aspects of the contact situation, however, can be controlled to some extent: the situational structure of the class and the interaction processes within and between teams. Structure and process will influence what we described earlier as a core of this model: identity relationships.

Assignment to and Composition of Teams

When creating teams in the classroom, instructors often convey that social cate-gory is the basis of assignment, whether intentional or not. Those in numerical minority are often spread out to ensure representation in all teams, thereby rein-forcing their external minority status within the team structure. This can often result in minority members being the only out-group member on each team. Being in a distinct minority increases the self-focus of minority members (Mul-len, 1983) and can result in increased in-group favoritism (Sachdev & Bourhis, 1984). Unequal numerical representation on teams is associated with reduced benefits of CLTs with respect to intergroup acceptance (Miller & Davidson-Podgorny, 1987). Although solo status will particularly exacerbate category dis-tinctiveness, other numerically unequal representations of categories may have similar effects, making it advisable, perhaps, to equalize the frequency of cate-gory representation in some settings or for some teams even if it means that other teams must be homogeneous. By periodically rotating team membership or creating different teams for different subject matters, one can ensure that students have more intimate experience with all class members. Contact needs to be extensive enough and involve a sufficiently large sample in order for positive affect to generalize to the outgroup (Ashmore, 1970; Gurwitz & Dodge, 1977).

When a heterogeneous team contains persons whose social category memberships cross (i.e., members differ on one category yet share a common identity on another dimension), the salience of social category distinctions will be decreased in comparison to conditions in which members differ on both categories (Vanbeselaere, 1987). We have reported elsewhere (N. Miller & Harrington, 1990a) a study that used physiological measures that are not under voluntary control and not ordinarily perceptible as a means to assess positive and negative affective response to social stimuli (cf. Cacioppo, Petty, Losch, & Kim, 1986). Facial electromyograph (EMG) activity varied directly as a function of the target's group memberships. Positive affect was greatest toward targets who shared two categories with the perceiver, lowest for targets who differed on both dimensions, and intermediate for targets whose memberships crossed (similar on one dimension but different on another).

In addition to the use of crosscutting or multiple categories to diffuse group boundaries, students can by recategorized along a different dimension that does not correlate or converge with category membership. They may be grouped by their interests in certain aspects of the subject matter, as one example. There are other ways in which the salience of group boundaries can be reduced, such as assignment to teams on the basis of unique and individualizing attributes in order to maximize heterogeneity of skills and abilities.

In a laboratory simulation, individuating subjects at the time they were assigned to heterogeneous teams led to more favorable evaluations of outgroup members than when assignments were based on category membership. In addition, minority subjects displayed more bias in their reward allocations than majority subjects when the team was constructed on the basis of category membership but lower bias when constructed on the bias of unique attitudes (N. Miller, Brewer, & Edwards, 1985). In a conceptual replication utilizing random, rather than individual-based, assignment, in comparison to category-based assignment, similar results were obtained (N. Miller & Harrington, 1990a). Thus, even simple random assignment of persons to teams reduced the ingroup favoritism produced by explicit category-based assignment. It is important to note that these studies only manipulated ostensible, not actual, homogeneity or heterogeneity among team members.

Task and Role Assignment

Often tasks require a division of labor such that subgroups of persons on the team work together to complete a particular aspect of the team task. This form of structuring the setting can have important implications for the learning process. Assignment of subgroups to specific task roles, in such instances, should crosscut rather than converge with category membership to avoid strengthening group boundaries. We caution, however, that simply reducing category salience by means of crosscutting role assignments may not be sufficient to reduce ingroup favoritism. Crosscutting tasks can actually increase the competitive social comparison process as long as social identity remains salient and there are no avenues to negotiate a positive personal identity (N. Miller & Harrington, 1990a).

If student preferences are the basis of team composition, existing social boundaries will be maintained. It is, therefore, worth considering the potential problems that can occur when the use of CLT is rare within the school in general and within the same classroom. If the use of CLT reflects an occasional choice of the teacher, only to return to the individual-based and highly competitive structure of the traditional class, then less impact can be expected. Moreover, as often happens, resegregation occurs for student-selected interactions such as those on the playground (Rogers, N. Miller, & Hennigan, 1981). The frequency of CLT use and classroom reward systems will suggest to students what types of interaction receive the most reinforcement.

Principle 2: Minimize Threats to Identity

There are situational features that are likely to produce a general state of negative affect, particularly in a task-oriented context like the classroom, where evaluation and comparison occur as well as the threat of a negative outcome.

Group Process and Personal Threat

Peer tutoring, as used, for instance, by Slavin (1978) in STAD, can carry the threat of status effects when all students learn the same material and, as a consequence of the fact that scholastic achievement and racial-ethnic identity are often linked, one group more often tutors the other group. In contrast, each person can become an expert in his or her own area, as in Jigsaw methods (Aronson, Blaney, Stephan, Sikes, & Snapp, 1978). The discussion of a decision problem, the solution of which is a cooperative benefit to all members, leads to high levels of cooperation (Dawes, 1987, cited by Messick & Mackie, 1989). Having to reach an intrateam consensus about the choice that the team makes, however, can produce competition (Insko, Hoyle, Pinckley, Hong, & Slim, 1988) and be dysfunctional. Teacher-directed training might focus, then, on the value that specific differences can bring to team activities. Team discussion can focus on how differences in expression and its interpretation can lead to serious misjudgments of others. Such discussion can also result in the identification of common values and attitudes among students. Consensus should not be regarded as necessary, but rather, norms for tolerating dissenting views should be encouraged. Support for differences in viewpoints can build relationships across group categories. Whites who received social support from either a black or a white teammate reduced their conformity to a majority (Boyanowsky & Allen, 1973).

Task Threat and Power

Perceptions of threat increase tension and heighten competitiveness (Deutsch & Krauss, 1962). When that threat is external and common to the group, it often has a functional and positive effect on intragroup attitudes and relations (LeVine & Campbell, 1972), producing greater cohesion within the group yet heightening conflict between groups. Conceptually distinct from threats to identity, task threat can best be conceptualized in team settings as the expectation of failure. Threat, therefore, can have dysfunctional effects within the group. Threat of time pressure on a task, for example, has been shown to produce feelings of stress, perceptions of increased task difficulty, and less satisfaction with the group solution (Kelly & McGrath, 1985). When negative consequences for task performance cannot be externalized, that is, attributions of failure are directed toward the team, threat produces greater ingroup bias such that outgroup members on the heterogeneous team are devalued relative to ingroup members (N. Miller & Harrington, 1990a).

In addition to the fact that tasks must often be broken down into subunits that require role specification, it is important to note that such roles often differ in status. In groups may try to appropriate the most valued, task-relevant, or status-enhancing dimensions for their own group (Mummenday & Schreiber, 1983). Equal-status roles and equal participation in decision making, therefore, help to equalize the distribution of power in teams. When decision-making power is salient, identity needs can become threatened and be restored by self-serving evaluations. Merely restructuring group boundaries is not sufficient to decrease bias in a cooperative setting as long as category membership is the only salient feature of identity. However, even in the absence of personalization per se, when subjects in a crosscutting condition do not prejudge their partners because of their category membership, they are more accepting of outgroup members than are subjects whose category membership is reinforced by the basis of task assignment (N. Miller & Harrington, 1990a).

Reward and Recognition

In STAD, gain scores for individuals are used to ensure that each team member has the opportunity to make an equitable contribution to the team, irrespective of initial differences in skill level. When contributions can be viewed objectively, reward allocations have been shown to reflect performance distinctions rather than group discrimination, irrespective of whether performance is perceived (Sachdev & Bourhis, 1987), self-assigned (Finchilescu, 1986), or actual (Ng, 1986). Therefore, if norms for fairness are encouraged, team members' resulting mutual evaluations of one another will counter tendencies toward simplistic category-based responding.

From our own perspective, competitive reward systems, either within or between teams, will be dysfunctional. Competition actually increases anxiety (Wilder & Shapiro, 1989). On first thought, our earlier arguments might seem to suggest that within-team rewards should only be awarded at the team level and not to individual team members because the latter might invoke intrateam competition. Though such a view may have merit, especially when, for whatever reasons, receipt of rewards becomes correlated with category membership, it is important to note that needs for either social or individual identity are not likely to operate to the exclusion of each other. Individual identity needs and the quest for uniqueness, as opposed to needs for similarity to and identification with other group or team members, become salient when social identity needs are unthreatened and when one feels secure about one's social category membership as well as one's acceptance on the heterogeneous team. In other words, in team settings the more optimally a team functions, the more secure is the social identity of its members, and consequently, their individual identity needs become more salient. When the team task is organized so that each individual's unique contributions are identifiable, as must be the case when rewards are dispersed on an individual basis, each team member can experience recognition as a unique contributor and thereby fulfill individual identity needs. Yet, at the same time, members can identify with the accomplishment and receive reward for the success of the entire team. Thus, although such individual recognition may not contribute to the benefits of cooperative team interaction (N. Miller & Davidson-Podgorny, 1987), it does contribute to personal identity needs. And when rewards are distributed on the basis of gain scores, as in STAD, their attainment is unlikely to be correlated with category membership. Therefore, we recommend that reward and recognition include both individual contribution to the team as well as performance of the team. Furthermore, the absence of attention to individual performance could result in the diffusion of responsibility (Latané & Nida, 1980) and disrupt the development of team performance standards for each other.

When a competitive interteam reward structure is imposed on the classroom, as in TGT (DeVries, Edwards, & Slavin, 1978), the stage is set to blame outgroup teammates whenever one's team fails, particularly if they are lower in social status. All the factors that promote category salience will work to increase the likelihood of such negative bias. Potential solutions lie not just in minimizing category salience but in reducing competitive reward structures. In a laboratory simulation, strong and consistent effects were found for interteam reward structures (N. Miller et al., 1985). Competition between teams resulted in more ingroup bias within the team than did cooperation; this occurred across all other experimental conditions, and outgroup devaluation was always the major source of bias, despite the fact that there was a cooperative structure within the team.

Principle 3: Provide Opportunities for Personalization

The focus here is on the self-other relationship. To know and be known by others is a large part of life. Relationships with a moderate or high level of intimacy become increasingly more important during the school stage, and their development is a cornerstone of socialization. In the following sections we describe our position and contrast it with other approaches to personalization.

Personalization

Newcomb (1961) described the development of relationships. In the early phases, disclosure is a function of the similarity of biographical characteristics; in the later stages, however, disclosure is based on discovered similarities in intimate areas of personality. D. A. Taylor (1979) argues that the exchange of intimate information is central to the formation of close relationships. This process whereby one comes to know and be known as a unique individual is what we refer to as personalization. In part, the development of relationships can be explained by the similarity-attraction hypothesis (Byrne, 1971), because the greater the disclosure, the greater the likelihood that similarities will be discovered. Additionally, those who disclose more intimately may be viewed as more trusting, friendly, and warm (Dalto, Ajzen, & Kaplan, 1979), as long as the intimacy of disclosure is not viewed as a violation of social norms (Derlega & Grzelak, 1979). Furthermore, similarity and liking show a reciprocal relationship; people will perceive themselves as more similar to those they like (Byrne & Griffit, 1973). In addition to changes in perceptions of others as a function of their disclosures, one who discloses intimately to another may infer liking for the other as a function of self-perception processes (Bem, 1972). This reciprocal nature of disclosure is central to our position on personalization processes.

Individual members of a group are reacted to more favorably than the group itself (Rothbart & John, 1985; Sears, 1983), and it has been argued that individuation is the result of a dyadic relationship between persons (Whitley, Schofield, & Snyder, 1984). Furthermore, individual interaction is likely to be less threatening, and a lowered anxiety level permits the processing of more individuating information (Wilder, 1986). In turn, the disclosure of unique information leads to more complex and differentiated perceptions of others, which, if informative, can override initial categorization (Kreuger & Rothbart, 1988). Therefore, when a subtask is suitable for dyads, it will be constructive to assign it to a heterogeneous pair within the team. Alternatively, one can begin with dyads, and then proceed to small teams. As students develop the appropriate skills and learn to work in small groups, team membership can be rotated. Eventually, the whole class can operate as an effective, pesonalized team.

Perception of threat should increase task focus, and this, in turn, may discourage the development of personalized interaction (Roth & Kubal, 1975). In a laboratory simulation that compared the consequences of personalized and non-personalized interaction, students were given instructions either to form an accurate impression (personalized focus) or to evaluate the quality of ideas (task focus) of their teammates (N. Miller et al., 1985). An effect parallel to that of a cooperative versus a competitive reward structure, mentioned earlier, was found in the comparison of impression orientation with task focus instructions. When compared with a natural orientation (no instructions), a task focus resulted in more bias; conversely, an interpersonal orientation eliminated ingroup favoritism. When reward structure and impression orientation were examined in conjunction, the task focus had its greatest impact in competing conditions, producing the most bias, whereas the interpersonal orientation had its greatest impact in cooperative conditions, resulting in the least bias. These additive effects are consistent with a view that reward structures influence the interaction process by enhancing or inhibiting an interpersonal focus.

A similar study (N. Miller & Harrington, 1990a) manipulated instructions designed to lead to personalized versus impersonal contact, under conditions in which external social status was also experimentally varied (high, equal, or low). Personalization instructions led to significantly more positive team interaction than the impersonal instructions. A significant interaction between type of contact (personal vs. impersonal) and status showed that personalization reduced ingroup bias among equal- and high-status members, whereas low-status members, who deferentially rated high-status members more positively in impersonal contact, did not evaluatively differentiate them from others in personal contact. This pattern of results shows that personalized contact can eliminate the negative self-fulfilling carryover effects typically found when group members have low external status.

Contrasts with Other Theoretical Approaches

We contrast our approach with four other models. Brewer and N. Miller (1984) proposed a model of decategorization of outgroup members. The first feature of this model is differentiation within the group: Differences among outgroup members are perceived, thus reducing homogeneity (interchangeability) and thereby increasing complexity of the group. The second feature is the personalization of individual outgroup members; that is, one comes to know the personal components of outgroup members' identities. We have extended this model (N. Miller & Harrington, 1990b) to emphasize the reciprocal nature of these processes – the differentiation of self from the ingroup and the personalization of self vis à vis the other through mutual self-disclosure.

Hewstone and Brown (1986) distinguish between interactions that are intergroup (the other perceived as an outgroup member) and those that are interpersonal (the other as an individual) and argue that these are governed by separate and distinct processes. Although they may concede that perceptions of the other as an outgroup member can pejoratively influence and even prevent interpersonal relationships, they argue that changes in interpersonal relations between members of different groups, as a result of CLT, for example, will do nothing to alter perceptions of the outgroup or even the same person when that person is seen as an outgroup member. We have contrasted our approaches before (Harrington & N. Miller, in press) and will note here how the interpersonal-intergroup distinction can be revealing and concealing, convenient yet misleading. The distinction is meaningful with respect to the two sources of identity: group memberships and personality characteristics. However, it unnecessarily creates two processes for the same underlying goal, which is to maintain or enhance a positive identity, as seen by self and others in that situation. It may be a convenient dichotomy for the purpose of discussion but is, in our view, clearly misleading. Demographics may represent the sum total of what we know about a stranger; for a personal friend, that same information accounts for only a fraction of what we know about the person. In any event, a teammate does not cease to be recognized as, for example, being black, female, or taller; that information merely becomes less important. In contrast to a dichotomous, dual-process model, we argue that the social-personal distinction can best be understood as a "proportional attention" dimension (Harrington & N. Miller, 1992). With more personalized contact, the other's complexity increases, and in turn, social charactersitics become relatively less salient. Simultaneously, the probability increases that perceived similarity between self and other will develop.

According to Brewer (1988), people are initially categorized by social features. Whether further information will be sought depends in part on the person being viewed as relevant to the perceiver but also on the insufficiency or inadequacy of the initial category as a basis for organizing the information about the person. In other words, the perceiver will first attempt to type the person within the category. If a type does not fit, the perceiver may then attempt to subtype – viewing the person as a special subcategory within the broader social category (e.g., "an educated black"). Only if both the target person is relevant and the perceiver is personally involved will perceptions tend toward personalization of the target. This is an attention-based, information-processing model. It suggests that participation in a CLT can provide these conditions, namely, relevance of targets and involvement of perceivers. These conditions in themselves, however, do not produce the reciprocal disclosure process we see as integral to personalization.

Fiske and Neuberg (1990), in a corresponding model, propose what we see as essentially a confirmation-disconfirmation model of impression formation, in which persons assess the fit between the other's salient features and a category label. There is a bias toward confirmation of the fit. Initially, the other is categorized by salient features, and then, additional information becomes assimilated to that category. If, however, either the type or the amount of countertypical information increases, perceivers will alter their cognitive strategy and attempt to re-categorize the other with a new label. Only if the initial category is found to be grossly inadequate and a new category cannot be found will the perceiver attempt a piecemeal approach to integrating the other. This too may be unsuccessful, in which case the perceiver may return to the original category as the best fit. In addition to these perceptual and cognitive processes, Fiske and Neuberg propose that motivational factors also will influence impression formation. The underlying motivation is for approval, whether that be from the other, a third-party authority, or self. Approval may be based on accuracy of impression or confirmation of a bias.

By implication, this approach suggests two strategies for implementation within CLT to develop personalization of participants. First, dependent outcomes (viz., outcome interdependence or common fate) may require greater attention to situationally relevant attributes of individuals and a greater need for accuracy in impression formation. Second, the teacher may instruct students to form accurate impressions of one another (for approval) and justify these instructions by reference to task goals. However, we propose that dependent outcomes, in themselves, do not guarantee personalization. Moreover, the teacher cannot be sure what constitutes "accuracy." Accuracy, from our viewpoint, is in the "eye of the receiver," not the perceiver.

This approach, although it includes motivational contributions, is, like Brewer's, primarily an information-accounting model that is other centered. It assumes that persons require a single feature around which to organize information, people cannot abide inconsistency, information is sought by the perceiver rather than provided by the target, and the affective dimension of information is secondary and of less consequence. It is on these points that our model differs from these two models. We have emphasized that the process of personalization just as much requires changes in one's self-perceptions as in one's perceptions of others. In contrast to laboratory studies on impression formation in which information about the target is provided by the experimenter, for the other to become personalized (in natural interaction), the other must willingly disclose self and is only likely to do so in a reciprocal manner (Rubin, 1975). Moreover, the development of interpersonal competencies is essential to cooperative behaviors on a heterogeneous team. Students need to develop skills in expressing themselves to others, listening to others, understanding differences, and so on, to be effective teammates. These points are addressed by Principle 4.

Principle 4: Develop Students' Interpersonal Competencies

To discuss the development of students' interpersonal competencies we borrow, for a moment, a model from a different discipline. When police evaluate potential suspects, they look for the joint presence of three characteristics: opportunity, motive, and means. Committing a particular act requires the contact opportunity for the act to occur, a reason sufficient to motivate the act, and access to a method whereby the act can occur. For students of various backgrounds to behave cooperatively together, they need an opportunity to interact in a situation in which cooperative behaviors can be manifested; they need a motivation to behave cooperatively, a reason to believe that such actions will be beneficial to them; and they need some skill in particular behaviors that we label as cooperative. Too often, intergroup conflict is viewed as an "attitude problem" that requires an "attitude adjustment." Then, as so often happens, attitudes fail to determine behavior.

Self-efficacy

Bandura's (1977) self-efficacy model suggests that students need to believe that (1) behaving in particular ways will lead to certain consequences – response efficacy; (2) such consequences are obtainable – outcome expectancies; and (3) one can perform the behaviors – self-efficacy. Assuming that the outcomes are worthy of attainment for the person, what is often lacking as the link between attitude (motivation to perform) and the behavior itself is the skill or competency to perform. In addition to expectations about self, expectations about environmental support can be instrumental to the development of such skills. Recognizing that behavioral change or skill development is a gradual process, skills can be learned and reinforced by vicarious experiences or modeling, feedback and direct reassurance from significant others, appropriate incentives for performance, opportunities for incremental performance accomplishments, and attributions of success to ability. Whether training is in skills like self-monitoring, self-evaluation, and self-reinforcement, or in skills such as interpersonal problem solving and communication, skills-training approaches emphasize the value of practice (Meichenbaum, 1975).

A variety of techniques, including modeling, self-statements, and imaginal rehearsal, have been used to address the problems that students can manifest in school and that can be disruptive to learning and cooperative interaction: aggression, impulsivity, interpersonal anxiety, test anxiety, and depression (Kendall & Hollon, 1979). Those having problems with aggression, for example, are often lacking in verbal skills (Bandura, 1973); therefore, the development of the ability to communicate can reduce the tendency toward acting out in the classroom. The positive effects of modeling self-disclosure, with appropriate verbal cues, have been demonstrated in dyads (Ehrlich & Graeven, 1971) and may even involve the use of peer models (Cohen & Przybycien, 1974). Care must be taken, however, that self-disclosure is not followed by critical comments about the disclosure, because that may elicit anger and aggression; learning to express one's feelings and cognitively reinterpret the other's expressions can reduce hostility (Green & Murray, 1973). Finally, the acquisition of role-taking ability, which can be fostered in peer discussions, has long been regarded as an important developmental process (Piaget, 1928) and the basis by which one comes to know and understand others – what Mead (1934) called empathy.

Goals of CLT

Returning to our opening comments, we proposed that there are several purposes for the use of CLT. Traditionally, information acquisition is the principal, if not the only, goal of the classroom; the development of positive interpersonal relations and the social skills to obtain them are secondary. We argue that these latter goals are, at least, of equal importance. We have proposed that social skills can be developed as instrumentally relevant to learning goals. A second aim is to improve behaviors with new outgroup members when teams are reformed; this form of generalization is somewhat different from attempts to change attitudes about a group. In our own research our measures of generalization typically are designed to test whether new outgroup members are interacted with as individuals (interpersonal) rather than to assess general attitudes toward the out-group. It is the team skills, we contend, that generalize in new teams. A third goal is generalization to members of all kinds of outgroups, not simply members of those groups encountered in the CLT. Thus, team experience is intended to be cumulative, building on successes.

These are other-centered descriptions of our goals – how one approaches others. Self-referenced descriptions of these same goals are (1) guided self-discovery through mutual disclosure, (2) development of some degree of openness to others or reduced anxiety with outsiders (W. G. Stephan & C. W. Stephan, 1984), and (3) acquired skills in personal relations and cooperative behaviors. Viewed in a different way, the development of these personal goals may parallel the three stages of compliance, identification, and internalized values (Kelman, 1958). Students may begin the process of mutual discovery in compliance with the teacher's instructions and guidance. Then, as they become more comfortable sharing, helping, providing feedback, disclosing to others, listening, and taking the role of the other, they can identify with the personal nature of the other, the more intimate areas of self. Finally, when these values for recognizing the uniqueness of each individual become internalized, students will be able to relate comfortably to others from a variety of outgroups, even those with whom they have had no previous experience.

Final Remarks

Laboratory studies suggest that persons seek confirmation of their early impressions (Rothbart & John, 1985) and that it takes increasingly salient counterstereotypic information to force a shift. Data from classroom interventions suggest that even after cross-racial friendships develop, attitudes toward the outgroup do not change. Acquaintance develops normally (selectively) within classes independent of CLT. CLT, however, provides a structure that can promote acquaintance beyond the social category similarity criteria ordinarily used. We have described a process whereby initial encounters among students are structured by the teacher and directed by guidelines for the development of the acquaintanceship process in learning teams. On this basis, one can foster the norms for respect, openness, and sharing that are essential for effective team functioning and relevant to the specific curricula proficiency goals that are the manifest purpose of the CLT. We do not expect that all cross-ethnic acquaintances will evolve into friendships. However, where individual friendships do develop, access is gained to friendship networks (friends of friends), which can be a major source of increasing cross-ethnic friendships (Slavin, 1985). When possible, structured playground activities can also be used to further promote cross-ethnic relationships (N. Miller, Rogers, & Hennigan, 1983).

We propose that it is a reasonable goal to teach students to delay judgment about others until a valid basis is formed. The accomplishment of this goal requires a gradual process of skills development; that is, it is competency based. Students will feel better about themselves as they develop both a confidence in their interaction competencies and a trust in other people that does not require a ''better than'' orientation but, instead, accepts a ''different from'' judgment as adequate and appropriate. As members of a team, they can work toward a win-win or common benefit of interaction. Because the self is an outgroup member to many others, these interpersonal competencies help reduce the anxiety or threat that others may experience by making them feel more comfortable during the interaction. The outcomes, thus, are twofold.

Although we have discussed the role of increased similarity that can result from personalization, the point is not to teach that similarity, per se, is the ideal – this just reinforces the original source of bias (similar is good; different is bad). Rather, similarity provides a bridge across which to develop personalization – it is a means to an end, which is learning to value differences as well as similarities in each other. In addition, there are many dimensions of similarity – not just social category dimensions. Frustration with the task, interest in a task, liking or disliking of different task components, knowledge or lack of it regarding different task components, and personal experiences relevant or not relevant to the task are not only some examples upon which a common humanity can be found for students in learning teams but also relevant topics of self-disclosure within the context of CLT. There will be self-other similarities across social categories on some of these, if not this time, the next.

The recommendations we have made with respect to the structure and process of student interaction, we believe, require as much attention as the content of the learning materials. We think these, in conjunction with CLT in general, should be emphasized in teacher education as well as in the expectations of teachers within the school system. The benefits to society seem to justify it.

References

Allen, V. L., Wilder, D. A., & Atkinson, M. L. (1983). Multiple group membership and social identity. In T. R. Sarbin & K. E. Scheibe (Eds.), *Studies in social identity*. New York: Praeger.

Aronson, E., Stephan, C., Sikes, J., Blaney, N., & Snapp, M. (1978). *The Jigsaw classroom*. Beverly Hills, CA: Sage.

Ashmore, R. D. (1970). Solving the problem of prejudice. In B. E. Collins (Ed.), *Social psychology* (pp. 246–296). Reading, MA: Addison-Wesley.

Bandura, A. (1973). *Aggression: A social learning analysis*. Englewood Cliffs, NJ: Prentice-Hall.

(1977). Self-efficacy: Toward a unifying theory of behavioral change. *Psychological Review, 84*, 191–215.

Bem, D. J. (1972). Self-perception theory. In L. Berkowitz (Ed.), *Advances in experimental social psychology* (Vol. 6) (pp. 1–62). New York: Academic Press.

Berger, J., & Zelditch, M., Jr. (1985). *Status, rewards, and influence: How expectations organize behavior*. San Francisco: Jossey-Bass.

Boyanowksy, E. O., & Allen, V. L. (1973). Ingroup norms and self-identity as determinants of discriminatory behavior. *Journal of Personality and Social Psychology, 25*, 408–418.

Brewer, M. B. (1979). In-group bias in the minimal intergroup situation: A cognitive-motivational analysis. *Psychological Bulletin, 86*, 307–324.

(1988). A dual process model of impression formation. *Advances in Social Cognition, 1*, 1–36.

Brewer, M. B., & Miller, N. (1984). Beyond the contact hypothesis: Theoretical perspectives on desegregation. In N. Miller & M. B. Brewer (Eds.), *Groups in contact: The psychology of desegregation* (pp. 281–302). New York: Academic Press.

Byrne, D. (1971). *The attraction paradigm.* New York: Academic Press.

Byrne, D., & Griffit, W. (1973). Interpersonal attraction. *Annual Review of Psychology, 24,* 317–336.

Cacioppo, J. T., Petty, R. E., Losch, M. E., & Kim, H. S. (1986). Electromyographic activity over facial muscle regions can differentiate the valence and intensity of affective reactions. *Journal of Personality and Social Psychology, 50,* 260–268.

Cohen, S., & Przybycien, C. A. (1974). Some effects of sociometrically selected peer models on the cognitive styles of impulsive children. *Journal of Genetic Psychology, 124,* 213–220.

Dalto, C. A., Ajzen, I., & Kaplan, K. J. (1979). Self-disclosure and attraction: Effects of intimacy and desirability on beliefs and attitudes. *Journal of Research in Personality, 13,* 127–138.

Darley, J. M., & Gross, P. H. (1983). A hypothesis-confirming bias in labeling effects. *Journal of Personality and Social Psychology, 44,* 20–33.

Derlega, V. J., & Grzelak, J. (1979). Appropriateness of self-disclosure. In G. Chelune (Ed.), *Self-disclosure: Origins, patterns, and implications of openness in interpersonal relationships* (pp. 151–176). San Francisco: Jossey-Bass.

Deutsch, M., & Krauss, R. M. (1962). Studies of interpersonal bargaining. *Journal of Conflict Resolution, 6,* 52–76.

DeVries, D., Edwards, K., & Slavin, R. (1978). Biracial learning teams and race relations in the classroom: Four field experiments in Teams-Games-Tournaments. *Journal of Educational Psychology, 70,* 356–362.

Duncan, B. L. (1976). Differential social perception and attribution of intergroup violence: Testing the lower limit of stereotyping of blacks. *Journal of Personality and Social Psychology, 34,* 590–598.

Ehrlich, H. J., & Graeven, D. B. (1971). Reciprocal self-disclosure in a dyad. *Journal of Experimental Social Psychology, 7,* 389–400.

Finchilescu, G. (1986). Effect of incompatibility between internal and external group membership criteria on intergroup behavior. *European Journal of Social Psychology, 16,* 83–87.

Fiske, S. T., & Neuberg, S. L. (1990). A continuum of impression formation, from category-based to individuating processes: Influences of information and motivation on attention and interpretation. In M. Zanna (Ed.), *Advances in experimental social psychology* (Vol. 23, pp. 1–74). New York: Academic Press.

Green, R., & Murray, E. (1973). Instigation to aggression as a function of self-disclosure and threat to self-esteem. *Journal of Consulting and Clinical Psychology, 40,* 440–443.

Gurwitz, S. B., & Dodge, K. A. (1977). Effects of confirmations and disconfirmations on stereotype-based attributions. *Journal of Personality and Social Psychology, 35,* 495–500.

Harrington, H. J., & Miller, N. (1992). Research and theory in intergroup relations: Issues of consensus and controversy. In J. Lynch, M. Modgil, & S. Modgil (Eds.), *Cultural diversity in the schools: Consensus and controversy.* London: Falmer Press.

Hewstone, M. (1990). The "ultimate attribution error"? A review of literature on intergroup causal attribution. *European Journal of Social Psychology, 20,* 311–336.

Hewstone, M., & Brown, R. (1986). Contact is not enough: An intergroup perspective on the "contact hypothesis." In M. Hewstone & R. Brown (Eds.), *Contact and conflict in intergroup encounters* (pp. 1–44). Oxford and New York: Basil Blackwell.

Insko, C. A., Hoyle, R. H., Pinkley, R. L., Hong, G., & Slim, R. M. (1988). Individual-group discontinuity: The role of a consensus rule. *Journal of Experimental Social Psychology, 24,* 505–519.

Johnson, D. W., & Johnson, F. P. (1987). *Joining together: Group theory and group skills.* Englewood Cliffs, NJ: Prentice-Hall.

Johnson, D. W., Johnson, R., & Maruyama, G. (1983). Interdependence and interpersonal attraction among heterogenous and homogenous individuals: A theoretical formulation and meta-analysis of the research. *Review of Educational Research, 52,* 5–54.

Kelly, J. R., & McGrath, J. E. (1985). Effects of time limits and task types on task performance and interaction of four-person groups. *Journal of Personality and Social Psychology, 49,* 395–407.

Kelman, H. C. (1958). Compliance, identification, and internalization: Three processes of attitude change. *Journal of Conflict Resolution, 2,* 51–60.

Kendall, P. C., & Hollon, S. D. (Eds.). (1979). *Cognitive-behavioral interventions: Theory, research, and procedures.* New York: Academic Press.

Krueger, J., & Rothbart, M. (1988). The use of categorical and individuating information in making inferences about personality. *Journal of Personality and Social Psychology, 55,* 187–195.

Latané, B., & Nida, F. (1980). Social impact theory and group influence: A social engineering perspective. In. P. D. Paulus (Ed.), Group Influence (pp. 3–34). Hillsdale, NJ: Erlbaum.

Lemyre, L., & Smith, P. M. (1985). Intergroup discrimination and self-esteem in the minimal group paradigm. *Journal of Personality and Social Psychology, 49,* 660–670.

LeVine, R. A., & Campbell, D. T. (1972). *Ethnocentrism: Theories of conflict, ethnic attitudes, and group behavior.* New York: John Wiley.

Lord, C. G., Ross, L., & Lepper, M. R. (1979). Biased assimilation and attitude polarization: The effect of prior theories on subsequently considered evidence. *Journal of Personality and Social Psychology, 37,* 2095–2109.

McGuire, W. J., & Padawa-Singer, A. (1978). Trait salience in the spontaneous self-concept. *Journal of Personality and Social Psychology, 33,* 743–754.

Mead, G. (1934). *Mind, self, and society.* Chicago: University of Chicago Press.

Meichenbaum, D. (1975). A self-instructional approach to stress management: A proposal for stress inoculation training. In C. Spielberger & I. Sarason (Eds.), *Stress and anxiety* (Vol. 2, pp. 337–360). New York: Wiley.

Messick, D. M., & Mackie, D. M. (1989). Intergroup relations. *Annual Review of Psychology, 40,* 45–81.

Miller, D. T., Turnbull, W., & McFarland, C. (1988). Particularistic and universalistic evaluation in the social comparison process. *Journal of Personality and Social Psychology, 55,* 908–917.

Miller, N., Brewer, M. B., & Edwards, K. (1985). Cooperative interaction in desegregated settings: A laboratory analogue. *Journal of Social Issues, 41,* 63–81.

Miller, N., & Davidson-Podgorny, G. (1987). Theoretical models of intergroup relations and the use of cooperative teams as an intervention for desegregated settings. *Review of Personality and Social Psychology, 9,* 23–29.

Miller, N., & Harrington, H. J. (1990a). A model of social category salience for intergroup relations: Empirical tests of relevant variables. In R. Takens (Ed.), *European perspectives in psychology* (pp. 205–220). New York: John Wiley.

(1990b). A situational identity perspective on cultural diversity and teamwork in the classroom. In S. Sharan (Ed.), *Cooperative learning: Theory and application* (pp. 39–75). New York: Praeger.

Miller, N., Rogers, M., & Hennigan, K. (1983). Increasing interracial acceptance: Using cooperative games in desegregated elementary schools. In L. Bickman (Ed.), *Applied Social Psychology Annual* (Vol. 4, pp. 199–216). Beverly Hills, CA: Sage.

Mullen, B. (1983). Operationalizing the effect of the group on the individual: A self-attention perspective. *Journal of Experimental Social Psychology, 19,* 295–322.

Mummenday, A., & Schreiber, H. (1983). Better or just different? Positive social identity by discrimination against, or by differentiation from, outgroups. *European Journal of Social Psychology, 13,* 389–397.

Newcomb, T. M. (1961). *The acquaintance process.* New York: Holt, Rinehart & Winston.

Ng, S. H. (1986). Equity, intergroup bias and interpersonal bias in reward allocation. *European Journal of Social Psychology, 16,* 239–255.

Park, B., & Judd, C. M. (1990). Measures and models of perceived group variability. *Journal of Personality and Social Psychology, 59,* 173–191.

Piaget, J. (1928). *Judgment and reasoning in the child.* New York: Harcourt, Brace.

Rogers, M., Miller, N., & Hennigan, K. (1981). Cooperative games as an intervention to promote cross-racial acceptance. *American Educational Research Journal, 18,* 513–518.

Roth, S., & Kubal, L. (1975). The effects of noncontingent reinforcement on tasks of differing importance: Facilitation and learned helplessness effects. *Journal of Personality and Social Psychology, 32,* 680–691.

Rothbart, M., & John, O. P. (1985). Social categorization and behavioral episodes: A cognitive analysis of the effects of intergroup contact. *Journal of Social Issues, 41,* 81–104.

Rubin, Z. (1975). Disclosing oneself to a stranger: Reciprocity and its limits. *Journal of Experimental Social Psychology, 11,* 233–260.

Sachdev, I., & Bourhis, R. Y. (1984). Minimal majorities and minorities. *European Journal of Social Psychology, 14,* 35–52.

(1987). Status differentials and intergroup behavior. *European Journal of Social Psychology, 17,* 277–293.

Sears, D. O. (1983). The person-positivity bias. *Journal of Personality and Social Psychology, 44,* 233–250.

Slavin, R. E. (1978). Student teams and achievement divisions. *Journal of Research and Development in Education, 12,* 39–49.

Snyder, M., & Swann, W. B. (1978). Behavioral confirmation in social interaction: From social perception to social reality. *Journal of Experimental Social Psychology, 14,* 148–162.

Steele, C. (1988). The psychology of self-affirmation: Sustaining the integrity of the self. In L. Berkowitz (Ed.), *Advances in experimental social psychology* (Vol. 21, pp. 261–302). New York: Academic Press.

Stephan, W. G., & Stephan, C. W. (1984). Intergroup anxiety. In N. Miller & M. B. Brewer (Eds.), *Groups in contact: The psychology of desegregation* (pp. 229–355). New York: Academic Press.

Tajfel, H., & Turner, J. C. (1979). An integrative theory of intergroup conflict. In W. G. Austin & S. Worchel (Eds.), *The social psychology of intergroup relations* (pp. 33–47). Monterey, CA: Brooks/Cole.

Taylor, D. A. (1979). Motivational bases. In G. Chelune (Ed.), *Self-disclosure: Origins, patterns, and implications of openness in interpersonal relationships* (pp. 110–150). San Francisco: Jossey Bass.

Taylor, D. M., & Dubé, L. (1986). Two faces of identity: The ''I'' and the ''we.'' *Journal of Social Issues, 42,* 81–98.

Tesser, A. (1988). Toward a self-evaluation maintenance model of social behavior. In L. Berkowitz (Ed.), *Advances in experimental social psychology* (Vol. 21, pp. 181–222). New York: Academic Press.

Vanbeselaere, N. (1987). The effects of dichotomous and crossed social categorization upon intergroup discrimination. *European Journal of Social Psychology, 17,* 143–156.

Whitley, B. E., Schofield, J. W., & Snyder, H. N. (1984). Peer preferences in a desegregated school: A round robin analysis. *Journal of Personality and Social Psychology, 46,* 799–810.

Wilder, D. A. (1986). Social categorization: Implications for creation and reduction of intergroup bias. In L. Berkowitz (Ed.), *Advances in experimental social psychology* (Vol. 19, pp. 291–355). New York: Academic Press.

Wilder, D. A., & Shapiro, P. (1984). The role of outgroup salience in determining social identity. *Journal of Personality and Social Psychology, 47,* 342–348.

. (1989). The role of competition-induced anxiety in limiting the beneficial impact of positive behavior to an out-group member. *Journal of Personality and Social Psychology, 56,* 60–69.

Zajonc, R. B. (1968). Attitudinal effects of mere exposure. *Journal of Personality and Social Psychology Monographs, 9* (2, Pt. 2), 1–27.

10 The Impacts of Role Reversal and Minority Empowerment Strategies on Decision Making in Numerically Unbalanced Cooperative Groups

Geoffrey M. Maruyama, Sharon Knechel, and Renee Petersen

There seems to be widespread agreement that schools within the United States are facing a crisis. Schools seem to be faring poorly in dealing with the diverse needs and demands of our heterogeneous society. Many students leave schools without having developed either strong intellectual skills or adaptive social skills. Further, large numbers of both teachers and students are frustrated by their educational systems.

In part, the problems and frustrations of schools today stem from traditional approaches to education, which (1) are too often high on repetitiveness, drills, and rote learning; (2) rely too heavily on teacher-centered instruction; and (3) have taken a right answer/wrong answer approach to problems. As an example of the first problem, the reading series books used during the elementary years often make reading drudgery, focus student attention on tedious work such as filling out worksheets, and result in teachers spending more time working with skilled readers than with less skilled readers (e.g., Taylor & Frye, 1988). With respect to the second problem, teacher-centered instruction requires that they drive events and impose either individualistic or competitive goals within the classroom. Individualization of instruction can isolate students and eliminate the motivational effects of peers, and competition between students can make peer interaction stressful. Finally, the right answer/wrong answer approach removes from study issues about which right answers are not clear or implies a single right way of thinking about problems (e.g., Boyer, 1983; Goodlad, 1984). In effect, students may learn that school is boring, that school friendships are not

The authors would like to thank Christopher Gustilo and Donna Isham for their help in the role reversal study, and Joseph Erickson, Kerry Frank, Judith LeCount, Patricia Lindberg, Danni Luo, and Mary Beth Stanne for their help with the minority empowerment study. The data contained here were presented at the 1988 meeting of the American Educational Research Association. Support for this proejct was provided by a Hewlett Foundation grant to the University of Minnesota Conflict Project.

particularly important to academic success, and that school addresses only topics that have right answers.

Of course, educational innovations attempt to remedy the shortcomings of today's schools. They begin by providing support, skills, and tools so teachers can create a climate that positively engages the students and helps them develop positive feelings about the school experience. Because peers play a central role in socialization and can be viewed by teachers as resources within the classroom (e.g., Maruyama, 1982), a number of innovations focus on building peer support and encouragement for instruction. Finally, attempts are being made to address issues about which there is disagreement and, thereby, to build critical thinking skills in students.

Cooperative group learning techniques, which provide task interdependence and shared outcomes for students within work groups, provide structure for creating a positive classroom climate that engages students and builds their skills. The techniques foster peer friendships (e.g., D. W. Johnson, R. T. Johnson, & Maruyama, 1983) and improve student achievement (e.g., D. W. Johnson, Maruyama, R. T. Johnson, Nelson, & Skon, 1981). In addition, when a constructive controversy format is incorporated (e.g., D. W. Johnson & F. P. Johnson, 1987), students can examine within a generally positive class climate issues on which there is disagreement and think critically about opposing positions. Finally, through peer tutoring, encouragement, and support, cooperative groups generally can help move the focus away from the tedium of work. Thus, it is not surprising to find that use of cooperative approaches in schools has increased dramatically in popularity over the last decade.

Even though cooperative learning has received increased attention and support, there is still much to be learned about how and why it works, and its limitations. There are many barriers to the development of a positive class climate and positive peer relations. One barrier addressed in this chapter is children's status, which affects how students resolve naturally occurring disagreements or divergent views (e.g., Cohen, 1986). Though the constructive controversy framework provides a structure for addressing disagreement, it likely does not go far enough in teaching the skills for effective and constructive persuasion. In fact, it has been used more to improve learning and to foster critical thinking than to resolve actual conflicts. The controversy approach builds social skills and allows careful presentation of alternative views, but it does not address complexities linked to (1) actual opinions that may be held strongly, (2) numerically unbalanced groups, and (3) strategies for arguing effectively against a larger group. Thus, it may not help much when value differences threaten to fragment the class, for such differences evoke processes of in-group cohesion and pressures to conform (e.g., Nail, 1986).

This chapter describes our initial attempts to develop an approach that over-comes pressures toward conformity and promotes friendship devleopment and respect in the face of disagreements. The approach is intended to lay the ground-work for making effective, informed decisions about complex and controversial issues. Its conceptual framework comes from the literatures on cooperative learn-ing and social influence. It integrates the literatures on cooperative goal struc-tures, structuring controversy within cooperative groups, role reversal, and so-cial influence processes; special attention is given to strategies that increase the effectiveness of persons holding numerically subordinate perspectives (i.e., a literature typically called "minority influence"). Although it builds on the work of the Johnson brothers, the extension to numerically unbalanced groups and the development of interaction strategies from the minority influence literature are new.

The extension to unbalanced groups and minority influence tactics is important for a number of reasons. First, it integrates literatures on group functioning that have developed independently yet seemingly are strongly interconnected. Sec-ond, in heterogeneous classes, views on any issue are likely to differ. The nu-merically balanced controversy is of limited applicability in such a setting. Third, skills taught as part of minority empowerment strategies are likely to increase the capacity of group members to help their groups make informed, thoughtful decisions and to resolve conflicts that emerge. Fourth, teaching students that disagreements are permitted, that they can be learning experiences, and that peo-ple can be friends with others with whom they disagree fosters a classroom cul-ture of intergroup acceptance. Thus, the work is not only conceptually integra-tive but may have broad applicability.

This chapter will follow the structure implicitly suggested earlier. First, it will summarize the literatures on cooperative learning, controversy, role reversal, and minority social influence. Then, these literatures will be integrated to gen-erate a conceptual model for addressing controversial issues. Finally, the con-ceptual framework that is developed will be applied in empirical studies to two controversial issues, one contemporary and concrete (viz., whether or not to support a proposition declaring English as the official language of the United States) and the other more historical and hypothetical (viz., how to distribute scarce supplies of penicillin during World War II). For the English-language question, controversy groups were formed on the basis of subjects' actual opin-ions as well as by arbitrary assignment to positions.

Cooperative Learning Techniques

The conceptual basis for using cooperative goal structures is primarily drawn from field theory (e.g., Lewin, 1935; Deutsch, 1949). According to field theory, motivations toward accomplishment of desired goals reflect a state of tension within individuals; the drive to accomplish a goal motivates behavior. Deutsch (1949) articulated three distinct ways of structuring goals: cooperative, competitive, and individualistic. Cooperative goals link individuals together, positively correlating their goal attainments. From the definition, there obviously can be a range of everyday collaborative activities that should be called cooperative. Besides "purely" cooperative activities, there are activities that require independent performance (e.g., studying with others to prepare for a test) or that allow both group outcomes and individual outcomes (e.g., sports performance). Variations in the array of research approaches commonly viewed as cooperative learning techniques reflect the range of collaborative endeavors present in everyday life.

Two points are important here. First, research examining social interaction and acceptance outcomes strongly favors cooperative goal structures (e.g., D. W. Johnson et al., 1983) over competitive or individualistic ones. Second, important differences in performance do not seem to appear when different cooperative learning techniques are compared with one another (e.g., D. W. Johnson et al., 1981).

This paper will employ the cooperative learning approach of D. W. Johnson and F. P. Johnson (1987) and of D. W. Johnson, R. T. Johnson, and K. Smith (1986) because (1) it reflects a relatively pure example of a cooperative goal structure, (2) its impact on social interaction variables may be somewhat greater than other cooperative strategies and (3) it has been developed for addressing controversy and conflict. To elaborate on the last point, their cooperative learning model structures controversy in specific stages leading to an outcome, there is positive interdependence and individual accountability built into it, and the end product is a product of the entire group.

To summarize, then, the accumulation of empirical work to date strongly supports use of a cooperative goal structure to facilitate both academic achievement and social relationships. Furthermore, this structure seems to be well suited for developing ways of addressing conflict (e.g., Deutsch, 1973). It is not surprising to find that the best developed means for structuring conflict not only employs cooperative goal structures but has been developed by cooperative learning researchers.

Controversy

Controversy can take on a number of different affective and cognitive meanings in our culture but is typically viewed negatively (e.g., Deutsch, 1973: D. W. Johnson, R. T. Johnson, & Smith, 1986). In contrast, D. W. Johnson and F. P. Johnson (1987) have attempted to give it a much more positive connotation. They define it as "the conflict that arises when one person's ideas, information, conclusions, theories, and opinions are incompatible with those of another person'' (p. 224). They view decisions as inherently controversial because they require decision makers to choose between alternatives. To the extent that viable alternative choices exist, controversy becomes an important part of decision making and a necessary stage in attempting to reach a common position. Furthermore, avoiding conflict can yield poor-quality decisions because competing views are not carefully articulated and the group most likely will settle somewhat arbitrarily on either the majority's position or one that everyone can accept. The absence of a careful analysis of alternative views and their bases can greatly limit positions that are acceptable to all group members. In effect, even though controversy can be destructive, carefully structuring it within a cooperative setting can lead to more detailed examination of the available arguments and to constructive results.

Research on controversy shows that conflict can be constructive (e.g., D. W. Johnson & F. P. Johnson, 1987; Tjosvold, 1982) and that it can improve communication and enjoyment of learning (e.g., D. W. Johnson, R. T. Johnson, & Smith, 1986); promote positive self-esteem, cognitive development, and personality development (e.g., D. W. Johnson, 1980); and foster more effective decisions (e.g., Smith, Peterson, D. W. Johnson, & R. T. Johnson, 1986). The positive outcomes for controversy seem to have emerged because they force complex thinking and effective communication, two fundamental educational skills. Most important, the structure has imposed a framework for addressing divergent perspectives in nonadversarial ways. Furthermore, role reversal (the topic of the next section) helps individuals to detach themselves from their own views. Lessened ownership of ideas should facilitate a more open exchange about strengths and weaknesses of particular views.

Before discussing the structure employed by the controversy model (e.g., D. W. Johnson & F. P. Johnson, 1987), it is worth considering in detail how addressing controversy can improve group functioning and group decisions. Initially, effective use of a controversy orientation requires that problems be addressed; all too often, conflict is not stated and therefore is left unattended. Awareness of conflict should arouse motivation to resolve it. Next, because the structure addresses divergent views, it encourages creative thinking, which should help in reformulating problems if disagreements are difficult to resolve and in generating novel and varied patterns of decisions.

In terms of the thought processes of group members, controversy will force group members to realize that others have a different conclusion and that their own conclusions will be challenged and contested. This often produces uncertainty about the correctness of one's view. In attempting to resolve conflict, group members are likely to search for additional information, different experiences, and a better cognitive position; in addition, they should pay more attention to and attempt to understand the conclusions and rationale of the persons with whom they disagree. Finally, as part of formulating their position for presentation, they are likely to engage in cognitive rehearsal of their position and rejoinders to it.[1] Empirical work suggests that the cognitive activity can result in reconceptualization of one's own position, better understanding of the positions of others, integration of the information and reasoning of others with one's position, some attitude change, and use of complex reasoning strategies (see D. W. Johnson, R. T. Johnson, & Smith, 1986).

Because the structure of the controversy model is the basis for the empirical work reported here, it will be described in some detail. In a typical scenario, students are given reading and reference materials covering the range of tenable views preceding the controversy exercise. Immediately prior to the exercise, students receive a clear description of their task, including the position each will initially advocate (often including a summary of key arguments supporting the position), and the specific stages of the controversy procedure (e.g., D. W. Johnson & F. P. Johnson, 1987). Students are divided into groups, generally groups of four, such that two students advocate each position. If students hold strong views about the issue, groups are most typically assigned with one person on each side whose personal views are consistent with the position he or she promotes.

The five stages of the controversy exercise as follows: (1) Each pair plans their position and arguments; (2) each pair presents their position to the other pair; (3) in open discussion each pair argues their side as forcefully and persuasively as possible; (4) each pair argues the opposing pair's position forcefully and persuasively (this role reversal stage typically does not include exchange of materials but involves arguing from notes and memory); and (5) both pairs stop advocating particular positions and attempt to reach a consensus on the view they believe is best supported by evidence and logic.

The controversy process ideally improves logical thinking and communication skills, promotes a better understanding of the issue being discussed, and provides a positive context for dealing with disagreement. The balanced groups and arbitrary assignment of students to positions can help students develop skills independently from engaging in actual disagreements. At the same time, however, the structure may limit applicability to naturally occurring controversies. Both conceptually and empirically it makes sense to add to the model the complexity

---

1 It may seem that cognitive rehearsal has been conceptualized as both solidifying one's position (e.g., belief inoculation) and increasing openness to change (the position of D. W. Johnson, R. T. Johnson, & Smith, 1986). It may be that the controversy structure focused attention on careful consideration of two sides of an issue, while the attitude studies primarily focused on refuting the other's position while strengthening your own (in effect, it implicitly took a competitive approach to disagreement). Clearly, however, this explanation awaits an empirical test.

of numerically unbalanced groups and actual opinions. Before turning to that discussion, however, a particular aspect of the controversy model, role reversal, will be discussed briefly.

Role Reversal

As a means of resolving conflicts about controversial issues, Muney and Deutsch (1968) advocated use of role reversal, an approach in which individuals discussing an issue are requested to present a perspective opposed to their own. Role reversal is likely to work only when the situation contains mixed motives, namely, a combination of cooperative and competitive goals (e.g., D. W. Johnson, 1971). In a purely cooperative setting, individuals generally are open and receptive to new information, so role reversal is not needed. In a purely competitive setting, either communication typically shuts down or the setting resembles debate, in which the focus is on winning or losing (Deutsch, 1962). Most group decision situations, however, involve aspects that are cooperative (there is need to reach an acceptable decision) and competitive (members have their own preferences), so role reversal should be effective.

Role reversal works because it counters three tendencies common in conflict situations that limit effective decision making: (1) Receivers evaluate messages of senders from the receivers' frame of reference; (2) receivers distort their opponents' messages and intentions; and (3) individuals communicate in ways that have high likelihoods of being misleading, misunderstood, or cut off (e.g., D. W. Johnson, 1971). Simply changing positions, however, is not sufficient. To be most effective, role reversers need to demonstrate credibility, displaying (1) accurate understanding of the message and perspective of others, (2) warmth toward and acceptance of others, and (3) authentic and genuine behavior.

Conceptually, effective role reversal acts by increasing listeners' understanding of the content and context of messages, which helps clarify positions and reduce misunderstandings; by leading individuals to realize that their views are being heard and understood; by giving the perception that the listeners are well intentioned; by reducing self-defensiveness; by increasing awareness of the strengths of the others' perspective and the weaknesses of one's own; and by increasing liking and perceived similarity between individuals. Factors inhibiting effectiveness of role reversal are strength of a priori commitment to a particular view and degree of incompatibility between different views.

Finally, role reversal helps individuals look carefully at the complexity of particular issues, which builds critical thinking and analytical skills. In effect, careful exposure to both sides of an issue makes simple conclusions more difficult and prevents schematic or simplistic solutions.

Interestingly, recent work on preventing bias in human social judgments has found effective strategies that have much in common with role reversal. Most notable is the strategy Lord, Lepper, and Preston (1984) called "consider the opposite," in which subjects are induced to look at individuals and social issues in ways that make salient perspectives opposite to the ones currently held. In both domains the technique countered common tendencies to attend to and be influenced primarily by confirming information. One could argue that the consider-the-opposite strategy produces the kinds of processes that role reversal does, but without the interpersonal dynamics. Both approaches help lessen individuals' tendencies to draw simplistic conclusions. Thus, this body of research affirms the value of role reversal techniques. However, the interpersonal nature of role reversal requires participants to develop social skills (e.g., communication) and skill in effective group decision making.

To summarize, role reversal facilitates effective communication. It changes perceptions of others as well as attitudes toward issues. Most important, it helps increase discussion and understanding of issues, thus improving decision making. Finally, when embedded in a cooperative goal structure, it fosters positive perceptions of others.

Social Influence Processes in Numerically Unbalanced Groups

The final literature to be discussed is that on social influence processes. A portion of it considers the effects of numerical majorities and minorities on each other – the conformity and minority influence literatures. The former literature is primarily American, dating back to work by Sherif (1935), Asch (e.g., 1956), Festinger (1950), and others. It examines a number of basic and fundamental pressures one faces within groups and organizations. Most important among these is the pressure to behave like other group members. Although individuals differ in their willingness to accept the views of others (e.g., Maslach, Stapp, & Santee, 1985; Snyder & Fromkin, 1980), the pressures to conform are powerful enough to have warranted investigation independently of variability among individuals in their susceptibility to influence. A complete understanding of social influence processes requires an understanding of this variability. Nonetheless, there are powerful and predictable forces within groups that at an aggregate level shape behaviors and often affect attitudes of group members. Even individuals who resist those influences are markedly affected by them. Therefore, examining social pressures exerted by majorities is an important part of the investigation of social influence processes.

The literature on the influence of numerical minorities developed in Europe independently of the majority influence literature (e.g., Moscovici, 1976). It proposes a more dynamic view of social influence processes. It recognizes that minorities are at a disadvantage in attempting to shape attitudes and behaviors of groups in which they participate, and focuses on how their influence can be increased.

Over the last few years, there has been a resurgence of interest in social influence processes coupled with a desire to compare, contrast, and even integrate the majority and minority influence literatures (e.g., Latane & Wolf, 1981; Levine, 1980; Levine & Russo, 1987; Maass & Clark, 1984; Nail, 1986; Nemeth, 1986; Tanford & Penrod, 1984). Before describing the attempts to juxtapose these two literatures, however, each will be examined in more detail.

Majority Influence

Recent work on social influence processes has been driven by the minority influence perspective's attempts to look at group interactions as dynamic processes involving mutual attempts at social influence. Because majorities exert the most prominent force within any group and consequently have the greatest influence (e.g., Tanford & Penrod, 1984), this work has brought the majority influence literature back into prominence as well. As suggested, however, the clearest delineation of *how* majorities exert influence has come from the minority influence perspective. "How" will be discussed later, when the focus shifts to influence strategies for minorities.

Nail (1986) recently consolidated and advanced the majority influence literature by providing a three-dimensional framework for responses to social influence. His paper reflects the orientation of the majority influence literature, which primarily has examined how the target of influence responds to social forces. Because that framework carefully delineates a range of responses to social influence, however, it warrants inclusion here. Further, it provides important contextual information for any dynamic model of social influence.

The three dimensions of Nail's (1986) framework are (1) initial or preinteraction agreement/disagreement, (2) postexposure or postinteraction public congruence/noncongruence, and (3) postexposure or postinteraction private agreement/disagreement. Nail's model examines consistency between the source(s) and target(s) of influences before and after the influence attempt. It allows researchers to look at four possible outcomes when persons initially agree, and four when they initially disagree. When *persons initially agree,* the target person can agree with the other (congruence), behave consistently with the other but disagree (compliance), or behave inconsistently with the other but actually agree (anticompliance), or behave inconsistently with the other and disagree (anticonversion). When *persons initially disagree,* the target can change in both attitude and behavior (conversion), in only the behavior (compliance), in only the attitude (anticompliance), or in neither (independence).

Nail's framework fits nicely with a dynamic model of social influence. For example, the case of anticompliance following initial disagreement (change in private attitude without change in public behavior) is difficult to imagine in the conformity literature but central to the minority influence literature, in which members of the majority often maintain public solidarity with their group while beginning to doubt and question the majority position. Thus, Nail's framework provides a perspective and terminology for examining group interactions.

One additional interesting aspect of Nail's work is his use of Deutsch and Gerard's (1955) notions of informational and normative social influence. Compliance is seen as produced by normative influence, in which individuals agree with the group's perspective to avoid sanctions or gain acceptance. In such instances the group's views do not necessarily provide information about reality. It is only necessary for those views to be understood so that public behavior is appropriate. Informational influence, in which group members' views are used to provide information about reality, is likely to lead to private attitudinal acceptance as well as congruent behaviors. Perhaps the most important aspect of the distinction is that it acknowledges multiple types of influence, for it may be that in the absence of interventions designed to shape peer interactions, neither informational nor normative social influence operates very strongly (e.g., Maruyama, Miller, & Holtz, 1986). Further, even when influence occurs, it is often difficult to sort out whether acquiescent or conforming behaviors of individuals reflect their perception that others understand more than they do or that others will punish them if they disagree. Nevertheless, the conceptual distinction allows better specification of the processes that occur, and the informational and normative social influence distinction will be helpful for integrating the literatures discussed here.

As noted earlier, the majority influence literature has studied how majority influence occurs. Researchers who examined the dynamics of social influence provide the most complete specification (e.g., Nemeth, 1986). They conclude that majorities exert their influence by presenting a united front; by generating and sustaining a focus on the position they hold and why the minority disagrees with it; by inducing stress (arousal) in the group, which helps to move the group to the dominant response; by implicitly withholding social acceptance from those who disagree; and by focusing on rapidly attaining consensus or at least agreement. Even though their influence attempts may suggest expertise and, therefore, informational influence (e.g., Duval, 1976), there is a strong normative influence component. Consequently, majorities are more likely to change others' public pronouncements and behavior than to change their private attitudes.

To summarize, the majority influence literature has focused on the impacts of the most powerful source of influence in a group situation, namely, the majority.

It separates changes in behavior from changes in attitudes, it looks at movement away from the majority position as well as toward it, and it has described the ways in which majorities shape the behaviors of others.

Minority Influence

As noted earlier, the literature on minority social influence comes from a much different tradition. Although its dynamic field-oriented focus is consistent with much work in American psychology, it has been viewed as a contrast to the majority influence literature. Even among recent reviews there has been disagreement about whether the two literatures should be integrated (e.g., Latane & Wolf, 1981; Tanford & Penrod, 1984) or viewed as distinct (e.g., Nemeth, 1986). The minority influence literature begins with the well-established assumption that minorities are at a disadvantage compared with the majority. From there, it attempts to understand why group decisions sometimes fail to follow majority positions. In many situations groups fragment rather than accept a majority view; in others, they adopt a position initially held only by a small proportion of group members. Thus, the challenge for minority influence researchers is to try to explain the factors that account for diminished influence of majorities and enhanced influence of minorities.

The minority influence literature has identified characteristics of the individuals involved and of the settings that shape group decisions. The impact of these characteristics depends upon the perceptions of and, subsequently, causal attributions made by majority group members. For example, for a particular issue minority group members are often more effective when they display *consistency* in their beliefs over time and despite pressure to change. Increased social influence occurs when the consistency is interpreted as reflecting certainty and confidence about the issue. If, however, the minority group members are viewed as *rigid* in interpersonal style and beliefs (i.e., across all issues), consistency will not be enough, for attributions will be made to the persons rather than to the issue. Finally, individuals who differ both in physical characteristics and in opinions (called "double minorities") have been found to be ineffective when their physical differences are viewed as accounting for the opinion differences. For example, a woman arguing for women's issues among men is likely to be ineffective. In such instances, the attributions likely are made to self-interest rather than access to information, thereby justifying disagreement and preventing successful influence. To be effective, a minority must appear to be flexible in style, be reasonable to interact with, lack self-interest in the issue, and be firm on the issue.

Aside from personal characteristics, the influence of minorities depends on the nature of the opinions held. As *discrepancy* between the views of the majority and minority increases, potential for persuasion obviously increases but so does the likelihood of the minority being labeled as personally strange, leading to a discounting of their positions by the majority. The limited literature on minority influence and discrepancy of opinion suggests that influence depends both on amount of discrepancy and on whether the discrepant views are on the same general side of the issue (e.g., Fishbein & Lange, 1990). Interestingly, none of the work seems to have examined the effects of group members' level of commitment to their views.

A second factor related to the nature of the opinions held is cultural zeitgeist, or the general set of prevailing cultural norms. Not surprisingly, when the zeitgeist favors a particular view, influence is much greater than when the zeitgeist opposes that view. Perhaps this finding should be linked to the group polarization or "risky shift" literature (e.g., Dion, Baron, & Miller, 1970), which examined as one reason for groups accepting increased risk an explanation labeled "rhetoric of risk." That view suggests that certain risky choices can be presented in a more powerful way than can alternative views because they sound important and "American." It is possible that the zeitgeist is supportive of appeals that are consistent with it and therefore appear "right" and "reasonable."

Nemeth (1986) has gone beyond the "effectiveness of influence" issue to look at the benefits of using a process in which minority perspectives are listened to and considered. She suggests that majorities and minorities stimulate different processes for problem solving and that successful use of a minority influence orientation will improve the group's decision-making processes independently of the correctness of the views of the minority. That is, minorities force the group to consider other perspectives. Further, because minorities, in contrast to majorities, typically do not compel compliance, their impact may occur via informational influence on private beliefs rather than on public behaviors.

In terms of the group processes, Nemeth's (1986) arguments parallel those of D. W. Johnson (e.g., D. W. Johnson & F. P. Johnson, 1987) when he describes role reversal and controversy. She contends that minorities force consideration of alternative views and divergent thinking, which produces more novel and higher quality group decisions. Increased understanding of alternative views should decrease group member confidence in their position and prepare them to make less biased decisions. Then, because overtly addressing conflict requires additional attention by group members, the decision-making process should be improved. Further, by removing the stigma of disagreeing, the minority influence orientation reduces stress and allows individuals to express their ideas even though those ideas may be wrong or not held by the majority.

To summarize, active minorities can force the groups to which they belong to consider a range of alternative views before making a decision. In terms of both process and outcome, this approach should be superior to one driven primarily by conformity processes. Before moving on there is one additional point worth making, which is that many of the minority influence studies have chosen as their tasks issues like blue/green color discrimination. In other words, the work has not typically involved tasks about which subjects have strong feelings or beliefs, which may limit its applicability to real-world decision processes.

Integration of Perspectives

Thus far, this chapter has provided an overview of literatures on cooperative learning, structured constructive controversy, role reversal, and social influence processes. As noted earlier, the first three literatures have generally developed independently of the social influence literature, despite substantial overlap in their focus on effective group functioning. The present section attempts to integrate these literatures in a way that focuses attention on the application to educational settings.

The basic principles need restating. First, decision making requires choosing between alternatives. Thus, controversy is inherently present in decision making. Second, groups making decisions are by definition cooperative; their members share one or more common goals as they select some common rules, norms, or guides to behavior. Third, group decision making entails influencing individuals who prefer alternative views. These principles lay the foundation for viewing social influence, cooperation, and controversy as intertwined; in making decisions groups cooperatively engage in processes involving both controversy and social influence.

Making effective decisions, however, depends on the approach taken. For example, if processes like structured controversy and role reversal are not used, the majority will likely force convergent thinking and agreement with its position. There is little reason to believe that group processes would differ from the conformity processes described in the majority influence literature. Notable also is that those processes are not very likely to change beliefs, even if behaviors change to conform to the majority.

Integration of the minority influence literature with the controversy and role reversal literatures seems to provide a framework for effectively addressing conflict and making decisions. The controversy framework coupled with role reversal certainly sets up a structure for addressing conflict and should force groups to engage in many of the processes (e.g., divergent thinking) that Nemeth (1986) has discussed in her conceptualization of the minority influence literature. At the same time, however, if minorities are overly concerned about acceptance or if they attempt to use strategies such as compromise or accommodation, the attributional framework suggests that they will be viewed as uncommitted to their views, which will diminish their influence. In effect, one likely shortcoming of the controversy framework is that it ignores the effects of social influence processes on group interaction. An important shortcoming of the minority influence literature is its inattentiveness to structural features that could produce more effective decision making in groups. From the latter literature, effective decisions occur when there is a fortuitous combination of personal characteristics possessed by individuals in the minority and personal and societal beliefs of group members. Integration of the literatures will provide both a structure for the interaction and a framework that attends to attributional processes of group members.

A structure that results in effective decision making must be a *cooperative goal structure*. To deflect competitive or antagonistic elements as persons try to influence one another, the *structured controversy* framework is needed. It keeps the focus on the issues and controls the process and structure of disagreement. As noted earlier, however, the controversy model has been applied only to balanced groups and typically has minimized or controlled differences in initial opinions. Further, it has been used to build skills more than to address active bases of disagreement. Its effectiveness in "real" situations with "real" issues is not clear. *Role reversal* has the potential to assist the controversy process, for it requires group members to carefully listen to and try to understand the views of other group members. Also, by forcing them to attend carefully to the issues, it should help lessen the tendency for individuals to allow heuristics to shape their positions. The effectiveness of role reversal, however, may be lessened when commitment to initial views is high and when opinion discrepancy is large. In such instances individuals are less receptive to divergent information and more likely to attribute the opinion discrepancy to the personal characteristics or situation of the individuals holding alternative views. Furthermore, it is not clear how well role reversal works in unbalanced groups. Finally, the *minority influence* literature has highlighted skills needed for being an effective minority. These skills begin with effective communication. An effective minority maintains its beliefs, draws attention away from deviants and toward the full array of member views, deals with pressure from other group members successfully, and displays interpersonal styles that lead other group members to view them as competent, generally flexible, and personally committed.

To summarize, integration of the various views seems logically to lead to a hybrid that builds on the strengths of both the controversy and the minority influence conceptual perspectives while trying to overcome their potential weaknesses. That hybrid incorporates the cooperative learning and structured controversy framework of D. W. Johnson and F. P. Johnson (e.g., 1987) but adds to it training of skills for effective influence from the minority influence literature. Thus, it yields a combination of structural and personal characteristics that facilitate effective decision making. The interpersonal training, which we will call *minority empowerment,* should help individuals holding minority perspectives to understand both why minorities are typically ineffective and what they can do to maximize the likelihood that their views are carefully attended to.

Operationalization of the Minority Empowerment Model

This section describes our first two efforts to operationalize the minority empowerment model. We selected college students as subjects. Our goal was to develop and improve the techniques on a college-aged population before attempting to use them in secondary and upper elementary classrooms. As will be seen from the findings to be reported, we are still working to strengthen and modify the techniques so their effects become both robust and consistent.

Our first study examined dynamics of majority and minority influence in a cooperative learning group exercise promoting controversy. We constructed the cooperative groups so four individuals argued for one position and two for the other. We used the controversy model of D. W. Johnson and F. P. Johnson (1987) to provide a structure in which persons could freely express differing ideas. We assumed that the unbalanced groups would not upset the general positive atmosphere.

In the treatment conditions, persons holding minority opinions were provided with ways to increase their influence on the decision, to lessen the focus of the group on them or their opinions (e.g., Duval, 1976), and to enhance their interpersonal effectiveness. The strategies, drawn from the minority influence literature (e.g., Maass & Clark, 1984; Nemeth, 1986), blended effective individual styles with effective orientations to disagreement. They included being consistent, focusing on issues and the process of controversy, appearing confident and competent, avoiding the appearance of seeking personal acceptance, and, when possible, appealing to the broader values and beliefs of group members.

The topic, one with both professional and personal relevance to the students, was the "English as the official language" proposition. It had recently been introduced in Minnesota and had received newspaper coverage in the major metropolitan and student newspapers. Therefore, although their beliefs about it were probably not strong, it was a topic about which they were likely to have an opinion. Further, when possible we assigned students to positions that they personally held.

Overall, then, the first study used a cooperative learning structure to integrate the dynamics of processes of majority influence (conformity), minority influence, and structured controversy. It attempted to provide a climate and structure that can be used to address controversial topics in natural settings, even in groups in which opinions are not evenly split and in which participants argue for positions that they strongly believe. Finally, it tested whether principles of effective minority influence when used in an educational intervention would increase minority effectiveness.

Specifically, the uneven split was always a majority of four against a minority of two; the setting was an hour-long class exercise (preceded by premeasures plus relevant information for the exercise topic). In over half of the groups the majority/minority split reflected subjects' reported opinion differences. Minority position individuals in half of the groups received written information about minority strategies for increasing one's influence. (For a more detailed description of the subject population, the design, the materials provided to subjects, and the instruments used, see Knechel, Maruyama, & Petersen, 1990.) These elements yielded a 2 (subjects divided by actual opinion vs. arbitrarily) × 2 (minority given strategies vs. not) × 2 (majority opinion favors vs. opposes the initiative) design.[2]

At the group level, the relatively small number of groups (20) limited the power of our analyses; there were no significant effects.[3] At the same time, there were patterns to the findings that intrigued us (see Table 10.1). Notably, the 7 groups in which individuals were assigned arbitrarily to their positions all selected the majority position. In contrast, when group members argued for their personal views, 12 of 13 groups (vs. 4 of 7 for the arbitrary groups) chose to be opposed to the initiative. There also appeared to be tendencies within the personal-view groups for the minority strategies to affect group decision processes. For example, those 3 groups in which minority members were *not* given strategies and yet prevailed never made decisions by consensus. In contrast, 3 of 4 groups in which the minority had strategies and opposed the proposition made their decisions by consensus. The 5 groups in which the majority opposed the proposition chose the majority position. The 2 groups in which minority members were given strategies, however, made decisions by majority rules, whereas 2 of the 3 groups in which minority members were not given strategies agreed with the position of the majority in a consensual decision. Notably, it appeared that the minority strategies worked better when real opinions were being argued, which is an exciting finding if replicable. Cast in terms of conceptual views, the arbitrary-opinion groups functioned much as the conformity literature would pre-

2 Note that we controlled only whether or not students in the numerical minority were given specific strategies to consider. We initially attempted to divide all groups according to actual opinions but were left with some unmatched participants, who were then arbitrarily assigned to positions. Because more participants initially favored the proposition, there were more groups with majorities favoring the proposition than with majorities opposing it.

3 Groups in the present studies were of size 6 or larger (including observers). Further, there was some loss of subjects when we attempted to select groups to reflect particular configurations of actual opinions, because attitudes rarely conform to a normal curve or a flat, equal-frequency distribution. The lack of power of the analyses was and will likely continue to be a problem.

Table 10.1. *Group decisions, method of decision making and number of arguments generated in support of the group decision, broken down by assigned majority position and whether or not the minority group members were given strategies* (N = 20 groups)

Majority positions: Minority strategies:	Favors		Opposes	
	No	Yes	No	Yes
Arbitrary-opinion groups				
Decision: favors	M5	C5		
		O5		
		M5		
Decision: opposes			C5	C5
				C4
Actual-opinion groups				
Decision: favors	C5			
Decision: opposes	O3	C4	C5	M4
	O3	C2	C1	M4
	O5	C5	M3	
		M5		

Note: The letters in the entries refer to the obtained type of decision making (C = consensus, M = majority rules, O = other). The letter is followed by the number of arguments generated in support of the decision. Groups indicating a decision method other than consensus or majority rules listed the following: one member (a minority member) "would not change her mind"; "we each had our own predetermined decision"; or "other" was checked as the method without further specification. Note that the table is organized by outcome as well as condition, which helps account for its unbalanced appearance.

Source: Adapted from Knechel, Maruyama, & Petersen (1990).

dict: Group decisions matched the majority view. In actual-opinion groups, minority influence strategies (although not statistically significant) seemed more effective in influencing the group decision and/or means of decision making. This suggests that commitment to the issue may be an important prerequisite for making the kind of impression on others that can counter pressures toward conformity. Commitment seemingly ought to diminish one's willingness to change, which not only keeps attention focused on the issue but also can increase the credibility of the position being supported.

At the individual level, majority members compared with minority group members were more satisfied with the experience and felt they were more influential, but they also changed more in response to the interactions than did minority group members in their intention to support the initiative. These results cannot be attributed to minority empowerment strategies, but in this setting, the presence of a minority who argued for an alternative position produced interesting effects on the groups' consideration of the issue.[4] Notably, the findings fit the majority influence literature's expectation of a powerful, satisfied majority but at the same time are consistent with the minority influence notion of latent minority influence. In addition, as predicted by the cooperative learning literature, minority and majority members viewed each other favorably – and more favorably than they were viewed by observers who did not participate in the controversy.

Group observers' assessments of the arguments provided a detailed picture of the processes involved. The most powerful arguments (selected a priori) were persuasive, even though their impact failed to reach statistical significance. Differences were also noted in how the members postured their arguments based on their group status. The number of arguments presented by the minority particularly affected the majority's satisfaction, attitudes, and intentions. The greater the number of minority arguments, the greater the change in the attitudes and behavioral intentions of the majority. The conformity literature does not predict such a finding. Minority members who presented a greater number of arguments reported greater satisfaction. The number of arguments presented by the majority was not related to minority members' change in behavioral intention or attitudes or to their satisfaction with the final decision.

Overall, then, though not significant, the group, individual, and observational outcomes are generally consistent with one another and with predictions of the minority influence literature (e.g., Nemeth, 1986). Although they are weaker than we might have hoped, given the small number of groups they are perhaps not surprising. The differences between actual- and arbitrary-opinion groups are worthy of further investigation, and the minority influence manipulation appears to have had some effects. In addition, the structured controversy activity seemed to foster a positive climate, for participants generally were interested in working with one another again.

One additional consideration, not addressed in the first study, was how role reversal might augment or modify the findings. We excluded it from the first study because of uncertainty about the effects it might have in unbalanced groups, for example, about how well students might do in presenting minority positions during role reversal, about sample size (which was not sufficient to have added another independent variable), and about overall time taken by the exercise. The exclusion of role reversal, however, should be viewed as part of our incremental approach to the problem area. A second study examined role reversal in unbalanced groups.

---

4 Alternatively, this could be an artifact of the sample, because more participants initially favored the propositions, and the predominant shifts were toward opposing the proposition.

Prior work on role reversal has been sufficiently supportive to have made it an integral part of the Johnson and Johnson controversy model. At the same time, that research typically has not examined changes from pretest to posttest group opinions and individual attitudes and has not studied numerically unbalanced groups. Therefore, we examined the effect of these features. The topic was "distribution of penicillin in North Africa during World War II" (see D. W. Johnson & F. P. Johnson, 1987). The 42 subjects were divided into groups of 6 (4 majority, 2 minority) based on pretest options.

There were no significant group-level effects. Not surprisingly, because we made no attempt to empower the minority, 6 or 7 groups chose the majority position prior to role reversal; after role reversal, 5 of 7 still chose the majority position. Role reversal increased both the number of groups reaching the decision by a consensus (from 1 to 3) and the number of arguments supporting the decision. Alternatively, these two changes could be due to the additional time given for discussion.

At the individual level, the findings were very interesting. For both intentions and attitudes, minority group members changed appreciably, moving significantly further away from the initial majority position prior to role reversal and then moving significantly back to their initial views after role reversal. The other individual measures (ideas, influence, satisfaction) showed no majority/minority differences, although the satisfaction of all subjects increased from the first decision time to the second.

The findings suggest that prior to role reversal, the will of the majority won out, but at a cost of alienating the minority, who even more strongly opposed the group decision. They look much like what one might expect from the conformity literature, but with a strong "backlash" effect. After role reversal, however, minority members tempered their views, moving back essentially to their initial views, and satisfaction of all group members increased.

According to the theory, the effects of role reversal would come from having to think through the others' perspective and from hearing the others articulate your position. Thus, a priori it seems that there is no strong reason to expect that perspective taking would occur *only* for the minority. On the other hand, if, due to pressures produced by conformity processes, the minority ineffectively presented its views, this would impair the perspective taking of the majority. If so, perspective taking could have produced change in the minority members' views but not in those of the majority members. Regardless of the "true" explanation, the findings are intriguing, for they emerge strongly despite the small sample. Because data collected prior to role reversal are not commonly reported in the paradigm used, our findings could reflect an unanticipated reaction to majority influence processes in a structured controversy setting, or they could result from our use of unbalanced opinion groups.

Finally, finding shifts only in the minority has potentially important implications, for role reversal produces a structure that should help articulate the minority position. It may possibly do so only if the minority view is clearly and persuasively presented. In the absence of an effective minority, the typical result may be minority frustration (because of their ineffectiveness) and alienation. If such processes occurred in our study, the role reversal experience apparently was strong enough to counter the negative reactions and bring minority members back to their initial opinion. Most important for our future work are the implications of increasing minority effectiveness. An intervention that increases the clarity and persuasiveness of persons holding the minority position could enhance the effectiveness of role reversal in shaping views of majority group members.

Conclusion

The two studies presented here provide data that generally seem consistent with the minority empowerment model. The minority empowerment strategies seem to have some effects within the controversy framework, and role reversal seems to operate in a somewhat unexpected, although not unpredictable, way in numerically unbalanced groups. The results give us reason to follow up our initial studies, for the merging of the approaches reviewed here seems promising. Ultimately, we will attempt to merge minority empowerment and role reversal within the controversy framework and develop the approach so it can be applied to classrooms. Particularly important are extensions to younger students, for controversy skills ideally would be developed early and refined throughout the school years.

In the two studies the minority influence strategies given to minority group members were not specially highlighted, no illustrations of them were given, and subjects had no time allocated for practicing them. Thus, it should probably not be surprising to find only modest effects. Our current efforts are built around strengthening the minority empowerment manipulation, as well as integrating it with a structure that includes role reversal.

To the extent that the majority empowerment processes we are developing can be modified to enhance the status of persons holding less popular views, they can help students think more carefully about their beliefs and can also help teachers and students work with naturally occurring diversity in the heterogeneous classes of today and tomorrow. The studies reported here provide a glimmering of the possibilities for developing alternative educational strategies and interventions to effectively address different or dissenting opinions on topics that do not always lend themselves to a "right answer" point of view.

References

Asch, S. E. (1956). Studies of independence and conformity: A minority of one against a unanimous majority. *Psychological Monograph, 70*(9, Whole no. 417).

Boyer, E. L. (1983). *High school.* New York: Harper & Row.

Cohen, E. (1986). *Designing group work: Strategies for the heterogeneous classroom.* New York: Teachers College Press.

Deutsch, M. (1949). A theory of cooperation and competition. *Human Relations, 2,* 129–152.

(1962). Cooperation and trust: Some theoretical notes. In M. Jones (Ed.), *Nebraska symposium on motivation* (pp. 275–319). Lincoln: University of Nebraska Press.

(1973). *The resolution of conflict.* New Haven, CT: Yale University Press.

Deutsch, M., & Gerard, H. B. (1955). A study of normative informational influences upon individual judgment. *Journal of Abnormal and Social Psychology, 51,* 629–636.

Dion, K. L., Baron, R. S., & Miller, N. (1970). Why do groups make riskier decisions than individuals? In L. Berkowitz (Ed.), *Advances in experimental social psychology* (Vol. 5, pp. 466–479). New York: Academic Press.

Duval, S. (1976). Conformity on a visual task as a function of personal novelty on attributional dimensions and being reminded of the object status of self. *Journal of Experimental Social Psychology, 12,* 87–98.

Festinger, L. (1950). Informal social communication. *Psychological Review, 57,* 271–282.

Fishbein, M., & Ajzen, I. (1975). *Belief, attitude intention and behavior: An introduction to theory and research.* Reading, MA: Addison-Wesley.

Fishbein, M., & Lange, R. (1990). The effects of crossing the midpoint on belief change: A replication and extension. *Personality and Social Psychology Bulletin, 16,* 189–199.

Goodlad, J. I. (1984). *A place called school: Prospects for the future.* New York: McGraw-Hill.

Johnson, D. W. (1971). Role reversal: A summary and review of the research, *International Journal of Group Tensions, 1*(4), 318–334.

(1980). Group processes: Influences on student/student interaction on school outcomes. In J. McMillin (Ed.), *Social psychology of school learning* (pp. 123–168). New York: Academic Press.

Johnson, D. W., & Johnson, F. P. (1987). *Joining together: Group theory and group skills* (3rd ed.). Englewood Cliffs, NJ: Prentice-Hall.

Johnson, D. W., Johnson, R. T., & Maruyama, G. (1983). Interdependence and interpersonal attraction among heterogeneous and homogeneous individuals: A theoretical formulation and meta-analysis of the research. *Review of Educational Research, 53,* 5–54.

Johnson, D. W., Johnson, R. T., & Smith, K. (1986). Academic conflict among students: Controversy and learning. In R. Feldman (Ed.), *Social psychological applications in education* (pp. 199–231). Cambridge: Cambridge University Press.

Johnson, D. W., Maruyama, G., Johnson, R. T., Nelson, D., & Skon, L. C. (1981). Effects of cooperative, competitive, and individualistic goal structures in achievement: A meta-analysis. *Psychological Bulletin, 89,* 47–62.

Knechel, S., Maruyama, G., & Petersen, R. P. (1990). The effects of strategies for enhancing minority influence on decision making in educational groups. In H. C. Waxman & C. D. Ellett (Eds.), *The study of learning environments* (Vol. 4, pp. 68–79).

Latane, B., & Wolf, S. (1981). The social impact of majorities and minorities. *Psychological Review, 88*(5), 438–453.

Levine, J. M. (1980). Reaction to opinion deviance in small groups. In P. B. Paulus (Ed.), *Psychology of group influence* (pp. 375–429). Hillsdale, NJ: Erlbaum.

Levine, J. M., & Russo, E. M. (1987). Majority and minority influence. In C. Hendrich (Ed.), *Group processes: Review of personality and social psychology* (vol. 8, pp. 13–54). Beverly Hills, CA: Sage.

Lewin, K. (1935). *A dynamic theory of personality.* New York: McGraw-Hill.

Lord, C. G., Lepper, M. R., & Preston, E. (1984). Considering the opposite: A corrective strategy for social judgment. *Journal of Personality and Social Psychology, 47,* 1231–1243.

Maass, A., & Clark, R. D., III (1984). Hidden impact of minorities: Fifteen years of minority influence research. *Psychological Bulletin, 100,* 190–206.

Maruyama, G. (1982). What causes achievement?: An examination of antecedents of achievement in segregated and desegregated classrooms. In D. E. Bartz & M. L. Maehr (Eds.), *The effects of school desegregation on motivation and achievement* (pp. 1–36). Greenwich, CT: JAI Press.

Maruyama, G., Miller, N., & Holtz, R. (1986). The relation between popularity and achievement: A longitudinal test of the lateral transmission of volume hypothesis. *Journal of Personality and Social Psychology, 51*(4), 730–741.

Maslach, C., Stapp, J., & Santee, R. (1985). Individuation: Conceptual analysis and assessment. *Journal of Personality and Social Psychology, 49*(3), 729–738.

Moscovici, S. (1976). *Social influence and social change.* New York: Academic Press.

Muney, B. F., & Deutsch, M. (1968). The effects of role reversal during the discussion of opposing viewpoints. *Journal of Conflict Resolution, 12,* 345–357.

Nail, P. R. (1986). Toward an integration of some models and theories of social response. *Psychological Bulletin, 100,* 190–206.

Nemeth, C. J. (1986). Differential contributions of majority and minority influence. *Psychological Review, 93,* 23–32.

Sherif, M. (1935). A study of some factors in perception. *Archives of Psychology, 27,* 1–60.

Smith, K., Petersen, R., Johnson, D. W., & Johnson, R. T. (1986). The effects of controversy and concurrence seeking on effective decision making. *Journal of Social Psychology, 126*(2), 237–248.

Snyder, C. R., & Fromkin, H. L. (1980). *Uniqueness: The human pursuit of differences.* New York: Plenum Press.

Tanford, S., & Penrod, S. (1984). Social influence model: A formal integration of research on majority and minority influence processes. *Psychological Bulletin, 95,* 189–225.

Taylor, B. M., & Frye, B. J. (1988). Pretesting pretesting: Minimize time spent on skill work for intermediate readers. *Reading Teacher, 42,* 100–104.

Tjosvold, D. (1982). Effects of approach to controversy within a cooperative or competitive context on organizational decision making. *Journal of Applied Psychology, 65,* 590–595.

Part V

Conclusion

*Rachel Hertz-Lazarowitz, Valerie Benveniste Kirkus,
and Norman Miller*

This volume has presented current research on cooperative learning from the disciplines of developmental, educational, and social psychology. In offering this broad perspective it introduces some challenging questions for scholars and practitioners who hope to merge these findings into a comprehensible whole. In approaching this integrative task we first will clarify our view of a fundamental issue that seldom is addressed directly in commentary chapters such as this: Is cooperative interaction among students important primarily as a means of reaching end goals such as enhancing academic achievement and increasing positive interpersonal and intergroup relations, or is there a place for cooperation in schools as an end product that is valuable in and of itself? We hold to the latter position, and it is through this filter that we interpret the literature and offer our suggestions for educational practice. We also recognize, however, the value of individualistic and competitive learning structures in the classroom and view them as complementary to, rather than oppositional to, cooperative learning structures. As suggested by Maruyama (1991), blends of cooperative, individualized, and competitive activities may best serve to prepare children with the academic and social skills needed for rich, productive, and fulfilling futures. Research can proceed, however, irrespective of one's stand on such value issues.

The nature of current research makes evident the emergence of this balanced view. As inquiry on cooperation enters the 1990s, scientists are moving away from framing research questions dichotomously. A question such as, "Which form of learning [cooperative, competitive, individualized] produces superior achievement and social skills?" oversimplifies the issue. Such polarization is often useful in the early stages of investigation, but it soon becomes a limiting factor. Thus, the question now more commonly asked about cooperative classroom interactions is, "Which specific situational determinants facilitate which specific academic and social outcomes?" The identification of underlying cognitive and social processes, as well as person characteristics, that act as mediating and moderating variables in cooperation is far from complete. Hertz-Lazarowitz (see Chapter 4) points out that investigation of such interaction effects is conspicuously absent. Although her multidimensional model of mirrors in the class-room provides a framework for using observational research to approach such complexity, this type of analysis is still in its infancy.

In this concluding chapter we systematically consider process events and de-velopmental factors that have bearing on the outcomes of cooperative classroom interventions. Although our discussion is designed to be systematic and provide scope, we do not attempt to cover comprehensively all of the relevant literature. We organize our discussion into two sections. First, we summarize and discuss the literature on causal mechanisms that facilitate and debilitate achievement outcomes produced by cooperative interaction. Next, we review the literature on children's social development, focusing on the progressive stages in children's social understanding and how these differences may influence the efficacy of classroom interventions designed to promote positive intra- and interpersonal affective outcomes. Last, we close with a restatement of the basic tenets under-lying our view of this integration of research areas in developmental social psy-chology. We hope that this volume will encourage a more widespread use of cooperation and at the same time contribute to the unification of these areas. We also hope that our following discussion will increase understanding of relevant conceptual issues and thereby enable teachers and practitioners to undertake changes in the structure and implementation of cooperative interventions that are respon-sive to varying classroom dynamics, as well as to specific goals, activities, or priorities.

Cognitive and Affective Outcomes in the Classroom: Positive and Negative Effects

The literature here (and the literature on cooperative learning in general) is weighted toward presenting information about the positive outcomes (and ease of imple-mentation) of working in cooperative groups. Far less attention is given to poten-tial negative effects. As noted by D. W. Johnson and R. T. Johnson (Chapter 8), however, there is much complexity in and many essential requirements for groups to function successfully. Included in this list are (1) sharing a common fate; (2) striving for mutual benefits; (3) having a long-term time perspective; (4) having a shared identity, as an individual and as a group member; and (5) mutual obligation, responsibility, and investment. The risk of failing to establish these conditions, and, thereby, failing to induce positive benefits, is evident. We have chosen to devote a considerable portion of this concluding chapter to the negative effects of working in groups, as established in social psychological research. This somewhat uneven discussion should not be construed as an indication that we do not have confidence in the efficacy of cooperative interventions to improve intergroup relations and enhance academic achievement in the classroom. On the contrary, identifying the conditions under which cooperative group learning may lead to negative achievement or negative affective outcomes is necessary to avoid them. Thus, we address an often-neglected area in the literature on cooperative education and thereby provide educators with an awareness of factors that are relevant to maximizing the positive effects of cooperative classroom interventions.

Process Gain: Cognitive Processes and Positive
Achievement Outcomes

Distinct cognitive processes have been hypothesized to underlie the gains in achievement produced by different cooperative learning methods (e.g., Group Investigation, Jigsaw, Learning Together, Cooperative Integrated Reading and Composition [CIRC], Reciprocal Teaching). As noted by Slavin (Chapter 7), however, achievement is oftentimes measured differently within each. Is achievement to be conceptualized best as individual performance? as a group product? as knowledge that is measured by an exam? as problem-solving ability? or as task or production efficiency? Though the use of conceptually distinct dependent measures, as well as uniquely structured cooperative interventions, may seem to suggest that distinct causal processes are associated with each, it is more likely that each is influenced by multiple, overlapping, and complex causal mechanisms (Knight & Bohlmeyer, 1990). In the following sections we discuss social psychological factors that moderate cognitive and affective outcomes when cooperative team learning procedures are applied in classroom settings.

A number of cognitive process factors have been suggested as underlying causal mechanisms for the increased achievement produced by cooperative learning, including (1) observational learning through modeling of effective learning strategies (Bandura, 1977; Harris, 1978; Lippett, Polansky, & Rosen, 1952; Schunk, 1981, 1986, 1987); (2) cognitive restructuring and reprocessing that occurs as a result of the need to integrate new or conflicting information brought to one's attention by other group members (Brown & Palincsar, 1989; O'Donnell & Dansereau, Chapter 6, this volume; Piaget, 1926); (3) increased organizational efficiency due to increased sources of information (other students as well as the teacher) and more immediate feedback (D. W. Johnson & R. T. Johnson, 1989; Slavin, Chapter 7, this volume); (4) increased practice, rehearsal, and elaboration (O'Donnell & Dansereau, Chapter 6, this volume; Webb, Chapter 5, this volume); and (5) development of self-regulation of learning through the development of skills such as instrumental help-seeking (Corno, 1986; Nelson-Le Gall, Chapter 3, this volume; Pintrich & DeGroot, 1990) and assuming responsibility for the division of assignments into smaller subtasks, producing a manageable and prioritized hierarchy of goals (Sharan & Shaulov, 1990).

A number of affective and motivational factors are also suggested as aiding cognitive gains. Often-cited motivational advantages of cooperative team interventions include (1) increased attention due to dramatic shifts from standard classroom procedures normally operational during the majority of the school day (Bossert, 1989); (2) responsibility for one's own learning, resulting in personal empowerment – that is, increased intrinsic motivation to learn due to self-determination, as opposed to extrinsic motivation that may rest, for example, on the need to complete a project or to get a good grade (Sharan, 1990; Knight & Bohlmeyer, 1990); (3) peer support that leads to increased task engagement and perseverance in the face of failure (D. W. Johnson and R. T. Johnson, 1989; D. W. Johnson, R. T. Johnson, Pierson, & Lyons, 1985); (4) peer norms that encourage individual effort and discourage the social loafing produced by additive and interdependent group rewards (Slavin, 1983, and Chapter 7, this volume); and (5) the absence of negative consequences for talking in class, which, in turn, removes both the barriers to, and stigma associated with, giving and receiving help (Nelson-Le Gall, Chapter 3, this volume; Webb, 1985, and Chapter 5, this volume), and (6) mastery goals oriented toward learning (as opposed to performance goals oriented toward positive self-presentation or performance evaluation) due to changes in classroom norms and structures (Dweck, 1986; Rosenholtz & Simpson, 1984; Schunk, 1984).

Bossert (1989) notes, however, that research has not ruled out the possibility that the achievement advantages often found in the comparison between cooperative and control groups may not be due to the cooperative structure itself but to differences in instructional quality between groups. This argument is particularly pertinent to models of cooperative learning such as CIRC, Reciprocal Teaching, and Scripted Cooperation, in which very specific teaching and learning strategies are included in task instructions. This problem was avoided in Sharan, Kussel, & Hertz-Lazarowitz, colleagues' study (1984) that compared achievement differences on similar curriculum presented by Group Investigation, Student Teams Achievement Divisions (STAD), and whole-class instruction methods. Teachers in each group were provided with detailed, structured lesson plans to ensure equivalent presentation of material across manipulations.

Process Loss: Cognitive Processes and Less than Optimal Achievement Outcomes

As many of the contributors to this volume have pointed out, situational determinants have been identified in which negative or less than optimal achievement outcomes are likely to occur. As with process gain, process loss in groups is often specific to the task and to the method of measurement. Types of process loss were briefly discussed in Chapters 7 and 8. In Chapter 7, Slavin explains that measuring achievement through the creation of a group product is often misleading in that it is a reflection of pooled, rather than individual, learning. He notes that a single group goal or product may also create a situation in which individual effort is decreased as a consequence of the diffusion of responsibility made possible when tasks are assigned to groups as opposed to individuals. D. W. Johnson and R. T. Johnson (with reference to Kerr & Bruun, 1983) discuss how a group member falls into the "free-rider effect," that is, reduces his or her individual effort by taking advantage of the efforts of others, or its companion, the "sucker effect" (Kerr & Bruun, 1983), in which an able group member reduces his or her effort due to perceived free riding or inferiority of prior output by others. These phenomena all fall within the broader category of "social loafing" (Latane, Williams, & Harkins, 1979; Harkins & Szymanski, 1989).

Social Loafing. Social loafing refers to reduction of effort and performance on the part of individuals that occurs when tasks are structured so that a group shares a single goal and individual contributions cannot readily be monitored (e.g., such as pushing a car out of the mud or keeping a school-campus clean). This effect was discussed over a century ago, in the late 1880s by Max Ringelmann, a French agricultural engineer. He asked subjects to pull on a rope as hard as they could, either alone or in groups, and measured their efforts with a strain gauge in kilograms of pressure. When pulling alone, individuals exerted an average of about 85 kilograms of pressure, but when working in a group of seven, this individual average dropped to about 65 kilograms of pressure. This effect has been reliably replicated in laboratory settings, not only with physical tasks such as cheering (Latané, Williams, & Harkins, 1979), pumping air with a bicycle pump (Kerr & Bruun, 1981), and folding paper (Zaccaro, 1984), but also with perceptual tasks (Weldon & Gargano, 1988), as well as across very different cultures (Gabrenya, Wang, & Latané, 1985). Though the tendency to loaf has not often been specifically studied in classroom settings, it has been confirmed with cognitive tasks such as evaluating essays (Petty, Harkins, & Williams, 1980), reacting to proposals (Brickner, Harkins, & Ostrom, 1986), brainstorming and vigilance tasks (Harkins & Petty, 1982), and solving mazes (Jackson & Williams, 1985).

Why do individuals exert less effort when working in a group than when working alone? A key factor is the inability of self or others to evaluate one's individual contribution to the overall group product. That is, an individual's efforts become "lost in the crowd" (Harkins & Szymanski, 1987, 1989; Szymanski & Harkins, 1987). When no one will know how hard one works, one cannot be held responsible for the group outcome. Consequently, the tendency to loaf cannot be identified and therefore cannot be subjected to group sanctions. Structuring a task, then, so that individual efforts are identifiable *and* can be compared with that of others helps to combat process loss through decreased effort. Identifiability of individual performance alone is insufficient and will not eliminate social loafing (Harkins & Jackson, 1985). Importantly, the tendency to loaf is also considerably reduced in tasks that are challenging, appealing, or involving (Brickner et al., 1986; Jackson & Williams, 1985), qualities that teachers strive to include in all class lessons or activities. The larger the group, the less identifiable any single member, but the increase in these motivational losses as a function of group size usually begins to level off sharply when group size is increased beyond four members (Ingham, Levinger, Graves, & Peckham, 1974). Thus, such losses are likely to be seen even within the small teams ordinarily used in cooperative team learning.

Influences of Task Structure.   When pursuing a group goal, the task structure, as well as group size, influences individual effort and motivation. Steiner (1972) identified four types of task structures in group work: disjunctive, conjunctive, additive, and discretionary. In a disjunctive task, the *most* able member of the group is most influential in attaining the group goal. A disjunctive task may be one in which there is one correct solution or the group is required to produce a single group project. Generally, all of the members of the team have access to the same resources or information. Slavin (see Chapter 7) uses the example of group work in science as a common example of disjunctive interdependence. It is apparent that in a task such as balancing chemical equations, one or two members of the group may be capable of solving all the problems. The less capable members of the group, then, may suffer motivation losses because they perceive (often accurately) that their efforts are *dispensable* and will not help to attain the group goal (Kerr & Bruun, 1983).

Disjunctive tasks also lead to the "rich do get richer effect" (Cohen, Lotan, & Catanzarite, 1990). As noted by Webb (Chapter 5) and D. W. Johnson and R. T. Johnson (Chapter 8), high-ability students are usually verbal during problem solving. Increased verbalization forces cognitive restructuring and reprocessing of information, as well as rehearsal and practice of relevant information and skills. This, in turn, leads to increases in achievement for high-ability students, whereby the "rich get richer" (Cohen et al., 1990, p. 210). In disjunctively structured tasks, then, ability status is salient, becomes a major influence in peer interaction, and may produce less than optimal patterns of task engagement for students of average and low ability. Additionally, a disjunctive task structure may also lead to unequal role assignments within the group, with divisions of labor such as "I'll solve the problem, and you write down the answer on the worksheet'' (Sheingold, Hawkins, & Char, 1984; also cited by Johnson & Johnson, Chapter 9).[1]

Steiner (1972) defines a conjunctive task as one in which the least able member of the group is most influential to attaining the group goal. With this structure, motivation loss is likely to occur among the more able members of the group, who perceive that maximum effort will not reap equivalent gains. In this structure, members of the group perform (essentially) the same chore or subtask, but the performance of the group is based on that of the weakest member of the team. (Mountain climbing is often used as an example. The climbers are linked together by a rope and can proceed no faster than the slowest member of the group.) Conjunctive structures occur in academic and nonacademic classroom activities. For example, the group may be allowed to go on to centers or other ''free-time'' activities only when all of its members have completed the task. A problem that may result with the use of conjunctive task structures is that high-ability students sometimes report feeling frustrated (Slavin, 1991; Willis, 1990), and parents of high-ability students become concerned that their children's academic growth is slowed when they are assigned to groups with lower ability students. Empirical studies can allay parental concerns by demonstrating that students will be exposed to the same content as in traditionally structured activities, and that gifted children benefit from the cognitive reorganization and content elaboration required when instructing others (see Johnson & Johnson, 1989; Slavin, Chapter 8). It is less clear, however, if such explanations or increased exposure to cooperative task structures will attenuate the frustration and negative affect of the students themselves. It may be best to avoid conjunctively structured tasks.

Additive tasks are structured such that the coordinated efforts of all members are important to goal attainment. Though a group can often accomplish together what an individual cannot on his or her own (e.g., cleaning-up-after centers), each member's contribution, as discussed earlier, is oftentimes reduced unless it can be individually identified and evaluated. In addition, in group brainstorming activities, ''production blocking'' typically occurs (Diehl & Stroebe, 1987; Hill, 1982; Lamm & Trommsdorff, 1973). That is, contrary to popular belief, when an individual works alone he or she generates more ideas than when working in a group. Diehl and Stroebe (1987) posit two causes for production blocking: first, because one must wait one's turn to speak in a group, ideas are forgotten, and second, because social norms dictate listening to others when they speak, listen-

---

1 Such naturally formed divisions of labor are likely to divide students into ability levels within groups. When groups are racially/ethnically heterogeneous, and when ability, for whatever reason, is correlated with such social distinctions, negative effects on intergroup acceptance are also likely (see Miller & Harrington, Chapter 9, this volume).

ing time is not used to generate ideas. Obviously, these coordination losses are not limited to brainstorming activities but apply to many situations in which small groups engage in problem solving. Giving group members the opportunity to generate (and write down) ideas individually, prior to group participation, will only partially help to minimize this inefficiency.

Discretionary tasks are those that require a group decision for which there is no right or wrong, or either-or, answer. Instead, there is a choice among several possible alternatives. Choosing a topic for Group Investigation (Sharan & Hertz- . Lazarowitz, 1980) is an example of a discretionary task. Other examples may include investigating alternatives to reduce pollution, learning about aspects of Native American culture, or researching policy or value issues, such as capital punishment or abortion. (See Chapter 4, which details more thoroughly tasks of this nature.) Some of the problems that Diehl and Stroebe discuss apply to discretionary tasks as well.

Methods for coping with many types of motivation and process loss (in the form of prescriptive external conditions) have been developed to ameliorate these debilitating effects. For example, structuring the task so that the superordinate goal must be attained through the additive cooperation of all group members (rather than being conjunctively based on the performance of the least able member of the group or disjunctively based on the performance of the most able group member) significantly reduces the free-rider effect. Also effective is designing the task so that it is personally relevant to group members (Brickner et al., 1986). Structuring individual accountability for a group member's contribution will increase the likelihood of evaluation of individual contributions (Harkins & Jackson, 1985). This last suggestion, however, may carry with it the potential for erosion of intrinsic motivation due to the imposition of external rewards for performance. (This problem will be discussed in greater detail under Affect and Individual Motivation.)

Presence Effects. Social loafing, free riding, sucker effects, and production blocking explain process loss when working with others in the creation of a group product. The issue to which we now turn, presence effects, examines the effects of the presence of others on measures of individual performance or on the creation of an individual product. Whereas social loafing occurs in tasks that are structured such that a group shares a single goal, presence effects occur in tasks for which there is an individual goal (e.g., competing in a race, playing a piano concerto, individual problem solving).

The results of research on how the presence of others affects individual performance is seemingly contradictory. The ambiguity is easily demonstrated in controlled experimentation as well as in the intuitive interpretations of everyday experiences. Consider the following examples:

Erica is an outstanding gymnast who hopes one day to try out for the Olympics. She trains hard daily but notices that she practices better with a partner than alone. Her best performances have been during actual meets where she was competing against other aspiring Olympiads.

Brian, a high school senior, is an aspiring politician. He's running for student-body president and has written what he considers to be a terrific campaign speech. When he rehearses at home, in front of his friends and family, he delivers his oratory with accuracy and self-confidence. At the election assembly, however, he gets flustered, stutters, and forgets the main points of his speech.

Zajonc (1965) examined the literature on positive and negative task performance changes in the presence of others and reconciled these contradictory effects by applying a well-established principle from Hullian learning theory (Hull, 1952): the effect of arousal on task performance depends on how well practiced one is on the task. Applied to social structures, Zajonc argued that the presence of others causes uncertainty and thereby increases arousal. Increases in arousal facilitate the performance of *dominant* response patterns. Thus, according to this drive theory of social facilitation, the complexity of the task is crucial. Performance on easy tasks is enhanced because the dominant response is likely to be correct. On more difficult tasks the dominant response is, instead, likely to be incorrect. On these latter tasks, therefore, the presence of others will impair performance. Much research supports this interpretation (for a review see Geen, 1991). Geen and Bushman (1987) and Baron, Moore, and Sanders (1978) suggest alternative explanations of these data. Geen and Bushman elaborate on Cottrell's (1972) suggestion that it is *evaluation apprehension*, the belief (or realization) that others are actively evaluating one's performance, not simply the mere presence of others, that is crucial. Baron's (1986) *distraction-conflict theory* argues that the presence of others causes attentional conflict. One's attempt to direct concentration simultaneously to both the task at hand and to co-actors or observers causes increases in arousal that lead to either social facilitation or debilitation, depending on the complexity or difficulty of the task.

Although the underlying explanations of presence effects on performance that are stipulated by drive theory, evaluation apprehension, distraction-conflict theory and other processes such as unpredictability (Guerin & Innes, 1982), objective self-awareness (Duval & Wicklund, 1972), or self-presentational motivation (Bond, 1982) do differ, the empirical outcomes they seek to explain and the inferences that may be drawn from them are the same: performance on simple tasks improves, whereas that on complex tasks diminishes as a consequence of the presence of others. Presence effects have implications for individual performance under all types of classroom learning – cooperative, competitive, and individualistic. It is reasonable to assume further that presence effects are moderated by individual differences in social anxiety and ability. That is, although the presence of another might decrease the performance of one student (as in the case of Brian), it may enhance that of another (e.g., Brian's competitor).

Presence effects may explain why dyads observed by an active or a passive "monitor" were outperformed by a no-monitor control condition in their understanding of text in a scripted learning task (O'Donnell et al., 1986). This suggests that to avoid giving students failure experiences, it may be better to assign complex or difficult tasks under conditions where each can work alone, or with only one partner, but not in the presence of others whose primary activity is surveillance. In cases where this is not possible, task materials and requirements should be structured to convert complex problems into simpler subtasks that consequently will not elicit the negative effects of observation by others.

Despite the various negative effects discussed, it is important to keep the broader perspective of group performance effects in mind. It has been known for some time that groups perform better than the average individual on a broad array of problems and decisions (for reviews see Hastie, 1986; Hill, 1982; Kelley & Thibaut, 1969; Stasser, Kerr, & Davis, 1990). Interestingly, however, recent studies comparing the collective information processing of four-member groups with that of individuals have found that the group can perform at a level equal to that of its single most able member under conditions where the task is complex and where there is adequate time for performing it (Laughlin, Vanderstoep, & Hollingshead, 1991). These are circumstances that can characterize many types of classroom tasks.

Affect and Intergroup Relations

In addition to evidence that under some circumstances the ordinarily beneficial academic effects of cooperation are diminished, or even fall below those of control conditions (Julian & Perry, 1967; Scott & Cherrington, 1974; for reviews see Michaels, 1977, and Slavin, 1977), we also have known for some time that under certain conditions cooperation produces negative affective outcomes. Intergroup competition and task failure are conditions frequently associated with negative affect (D. W. Johnson & R. T. Johnson, 1989; M. Sherif, Harvey, White, Hood, & C. Sherif, 1961). Ingroup-outgroup boundaries, which are at the core of affective biases, are often correlated with status factors (Berger, Cohen, & Zelditch, 1972; Cohen, Lotan, & Catanzarite, 1990) and are also very easily created artificially in the laboratory or school (M. Sherif et al., 1961; Tajfel, 1969, 1970). Conditions that make ingroup-outgroup boundaries salient, and thereby increase bias, include intergroup competition, task (as opposed to interpersonal) focus (Miller & Harrington, 1990), and task failure (Worchel, Andreoli, & Folger, 1977).

Scapegoating is the blaming or singling out of a lower status or outgroup member as responsible for failure (Worchel et al., 1977; Worchel & Norvell, 1980). In competition, where task orientation is salient and failure guaranteed to at least one group, it is unimportant whether ingroup-outgroup distinctions naturally occur or are artificially created in order for the frustration inherent in them to beget scapegoating. The scapegoated individual or group is then the target of negative affect and/or increased prejudice. That is, lower status, or outgroup membership, interacts with negative affect and other cues for aggression to augment aggressive responding toward persons who are members of these categories (Carlson, Marcus-Newhall, & Miller, 1990).

Just as circumstances can be manipulated to help minimize the adverse effects on task performance and proficiency that are sometimes inherent in cooperative team learning, conditions can also be structured to help protect against negative affective outcomes. Chapter 9 focuses specifically on this issue and suggests that teams be formed and tasks designed to reduce both threat to self-esteem and the salience of intergroup boundaries, thereby decreasing category-based responding (Miller & Davidson-Podgorny, 1987; Miller & Harrington, 1990). In addition to the principles for the formation of teams, other teacher-imposed structures can help facilitate positive intergroup relations. Most often recommended is modifying the reward or incentive structure so that intergroup competition is eliminated (Hewstone, 1988; D. W. Johnson & R. T. Johnson, 1989; D. Solomon, Watson, Schaps, Battistich, & J. Solomon, 1990). More recently, interventions have been designed to include specific group process interaction skills such as turn-taking, listening, and offering and accepting constructive criticism and meaningful praise as ways to facilitate social and interpersonal understanding and acceptance (Hepler & Rose, 1988; D. W. Johnson & F. P. Johnson, 1987; Lew, Mesch, D. W. Johnson, & R. T. Johnson, 1986; Maruyama, Knechel, & Petersen, Chapter 10, this volume; Warring, D. W. Johnson, Maruyama, & R. T. Johnson, 1985).

Affect and Individual Motivation

Reward structure is often specified in cooperative interventions (such as STAD or Teams Games Tournaments). Reward conditions that may decrease intrinsic motivation, however, are of concern. Reward structure can alter the perception of a task and thereby shift its affective valence, as shown by studies of the *overjustification effect*. Lepper and Greene (1975) divided preschool children into two groups, experimental and control, each of which played with jigsaw puzzles. The control group received no specific instructions, whereas the experimental group was told that if they worked on the puzzles, they would be rewarded with a fun activity later. After playing with the puzzles, the children from both groups were then allowed to engage in the "fun" (or rewarding) later activity. A few weeks later the children were again exposed to puzzles. Those who had worked on them with the promise of reward spent *less* time playing with the puzzles in this postmeasure than those in the control group. In short, the manipulation changed the children's perception of the task from play into work – the task was no longer valued or fun in and of itself but only as a means to a more rewarding end. The theories underlying the overjustification effect stem from self-perception and cognitive-evaluative traditions wherein incentive is viewed as focusing attention on the promised reward rather than the enjoyment of the challenge (and mastery) of the task. Such evidence (e.g., Anderson, Manoogian, & Reznick, 1976; Boggiano & Ruble, 1979; Boggiano, Ruble, and Pittman, 1982; Harackiewicz, Sansone, & Manderlink, 1985) supports the recommendations of Hertz-Lazarowitz (see Chapter 4) and Sharan and Shaulov (1990) that caution is advised when structuring external rewards into cooperative learning programs. Sharan and Shaulov contend that "calculated use of external rewards for improving student achievement might stimulate harder work for better grades but will not contribute effectively to pupils' inherent interest in the content and process of learning" (1990, p. 174). Newman (1990) notes that an intrinsic versus extrinsic goal orientation also affects the nature of help-seeking behaviors. An intrinsically motivated student is likely to perceive help-seeking instrumentally, as a means toward achieving task mastery, whereas an extrinsically motivated child is likely to view help-seeking as an expedient means of obtaining the reward associated with task completion. Research on motivation and learning efficiency (Atkinson, 1974) and developmental components of motivation (Connell & Ryan, 1987) suggests that judicious use of external incentives may be beneficial in that they facilitate *initiation* of achievement tasks, which can then better be pursued to completion through intrinsic competence motivation (Harter, 1978, 1981).

Although motivation losses were discussed in conjunction with group productivity and process loss, it is unlikely that negative affect normally will arise from these losses. There are, however, important affective consequences of negative motivational patterns that are experienced by some children in cooperative classroom structures. Low-achieving students (particularly those age 11 and above) can be embarrassed by their performance or inability when working with others in cooperative groups (Dweck & Leggett, 1988; Newman & Golden, 1990). Self-esteem deteriorates along with motivation to achieve, resulting in acting-out behavior designed to shift attention away from one's inadequacies. For these students, participating in cooperative learning activities may increase the negativity of school experiences, not only increasing individual motivation loss, but also disrupting group work and learning of others (cf. Bossert, 1989).

Summary

To restate our earlier caveat, the purpose of the foregoing is not intended to discourage the use of cooperation in school settings but to illustrate some of the obstacles that may confront students and teachers in the classroom. Through an understanding of circumstances and processes that ameliorate less than optimal achievement, as well as negative affective and motivational outcomes, teachers can more effectively make cooperative interventions beneficial. Though process and motivation losses do occur in groups, the literature provides us with some remedies in the form of structural conditions that help to lessen their effects. As indicated, most important to optimizing student achievement in cooperative learning activities is to structure tasks such that each individual's contribution is identifiable and can be noted by other group members. It is also important to design the task so that it is challenging and personally relevant to group members (Brickner et al., 1986). Positive intergroup affect can be facilitated by decreasing social category salience when forming and working in groups, eliminating intergroup competition, and including direct instruction in group interaction skills, thereby making these skills a normative part of the cooperative activity.

Developmental Considerations for Cooperative Classroom Interventions

Research on children's social cognition provides a foundation for understanding the affective implications of cooperative interactions in the classroom across different grade levels. Development of understanding of self in relation to others results from interactions between physical maturation and social experience. The extent to which developmental changes in personal perceptions *cause* intergroup interactional patterns or are *resultant to* them cannot be determined. First, we discuss the development of children's understanding of knowledge of intentions, and how their limited cognitive capacity in early childhood may be partially overcome by direct instruction in role-taking strategies. Next, we examine stages in understanding of ability and its relation to children's interpretation of helping behaviors as well as their choice of potential workmates. Last, we consider how organizational features of classrooms (e.g., cooperative, competitive, or individualistic task structures) might influence the content and course of children's social perceptions, and how these patterns may change with the implementation of differing classroom structures.

Development of Knowledge of Intentions

The ability to take the perspective of another is critical to social maturity. This section provides a basis for understanding the reciprocal influences of maturation and social context (in school) on the affective and cognitive components of social perspective taking. Ages associated with perspective-taking stages vary between and within cultures, and the context of the social setting is an important mediator of this ability. Recent research with siblings indicates that in familiar and personally meaningful contexts children are capable of greater subtlety of social understanding (Dunn, 1992) than when measured in more formal settings (Flavell, 1985; Keasey, 1978; Shantz, 1983; Shultz, 1980). The descriptions and approximate age ranges as established in laboratory research (Selman, 1980) are useful for understanding levels of social perspective-taking in the classroom.

Children begin at Level 0, which is the predominant mode of social cognition up to about age 5 or 6. At this level they are egocentric and lack awareness of the existence of any perspective other than their own. Through maturation and experience, they progress to Level 1, where they remain until approximately age 8. At Level 1 they become capable of differentiated and subjective perspective-taking, developing the ability to recognize that others can have perspectives different from their own. They believe, however, that this only occurs when the other person has *received different information*. That is, in a given situation, Level 1 children assume that individuals given the same information will respond, invariantly, just as they would.

Children are in Level 2 until approximately 11 or 12 years of age. At this level they develop the capacity for self-reflective and second-person reciprocal role-taking. That is, they grow to understand that even when given the same information, points of view or affective responses may conflict. Also, importantly, they understand that individuals may have a dual social presentation: outward appearance for impression management of others and an inward, perhaps hidden, reality. Children at this age are capable of adult-like normative discrimination that mediates expression and interpretation of cognition and affect.

The next levels involve sophisticated social understanding that is not always automatically employed once attained. That is, even if one is capable of such reasoning, whether one uses these advanced skills depends on personal and situational circumstances. Even adults may not generally engage in these levels of understanding although they are in their cognitive repertoire. Level 3 understanding generally develops from roughly 10 to 15 years of age. At this level one can engage in third-person and mutual perspective-taking, wherein one can simultaneously consider both one's own and another person's point of view and also step outside this perspective to simultaneously take the perspective of a third, uninvolved person. One has the ability to anticipate and predict differing affective and cognitive responses depending on one's role (e.g., in the same situation the mother may feel one emotion, while self feels another, and sibling yet a third). One is aware that one can simultaneously hold more than one role (e.g., be brother and son), and this realization cannot always be cognitively or emotionally explained, thereby creating internal conflict or ambivalence. Level 4, the most advanced level, includes all previous skills as well as the additional ability to take into account more abstract points of view, such as that of differing societies.

It is important to consider students' developmental level of perspective-taking when assigning group tasks. Affective correlates resulting from interpersonal interactions in the classroom are directly influenced by the child's ability to take the perspective of another. An accurate understanding of intention is important to help-giving and help-receiving, as discussed by both Webb (Chapter 5) and Nelson-Le Gall (Chapter 3). For example, Webb points out that children ask for and receive different kinds of help (from simply giving answers to elaborate explanations), and Nelson-Le Gall describes the barriers to children's effective help-seeking. It is important that student requests for help be perceived as sincere, rather than as lazy, as when asking for only the answer rather than help in understanding the underlying process or asking for help before trying to solve the problem on one's own (Wilkinson & Spinelli, 1983). Here, again, we recommend direct instruction in social and communication skills for children to use with peers during cooperative group tasks, not only to convey that which is normatively appropriate but also to minimize the possibility of a student becoming a neglected and ineffective classroom communicator – one whose intentions are not clearly discernible by peers. Garnica (1981, p. 76) gives the following example. Two children are coloring pictures in a kindergarten classroom, and each requests the use of a marker from another child. The efficient "bidder" makes the request clearly and directly ("I need green. When you're done, can I use it?") and is successful in meeting his need. The ineffective child makes requests that are not necessarily to the point and are inadequately revised when initially ineffective (e.g., "How are you doing with that pink?") and is unsuccessful in obtaining a marker.

Understanding of intention is also important to conflict resolution during cooperative learning tasks. Cooperative learning in the primary grades should include direct instruction of each student's role and responsibility. In addition, basic interpersonal skills, such as listening and turn-taking, should not be taken for granted but actively taught. When outside of the familiar context of the family, young children generally have an imperfect understanding of the intent and *affect* of others. That is, they do not usually integrate the co-occurrence of conflicting affect or affect that changes from one circumstance to another. A common occurrence in primary classrooms involves misattributions for the unintentional acts of others. For example, a child may be angry that a classmate has (accidentally) spilled paint on a drawing or knocked down a tower of blocks, because he or she does not realize that unintentional acts such as these, though they *result* in unhappy personal outcomes, are not committed out of malice. Additionally, it is not understood that one can be happy that their six new kittens have found good homes and at the same time be sad that he or she won't be able to play with them after they leave. Such combinations of affect, as perceived in oneself as well as projected onto others, are experienced in temporal order until about age 8 (Harter, 1986). In the former example, the offended child may initially experience anger but with explanation may move to a more accurate behavioral attribution in which no residual anger is experienced. Recognition of simultaneous conflicting emotions usually develops at about age 8 or 9 but may not always be *automatic*. Children in the middle grades, therefore, will benefit from lessons designed specifically to augment perspective-taking ability and social sensitivity.

Beginning at about the sixth or seventh grade, students become capable of accurate and differential role-taking and at this time will benefit from practice in assuming the perspective of another during cognitive controversy, such as described in Chapter 10 by Maruyama, Knechel, and Petersen. Activities in which they must assume differing roles and responsibilities in group tasks are beneficial from this stage forward and will facilitate interpersonal and intergroup acceptance. Prior to this stage, however, use of the minority empowerment model of Maruyama and colleagues, which employs role reversal, may prove of little value. And if used at these grades, students will need close supervision to avoid the conflict inherent in this model. Due to the nonautomatic nature of the employment of perspective-taking skills, we suggest direct instruction in self-other differential role-taking at all grade levels prior to classroom implementation of such activities.

Development of Social Conceptions of Task Difficulty and Ability

Cognitions about ability carry affective valences, which, in turn, influence the immediate and future behavior of students in and out of school. Perception of personal ability moves through developmental levels before reaching adultlike (normative) conceptions (Flavell, 1985; Graham & Barker, 1990; Nicholls, 1984). Toddlers, up until approximately 2 to 3 years, often are unaware of the notions of success or failure, correct or incorrect (Lutkenhaus, Bullock, & Geppert, 1987; Nicholls, 1984, 1987). Self-perceptions of ability, then, are probably of little or no influence on behavior prior to age 3, when children develop this discriminatory capability for many tasks. During the first level, from about ages 3½ or 4 to 7, children's understanding of ability is *egocentric*. They can consider ability and task difficulty only in terms of their own, subjective probability of success. Tasks are judged as "hard" if they are "hard for me" and "easy" if they are "easy for me." The objective level of difficulty cannot be ordered: Tasks are either attainable or not. A child does not understand that a five-piece jigsaw puzzle is "harder" than the four-piece puzzle, or that he or she will be successful in solving the four-piece puzzle sooner than the five-piece one. In this stage effort and ability are undifferentiated and seen as roughly equivalent. That is, egocentric children assert that individuals are capable of equal achievement with the application of equal effort: One is not "smarter" than another, but one may "try harder." Children at this developmental level expect to be able to influence the outcomes of tasks through effort.

Children enter the "objective" stage beginning at about age 7, when comparison processes begin to play a role in understanding but are still not fully developed. At this level tasks can be ordered in terms of complexity and are recognized independently of one's own expectations of success (i.e., a five-piece puzzle is seen as harder than a four-piece puzzle). Whether or not peers can successfully complete the task, however, generally does not enter into the concept of ability or difficulty, and normative difficulty is still confused. "Hard" is still the same as "hard for me," even if the task is easily accomplished by peers.

"Normative" social comparison processes, in which children attain adultlike conceptions of ability, begin to surface between the ages of approximately 10 to 12. Task difficulty begins to be understood in terms of the success rates for others. Tasks on which fewer peers can succeed are judged as "hard," and "hard" can be distinguished from "hard for me." Thus, task difficulty can be conceptualized as divided into two general categories: tasks that are (1) individually difficult, that is, easy to hard for me, and (2) normatively difficult, that is, easy to hard for most people, a distinction based on social comparison.

At this point in children's development, when ability and effort are fully differentiated and understood as independent constructs, the perceived relationship between the two changes substantially. In other words, up until about age 10, children construe ability to be a malleable or changeable entity that can improve with the application of increased effort: The harder one works or tries, the smarter one will be or become. After these concepts become discrete, the perceived relationship changes. Ability is seen as a fixed trait, and the application of increased effort is an indication of an inverse relationship to ability. Consequently, the more effort a person applies, or the harder a person needs to try, the less able (dumber) that person must be (Dweck & Leggett, 1988; Graham & Barker, 1990; Nicholls, 1984, 1987). Additionally, at this time a parallel shift occurs in children's choice of workmates in school as a function of perceived ability differences. The high-ability student becomes the preferred workmate for all.

Graham and Barker (1990) performed a series of studies in which subjects between the ages of 5 and 12 observed two students (on videotape) working on a mathematics task, one of whom received unsolicited help from the teacher, whereas the other worked independently. The subjects, divided into four age-groups for analysis (5- to 6-, 7- to 8-, 9- to 10-, and 11- to 12-year-olds), were told that both students received identical scores on the math worksheet. They were then asked which student was smarter, which one tried harder, and which one the subject would rather work with in the future on a group math task. Ability and effort attributions followed expected patterns. The nonhelped student was perceived as smarter across all age levels and was perceived as working harder up to age 10. The 11- and 12-year-olds similarly perceived the nonhelped student as smarter but, contrary to the other groups, as applying *less* effort. The older students follow the reasoning that the more ability a student possesses, the less effort that student needs to apply to successfully complete the task. Equally interesting is subjects' choice of future workmate. The younger children preferred to work with the helped student, whereas the older children preferred to work with the nonhelped student. During the postexperimental debriefing, older children explained their choices with statements indicating preference due to the inferred superior ability of the nonhelped student. The younger children explained their choices with statements such as the subject felt he or she could be of help to the lesser ability student or, generally in the case of the youngest children, that he or she felt the teacher liked the helped student more.

Practical Implications. The currently observed developmental sequence of ability perceptions is approximately as follows. In early grades (preschool, kindergarten, first, and perhaps second) students see ability and effort as inextricably entwined. Ability is seen as a malleable entity that can be augmented with the application of effort. As children progress through the grades, they begin to perceive greater differentiation between ability and effort, until about the age of 10 to 12, when ability is generally seen as a relatively stable aspect of identity. Considered in terms of interpersonal relations, then, concepts of "smarter" and "dumber" are comparatively unimportant in the creation of status levels in the kindergarten, first, and second grades. Ability status becomes an increasingly important factor in self-identity and interpersonal relations through the middle grades, and by the sixth or seventh grade it becomes an important, stable aspect of student identity and social interactions. As noted, however, these observed age differences in social cognition may not remain as consistent if the social organization of schools undergoes a transition from traditional to more multidimensional and cooperative structures.

Self-perceptions of ability influence student behaviors and motivational patterns in all types of classroom structures: cooperative, competitive, individualistic. As discussed earlier, help-seeking behaviors especially are strongly influenced by self-identity. Recall that children as young as 5 (Graham and Barker, 1990) perceive students who receive help as less able than their nonhelped peers. With the implementation of more cooperative structures in classrooms, we may find, in accord with the social constructivist view of Vygotsky (discussed in Chapters 1 and 2) that these attributional patterns may shift as help-seeking comes to be perceived normatively as an instrumentally valuable means of acquiring skill mastery (see Nelson-Le Gall, Chapter 3). Additionally, this mastery-oriented view of help-seeking is compatible with intrinsic learning motivation as described by Harter (1978, 1981), Newman (1990), and Dweck (1986) – an approach that we value as fundamental to schooling.

The developmental sequence and causal analysis of ability perceptions is important in Webb's model as well (1982, 1989, Chapter 5, this volume) which looks at natural or spontaneous student exchanges as a function of ability status. Research on the effects of status cues and expectations on behavior consistently shows that those students who are of high-ability status are more influential in a group (Berger, Webster, Ridgeway, & Rosenholtz, 1986), initiate more social interaction (Cohen et al., 1990; Dembo & McAuliffe, 1987), and score higher in measures of achievement (Webb, 1985). In Chapter 5, Webb reports distinct patterns of interaction and achievement for specific configurations of ability within groups.

Cohen and her colleagues (1990) also focus on ability status and interpersonal interaction. In addition to observing patterns of verbal exchanges, an important dependent variable in Cohen's investigations is a sociometric measure of interpersonal affect. In her studies race is the independent variable of interest but is interpreted as a proxy for ability status. Cohen reasons that in multiethnic settings the specific status characteristic of ability springs from the diffuse status characteristic of race – that is, racial membership engenders concomitant expectations of competence. The developmental stage at which racial membership becomes a proxy for ability status, however, is uncertain.[2]

School Organization and the Construction of Social Cognition

The model presented focuses on the role of maturation in progressive understanding of perceptions of ability and appears to place relatively less emphasis on the social context in which this growth occurs. Others, however, stress the role of the school social organization in the formation of ability perceptions (e.g., Bos-

2 The extensive literature on young children's awareness of racial differences through the middle grades of school is not consistent (for a review, see Aboud, 1988), at least in part as a consequence of methodological problems, including reliance on forced-choice measures (which may confound in-group preference with out-group rejection), a neglect of the influences of social milieu on racial preferences, and a lack of controls for response sets, which are often found in young children (Aboud, 1988).

sert, 1979; Dweck, 1986; Dweck & Leggett, 1988; Elliot & Dweck, 1988; Rosenholtz & Simpson, 1984). They contend that children use effort as evidence of ability in the early elementary grades not solely due to limitations in their cognitive capacity relative to older children but also because teachers in early grades (particularly kindergarten, first, and second) link reward with, and stress the importance of, effort. These theorists (as well as McCarthey and McMahon, Bershon, and Nelson-Le Gall, Chapters 1 through 3, this volume) assume that children are active participants in their own socialization. The social context of the classroom, including task structure, teacher direction, and peer interaction, is an important mediator in the formation of social cognition. These factors have been discussed in detail in several chapters of this book. Context theorists such as Rosenholtz and Simpson (1984), however, have focused on the dimension of classroom structure and its role in shaping the development of ability perceptions.

Classroom structure ranges along a continuum from unidimensional to multidimensional (Bossert, 1979; Rosenholtz & Simpson, 1984) and is an important determinant of social comparison processes in children. In a classroom that is unidimensionally structured, academic tasks are undifferentiated, meaning that all class members work on similar tasks, only a limited number of different materials and methods are used during instruction, and materials and methods are qualitatively similar. This elicits uniformity of performances and products in the daily flow of academic work from students within each group. Similar tasks, materials, and methods, combined with stable student grouping patterns, make social comparison salient and allow students to compare readily their own performance with that of their peers. In this manner, over time, the social organization of conventional, unidimensional classrooms constructs a belief among its members that individual ability levels are unchangeable and relatively unaffected by increases in effort.

A multidimensional class structure, on the other hand, offers students independent choices regarding academic tasks, perhaps including which tasks to do or when or how to do them, thereby increasing and differentiating performance options. This reduces the ease of ability attributions based on peer comparison and places greater emphasis on *qualitative* differences among performances, which, in turn, fosters the development of identity based on personal attributes other than ability, a principle for the formation of student work groups that Miller and Harrington (Chapter 9) recommend. A multidimensional structure counters children's high susceptibility and ready conformity to a classroom ability-status hierarchy. Cooperative group learning is effective in facilitating the transition from a unidimensional to a multidimensional classroom structure (as noted by Hertz-Lazarowitz in Chapter 4 and others in this volume).

Summary

Identity development in children changes character as their understanding of social comparison develops. The lack of ability for reciprocal role-taking and normative social comparison noted in young children is attributed to perceptual and memory limitations as well as the protective social environment surrounding young children in school and at home. Mature social understanding, inversely, is due to both increases in cognitive capability and also to the progressively competitive structure of schooling through the elementary grades. The extent to which these observed developmental patterns in social cognition influence social organization remains an interesting question.

Closing Comments

As stated earlier, this volume hopes to contribute to the advancement of knowledge by bringing together recent scholarship about the dynamics of cognitive and interpersonal processes in cooperative learning from the distinct approaches of developmental, educational, and social psychology. In so doing, it demonstrates that it is oftentimes difficult for research in one area to consider the implications of research in others. For example, the chapters that make up Part I of this volume discuss child development as related to cognitive growth but do not consider in equivalent detail the concomitant formation of intrapersonal, interpersonal, and intergroup perceptions and attitudes. Similarly, the chapters in Part IV discuss social psychological principles of interpersonal and intergroup relations that have been formulated mainly through research with adults but which may not always be applicable to young children. Parts II and III attempt to integrate the theory underlying these literatures and offer recommendations for classroom interventions and practices. The primary interest of these chapters, however, is upon gains in achievement. Enhancement of positive social relations receives considerably less attention.

Additionally, difficulties in communication and theoretical disagreements occur within, as well as between, psychological disciplines. An example from the area of development has to do with the directing impetus of children's cognitive development. Is it self-directed, as argued by White (1959), Harter (1978), and others who hold to the theory of competence/effectance motivation, or other-directed, as in Vygotsky's theory of the social construction of knowledge? Echoing the sentiments expressed by Brown and Palincsar (1989), we hold that both representations are valid, and a combination of the two is probably most accurate.

Cooperative learning research that measures conceptually distinct dependent variables has created a situation in which the findings and recommendations of one group may seem to be in conflict with those of another. For example, intergroup competition when combined with group reward and individual accountability has been found to increase achievement (Slavin, 1980, and Chapter 7, this volume) but also has consistent negative effects on both intergroup relations (Bettencourt, Brewer, Croak, & Miller, in press; Johnson & Johnson, 1989; M. Sherif et al., 1961) and intrinsic motivation (e.g., Anderson, Manoogian, & Resnick, 1976; Boggiano & Ruble, 1979; Boggiano, Ruble, & Pittman, 1982; Harackiewicz et al., 1985; Lepper & Greene 1975).

The vast diversity of educational settings includes overcrowded urban ghettos, sparsely populated rural communities, and ethnically homogeneous and heterogeneous schools, each with unique combinations of needs. One environment may be that of a middle-class community in which family stability and strong lines of communication between school and home are supportive of and responsive to children's educational needs. A very different environment may be found in urban ghettos, where the academic achievement goals of disadvantaged youth are undermined by the obstacles of daily violence, uncertain futures, and feelings of disenfranchisement and hopelessness. The consideration of situation-specific needs, then, will always be a primary factor in the design, selection, and individualization of classroom interventions.

Because educational priorities and needs are not invariant across populations and cultures, the efficacy and desirability of particular cooperative interventions will vary. This volume's emphasis on theoretical foundations is designed to provide interventionists with an awareness of relevant issues when selecting or designing cooperative classroom procedures. A more widespread use of cooperation will provide new sources of information that identify new process, task, and situation variables for future study.

We close with a reemphasis of our concerns in two major areas. First, we strongly believe that facilitating positive interpersonal and intergroup relations is (at least) of equal importance to fostering academic achievement. Additionally, though the focus of harmonious social relations in this collection, as in much of the literature, is generally on interpersonal acceptance between diverse ethnic groups, we envision the principles herein as also promotive of *within*-group acceptance. We are sensitive to the profound concerns of urban schools in which hostilities *within* homogeneous racial/ethnic groups (in the form of juvenile gangs) are often as divisive as those between groups. We stress that this adds particular urgency to classroom strategies that facilitate intergroup and interpersonal acceptance.

Last, we also reemphasize that children, schools, and learning are innately social in all aspects, and it is our hope that the structure of schooling will begin a rapid transition toward working synergistically with this inclination of children to interact during learning. We see a need to speak of learning and social relations as one – we cannot disentangle the reciprocal influences of each on the other.

References

Aboud, F. (1988). *Children and prejudice*. Cambridge: MA: Basil Blackwell.

Anderson, R. Manoogian, S. T., & Resnick, J. S. (1976). The undermining and enhancing of intrinsic motivation in preschoolchildren. *Journal of Personality and Social Psychology, 34,* 915–922.

Atkinson, J. W. (1974). Strength of motivation and efficiency of performance. In J. W. Atkinson & J. O. Raynor (Eds.), *Motivation and achievement* (pp. 193–218). New York: John Wiley.

Bandura, A. (1977). *Social learning theory*. Englewood Cliffs, NJ: Prentice-Hall.

Baron, R. (1986). Distraction-conflict theory: Progress and problems. In L. Berkowitz (Ed.), *Advances in experimental social psychology* (Vol. 19, pp. 1–40). Orlando, FL: Academic Press.

Baron, R. S., Moore, D., & Sanders, G. S. (1978). Distraction as a source of drive in social facilitation research. *Journal of Personality and Social Psychology, 36,* 816–824.

Berger, J., Cohen, B. P., & Zelditch, M., Jr. (1972). Status characteristics and social interaction. *Annual Review of Sociology, 6,* 479–508.

Berger, J. Webster, M., Jr., Ridgeway, C., & Rosenholtz, S. J. (1986). Status cues, expectations, and behavior. *Advances in group processes, 3,* 1–22.

Bettencourt, B. A., Brewer, M. B., Croak, M. R., & Miller, N. (in press). Cooperation and the reduction of intergroup bias: The role of reward structure and social orientation. *Journal of Experimental Social Psychology.*

Boggiano, A. K., & Ruble, D. N. (1979). Perception of competence and the overjustification effect: A developmental study. *Journal of Personality and Social Psychology, 37,* 1462–1468.

Boggiano, A., Ruble, D. N., & Pittman, T. S. (1982). The mastery hypothesis and the overjustification effect. *Social Cognition, 1,* 38–49.

Bond, C. F., Jr. (1982). A self presentational view. *Journal of Personality and Social Psychology, 42,* 1042–1050.

Bossert, S. T. (1979). *Tasks and social relationships in the classroom: A study of instructional organization and its consequences*. New York: Cambridge University Press.

(1989). Cooperative activities in the classroom. In E. Z. Rothkopf (Ed.), *Review of research in education* (Vol. 15, pp. 225–250). Washington, DC: American Education Research Association.

Brickner, M., Harkins, S., & Ostrom, T. (1986). Effects of personal involvement: Thought-provoking implications for social loafing. *Journal of Personality and Social Psychology, 51,* 763–769.

Brown, A., & Palincsar, A. S. (1989). Guided, cooperative learning and individual knowledge acquisition. In L. Resnick (Ed.), *Knowing, learning, and instruction* (pp. 393–451). Hillsdale, NJ: Erlbaum.

Carlson, M., Marcus-Newhall, A., & Miller N. (1990). Effects of situational aggression cues: A quantitative review. *Journal of Personality and Social Psychology, 58,* 622–633.

Cohen, E. G., Lotan, R., & Catanzarite, L. (1990). Treating status problems in the cooperative classroom. In S. Sharan (Ed.), *Cooperative learning: Theory and research* (pp. 203–230). New York: Praeger.

Connell, J. P., & Ryan, R. M. (1987). A developmental theory of motivation in the classroom. *Teacher Education Quarterly, 11*, 64–77.

Corno, L. (1986). The metacognitive control components of self-regulated learning. *Contemporary Educational Psychology, 11*, 333–346.

Cottrell, N. B. (1972). Social facilitation. In C. G. McClintock (Ed.), *Experimental social psychology* (pp. 185–236). New York: Holt, Rinehart, & Winston.

Dembo, M. H., & McAuliffe, T. J. (1987). Effects of perceived ability and grade status on social interaction and influence in cooperative groups. *Journal of Educational Psychology, 79*, 415–423.

Diehl, M., & Stroebe, W. (1987). Productivity loss in brainstorming groups: Toward the solution of a riddle. *Journal of Personality and Social Psychology, 53*(3), 497–509.

Dunn, J. Siblings and development. *Current Directions in Psychological Science, 1*, 6–9.

Duval, S., & Wicklund, R. A. (1972). *A theory of objective self awareness*. New York: Academic Press.

Dweck, C. (1986). Motivational processes affecting learning. *American Psychologist, 41*(10), 1040–1048.

Dweck, C., & Leggett, E. (1988). A social-cognitive approach to motivation and personality. *Psychological Review, 95*, 256–273.

Elliot, E. S., & Dweck, C. S. (1988). Goals: An approach to motivation and achievement. *Journal of Personality and Social Psychology, 54*, 5–12.

Flavell, J. H. (1985). *Cognitive development*. Englewood Cliffs, NJ: Prentice-Hall.

Gabrenya, W. K., Wang, Y., & Latané, B. (1985). Social loafing on an optimizing task: Cross cultural differences among Chinese and Americans. *Journal of Cross-cultural Psychology, 16*, 223–242.

Garnica, O. K. (1981). Social dominance and conversational interaction – The omega child in the classroom. In J. L. Green & C. Wallat (Eds.), *Ethnography and language in educational settings* (pp. 229–252). Norwood, NJ: Ablex.

Geen, R. G. (1991). Social motivation. *Annual Review of Psychology, 42*, 377–399.

Geen, R. G., & Bushman, B. J. (1987). Drive theory: Effects of socially engendered arousal. In B. Mullen & G. R. Goethals (Eds.), *Theories of group behavior* (pp. 89–110). New York: Springer Verlag.

Graham, S., & Barker, G. B. (1990). The down side of help: An attributional-developmental analysis of helping behavior as a low-ability cue. *Journal of Educational Psychology, 82*, 7–14.

Guerin, B., & Innes, J. M. (1982). Social facilitation and social monitoring: A new look at Zajonc's mere presence hypothesis. *British Journal of Social Psychology, 21*, 7–18.

Harackiewicz, J. M., Sansone, C., & Manderlink, G. (1985). Competence achievement orientation, and intrinsic motivation: A process analysis. *Journal of Personality and Social Psychology, 48*, 493–508.

Harkins, S. G., & Jackson, J. M. (1985). The role of evaluation in eliminating social loafing. *Personality and Social Psychology Bulletin, 11*, 456–465.

Harkins, S. G., & Petty, R. E. (1982). Effects of task difficulty and task uniqueness on social loafing. *Journal of Personality and Social Psychology, 43*, 1214–1229.

Harkins, S. G., & Szymanski, K. (1987). Social loafing and social facilitation: New wine in old bottles. *Review of Personality and Social Psychology, 9*, 167–188.

(1989). Social loafing and group evaluation. *Journal of Personality and Social Psychology, 56*(6), 934–941.

Harris, M. B. (1978). Effectance motivation reconsidered. *Human Development, 21,* 34–64.

Harter, S. (1981). A new self-report scale of intrinsic versus extrinsic orientation in the classroom: Motivational and informational components. *Developmental Psychology, 17,* 300–312.

(1986). Cognitive-developmental processes in the integration of concepts about emotions and the self. *Social Cognition, 2,* 119–151.

Hastie, R. (1986). Review essay: Experimental evidence on group accuracy. In G. Owen & B. Grofman (Eds.), *Information pooling and group accuracy* (pp. 129–157). Greenwich, CT: JAI Press.

Hepler, J., & Rose, S. F. (1988). Evaluation of multi-component group approach for improving the social skills of elementary school children. *Journal of Social Service Research, 11*(4), 1–18.

Hewstone, M. (1988). Attributional bases of intergroup conflict. In W. Stroebe, A. Kruglanski, D. Bar-Tal, & M. Hewstone (Eds.), *The social psychology of intergroup conflict* (pp. 47–72). New York: Springer Verlag.

Hill. G. W. (1982). Group versus individual performance: Are $n + 1$ heads better than one? *Psychological Bulletin, 91,* 517–539.

Hull, C. L. (1952). *A behavior system.* New Haven, CT: Yale University Press.

Ingham, A. G., Levinger, G., Graves, J., & Peckham, V. (1974). The Ringelmann effect: Studies of group size and group performance. *Journal of Experimental Social Psychology, 10,* 371–384.

Jackson, J. M., & Williams, K. D. (1985). Social loafing on difficult tasks: Working collectively can improve performance. *Journal of Personality and Social Psychology, 49,* 937–942.

Johnson, D. W., & Johnson, F. P. (1987). *Joining together: Group theory and group skills* (3rd ed.). Englewood Cliffs, NJ: Prentice-Hall.

Johnson, D. W., & Johnson, R. T. (1989). *Cooperation and competition: Theory and research.* Edina, MN: Interaction Book Co.

Johnson, D. W., Johnson, R. T., Pierson, W. T., & Lyons, V. (1985). Controversy versus concurrence seeking in multi-grade and single-grade learning groups. *Journal of Research in Science Teaching, 2,* 835–848.

Julian, J. W., & Perry, F. A. (1967). Cooperation contrasted with intra-group and inter-group competition. *Sociometry, 30,* 79–90.

Keasey, C. B. (1977). Children's developing awareness and usage of intentionality and motives. In C. B. Keasey (Ed.), *Nebraska symposium on motivation* (Vol. 25, pp. 219–260). Lincoln: University of Nebraska Press.

Kelley, H. H., & Thibaut, J. W. (1969). Group problem solving. In G. Lindzey & E. Aronson (Eds.), *The handbook of social psychology* (Vol. 4, pp. 1–101). Reading, MA: Addison-Wesley.

Kerr, N. L., & Bruun, S. E. (1981). Ringelmann revisited: Alternative explanations for the social loafing effect. *Personality and Social Psychology Bulletin, 7,* 224–231.

(1983). Dispensability of member effort and group motivation losses: Free-rider effects. *Journal of Personality and Social Psychology, 44*(1), 78–94.

Knight, G. P., & Bohlmeyer, E. M. (1900). Cooperative learning and achievement: Methods for assessing causal mechanisms. In S. Sharan (Ed.), *Cooperative learning: Theory and research* (pp. 1–22). New York: Praeger.

Lamm, H., & Trommsdorff, G. (1973). Group versus individual performance on tasks requiring ideational proficiency (brainstorming). *European Journal of Social Psychology, 44,* 78–94.

Latané, B., Williams, K., & Harkins, S. (1979). Many hands make light the work: The causes and consequences of social loafing. *Journal of Personality and Social Psychology, 37,* 823–832.

Laughlin, P. R., Vanderstoep, S. W., & Hollingshead, A. B. (1991). Group versus individual problem solving: Four-person groups versus four independent individuals. *Journal of Personality and Social Psychology, 51,* 60–67.

Lepper, M. R., & Greene, D. (1975). Turning play into work: Effects of adult surveillance and extrinsic rewards on children's intrinsic motivation. *Journal of Personality and Social Psychology, 31,* 479–486.

Lew, M., Mesch, D., Johnson, D. W., & Johnson, R. (1986). Positive interdependence, academic and collaborative-skills group contingencies and isolated students. *American Educational Research Journal, 23,* 822–832.

Lippett, R. R., Polansky, N., & Rosen, S. (1952). The dynamic of power. *Human Relations, 5,* 37–64.

Lutkenhaus, P., Bullock, M., & Geppert, U. (1987). Toddlers' actions: Knowledge, control, and the self. In F. Halisch & J. Kuhl (Eds.), *Motivation, intention and volition* (pp. 73–86). Berlin: Springer-Verlag.

Maruyama, G. (1991). Meta-analyses relating goal structures to achievement: Findings, controversies, and impacts. *Personality and Social Psychology Bulletin, 17*(3), 300–305.

Michaels, J. W. (1977). Classroom reward structures and academic performance. *Review of Educational Research, 47,* 87–98.

Miller, N., & Davidson-Podgorny, G. (1987). Theoretical models of intergroup relations and the use of cooperative teams as an intervention for desegregated settings. In C. Hendrick (Ed.), *Review of personality and social psychology* (Vol. 8, pp. 41–67). Newbury Park: Sage.

Miller, N., & Harrington, H. J. (1990). A situational identity perspective on cultural diversity and teamwork in the classroom. In S. Sharan (Ed.), *Cooperative learning: Theory and research* (pp. 39–75). New York: Praeger.

Newman, R. S. (1990). Children's help-seeking in the classroom: The role of motivational factors and attitudes. *Journal of Personality and Educational Psychology, 82,* 71–80.

Newman, R. S., & Golden, L. (1990). Children's reluctance to seek help with schoolwork. *Journal of Educational Psychology, 82,* 92–100.

Nicholls, J. G. (1984). Achievement motivation: Conceptions of ability, subjective experience, task choice, and performance. *Psychological Review, 91*(3), 328–346.

   (1987). Conceptions of ability across the school years: Reflections on method. In F. Halisch & J. Kuhl (Eds.), *Motivation, intention and volition* (pp. 201–212). Berlin: Springer-Verlag.

O'Donnell, A. M., Dansereau, D. F., Hythecker, V. I., Larson, C. O., Rocklin, T. R., Lambiotte, J. G., & Young, M. D. (1986). The effects of monitoring on cooperative learning. *Journal of Experimental Education, 54,* 169–173.

Petty, R. E., Harkins, S. G., & Williams, K. D. (1980). The effects of group diffusion of cognitive effort on attitudes: An information-processing view. *Journal of Personality and Social Psychology, 1,* 81–92.

Piaget, J. (1926). *Language and thought of the child.* New York: Harcourt Brace.

Pintrich, P. R., & DeGroot, E. V. (1990). Motivational and self-regulated learning components of classroom academic performance. *Journal of Educational Psychology, 82,* 33–40.

Rosenholtz, S. J., & Simpson, C. (1984). The formation of ability conceptions: Developmental trend or social construction. *Review of Educational Research, 54*(1), 31–63.

Schunk, D. H. (1981). Modeling and attributional effects on children's achievement: A self-efficacy analysis. *Journal of Educational Psychology, 73,* 93–105.

(1984). Self-efficacy perspective on achievement behavior. *Educational Psychologist, 19*(1), 48–58.

(1986). Vicarious influences on self-efficacy for cognitive skill learning. *Journal of Social and Clinical Psychology, 4,* 316–327.

(1987). Peer models and children's behavioral change. *Review of Educational Research, 57,* 149–174.

Scott, W. E., Jr., & Cherrington, D. J. (1974). Effects of competitive, cooperative, and individualistic reinforcement contingencies. *Journal of Personality and Social Psychology, 30,* 748–758.

Selman, R. L. (1980). *The growth of interpersonal understanding.* New York: Academic Press..

Shantz, C. U. (1983). Social cognition. In J. H. Flavell & E. M. Markman (Eds.), *Handbook of child psychology: Cognitive development* (Vol. 4, pp. 495–556). New York: Wiley.

Sharan, S. (1990). Cooperative learning: A perspective on research and practice. In S. Sharan (Ed.), *Cooperative learning: Theory and research* (pp. 285–300). New York: Praeger.

Sharan, S., & Hertz-Lazarowitz, R. (1980). A Group-Investigation method of cooperative learning in the classroom. In S. Sharan, P. Hare, C. Webb, & R. Hertz-Lazarowitz (Eds.), *Cooperation in education* (pp. 14–76). Provo, UT: Brigham Young University Press.

Sharan, S., Kussel, P., Hertz-Lazarowitz, R., Bejarano, Y., Raviv, S., & Sharan, Y. (1984). *Cooperative learning in the classroom: Research in desegregated schools.* Hillsdale, NJ: Erlbaum.

Sharan, S., & Shaulov, A. (1990). Cooperative learning, motivation to learn, and academic achievement. In S. Sharan (Ed.), *Cooperative learning: Theory and research* (pp. 173–202). New York: Praeger.

Sheingold, K., Hawkins, J., & Char, C. (1984). "I'm the thinkist, you're the typist": The interactions of technology and the social life of classrooms. *Journal of Social Issues, 40,* 49–61.

Sherif, M., Harvey, O., White, B., Hood, W., & Sherif, C. (1961). *Intergroup conflict and cooperation: The Robber's Cave experiment.* Norman: University of Oklahoma, Institute of Group Relations.

Slavin, R. E. (1977). Classroom reward structure: An analytical and practical review. *Review of Educational Research, 47,* 633–650.

(1980). Cooperative learning. *Review of Educational Research, 50*(2), 315–342.

(1983). When does cooperative learning increase student achievement? *Psychological Bulletin, 94,* 429–445.

(1991). What cooperative learning has to offer the gifted. *Cooperative Learning, 11,* 22–23.

Solomon, D., Watson, M., Schaps, E., Battistich, W., & Solomon, J. (1990). Cooperative learning as part of a comprehensive classroom program designed to promote prosocial development. In S. Sharan (Ed.), *Cooperative learning: Theory and research* (pp. 232–260). New York: Praeger.

Stasser, G., Kerr, N. L., & Davis, J. H. (1990). Influence models and consensus processes in decision making groups. In P. B. Paulus (Ed.), *Psychology of group influence* (2nd ed., pp. 279–326). Hillsdale, NJ: Erlbaum.

Steiner, I. (1972). *Group process and productivity.* New York: Academic Press.

Syzmanski, K., & Harkins, S. G. (1987). Social loafing and self-evaluation with a social standard. *Journal of Personality and Social Psychology, 53,* 891–897.

Tajfel, H. (1969). Cognitive aspects of prejudice. *Journal of Social Issues, 25,* 79–97.

    (1970). Experiments in intergroup discrimination. *Scientific American, 223*(5), 96–102.

Warring, D., Johnson, D. W., Maruyama, G., & Johnson, R. (1985). Impact of different types of cooperative learning activities on cross-ethnic and cross-sex relationships. *Journal of Educational Psychology, 77,* 53–59.

Webb, N. W. (1982). Group composition, group interaction, and achievement in cooperative small groups. *Journal of Educational Psychology, 74*(4), 475–484.

    (1985). Student interaction and learning in small groups: A research summary. In R. Slavin, S. Sharan, S. Kagan, R. Hertz-Lazarowitz, E. Webb, & R. Schmuck (Eds.), *Learning to cooperate, cooperating to learn.* New York: Plenum Press.

    (1989). Peer interaction and learning in small groups. *International Journal of Educational Research, 13*(1), 21–40.

Weldon, E., & Gargano, G. M. (1988). Cognitive loafing: The effects of accountability and shared responsibility on cognitive effort. *Personality and Social Psychology Bulletin, 14,* 159–171.

White, R. (1959). Motivation reconsidered: The concept of competence. *Psychological Review, 66,* 297–323.

Wilkinson, L. C., & Spinelli, F. (1983). Using requests effectively, in peer-directed instructional groups. *American Education Research Journal, 20,* 479–501.

Willis, S. (1990). Cooperative learning fallout? *ASUD Update, 32,* 6–8.

Worchel, S., Andreoli, V. A., & Folger, R. (1977). Intergroup cooperation and intergroup attraction: The effect of previous interaction and outcome of combined effort. *Journal of Experimental Social Psychology, 13,* 131–140.

Worchel, S., & Norvell, N. (1980). Effects of perceived environmental conditions during cooperation on intergroup attraction. *Journal of Personality and Social Psychology, 38,* 764–772.

Zaccaro, S. J. (1984). Social loafing: The role of task attractiveness. *Personality and Social Psychology Bulletin, 10,* 99–106.

Zajonc, R. B. (1965). Social facilitation. *Science, 149,* 261–274.

Author Index

Subject Index